Microsoft®

EXCEL 2000

INTRODUCTORY EDITION

Sarah E. Hutchinson

Glen J. Coulthard

irwin McGraw-Hill

Boston   Burr Ridge, IL   Dubuque, IA   Madison, WI   New York   San Francisco   St. Louis
Bangkok   Bogotá   Caracas   Lisbon   London   Madrid   Mexico City
Milan   New Delhi   Seoul   Singapore   Sydney   Taipei   Toronto

MICROSOFT®
EXCEL 2000

INTRODUCTORY EDITION

McGraw-Hill Higher Education

A Division of The McGraw-Hill Companies

MICROSOFT® EXCEL 2000
INTRODUCTORY EDITION

Copyright © 2000 by The McGraw-Hill Companies, Inc. All rights reserved. Printed in the United States of America. Except as permitted under the United States Copyright Act of 1976, no part of this publication may be reproduced or distributed in any form or by any means, or stored in a database or retrieval system, without the prior written permission of the publisher.

This book is printed on acid-free paper.

1 2 3 4 5 6 7 8 9 0 WEB/WEB 9 0 9 8 7 6 5 4 3 2 1 0 9

ISBN 0-07-234802-X

Vice President/Editor in chief: *Michael W. Junior*

Publisher: *David Kendric Brake*

Sponsoring editor: *Trisha O'Shea*

Senior marketing manager: *Jodi McPherson*

Project manager: *Christina Thornton-Villagomez*

Production supervisor: *Debra R. Benson*

Designer: *AM Design*

Supplement coordinator: *Carol Loreth*

New Media: *Lisa Ramos-Torrescano*

Compositor: *GTS Graphics*

Typeface: *11/13 Stone Serif*

Printer: *Webcrafters, Inc.*

Library of Congress Cataloging-in-Publication Data

Hutchinson, Sarah E.
    Microsoft Excel 2000 / Sarah E. Hutchinson, Glen J. Coulthard.
   Introductory ed.
      p. cm. (Advantage series for computer education)
    ISBN 0-07-234802-X
    Includes index.
    1. Microsoft Excel for Windows.   2. Business—Computer programs.
  3. Electronic spreadsheets.   I. Coulthard, Glen J.   II. Title.
  III. Series.
  HF5548.4.M523H8763   2000
  005.369 dc—21   99-34913

http://www.mhhe.com

At McGraw-Hill Higher-Education, we publish instructional materials targeted at the higher-education market. In an effort to expand the tools of higher learning, we publish texts, lab manuals, study guides, testing materials, software and multimedia products.

At Irwin/McGraw-Hill (a division of McGraw-Hill Higher Education), we realize that technology will continue to create new mediums for professors and students to manage resources and communicate information with one another. We strive to provide the most flexible and complete teaching and learning tools available and offer solutions to the changing world of teaching and learning.

Irwin/McGraw-Hill is dedicated to providing the tools for today's instructors and students to successfully navigate the world of Information Technology.

- **Seminar Series**—Irwin/McGraw-Hill's Technology Connection seminar series offered across the country ever year, demonstrate the latest technology products and encourage collaboration among teaching professionals.

- **Osborne/McGraw-Hill**—A division of The McGraw-Hill Companies known for its best selling Internet titles *Harley Hahn's Internet & Web Yellow Pages* and the *Internet Complete Reference*, offers an additional resource for certification and has strategic publishing relationships with corporations such as Corel Corporation and America Online. For more information visit Osborne at www.osborne.com.

- **Digital Solutions**—Irwin/McGraw-Hill is committed to publishing Digital Solutions. Taking your course online doesn't have to be a solitary venture, nor does it have to be a difficult one. We offer several solutions, which will let you enjoy all the benefits of having course material online. For more information visit www.mhhe.com/solutions/index.mhtml.

- **Packaging Options**—For more information about our discount options, contact your local Irwin/McGraw-Hill Sales representative at 1-800-338-3987 or visit our Website at www.mhhe.com/it.

Preface
The Advantage Series

Goals/Philosophy

The Advantage Series presents the **What, Why, and How** of computer application skills to today's students. Each lab manual is built upon an efficient learning model, which provides students and faculty with complete coverage of the most powerful software packages available today.

Approach

The Advantage Series builds upon an efficient learning model, which provides students and faculty with complete coverage and enhances critical thinking skills. This case-based, "problem-solving" approach teaches the What, Why, and How of computer application skills.

The Advantage Series introduces the **"Feature-Method-Practice"** layered approach. The **Feature** describes the command and tells the importance of that command. The **Method** shows students how to perform the Feature. The **Practice** allows students to apply the feature in a keystroke exercise.

About the Series

The Advantage Series offers *three levels* of instruction. Each level builds upon the previous level. The following are the three level of instructions:

Brief: covers the basics of the application, contains two to four chapters, and is typically 120–190 pages long.

Introductory: includes the material in the Brief Lab manual plus two to three additional chapters. The Introductory lab manuals are approximately 300 pages long and prepare students for the *Microsoft Office User Specialist Proficient Exam (MOUS Certification)*

Complete: includes the Introductory lab manual plus an additional five chapters of advanced level content. The Complete lab manuals are approximately 600 pages in length and prepare students to take the *Microsoft Office User Specialist Expert Exam (MOUS Certification)*.

Approved Microsoft Courseware

Use of the Microsoft Office User Specialist Approved Coursework Logo on this product signifies that it has been independently reviewed and approved in complying with the following standards: Acceptable coverage of all content related to the Microsoft Office Exam entitled *Microsoft Excel 2000* and sufficient performance-based exercises that relate closely to all required content, based on sampling of text. For further information on Microsoft's MOUS certification program please visit Microsoft's Web site at http://www.microsoft.com/office/traincert/.

About the Book

Each lab manual features the following:

- **Learning Objectives:** At the beginning of each chapter, a list of action-oriented objectives is presented detailing what is expected of the students.

- **Chapters:** Each lab manual is divided into chapters.

- **Modules:** Each chapter contains three to five independent modules, requiring approximately 30–45 minutes each to complete. Although we recommend you complete an entire chapter before proceeding, you may skip or rearrange the order of these modules to best suit your learning needs.

- **Case Studies:** Each chapter, begins with a Case Study. The student is introduced to a fictitious person or company and their immediate problem or opportunity. Throughout the chapter students obtain the knowledge and skills necessary to meet the challenges presented in the Case Study. At the end of each chapter, students are asked to solve problems directly related to the Case Study.

- **Feature-Method-Practice:** Each chapter highlights our **unique "Feature-Method-Practice"** layered approach. The **Feature** layer describes the command or technique and persuades you of its importance and relevance. The **Method** layer shows you how to perform the procedure, while the **Practice** layer lets you apply the feature in a hands-on step-by-step exercise.

- **Instructions:** The numbered step-by-step progression for all hands-on examples and exercises are clearly identified. Students will find it surprisingly easy to follow the logical sequence of keystrokes and mouse clicks, and no longer worry about missing a step.

- **In Addition Boxes:** These content boxes are placed strategically throughout the chapter and provide information on advanced topics that are beyond the scope of the current discussion.

- **Self-Check Boxes:** At the end of each module, a brief self-check question appears for students to test their comprehension of the material. Answers for these questions appear in the Appendix.

- **Chapter Review:** The *Command Summary* and *Key Terms* provide an excellent review of the chapter content and prepare students for the short-answer, true-false and multiple-choice questions at the end of each chapter.

Easy

Moderate

Difficult

- **Hands-On Projects:** Each chapter concludes with six hands-on projects that are rated according to their difficulty level. The *easy* and *moderate* projects use a running-case approach, whereby the same person or company appears at the end of each chapter in a particular tutorial. The two *difficult* or *on your own* projects provide greater latitude in applying the software to a variety of creative problem-solving situations.

- **Appendix: Microsoft Windows Quick Reference:** Each lab manual contains a Microsoft Windows Quick Reference. This Quick reference teaches students the fundamentals of using a mouse and a keyboard, illustrates how to interact with a dialog box, and describes the fundamentals of how to use the Office 2000 Help System.

Features of This Lab Manual

Instructions: The numbered step-by-step progression for all hands-on examples and exercises are clearly identified. Students will find it surprisingly easy to follow the logical sequence of keystrokes and mouse clicks, and no longer worry about missing a step.

In Addition Boxes: These content boxes are placed strategically throughout the chapter and provide information on topics that are beyond the scope of the current discussion.

Self-Check Boxes: At the end of each module, a brief self-check question appears for students to test their comprehension of the material. Answers for these questions appear in the Appendix.

Feature-Method-Practice: Each chapter highlights our unique "Feature-Method-Practice" layered approach. The *Feature* layer describes the command or technique and persuades you of its importance and relevance. The *Method* layer shows you how to perform the procedure, while the *Practice* layer lets you apply the feature in a hands-on step-by-step exercise.

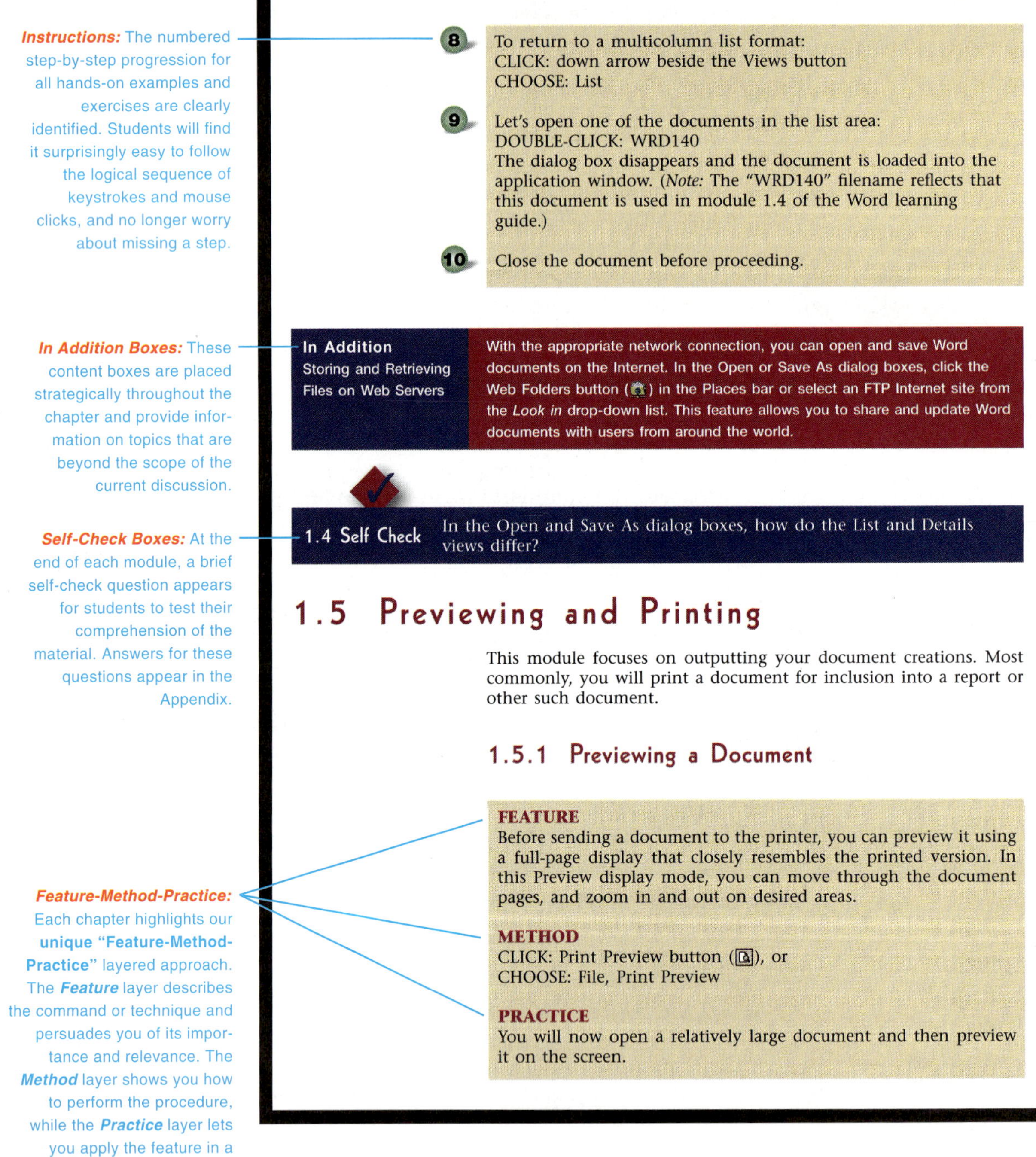

8 To return to a multicolumn list format:
CLICK: down arrow beside the Views button
CHOOSE: List

9 Let's open one of the documents in the list area:
DOUBLE-CLICK: WRD140
The dialog box disappears and the document is loaded into the application window. (*Note:* The "WRD140" filename reflects that this document is used in module 1.4 of the Word learning guide.)

10 Close the document before proceeding.

In Addition
Storing and Retrieving Files on Web Servers

With the appropriate network connection, you can open and save Word documents on the Internet. In the Open or Save As dialog boxes, click the Web Folders button ( ) in the Places bar or select an FTP Internet site from the *Look in* drop-down list. This feature allows you to share and update Word documents with users from around the world.

1.4 Self Check In the Open and Save As dialog boxes, how do the List and Details views differ?

1.5 Previewing and Printing

This module focuses on outputting your document creations. Most commonly, you will print a document for inclusion into a report or other such document.

1.5.1 Previewing a Document

FEATURE
Before sending a document to the printer, you can preview it using a full-page display that closely resembles the printed version. In this Preview display mode, you can move through the document pages, and zoom in and out on desired areas.

METHOD
CLICK: Print Preview button ( ), or
CHOOSE: File, Print Preview

PRACTICE
You will now open a relatively large document and then preview it on the screen.

EXCEL

Case Study

1-on-1 Tutoring Services

Dean Shearwater is helping to pay his university tuition by tutoring other university and high school students. Over the last two years, he has developed an excellent reputation for making complex topics simple and easy to remember. While he is an excellent tutor, last year he didn't earn as much as he had expected.

Dean thinks his lackluster earnings can be attributed to poor advertising and inadequate record keeping. This year, he has decided to operate his tutoring services more like a real business. His first priority is to learn how to use Microsoft Word so that he can prepare advertising materials, send faxes and memos, and organize his student notes.

In this chapter, you and Dean learn how to create simple documents from scratch, use built-in document templates, edit documents, and use the Undo command. You also learn how to preview and print your work.

1.1 Getting Started with Word

Microsoft Word 2000 is a **word processing** program that enables you to create, edit, format, and print many types of documents including résumés and cover letters, reports and proposals, World Wide Web pages, and more. By the time you complete this learning guide, you will be skilled in creating all types of documents and in getting them to look the way you want. In this module, you load Microsoft Word and proceed through a guided tour of its primary components.

1.1.1 Loading and Exiting Word

FEATURE

You load Word from the Windows Start menu, accessed by clicking the Start button (Start) on the taskbar. Because Word requires a significant amount of memory, you should always exit the application when you are finished doing your work. Most Windows applications allow you to close their windows by clicking the Close button (x) appearing in the top right-hand corner.

Teaching Resources

The following is a list of supplemental material, which can be used to teach this course.

Skills Assessment

Irwin/McGraw-Hill offers two innovative systems that can be used with the Advantage Series, ATLAS and **SimNet,** which take skills assessment testing beyond the basics with pre- and post-assessment capability.

- **ATLAS—(Active Testing and Learning Assessment Software)**—Atlas is our **live** in the application skills assessment tool. ATLAS allows Students to perform tasks while working *live* within the office applications environment. ATLAS is web-enabled and customizable to meet the needs of your course. Atlas is available for Office 2000.

- SimNet—(Simulated Network Assessment Product)—SimNet permits you to test the actual software skills students learn about the Microsoft Office Applications in a **simulated** environment. SimNet is web-enabled and is available for Office 97 and Office 2000.

Instructor's Resource Kits

The Instructor's Resource Kit provides professors with all of the ancillary material needed to teach a course. Irwin/McGraw-Hill is committed to providing instructors with the most effective instructional resources available. Many of these resources are available at our **Information Technology Supersite** www.mhhe.com/it. Our Instructor's Resource Kits are available on CD-ROM and contain the following:

- **Diploma by Brownstone**—is the most flexible, powerful, and easy-to-use computerized testing system available in higher education. The diploma system allows professors to create an exam as a printed version, as a LAN-based Online version and as an Internet version. Diploma includes grade book features, which automate the entire testing process.

- **Instructor's Manual**—Includes:
  —Solutions to all lessons and end-of-chapter material
  —Teaching Tips
  —Teaching Strategies
  —Additional Exercises

- **Student Data Files**—To use the Advantage Series students must have data files to complete practice and test sessions. The instructor and students using this text in classes are granted the right to post the student files on any network or stand-alone computer, or to distribute the files on individual diskettes. The student files may be downloaded from our IT Supersite at www.mhhe.com/it.

- **Series Web Site**—Available at www.mhhe.com/cit/apps/adv/.

Digital Solutions

PageOut Lite—allows an instructor to create their own basic Web site hosted by McGraw-Hill. PageOut Lite includes three basic templates that automatically convert typed material into HTML Web Pages. Using PageOut Lite an instructor can set up a homepage, Web links, and a basic course syllabus and lecture notes.

PageOut—is Irwin/McGraw-Hill's Course Webster Development Center. Pageout allows an instructor to create a more complex course Webster with an interactive syllabus and some course management features. Like PageOut Lite, PageOut converts typed material to html. For more information please visit the Pageout Web site at www.mhla.net/pageout.

OLC/Series Web Sites—Online Learning Centers (OLC's)/Series Sites are accessible through our Supersite at www.mhhe.com/it. Our OLC/Series Sites provide pedagogical features and supplements for our titles online. Students can point and click their way to key terms, learning objectives, chapter overviews, PowerPoint slides, exercises and Web links.

The McGraw-Hill Learning Architecture (MHLA)—is a complete course delivery system. MHLA gives professors ownership in the way digital content is presented to the class through online quizzing, student collaboration, course administration, and content management. For a walkthrough of MHLA, visit the MHLA Web site at www.mhla.net.

Packaging Options

For more information about our discount options, contact your local Irwin/McGraw-Hill Sales representative at 1-800-338-3987 or visit our Web site at www.mhhe.com/it.

Acknowledgments

This series of tutorials is the direct result of the teamwork and heart of many people. We sincerely thank the reviewers, instructors, and students who have shared their comments and suggestions with us over the past few years. We do read them! With their valuable feedback, our tutorials have evolved into the product you see before you.

Many thanks go to Kyle Lewis, Trisha O'Shea, Kyle Thomes, and Carrie Berkshire from Irwin/McGraw-Hill whose management helped to get this book produced in a timely and efficient manner. Special recognition goes to all of the individuals mentioned in the credits at the beginning of this tutorial. And finally, to the many others who weren't directly involved in this project but who have stood by us the whole way, we appreciate your encouragement and support.

The Advantage Team
Special thanks go out to our contributing members on the Advantage team.

> Verlaine Murphy
> Walt Musekamp
> Ingrid Neumann
> Catherine Schuler

Write to Us
We welcome your response to this tutorial, for we are trying to make it as useful a learning tool as possible. Please contact us at

Sarah E. Hutchinson—sclifford@mindspring.com
Glen J. Coulthard—glen@coulthard.com

Contents

PERFORMING CALCULATIONS

MANAGING WORKSHEETS AND WORKBOOKS

MICROSOFT®
EXCEL 2000

BRIEF EDITION

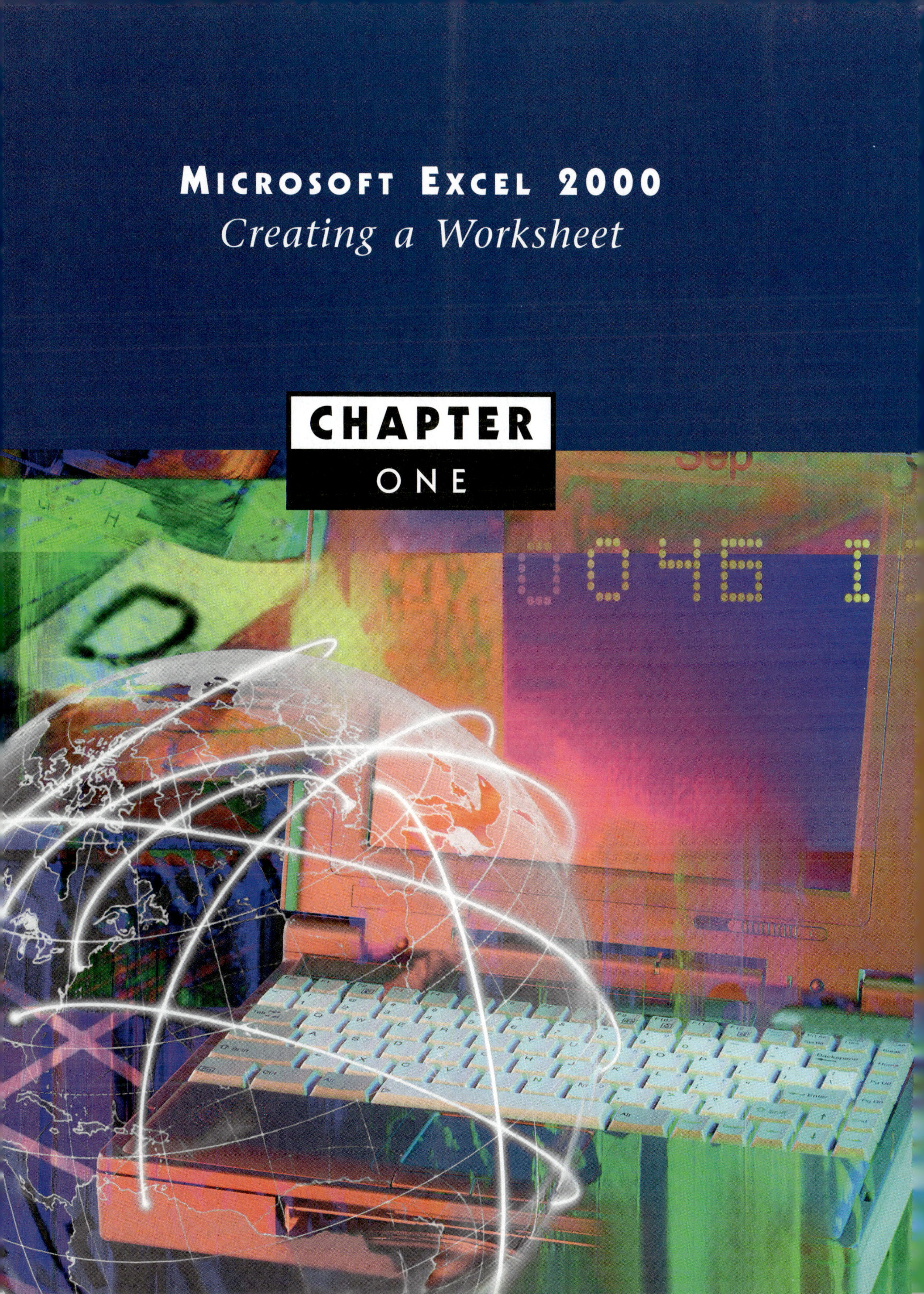

MICROSOFT EXCEL 2000
Creating a Worksheet
CHAPTER
ONE

Chapter Outline

Learning Objectives

After reading this chapter, you will be able to:

- Describe the different components of the application and workbook windows

- Select commands using the Menu bar and right-click menus

- Enter text, dates, numbers, and formulas in a worksheet

- Edit and erase cell data

- Use the Undo and Redo commands

- Start a new workbook

- Save, open, and close a workbook

EXCEL

Case Study

Rain Coast Air

Rain Coast Air is a small, privately owned airline charter company operating in the Pacific Northwest. The company's typical charter business consists of flying tourists to remote fishing lodges and transporting geological and forestry survey crews. Earlier this year, Rain Coast added a third aircraft to their fleet of float planes and retained two full-time and three part-time pilots. Along with the pilots, Rain Coast employs a dock hand and a mechanic. Hank Frobisher, the general manager, started the company and oversees all aspects of its operation.

To date, Rain Coast has been operating with a bare minimum of paperwork and manual record-keeping. All bookings are hand-written into a scheduling chart and the pilots fill out trip logs at the end of each flight. Invoices and receipts are simply turned over to a bookkeeping service as Hank cannot afford a staff accountant. Just lately, however, Hank is finding it increasingly difficult to obtain the information he needs to make key business decisions. To remedy this, he hired Jennifer Duvall, the daughter of one of his pilots, as an office assistant. Jennifer is enrolled in a Microsoft Excel course at the local community college and has expressed some enthusiasm in setting up worksheets for Rain Coast Air.

In this chapter, you and Jennifer learn how to work with Microsoft Excel. Specifically, you create new worksheets from scratch and enter text, numbers, dates, and formulas. Then you learn how to edit and modify cell entries and even practice using the Undo command. To complete the chapter, you practice saving and opening workbooks.

1.1 Getting Started with Excel

Microsoft Excel 2000 is an electronic spreadsheet program that enables you to store, manipulate, and chart numeric data. Researchers, statisticians, and business people use spreadsheet software to analyze and summarize mathematical, statistical, and financial data. Closer to home, you can use Excel to create a budget for your monthly living expenses, analyze returns in the stock market, develop a business plan, or calculate the loan payment required to purchase a new car.

Excel enables you to create and modify worksheets—the electronic version of an accountant's ledger pad—and chart sheets. A **worksheet** (Figure 1.1) is divided into vertical columns and horizontal rows. The rows are numbered and the columns are labeled from A to Z, then AA to AZ, and so on to column IV. The intersection of a column and a row is called a **cell.** Each cell is given a **cell address,** like a post office box number, consisting of its column letter followed by its row number (for example, B4 or FX400). Excel allows you to open multiple worksheets and chart sheets within its application window.

Figure 1.1

An electronic worksheet

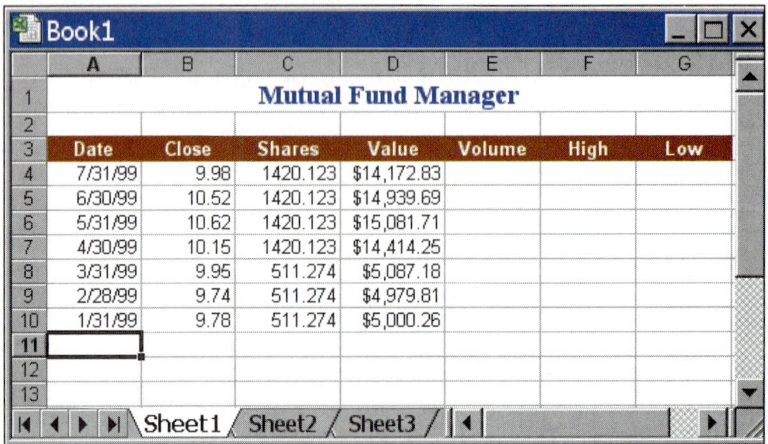

A **chart sheet** (Figure 1.2) displays a chart graphic that is typically linked to data stored in a worksheet. When the data is changed, the chart is updated automatically to reflect the new information. Charts may also appear alongside their data in a worksheet.

Figure 1.2

A chart sheet

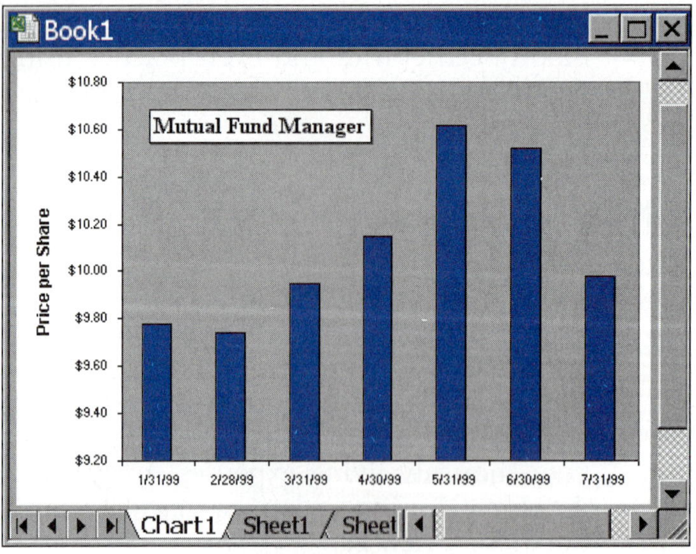

Related worksheets and chart sheets are stored together in a single disk file called a **workbook.** You can think of an Excel workbook as a three-ring binder with tabs at the beginning of each new page or sheet. In this module, you load Microsoft Excel and proceed through a guided tour of its application and document windows.

1.1.1 Loading and Exiting Excel

FEATURE

You load Excel from the Windows Start menu, accessed by clicking the Start button (Start) on the taskbar. Because Excel requires a significant amount of memory, you should always exit the application when you are finished doing your work. Most Windows applications allow you to close their windows by clicking on the Close button ($\boxed{\times}$) appearing in the top right-hand corner.

METHOD

- To load Excel:
  CLICK: Start button (Start)
  CHOOSE: Programs, Microsoft Excel
- To exit Excel:
  CHOOSE: File, Exit from Excel's Menu bar

PRACTICE

You will now load Microsoft Excel using the Windows Start menu.

Setup: Ensure that you have turned on your computer and that the Windows desktop appears.

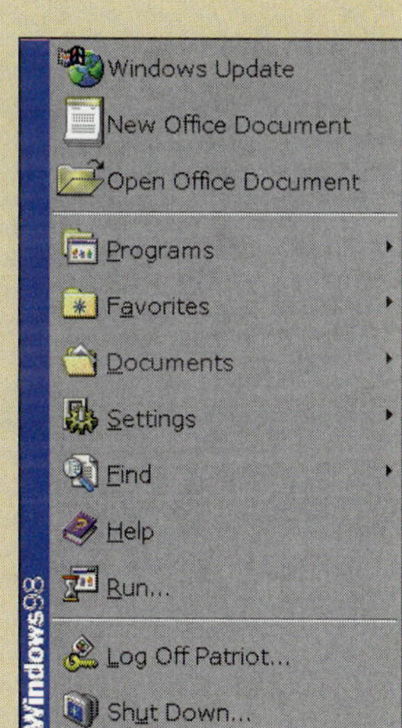

1 Position the mouse pointer over the Start button (Start) appearing in the bottom left-hand corner of the Windows taskbar and then click the left mouse button once. The Start pop-up menu appears as shown here.

2 Position the mouse pointer over the Programs menu option. Notice that you do not need to click the left mouse button to display the list of programs in the fly-out or cascading menu.

3 Move the mouse pointer horizontally to the right until it highlights an option in the Programs menu. You can now move the mouse pointer vertically within the menu to select an option.

4 Position the mouse pointer over the Microsoft Excel menu option and then click the left mouse button once. After a few seconds, the Excel application window appears.

6 An Office Assistant character, like "Rocky" (shown at the right), may now appear. You will learn how to hide this character in lesson 1.1.2.

In Addition Switching Among Applications	Each application that you are currently working with is represented by a button on the taskbar. Switching between open applications on your desktop is as easy as clicking the appropriate taskbar button, like switching channels on a television set.

1.1.2 Touring Excel

FEATURE

The Excel **application window** acts as a container for the worksheet and chart windows. It also contains the primary interface components for working in Excel, including the *Windows icons, Menu bar, Toolbars, Name box, Formula bar,* and *Status bar.* The components of a worksheet **document window** include *Scroll bars, Sheet tabs, Tab Split box,* and *Tab Scrolling arrows.* Figure 1.3 identifies several of these components.

PRACTICE

In a guided tour, you will now explore the features of the Excel application and document windows.

Setup: Ensure that you've loaded Excel.

1 Excel's application window is best kept maximized to fill the entire screen, as shown in Figure 1.3. As with most Windows applications, you use the Title bar icons—Minimize (▭), Maximize (▢), Restore (▱), and Close (▨)—to control the display of a window using the mouse. Familiarize yourself with the components labeled in Figure 1.3.

Figure 1.3

Excel's application window

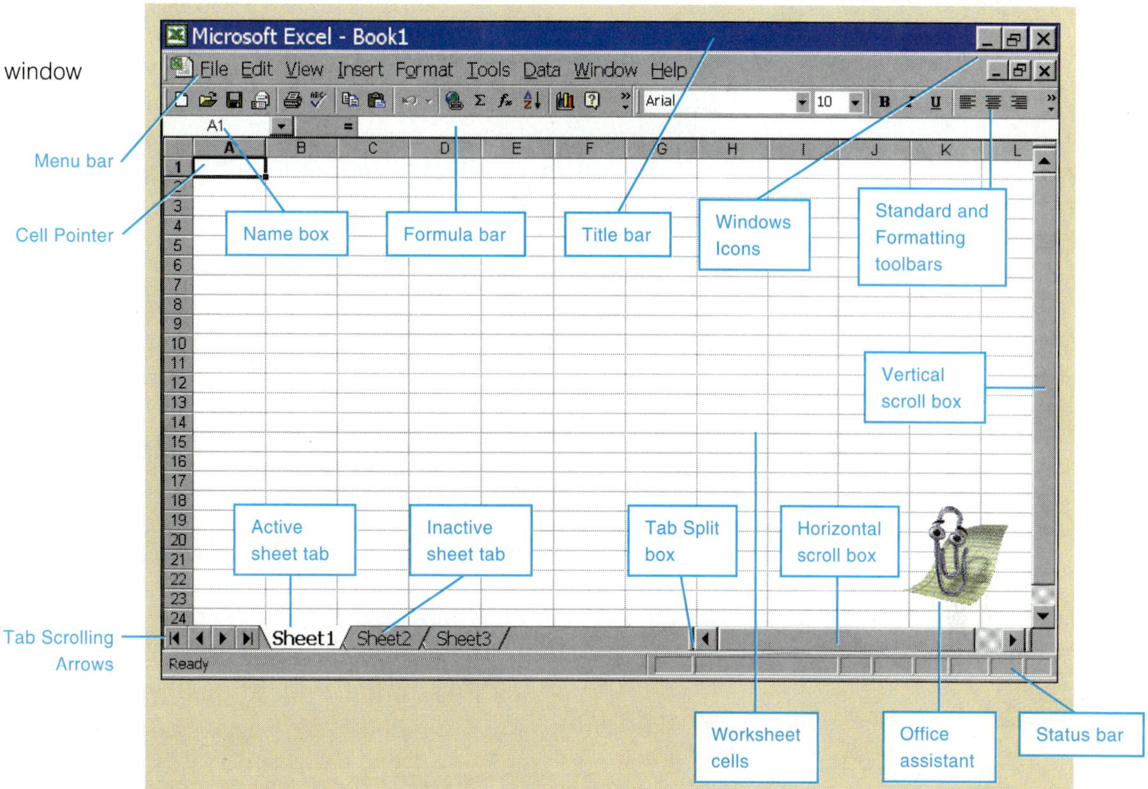

2 The Menu bar contains the Excel menu commands. To execute a command, you click once on the desired Menu bar option and then click again on the command. Commands that appear dimmed are not available for selection. Commands that are followed by an ellipsis (…) will display a dialog box. Pull-down menus that display a chevron (⯆) at the bottom display further menu options when selected.

To practice working with the Excel Menu bar:
CHOOSE: Help
This instruction tells you to click the left mouse button once on the Help option appearing in the Menu bar. (*Note:* All menu commands that you execute in this guide begin with the instruction "CHOOSE.")

3 To display other pull-down menus, move the mouse to the left over other options in the Menu bar. As each option is highlighted, a pull-down menu appears with its associated commands.

4 To leave the Menu bar without making a command selection:
CLICK: in a blank area of the Title bar

5 Excel provides context-sensitive *right-click menus* for quick access to menu commands. Rather than searching for the appropriate command in the Menu bar, you can position the mouse pointer on any object, such as a cell, graphic, or toolbar button, and right-click the mouse to display a list of commonly selected commands.

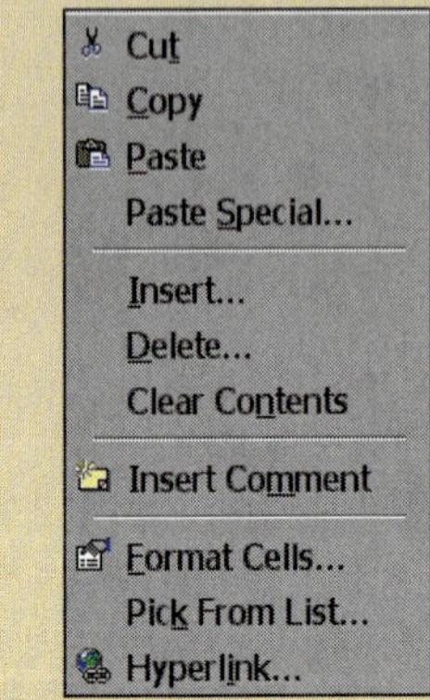

To display a cell's right-click menu:
RIGHT-CLICK: cell A1
The pop-up menu at the right should appear.

6 To remove the cell's right-click menu from the screen:
PRESS: ESC

7 If an Office Assistant character currently appears on your screen, do the following to hide it from view:
RIGHT-CLICK: *the character*
CHOOSE: Hide from the right-click menu
(*Note:* The character's name may appear in the command, such as "Hide Rocky.")

1.1.3 Customizing Menus and Toolbars

FEATURE
Some people argue that software becomes more difficult to learn and use with the addition of each new command or feature. In response to this sentiment, Microsoft developed **adaptive menus** that display only the most commonly used commands. By default, Microsoft Office 2000 ships with the adaptive menus feature enabled. However, you may find this dynamic feature confusing and choose to turn off the adaptive menus. Likewise, the Standard and Formatting toolbars are positioned side-by-side in a single row by default. Again, you may find it easier to locate buttons when these toolbars are positioned on separate rows.

METHOD
To disable the adaptive menus feature:
1. CHOOSE: Tools, Customize
2. SELECT: *Menus show recently used commands first* check box, so that no "✔" appears

To display the Standard and Formatting toolbars on separate rows:
1. CHOOSE: Tools, Customize
2. SELECT: *Standard and Formatting toolbars share one row* check box, so that no "✔" appears

PRACTICE

In this lesson, you disable the adaptive menus feature and display the Standard and Formatting toolbars on separate rows.

Setup: Ensure that you've completed the previous lesson.

1 To begin, display the Tools menu:
CHOOSE: Tools
You should now see the Tools pull-down menu. When a desired command does not appear on a menu, you can extend the menu to view all of the available commands by waiting for a short period, by clicking on the chevron (⌄) at the bottom of the pull-down menu, or by double-clicking the option in the Menu bar.

2 Let's turn off the adaptive menus feature and customize the Standard and Formatting toolbars. Do the following:
CHOOSE: Customize from the Tools pull-down menu
The Customize dialog box should now appear (Figure 1.4.)

Figure 1.4

Customize dialog box

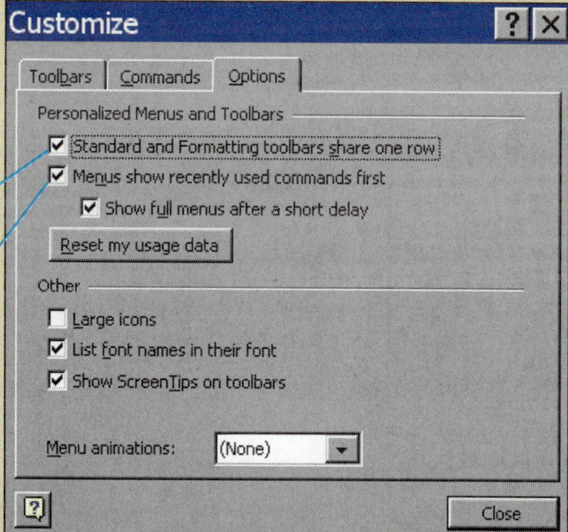

3 SELECT: *Menus show recently used commands first* check box, so that no "✔" appears

4 SELECT: *Standard and Formatting toolbars share one row* check box, so that no "✔" appears

5 To proceed:
CLICK: Close button

Figure 1.5 displays the Standard and Formatting toolbars as they should now appear on your screen. The Standard toolbar provides access to file management and editing commands, in addition to special features such as wizards. The Formatting toolbar lets you access cell formatting commands.

IMPORTANT: *For the remainder of this learning guide, we assume that the adaptive menus feature has been disabled and that the Standard and Formatting toolbars are positioned on separate rows.*

Figure 1.5

Standard toolbar

Formatting toolbar

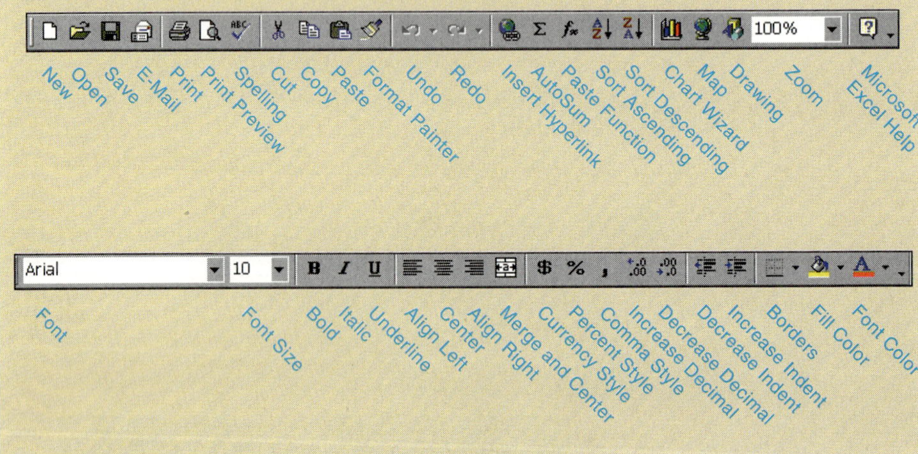

In Addition Moving Toolbars	You can move toolbars around the Excel application window using the mouse. A *docked* toolbar appears attached to one of the window's borders. An *undocked* or *floating* toolbar appears in its own window, complete with a Title bar and Close button. To float a docked toolbar, drag the Move bar (‖) at the left-hand side toward the center of the window. To redock the toolbar, drag its Title bar toward a border until it attaches itself automatically.

1.1 Self Check   How do you turn the adaptive menus feature on or off?

1.2 Creating Your First Worksheet

You create a worksheet by entering text labels, numbers, dates, and formulas into the individual cells. To begin entering data, first move the cell pointer to the desired cell in the worksheet. Then type the information that you want to appear in the cell. And finally, complete the entry by pressing (ENTER) or by moving the cell pointer to another cell. In this module, you learn how to navigate a worksheet, enter several types of data, and construct a simple formula expression.

1.2.1 Moving the Cell Pointer

FEATURE

You move the **cell pointer** around a worksheet using the mouse and keyboard. When you first open a new workbook, the cell pointer is positioned on cell A1 in the Sheet1 worksheet. Excel displays the current cell address in the **Name box,** appearing at the left-hand side of the Formula bar.

METHOD

Some common keystrokes for navigating a worksheet include:

- ⬆, ⬇, ⬅, and ➡
- HOME, END, PgDn, and PgDn
- CTRL + HOME to move to cell A1
- CTRL + END to move to the last cell in the active worksheet area
- F5 GoTo key for moving to a specific cell address

PRACTICE

You will now practice moving around an empty worksheet.

Setup: Ensure that Excel is loaded and a blank worksheet appears.

1 With the cell pointer in cell A1, move to cell D4 using the following keystrokes:
PRESS: ➡ three times
PRESS: ⬇ three times
Notice that the cell address, D4, is displayed in the Name box and that the column (D) and row (4) headings in the frame area appear boldface.

2 To move to cell E12 using the mouse:
CLICK: cell E12
(*Hint:* Position the cross mouse pointer over cell E12 and click the left mouse button once.)

3 To move to cell E124 using the keyboard:
PRESS: `PgDn` until row 124 is in view
PRESS: `↑` or `↓` to select cell E124
(*Hint*: The `PgUp` and `PgDn` keys are used to move up and down a worksheet by as many rows as fit in the current document window.)

4 To move to cell E24 using the mouse, position the mouse pointer on the vertical scroll box and then drag the scroll box upwards to row 24, as shown in Figure 1.6. Notice that a yellow Scroll Tip appears identifying the current row. When you see "Row: 24" in the Scroll Tip, release the mouse button. Then click cell E24 to select the cell.

Figure 1.6

Dragging the vertical scroll bar

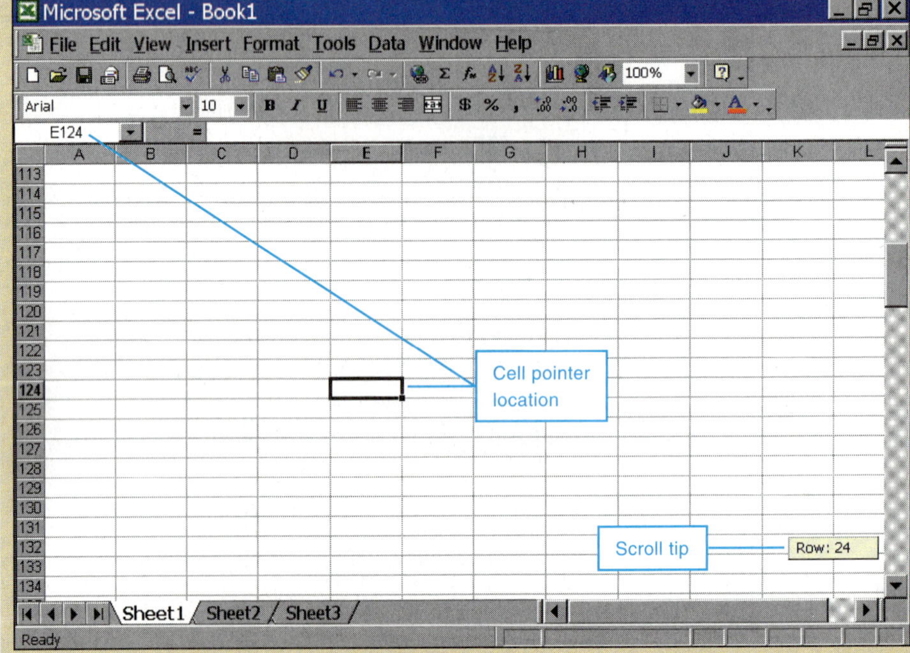

5 To move quickly to a specific cell address, such as cell AE24:
CLICK: once in the Name box
TYPE: **ae24**
PRESS: `ENTER`
The cell pointer scoots over to cell AE24. (*Hint*: Because cell addresses are not case sensitive, you need not use capital letters when typing a cell address.)

6 To move the cell pointer in any direction until the cell contents change from empty to filled, filled to empty, or until a border is encountered, press CTRL with an arrow key. For example:
PRESS: CTRL + → to move to column IV
PRESS: CTRL + ↓ to move to row 65536
The cell pointer now appears in the bottom right-hand corner of the worksheet.

7 To move back to cell A1:
PRESS: CTRL + HOME

1.2.2 Entering Text

FEATURE
Text labels are used to enhance the readability of a worksheet by providing headings, instructions, and descriptive information. Although a typical worksheet column is only eight or nine characters wide, a single cell can hold thousands of characters. With longer entries, the text simply spills over the column border into the next cell, if it is empty.

METHOD
TYPE: *a text string*
PRESS: ENTER

PRACTICE
In this example, you begin a simple worksheet by specifying text labels for the row and column headings.

Setup: Ensure that the cell pointer is positioned in cell A1 of the Sheet1 worksheet.

1 Let's begin the worksheet by entering a title. As you type the following entry, watch the Formula bar:
TYPE: Income Statement

2 To accept an entry, you press ENTER or click the Enter button (☑) in the Formula bar. To cancel an entry, you press ESC or click the Cancel (☒) button. To proceed:
PRESS: ENTER
Notice that the entry does not fit in a single column and must spill over into column B. This is acceptable as long as you don't place an entry into cell B1. Otherwise, you need to increase the width of column A.

After you press (ENTER), you may notice that the cell pointer moves to the next row. (*Note:* If your cell pointer remains in cell A1, choose Tools, Options from the Menu bar and click the *Edit* tab in the Options dialog box. Ensure that there is a check mark in the *Move selection after Enter* check box, as shown in Figure 1.7.)

Figure 1.7

Options dialog box: *Edit* tab

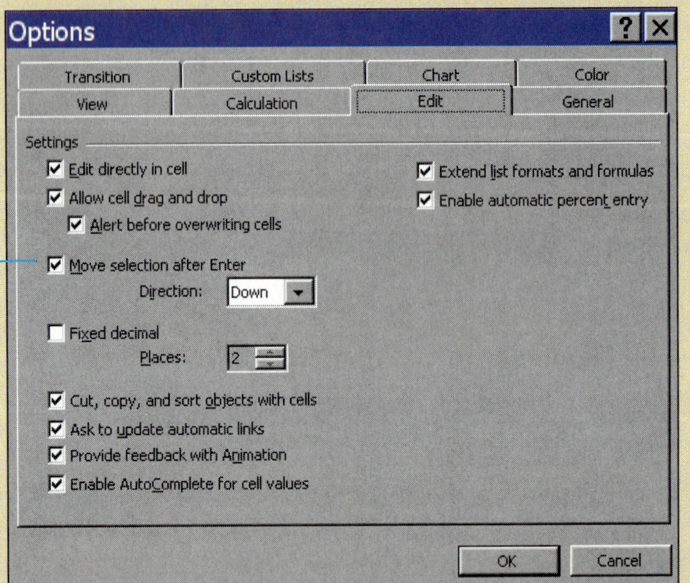

Ensure that this check box is selected and that the *Direction* drop-down list box displays Down.

3 Move the cell pointer to cell B3.

4 Enter the following text label:
TYPE: **Revenue**
PRESS: ⬇
Notice that pressing ⬇ provides the same result as pressing (ENTER).

5 To complete entering the row labels:
TYPE: **Expenses**
PRESS: ⬇
TYPE: **Profit**
PRESS: (ENTER)
All of the text data has now been entered into the worksheet.

1.2.3 Entering Dates

FEATURE
You enter dates into a cell using one of the common date formats recognized by Excel, such as mm/dd/yy (12/25/99) or dd-mmm-yy (25-Dec-99). Excel treats a date (or time) as a formatted number or value. Consequently, you can use date values to perform arithmetic calculations, such as finding out how many days have elapsed between two calendar dates.

METHOD
TYPE: *a date*, using a recognized date format
PRESS: ENTER

PRACTICE
You will now add date values as column headings.

Setup: Ensure that you have completed the previous lesson.

1 Move to cell C2.

2 To enter a month and year combination as a date value, you use the format mmm-yy. For example:
TYPE: **Sep-99**
PRESS: ➡
(*Note:* Pressing ➡ moves the cell pointer one cell to the right.)

3 In cell D2, do the following:
TYPE: **Oct-99**
PRESS: ➡
TYPE: **Nov-99**
PRESS: ➡
TYPE: **Dec-99**
PRESS: ENTER
Your worksheet should now appear similar to Figure 1.8.

Figure 1.8

Entering date values into a worksheet

	A	B	C	D	E	F	G
1	Income Statement						
2			Sep-99	Oct-99	Nov-99	Dec-99	
3		Revenue					
4		Expenses					
5		Profit					
6							

4 Move the cell pointer to cell C2. Looking in the Formula bar, notice that the entry reads "9/1/1999" and not "Sep-99." As shown here, a cell's appearance on the worksheet can differ from its actual contents.

1.2.4   Entering Numbers

FEATURE

Numbers are entered into a worksheet for use in performing cal-culations, preparing reports, and creating charts. You can enter a raw or unformatted number, like 3.141593, or a formatted num-ber, such as 37.5% or $24,732.33. It is important to note that phone numbers, Social Security numbers, and zip codes are not treated as numeric values, since they are never used in performing mathematical calculations. Numbers and dates are right-aligned when entered as opposed to text, which aligns with the left bor-der of a cell.

METHOD

TYPE: *a number*, using recognized symbols
PRESS: `ENTER`

PRACTICE

You will now add some numbers to the worksheet.

Setup: Ensure that you have completed the previous lesson.

1   Move to cell C3.

2   To enter a value for September's revenue, do the following:
TYPE: 112,500
PRESS: ➡
Notice that you placed a comma (,) in the entry to separate the thousands from the hundreds. Excel recognizes symbols such as commas, dollar signs, and percentage symbols as numeric format-ting.

3   In cell D3, do the following:
TYPE: 115,800
PRESS: ➡
TYPE: 98,750
PRESS: ➡
TYPE: 112,830
PRESS: `ENTER`

4   Move the cell pointer to cell C3. Notice that the Formula bar reads "112500" without a comma separating the thousands. Simi-lar to date values, numeric values may be formatted to display differently on the worksheet than the actual value stored.

1.2.5 Entering Formulas

FEATURE

You use formulas to perform calculations, such as adding a column of numbers. A **formula** is an expression, containing numbers, cell references, and/or mathematical operators, that is entered into a cell in order to display a result. The basic mathematical operators ("+" for addition, "-" for subtraction, "/" for division, and "*" for multiplication) and rules of precedence from your high school algebra textbooks apply to an Excel formula. In other words, Excel calculates what appears in parentheses first, multiplication and division operations (from left to right) second, and, lastly, addition and subtraction (again from left to right.)

METHOD

1. SELECT: the cell where you want the result to appear
2. TYPE: **=** (an equal sign)
3. TYPE: *the desired expression*, such as A4+B4
4. PRESS: ENTER

PRACTICE

You will now enter formulas into the worksheet that multiply the Revenue values by 60% to yield the related Expenses.

Setup: Ensure that you have completed the previous lesson.

1 Move to cell C4. Notice that the first step in entering a formula is to move to the cell where you want the result to display.

2 To inform Excel that you will be entering a formula, you type an equal sign. Do the following:
TYPE: **=**

3 In order to calculate September's expenses as 60% of the month's revenue, you multiply the cell containing the revenue value (cell C3) by 60%. Do the following:
TYPE: c3*60%
PRESS: ➡
The result, 67500, appears in the cell.

4 In cell D4, you will use a method called *pointing* to enter the required formula. With pointing, you use the mouse or keyboard to point to the cell reference that you want included in an expression. To illustrate:
TYPE: **=**
PRESS: ⬆
Notice that a dashed marquee appears around cell D3 and that the value "D3" appears in the Formula bar.

5 To finish entering the formula:
TYPE: *60%
PRESS: ➡
The result, 69480, appears in the cell.

6 For November's calculation, you will use the mouse to point to the desired cell reference. Do the following:
TYPE: =
CLICK: cell E3
Notice that cell E3 displays a dashed marquee to denote its selection.

7 To complete the row:
TYPE: *60%
PRESS: ➡
The result, 59250, appears.

8 Lastly, enter the formula for December by typing:
TYPE: =f3*.6
PRESS: ENTER
The result, 67698, appears in cell F4. Notice that you used the value .6 instead of 60% to yield this result. Your worksheet should now appear similar to Figure 1.9.

Figure 1.9

Entering formulas into a worksheet

	A	B	C	D	E	F	G
1	Income Statement						
2			Sep-99	Oct-99	Nov-99	Dec-99	
3		Revenue	112,500	115,800	98,750	112,830	
4		Expenses	67500	69480	59250	67698	
5		Profit					
6							

9 To illustrate the true power of Excel, you can change a cell's value and all the formulas in the worksheet that reference that cell are updated automatically. Do the following:
ELECT: cell F3
TYPE: 100,000
PRESS: ENTER
Notice that the Expense calculation for Dec-99 (cell F4) is immediately updated to display 60000.

10 To conclude this module, you will close the worksheet without saving the changes. From the Menu bar:
CHOOSE: File, Close

11 In the dialog box that appears:
CLICK: No command button
There should be no workbooks open in the application window.

12  To display a new workbook and worksheet for use in the next module:
CLICK: New button ([⬜]) on the Standard toolbar
A new workbook, entitled Book2, appears in the document area.

1.2 Self Check   Explain why a phone number is not considered a numeric value in an Excel worksheet.

1.3 Editing Your Work

What if you type a label, a number, or a formula into a cell and then decide it needs to be changed? Both novices and experts alike make data entry errors when creating a worksheet. Fortunately, Excel provides several features for editing information that has already been entered. In this module, you learn how to modify existing cell entries, erase the contents of a cell, and undo a command or typing error.

1.3.1 Editing a Cell's Contents

FEATURE
You can edit information either as you type or after you have entered data into a cell. Effective editing of a worksheet is an extremely valuable skill. In fact, few worksheets are created from scratch in favor of simply revising older worksheets. And, as a relatively new user of Excel, you will often find yourself engaged in modifying and maintaining worksheets created by other people.

METHOD
- To edit data as you type, press [BACKSPACE] and then correct the typographical error or spelling mistake.
- To replace a cell's contents entirely, select the cell and then type over the original data.
- To edit a cell whose contents are too long or complicated to retype, double-click the cell to perform **in-cell editing.** In this mode, the flashing insertion point appears ready for editing inside the cell. Alternatively, you can press the [F2] EDIT key or click in the Formula bar to enter Edit mode, in which case you edit the cell's contents in the Formula bar. Regardless, once the insertion point appears, you perform your edits using the arrow keys, [DELETE], and [BACKSPACE].

PRACTICE

In this lesson, you create a simple inventory worksheet. Then, you practice modifying the data stored in the worksheet cells.

Setup: Ensure that a blank worksheet appears in the application window.

1 SELECT: cell A1
(*Note:* For the remainder of this guide, you may use either the keyboard or mouse to move the cell pointer.)

2 Let's enter a title for this worksheet:
TYPE: **Staples Food Supplies**
PRESS: ⬇
TYPE: **Inventory List**
PRESS: **ENTER**

3 SELECT: cell A4

4 Now let's add some column headings:
TYPE: **Code**
PRESS: ➡
TYPE: **Product**
PRESS: ➡
TYPE: **Quantity**
PRESS: ➡
TYPE: **Price**
PRESS: **ENTER**

5 On your own, complete the worksheet as displayed in Figure 1.10. If you make a typing error, use **BACKSPACE** to correct your mistake prior to pressing **ENTER** or an arrow key.

Figure 1.10

Creating an inventory worksheet

	A	B	C	D	E
1	Staples Food Supplies				
2	Inventory List				
3					
4	Code	Product	Quantity	Price	
5	AP01B	Apples	200	0.17	
6	DM21P	Milk	40	2.28	
7	DB29G	Butter	35	3.91	
8	FL78K	Flour	78	1.25	
9	RS04G	Sugar	290	7.23	
10					
11					

6 As the editor for this worksheet, you've noticed that the column heading in cell D4 should read "Cost" and not "Price." To replace this entry:
SELECT: cell D4
TYPE: **Cost**
PRESS: ENTER
Notice that the new entry overwrites the existing entry.

7 You activate in-cell editing by double-clicking a cell. To practice, let's change the quantity of butter from 35 to 350 packages:
DOUBLE-CLICK: cell C7

Notice that the Status bar now reads "Edit" in the bottom left-hand corner, instead of the word "Ready." A flashing insertion point should also appear inside the cell.

8 To add a "0" to the end of the cell's contents:
PRESS: END to move the insertion point to the far right
TYPE: 0
PRESS: ENTER
Notice that the Status bar once again reads "Ready."

9 You can also activate Edit mode by pressing the F2 EDIT key or by clicking the I-beam mouse pointer inside the Formula bar. In this step, you edit one of the product codes. Do the following:
SELECT: cell A6
Notice that the text "DM21P" appears in the Formula bar.

10 To modify the "DM" to read "DN," position the I-beam mouse pointer over the Formula bar entry, immediately to the left of the letter "M." Click the left mouse button and drag the mouse pointer to the right until the "M" is highlighted. Now that the desired letter is selected:
TYPE: N
PRESS: ENTER
The letter "N" replaces the selected letter in the Formula bar.

1.3.2 Erasing a Cell

FEATURE
You can quickly erase a single cell, a group of cells, or the entire worksheet with a few simple keystrokes. To erase a cell's contents, select the cell and then press DELETE. If you would like to delete other characteristics of a cell, such as formatting attributes or attached comments, choose the Edit, Clear command from the Menu bar.

METHOD

After choosing the Edit, Clear command, select one of the following:

- *All*   Removes the cell contents, formatting, and comments
- *Formats*   Removes the cell formatting only
- *Contents*   Removes the cell contents only; same as pressing (DELETE)
- *Comments*   Removes the cell comments only

PRACTICE

You will now practice erasing information that is stored in the inventory worksheet.

Setup: Ensure that you have completed the previous lesson.

1 SELECT: cell A2

2 To delete the subtitle:
PRESS: (DELETE)
Notice that you need not press (ENTER) or any other confirmation key. Pressing (DELETE) removes the contents of the cell immediately.

3 SELECT: cell A9

4 In order to delete a group of cells, you must first select the cells. In this step, you select the inventory line item for Sugar. Do the following:
PRESS: (SHIFT) and hold it down
CLICK: cell D9
RELEASE: (SHIFT)
The four cells should now appear highlighted, as shown in Figure 1.11.

Figure 1.11

Selecting a group of cells to erase

	A	B	C	D	E
1	Staples Food Supplies				
2					
3					
4	Code	Product	Quantity	Cost	
5	AP01B	Apples	200	0.17	
6	DN21P	Milk	40	2.28	
7	DB29G	Butter	350	3.91	
8	FL78K	Flour	78	1.25	
9	RS04G	Sugar	290	7.23	
10					

5 To erase all of the cell information:
CHOOSE: Edit, Clear from the Menu bar
CHOOSE: All from the cascading menu

6 PRESS: CTRL + HOME to move the cell pointer to cell A1

1.3.3 Using Undo and Redo

FEATURE
The **Undo command** allows you to cancel up to your last 16 actions. The command is most useful for immediately reversing a command or modification that was mistakenly performed. If an error occurred several steps before, you can continue "undoing" commands until you return the worksheet to its original state prior to the mistake. Although somewhat confusing, you can undo an Undo command. The **Redo command** allows you to reverse an Undo command that you performed accidentally.

METHOD
To reverse an action or command:
- CLICK: Undo button (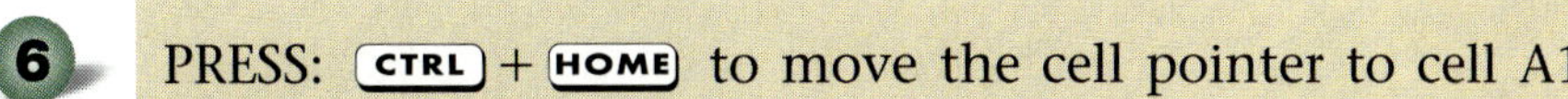), or
- CHOOSE: Edit, Undo, or
- PRESS: CTRL +z

To reverse an Undo command:
- CLICK: Redo button ( )

PRACTICE
Let's practice reversing common editing procedures using the Undo command.

Setup: Ensure that you have completed the previous lesson.

1 SELECT: cell A5

2 In order to practice using the Undo command, let's delete the contents of the cell:
PRESS: DELETE

3 To undo the last command or action performed:
CLICK: Undo button ( ) on the Standard toolbar
(*CAUTION:* The tip of the mouse pointer should be placed over the curved arrow and not on the attached down arrow.)

4 SELECT: cell C5

5 To modify the quantity of Apples:
TYPE: 175
PRESS: ENTER

6 To undo the last entry using a keyboard shortcut:
PRESS: CTRL + z
The value 175 is replaced with 200 in cell C5. (*Hint:* This shortcut keystroke allows you to continue entering data without having to reach for the mouse or choose a menu command.)

7 Let's view the commands that Excel has been tracking for the Undo command. To begin, position the mouse pointer over the down arrow attached to the Undo button ( ) on the Standard toolbar. Then click the down arrow once to display the drop-down list of "undoable" or reversible commands.

8 Move the mouse pointer slowly downward to select multiple commands. Your screen should appear similar to Figure 1.12.

Figure 1.12

Displaying reversible commands

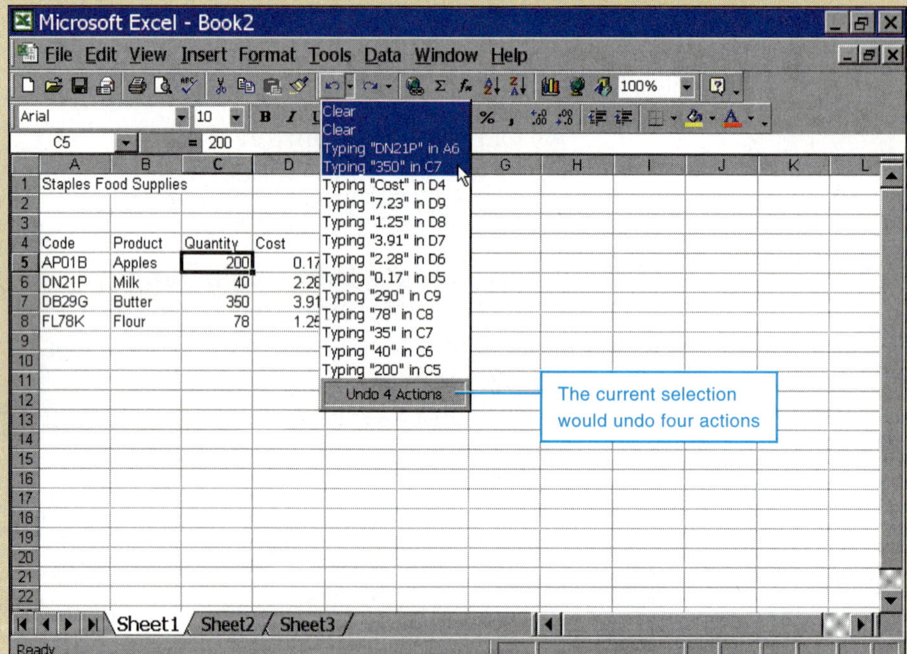

9 To remove the drop-down list without making a selection:
CLICK: down arrow attached to the Undo button ( )
(*Hint:* You can also click the Title bar, which provides a larger mouse target than the button's down arrow.)

10 To conclude this module, close the worksheet without saving the changes. Do the following:
CHOOSE: File, Close
CLICK: No command button

1.4   Managing Files

Managing the workbook files that you create is an important skill. When you are creating a workbook, it exists only in the computer's RAM (random access memory), which is highly volatile. If the power to your computer goes off, your workbook is lost. For security, you need to save your workbook permanently to the local hard disk, a network drive, or a floppy diskette.

Saving your work to a named file on a disk is similar to placing it into a filing cabinet. For important workbooks (ones that you cannot risk losing), you should save your work at least every 15 minutes, or whenever you're interrupted, to protect against an unexpected power outage or other catastrophe. When naming your workbook files, you can use up to 255 characters, including spaces, but it's wise to keep the length under 20 characters. Furthermore, you cannot use the following characters in naming your workbooks:

$$\backslash \quad / \quad : \quad ; \quad * \quad ? \quad " \quad < \quad > \quad |$$

In the following lessons, you will practice several file management procedures, including creating a new workbook, saving and closing workbooks, and opening existing workbooks.

Important: *In this guide, we refer to the files that have been created for you as the **student data files**. Depending on your computer or lab setup, these files may be located on a floppy diskette, in a folder on your hard disk, or on a network server. If necessary, ask your instructor or lab assistant where to find these data files. You will also need to identify a storage location for the files that you create, modify, and save. To download the Advantage Series' student data files from the Internet, visit McGraw-Hill's Information Technology Web site at:*

http://www.mhhe.com/it

1.4.1 Beginning a New Workbook

FEATURE

There are three ways to start creating a new workbook. First, you can start with a blank workbook and then enter all of the data from scratch. Next, you can select a workbook **template** that provides pre-existing data and design elements. A template is a time-saver that promotes consistency in both design and function. And, lastly, you can employ a **wizard** to help lead you step-by-step through creating a particular type of workbook.

METHOD

- To display a new blank workbook:
  CLICK: New button (□)
- To begin a workbook using a template or wizard:
  CHOOSE: File, New

PRACTICE

In this example, you use one of Excel's prebuilt templates to create a new workbook for an invoicing application.

Setup: Ensure that no workbooks are displayed in the application window.

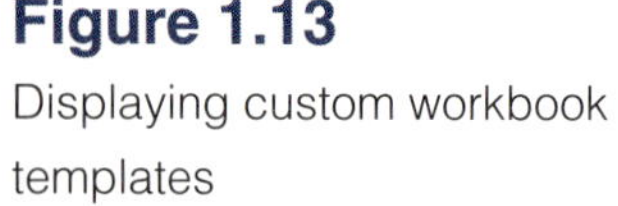

To view the templates that are available:
CHOOSE: File, New
The blank "Workbook" template icon appears on the *General* tab of the New dialog box. This workbook template is used by Excel when you click the New button (□) on the Standard toolbar.

The custom templates that are shipped with Excel and that have been installed onto your system appear on the next tab:
CLICK: *Spreadsheet Solutions* tab
Your screen should appear similar to Figure 1.13.

Figure 1.13

Displaying custom workbook templates

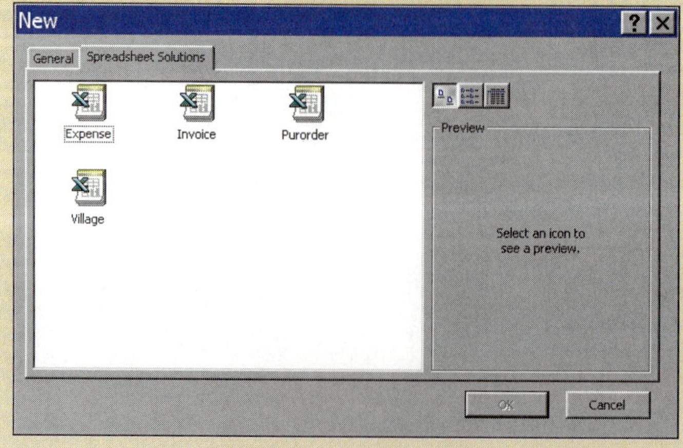

3 To create a new workbook based on the "Invoice" template:
DOUBLE-CLICK: Invoice template icon ( )
(*Note:* If you or your lab administrator has not installed the workbook templates, you must skip to step 7.)

4 A warning dialog box may appear stating that the template may contain a **macro virus.** A virus is a hostile program that is secretly stored and shipped inside of another program or document. As this template is provided by Microsoft and not from an unknown source, you can safely enable the macros and continue:
CLICK: Enable Macros

5 If other warning dialog boxes appear, click the appropriate command buttons to remove them from the screen. You should now see the Invoice template, as shown in Figure 1.14.

Figure 1.14

New workbook based on the
Invoice template

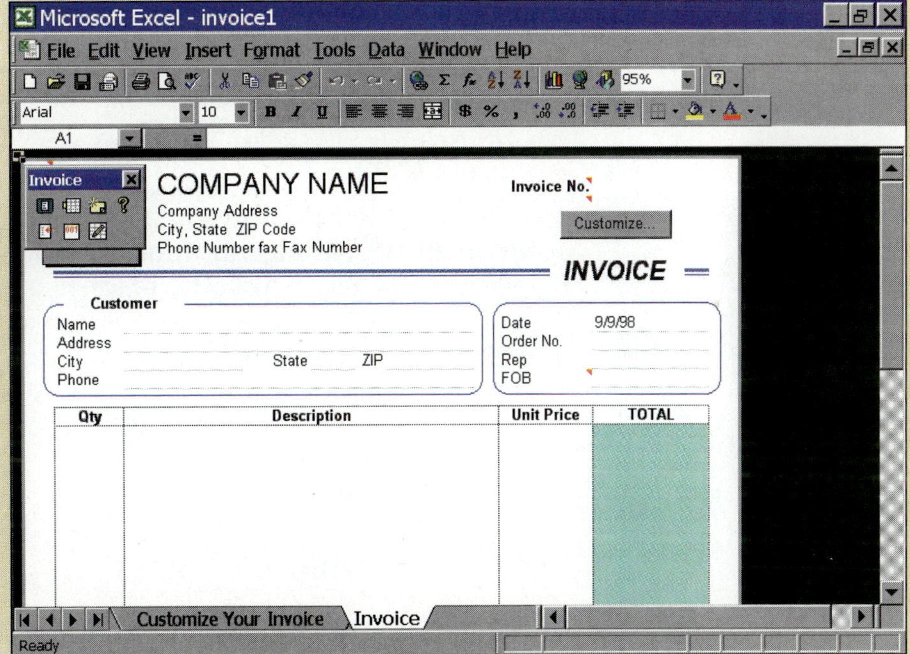

6 The workbook templates provided by Excel contain many advanced features. Rather than introducing these features now, let's close the workbook and continue our discussion of file management.
CHOOSE: File, Close
CLICK: No command button, if asked to save the changes

1.4.2 Saving and Closing

FEATURE

There are many options available for saving a workbook to a permanent storage location. The File, Save command and the Save button (🖫) on the toolbar allow you to overwrite an existing disk file with the latest version of a workbook. The File, Save As command enables you to save a workbook to a new filename or storage location. Once you have finished working with a workbook, you close the file to free up valuable system resources (RAM).

METHOD

- To save a workbook:
  CLICK: Save button (🖫), or
  CHOOSE: File, Save, or
  CHOOSE: File, Save As
- To close a workbook:
  CLICK: its Close button (☒), or
  CHOOSE: File, Close

PRACTICE

You will now practice saving and closing a workbook.

Setup: Identify a storage location for your personal workbook files. If you want to use a diskette, place it into the diskette drive now.

1 To create a new workbook from scratch:
CLICK: New button (▫)
TYPE: My Library into cell A1
PRESS: ENTER

2 To save the new workbook:
CLICK: Save button (🖫)

(*Note:* If you have not yet saved a workbook, Excel displays the Save As dialog box regardless of the method you chose to save the file. The filenames and directories that appear in your Save As dialog box may differ from those shown in Figure 1.15.)

Figure 1.15

Save As dialog box

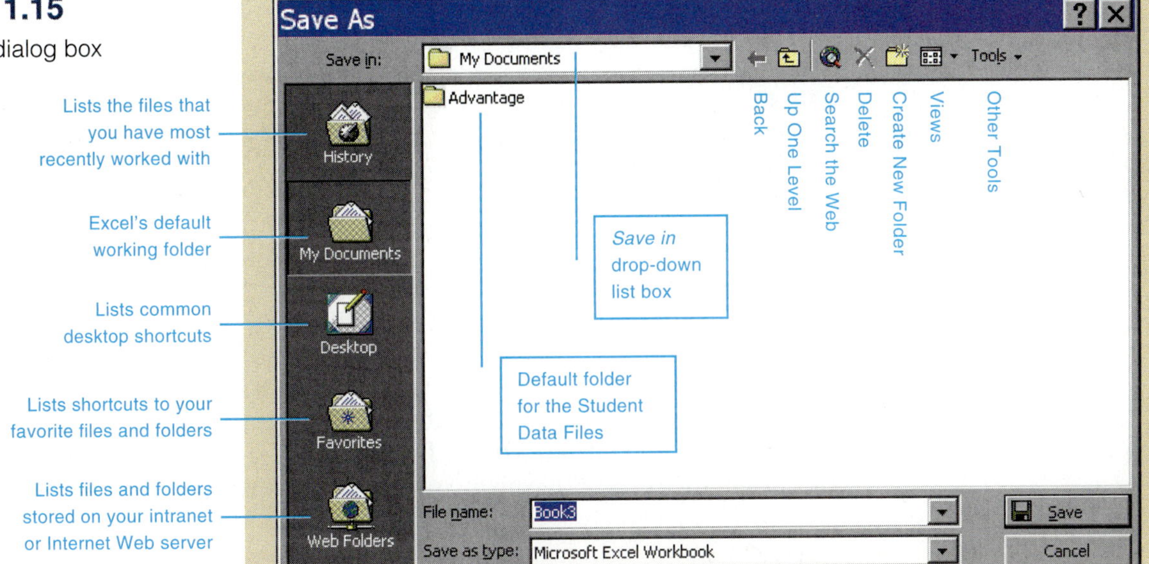

EXCEL

3   The **Places bar,** located along the left border of the dialog box, provides convenient access to commonly used storage locations. To illustrate, let's view the files in your "My Documents" folder:
CLICK: My Documents button (📁) in the Places bar

4   Let's browse the local hard disk:
CLICK: down arrow attached to the *Save in* drop-down list box
SELECT: Hard Disk C:
The list area displays the folders and files stored in the root directory of your local hard disk.

5   To drill down into one of the folders:
DOUBLE-CLICK: Program Files folder
This folder contains the program files for several applications.

6   To return to the previous display:
CLICK: Back button (⬅) in the dialog box

7   Now, using either the Places bar or the *Save In* drop-down list box:
SELECT: *a storage location for your personal files*
(*Note:* In this guide, we save files to the My Documents folder.)

8   Let's give the workbook file a unique name. Do the following:
DOUBLE-CLICK: the *workbook name* appearing in the *File name* text box to select it
TYPE: **My Library**

9   To complete the procedure:
CLICK: Save command button
Notice that the workbook's name now appears in the Title bar.

10   Let's close the workbook:
CHOOSE: File, Close

There are times when you'll want to save an existing workbook under a different filename. For example, you may want to keep different versions of the same workbook on your disk. Or, you may want to use one workbook as a template for future workbooks that are similar in style and format. Rather than retyping an entirely new workbook, you can retrieve an old workbook file, edit the information, and then save it under a different name using the File, Save As command.

In Addition Creating a New Folder	Folders can help you organize your work. They also make it easier to find documents and back up your data. For example, you can use a folder to collect all of the workbooks related to a single fiscal period. You can also specify a folder to hold all of your personal documents, such as resumes and expense reports. While the Windows Explorer should be used for most folder management tasks, Excel allows you to create a new folder from the Save As dialog box. After you navigate to where you want the folder to appear, click the Create New Folder button (). In the New Folder dialog box, type a name for the folder and press **ENTER**.

1.4.3 Opening an Existing Workbook

FEATURE

You use the Open dialog box to search for and retrieve existing workbooks that are stored on your local hard disk, a floppy diskette, a network server, or on the Web. If you want to load Excel and an existing workbook at the same time, you can use the Open Office Document command on the Start menu. Or, if you have recently used the workbook, you can try the Start, Documents command, which lists the 15 most recently used files.

METHOD

- CLICK: Open button (), or
- CHOOSE: File, Open

PRACTICE

You will now retrieve a student data file named EXC140 that displays the market penetration for snowboard sales by Canadian province.

Setup: Ensure that you have completed the previous lesson. There should be no workbooks displayed in the application window. You will also need to know the storage location for the student data files.

1 To display the Open dialog box:
CLICK: Open button (📂)

2 Using the Places bar and the *Look in* drop-down list box, locate the folder containing the student data files. (*Note:* In this guide, we retrieve the student data files from a folder named "Advantage.")

3 To view additional information about each file:
CLICK: down arrow beside the Views button (▦▾)
CHOOSE: Details
Each workbook is presented on a single line with additional file information, such as its size, type, and date, as shown in Figure 1.16. (*Hint:* You can sort the filenames in this list area by clicking on one of the column heading buttons.)

Figure 1.16

Open dialog box

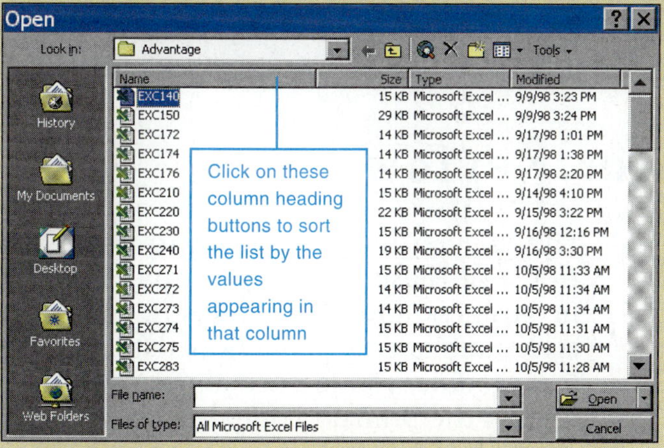

4 To return to a multicolumn list format:
CLICK: down arrow beside the Views button
CHOOSE: List

5   Let's open one of the workbooks in the list area:
DOUBLE-CLICK: EXC140
The dialog box disappears and the workbook is loaded into the application window. (*Note:* The "EXC140" filename reflects that this workbook is used in module 1.4 of the Excel learning guide.)

6   Now close the EXC140 workbook without saving the changes.

7   To exit Microsoft Excel:
CHOOSE: File, Exit

In Addition Opening and Saving Files of Different Formats	In the Open and Save As dialog boxes, you will notice a drop-down list box named *Files of type* and *Save as type* respectively. These list boxes allow you to select different file formats for opening and saving your files. For instance, you can save a workbook so that users with an earlier version of Excel are able to open and edit its contents. You can also open a file that was created using another spreadsheet software program, such as Lotus or Quattro Pro.

1.4 Self Check   In the Open and Save As dialog boxes, how do the List and Details views differ? What two other views are accessible from the Views button?

1.5 Chapter Review

This chapter introduced you to using Microsoft Excel 2000, an electronic spreadsheet program. Spreadsheet software is used extensively in business and other industries for performing statistical analyses and summarizing numerical data for inclusion into reports. In the first module, you learned about worksheets and were led on a guided tour of the primary components in Excel. Next, you created a worksheet from scratch by entering text, numbers, dates, and formulas. The third module spent time explaining the importance of editing a worksheet effectively. In the last module, you learned how to create, save, and open workbook files.

1.5.1 Command Summary

Many of the commands and procedures appearing in this chapter are summarized in the following table.

Skill Set	To Perform This Task . . .	Do the Following . . .
Using Excel	Launch Microsoft Excel	CLICK: Start button (Start) CHOOSE: Programs, Microsoft Excel
	Exit Microsoft Excel	CLICK: its Close button (x), or CHOOSE: File, Exit
	Close a workbook	CLICK: its Close button (x), or CHOOSE: File, Close
	Customize menus and toolbars	CHOOSE: Tools, Customize
Managing Files	Create a new workbook	CLICK: New button, or CHOOSE: File, New
	Use a template to create a new workbook	CHOOSE: File, New CLICK: *Spreadsheet Solutions* tab DOUBLE-CLICK: *a template*
	Locate and open an existing workbook	CLICK: Open button, or CHOOSE: File, Open
	Open files of different formats	SELECT: a format from the *Files of type* drop-down list box in the Open dialog box
	Save a workbook	CLICK: Save button, or CHOOSE: File, Save
	Save a workbook using a different filename, location, or format	CHOOSE: File, Save As
	Create a new folder while displaying the Save As dialog box	CLICK: Create New Folder button

Continued

Skill Set	To Perform This Task . . .	Do the Following . . .
Using Excel	Launch Microsoft Excel	CLICK: Start button ([Start]) CHOOSE: Programs, Microsoft Excel
Working with Cells	Navigate to a specific cell	CLICK: in the Name box TYPE: *the desired cell address*
	Enter text labels, numbers, and dates	TYPE: *the desired entry*
	Enter a formula	TYPE: *=expression*
	Replace a cell's contents with new data	TYPE: *a new entry*
	Activate Edit mode to revise a cell's contents	DOUBLE-CLICK: the desired cell, or CLICK: in the Formula bar, or PRESS: F2 EDIT key
	Delete cell contents	PRESS: DELETE
	Delete all information associated with a cell	CHOOSE: Edit, Clear, All
	Reverse or undo a command or series of commands	CLICK: Undo button, or CHOOSE: Edit, Undo, or PRESS: CTRL + z
	Reverse or undo an Undo command	CLICK: Redo button

1.5.2 Key Terms

This section specifies page references for the key terms identified in this chapter. For a complete list of definitions, refer to the Glossary provided in the Appendix.

adaptive menus, *p. 10*

application window, *p. 8*

cell, *p. 5*

cell address, *p. 5*

cell pointer, *p. 13*

chart sheet, *p. 6*

document window, *p. 8*

formula, *p. 19*

in-cell editing, *p. 21*

macro virus, *p. 29*

Name box, *p. 13*

Places bar, *p. 31*

Redo command, *p. 25*

template, *p. 28*

Undo command, *p. 25*

wizard, *p. 28*

workbook, *p. 6*

worksheet, *p. 5*

1.6 Review Questions

1.6.1 Short Answer

1. Explain the difference between an application window and a document window.
2. What is the difference between a toolbar and the Menu bar?
3. What is the fastest method for moving to cell DF8192?
4. What is significant about how dates are entered into a worksheet?
5. How do you enter a formula into a cell? Provide an example.
6. With respect to entering a formula, explain the term *pointing*.
7. How would you reverse the last three commands executed?
8. How do you create a new workbook based on a template?
9. How would you save a copy of the currently displayed workbook onto a diskette?
10. How would you save a workbook in Excel using the Lotus spreadsheet file format?

1.6.2 True/False

1. ____ The cell reference "100AX" is an acceptable cell address.
2. ____ Pressing (CTRL) + (HOME) moves the cell pointer to cell A1.
3. ____ An Excel worksheet contains over 64,000 rows.
4. ____ Once a formula has been entered into a cell, you cannot edit the expression.
5. ____ A formula may contain both numbers and cell references, such as A1*B7-500.
6. ____ Pressing (DELETE) erases the contents of a cell.
7. ____ Pressing (CTRL) +x will undo the last command executed.
8. ____ You can create a new folder from within the Save As dialog box.
9. ____ You access Excel's workbook templates using the File, Open command.
10. ____ You can open files in Excel that have been created using different application software programs.

1.6.3 Multiple Choice

1. Which mouse shape is used to select cells in a worksheet?
   a. arrow
   b. cross
   c. hand
   d. hourglass

2. Excel displays the current cell address in the:
   a. Name box
   b. Status bar
   c. Title bar
   d. Standard toolbar

3. Using a mouse, you move around a worksheet quickly using the:
   a. Status bar
   b. Tab Scrolling arrows
   c. Tab Split bar
   d. Scroll bars

4. When you enter a text label, Excel justifies the entry automatically between the cell borders as:
   a. left-aligned
   b. centered
   c. right-aligned
   d. fully justified

5. When you enter a date, Excel justifies the entry automatically between the cell borders as:
   a. left-aligned
   b. centered
   c. right-aligned
   d. fully justified

6. Which keyboard shortcut lets you modify the contents of a cell?
   a. CTRL
   b. SHIFT
   c. F2
   d. F5

7. Which is the correct formula for adding cells B4 and F7?
   a. =B4*F7
   b. +B4+F7
   c. $B4:F7
   d. =B4+F7

8. To save the current workbook using a different filename:
   a. CHOOSE: File, Save
   b. CHOOSE: File, Save As
   c. CLICK: Save button
   d. CLICK: File, Rename

9. To open a new blank workbook:
   a. CLICK: New button
   b. CHOOSE: File, Open
   c. CHOOSE: File, Blank
   d. CHOOSE: File, Template

10. To reverse an Undo command:
   a. CHOOSE: Edit, Go Back
   b. CHOOSE: File, Reverse Undo
   c. CLICK: Reverse button
   d. CLICK: Redo button

1.7 Hands-On Projects

1.7.1 Grandview College: Semester Information

This exercise lets you practice fundamental worksheet skills, such as moving around a worksheet and entering text labels.

1. Load Microsoft Excel and ensure that a blank worksheet is displayed.
2. To enter a title label for the worksheet:
   SELECT: cell A1
   TYPE: **Grandview Community College**
   PRESS: ENTER
3. In cell A2:
   TYPE: **Enrollment Statistics**
   PRESS: ⬇ twice
   The cell pointer should now appear in cell A4.
4. Let's add some row heading labels:
   TYPE: **Courses**
   CLICK: cell A7
   Notice that when you click a new cell location, the contents are moved from the Formula bar into the cell as if you had pressed ENTER.
5. TYPE: **Instructors**
   CLICK: cell A10
6. TYPE: **Students**
   PRESS: ENTER
7. On your own, enter the following text labels:

Move to cell	*TYPE:*
B5	**credit**
B6	**non-credit**
B8	**salaried**
B9	**contract**
B11	**full-time**
B12	**part-time**

8. To quickly move the cell pointer to the first column heading:
   CLICK: the Name box
   TYPE: **c4**
   PRESS: ENTER

9. In cells C4 and D4, enter the following column headings:
   TYPE: **Fall-99**
   PRESS: ➡
   TYPE: **Spring-00**
   PRESS: ENTER
10. To move the cell pointer to cell A1:
    PRESS: CTRL + HOME
11. Save the workbook as "Grandview Stats" to your personal storage location. (*Hint:* If you are unsure of where to store your personal files, select the "My Documents" folder.)
12. Close the workbook before proceeding.

1.7.2 Fast Forward Video: Store Summary

In this exercise, you will edit text labels in an existing worksheet, enter numbers and dates, and practice using the Undo command.

1. Open the data file named EXC172.
2. Save the workbook as "Video Stores" to your personal storage location.
3. To change the "Store" column heading to read "Location:"
   SELECT: cell B3
   TYPE: **Location**
   PRESS: ENTER
4. To correct a spelling mistake that occurs in the first location's name:
   DOUBLE-CLICK: cell B5
   PRESS: END
   PRESS: ⬅
   TYPE: **w**
   PRESS: ENTER
   The entry should now read "Downtown."
5. To expand upon the abbreviation used for the second location's name:
   SELECT: cell B6
   PRESS: F2
   PRESS: BackSpace to remove the last letter
   TYPE: **ream**
   The location name should now read "Coldstream."

6. To correct an error appearing in the second column heading:
   SELECT: cell D3
7. Position the I-beam mouse pointer to the right of the text in the formula bar and click the left mouse button once. The flashing insertion point should appear at the end of the word "Hour." Then do the following:
   TYPE: **s**
   PRESS: ENTER
   The entry now reads "Hours."
8. On your own, change the column heading "Tapes" to "Videos" and then correct the last heading so that it reads "Games."
9. Now let's put the current date on the worksheet:
   SELECT: cell D1
   TYPE: *the current date* using the format dd/mm/yy
10. Complete the following worksheet as shown in Figure 1.17.

Figure 1.17

Entering values into the Video Stores workbook

	A	B	C	D	E	F	G
1	Fast Forward Video			12/25/99			
2							
3		Location		Hours	Staff	Videos	Games
4							
5		Downtown		68	7	2,325	
6		Coldstream		68	5	1,790	
7		Westside		62	3	857	
8		Sahali Mall		74	9	2,114	
9							
10							

11. To delete the last column heading:
    SELECT: cell G3
    PRESS: DELETE
12. Now let's select the information for the Sahali Mall location:
    SELECT: cell D8
    PRESS: SHIFT and hold it down
    CLICK: cell F8
13. To erase all of the information in the selected cells:
    CHOOSE: Edit, Clear from the Menu bar
    CHOOSE: All from the cascading menu
14. To undo the deletion of the previous step:
    CLICK: Undo button ( ) on the Standard toolbar
15. Save and then close the workbook.

1.7.3 Sun Valley Frozen Foods: Variance Analysis

You will now practice creating a worksheet from scratch that includes text, values, and formulas.

1. To display a new workbook and a blank worksheet:
   CLICK: New button (□)
2. Enter the company name in cell A1:
   TYPE: **Sun Valley Frozen Foods**
   PRESS: ↓
   TYPE: **Today is:**
   PRESS: →
3. Enter today's date in cell B2:
   TYPE: *the current date* using the format dd-mmm-yy
   (*Hint:* The date 9/24/99 would be entered as 24-Sep-99.)
4. Complete the worksheet as shown in Figure 1.18.

Figure 1.18

Entering data into a blank worksheet

	A	B	C	D	E	F
1	Sun Valley Frozen Foods					
2	Today is:	25-Dec-99				
3				Budget	Actual	Variance
4	Income					
5		Sales		43,000	41,380	
6		Service		17,500	19,620	
7						
8						
9	Expenses					
10		Materials		11,500	12,340	
11		Fixed Overhead		6,700	6,700	
12		Other Costs		12,500	12,975	
13						
14						

5. To calculate the Sales variance:
   SELECT: cell F5
   TYPE: **=e5-d5**
   PRESS: ENTER
   The value –1620 appears in the worksheet.
6. Using the same method, calculate the remaining variances for cells F6, F10, F11, and F12.

7. SELECT: cell C7
    TYPE: **Total**
    SELECT: cell C13
    TYPE: **Total**
    PRESS: ENTER
8. To sum the Income and Expenses columns:
    SELECT: cell D7
    TYPE: **=**
    SELECT: cell D5
    TYPE: **+**
    SELECT: cell D6
    PRESS: ENTER
9. Using either the typing or pointing method, enter addition
    formulas in the remaining cells of row 7 and row 13.
10. Save the workbook as "Sun Variance" and then close the work-
    book.

1.7.4 Lakeside Realty: Current Listing Report

This exercise lets you practice adding and modifying text, numbers,
and formulas in an existing workbook.

1. Open the data file named EXC174.
2. Save the workbook as "Lakeside Listings" to your personal
    storage location.
3. In cell C7, you will now construct a formula to calculate the
    "Total Current Listings." Do the following:
    SELECT: cell C7
    TYPE: **= c3+c4-c5-c6**
    PRESS: ENTER
4. In cell A14, change the label from "Undeveloped" to read
    "Undeveloped Commercial."
5. In cell D14, you will enter the number of Undeveloped Com-
    mercial listings. As you do so, watch the formula in cell D16
    recalculate after you press ENTER. Do the following:
    TYPE: **19**
    PRESS: ENTER

6. The formula appearing in cell D16 for "Total Residential" incorrectly sums both the "Commercial" and "Undeveloped Commercial" listings. Therefore, you must edit the formula:
   SELECT: cell D16

7. Position the I-beam mouse pointer to the right of the formula in the Formula bar. Then, do the following:
   CLICK: the left mouse button and hold it down
   DRAG: the I-beam mouse pointer to the left to select "+D13+D14"

8. Once the selection is made, release the mouse button. Then:
   PRESS: DELETE

9. To complete the entry:
   PRESS: ENTER

10. In cell D18, enter a formula that adds up the Commercial (cell D13) and Undeveloped Commercial (cell D14) listings.

11. The Market Share column shows the proportional value of a particular row category as compared to either the Total Residential or Total Commercial results. To examine the formula used to calculate the Market Share for Single Family Houses, do the following:
    SELECT: cell F9
    Notice the expression displayed in the Formula bar.

12. Enter formulas in cells F10, F11, and F12 that calculate their respective market shares of the residential listings. (*Hint:* Divide each row value in column D by the Total Residential value in cell D16.)

13. Enter formulas in cells F13 and F14 that calculate their respective market shares of the commercial listings. (*Hint:* Divide each row value in column D by the Total Commercial value in cell D18.)

14. Save and then close the workbook.

1.7.5   On Your Own: Personal Monthly Budget

To practice working with text, values, and formulas, ensure that Excel is loaded and then display a blank workbook. You will now begin creating a personal budget. Enter a title that contains the words "My Monthly Budget." Under this title include your name and the current month. Now enter the following expense categories and a reasonable amount for each:

- Rent/Mortgage
- Food
- Clothing
- Car expenses
- Utilities
- Education
- Entertainment

In the same column as the labels, enter the words "Total Expenses." Then, beneath the column of numbers, enter a formula that sums the column. Now add a new column next to these budget figures that displays the percentage share for each budget category of the total expenses. For example, you would divide the value for Food by the Total Expenses value to calculate its share of the budget. Experiment with increasing and decreasing the budget expense figures to see their effect on the percentage share calculations. When completed, save the workbook as "My Budget" to your personal storage location and then close the workbook.

1.7.6   On Your Own: Personal Grade Book

To practice working with data and formulas, open the EXC176 workbook. Before continuing, save the workbook as "My Grades" to your personal storage location. Enter sample marks into column D of the worksheet.

Enter formulas that calculate the percentage grade for each test or assignment by dividing the "Mark" column by the "Out Of" column. Then, enter formulas that calculate the Term Percentages for display in cells F8 and F15. (*Hint:* Divide the total course marks achieved by the total marks possible.) Finally, enter a formula that calculates the average percentage of both courses for display in cell F17. Adjust some of the sample marks to ensure that the formulas are working correctly.

Save the workbook to your personal storage location. And, lastly, close the workbook and exit Microsoft Excel.

1.8   Case Problems: Rain Coast Air

Rain Coast Air, a small airline charter business on the West coast, is in the process of modernizing how it tracks and analyzes its business data. As an initial step, the new office assistant, Jennifer Duvall, is learning how to use Microsoft Excel. Her boss, Hank Frobisher, wants Jennifer to create a worksheet that will enable him to compare the monthly efficiency of each of his three planes. You see, Hank has an opportunity to purchase an additional float plane for well below market value. And, as a cost-conscious businessman, Hank wants to have a clear understanding of how his current equipment is performing before deciding to spend any money.

In the following case problems, assume the role of Jennifer and perform the same steps that she identifies. You may want to re-read the chapter opening before proceeding.

1.   Jennifer decides to create a new worksheet that she can use as a template for each month's report. She begins by loading Microsoft Excel and displaying a blank workbook. Her first step will be to enter the title and the row and column headings. Then, the workbook needs to be saved to disk so that it can be later retrieved as a starting point for the monthly reports.

     Jennifer creates the worksheet shown in Figure 1.19 and then saves it as "Aircraft Stats" to her personal storage location.

Figure 1.19

The Aircraft Stats worksheet

	A	B	C	D	E	F	G	H
1	Monthly Aircraft Performance							
2								
3	Month:	Sep-99						
4								
5	Aircraft	Revenue	Expenses	Net Rev.	Flight Hrs	Rev/Hour	Exp %	
6								
7	XL-3079							
8	RB-2100							
9	DZ-514							
10								
11	Total							
12								
13								

2. Satisfied that this format will provide Hank with the information he needs, Jennifer begins to fill in the first month's figures. Then, she enters the formulas required to summarize each aircraft's performance. Most of the data she uses is taken directly from the monthly revenue and expense summaries prepared by the bookkeeping service. The pilots' trip logs provide the rest of the data. After entering the data in Figure 1.20, Jennifer saves the workbook as "September Stats" to her personal storage location.

Figure 1.20

September's aircraft performance report

	A	B	C	D	E	F	G	H
1	Monthly Aircraft Performance							
2								
3	Month:	Sep-99						
4								
5	Aircraft	Revenue	Expenses	Net Rev.	Flight Hrs	Rew/Hour	Exp %	
6								
7	XL-3079	15,326	4,259		87			
8	RB-2100	17,210	3,876		95			
9	DZ-514	9,845	2,633		53			
10								
11	Total							
12								
13								

3. Now, Jennifer tackles entering the formulas for the worksheet:

- She constructs formulas for display in row 11 that add the values appearing in the Revenue, Expenses, and Flight Hrs columns. The three formulas are entered into cells B11, C11, and E11.
- She enters formulas in cells D7, D8, D9, and D11 that calculate the Net Revenue by subtracting the Expenses for an aircraft from the Revenue it generated.
- She calculates and displays the Net Revenue per Hour in cells F7, F8, F9, and F11. The calculation she uses is simply the Net Revenue from column D divided by the Flight Hours in column F.
- Lastly, she calculates the Exp % column, which divides the Expenses by the Revenue and then multiples the result by 100. She places the results in cells G7, G8, G9, and G11.

Unfortunately, Hank has already gone home. Jennifer decides to call it a day; she saves and closes the workbook. She is already looking forward to showing off her new creation to Hank in the morning.

4. The next morning, Jennifer opens the "September Stats" workbook and asks Hank to take a look at it. He is very pleased with the report and amazed at how quickly Excel can perform the calculations. Hank asks Jennifer what it would take to produce this report for another month. She explains that all she needs to do is enter the month's revenues, expenses, and flight hours into the appropriate cells; Excel then recalculates the worksheet automatically. Hank is outwardly impressed, realizing that he will finally have some decent information on which to base business decisions.

    After mulling over the worksheet, Hank decides it would be prudent to purchase the fourth aircraft. With some minor modifications to the worksheet, he realizes that this information would come in handy during his meeting with the bank's loan officer. Hank calls Jennifer over to his desk and explains the revisions he wants her to make.

    - The title of the report, explains Hank, should read "Rain Coast Air." And the aircraft should be identified by their names instead of their registration numbers. For example, the aircraft names are Eagle (XL-3079), Wanderer (RB-2100), and Sky Spirit (DZ-514).
    - An upholstery repair bill for $262 was accidentally charged against the Wanderer, when it was actually for the Eagle. Therefore, the expense figures need to be adjusted accordingly. (*Hint:* To change the cell entry from a value to a formula, edit the cell contents by inserting an equal sign (=) at the front of the entry and "-262" at the end of the entry. You need an equal sign to convert the cell contents from a value to a formula.)

    Jennifer makes the requested changes. She then saves the workbook as "Sept 99 Stats" and closes the workbook. As a last step, she exits Microsoft Excel.

MICROSOFT EXCEL 2000
Modifying a Worksheet

CHAPTER
TWO

Chapter Outline

2.1 Entering and Reviewing Data

2.2 Copying and Moving Data

2.3 Modifying Rows and Columns

2.4 Chapter Review

2.5 Review Questions

2.6 Hands-On Projects

2.7 Case Problems

Learning Objectives

After reading this chapter, you will be able to:

- Use several "Auto" features provided by Excel for entering and editing data and formulas

- Copy and move information with the Windows and Office Clipboards, and by using drag and drop

- Use the AutoFill feature and Fill commands to duplicate and extend data and formulas

- Insert and delete cells, rows, and columns

- Hide, unhide, and adjust rows and columns

Case Study

Granby Insurance Agency

The Granby Insurance Agency, located at the corner of 43rd and Main in Middleton's business district, is the city's largest private insurance company. Granby Insurance has always maintained a high profile in the community by sponsoring youth programs and providing assistance to the local charities. This sense of community was one of the main attractions for Scott Allenby, who recently joined the agency as their internal business manager.

Just last week, one of the agency partners purchased a new computer for Scott and made him personally responsible for generating the company's monthly profitability reports. With an increased workload, Scott knows that he must streamline operations and find a more efficient method for summarizing the data he receives. Fortunately, the computer came with Microsoft Excel installed and, after only a few days, Scott is now creating his own worksheets. Far from being comfortable with Excel's vast number of features, Scott has asked a knowledgeable friend to help construct a few simple workbooks for him to use.

In this chapter, you and Scott learn to modify and manipulate worksheet data. In addition to copying and moving information, you are introduced to inserting and deleting cells, rows, and columns. You also learn how to hide specific columns before generating reports.

2.1 Entering and Reviewing Data

Even novice users find it easy to build and use simple worksheets. In this module, you are introduced to some popular tools that can help speed your learning and improve your efficiency. Specifically, Excel provides three "Auto" features that may be used to enter repetitive data and perform calculations. Once you've practiced selecting ranges, you learn to use these three "Auto" features, called *AutoComplete, AutoCalculate,* and *AutoSum.*

2.1.1 Selecting Cells and Ranges

FEATURE

A **cell range** is a single cell or rectangular block of cells. Each cell range has a beginning cell address in the top left-hand corner and an ending cell address in the bottom right-hand corner. To use a cell range in a formula, you separate the two cell addresses using a colon. For example, the cell range B4:C6 references the six cells shown shaded below. Notice that the current or active cell, B4, is not shaded in this graphic.

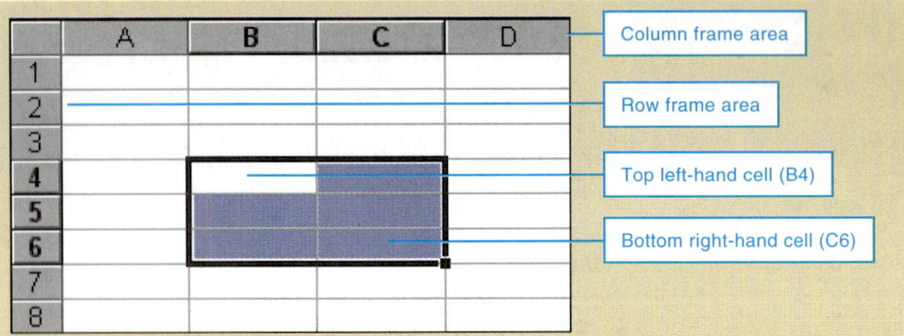

METHOD
To select a cell range using the mouse:
1. CLICK: the cell in the top left-hand corner
2. DRAG: the mouse pointer to the cell in the bottom right-hand corner

To select a cell range using the keyboard:
1. SELECT: cell in the top left-hand corner
2. PRESS: SHIFT and hold it down
3. PRESS: *an arrow key* to extend the range highlighting
4. RELEASE: SHIFT

PRACTICE
In this exercise, you open a workbook, save it to your personal storage location, and practice selecting single and multiple cell ranges.

Setup: Ensure that Excel is loaded.

1 Open the data file named EXC210.

2 In the next two steps, you will save the file as "My Gift List" to your personal storage location. Do the following:
CHOOSE: File, Save As
TYPE: My Gift List (but do not press ENTER)

3 Using the *Save in* drop-down list box or the Places bar:
SELECT: *your storage location* (for example, the "My Documents" folder)
CLICK: Save command button
(*Note:* Most lessons in this guide begin by opening a student data file and then saving it immediately using a new filename.)

4 Let's practice selecting cell ranges. To begin:
SELECT: cell A3
(*Hint:* The word SELECT tells you to place the cell pointer at the identified cell address using either the keyboard or the mouse.)

5 To select the range from cell A3 to E3 using the keyboard:
PRESS: (SHIFT) and hold it down
PRESS: ➡ four times
Although not explicitly stated in the above instruction, you release the (SHIFT) key once the range is selected.

6 The (CTRL) + (HOME) combination moves the cell pointer to cell A1. Pressing (HOME) by itself moves the cell pointer to column A within the same row. To move the cell pointer back to cell A3:
PRESS: (HOME)

7 To select the same cell range, but faster and more efficiently:
PRESS: (SHIFT) and hold it down
PRESS: (CTRL) + ➡ together
Notice that the entire range is selected. You may remember from the last chapter that the (CTRL) +arrow combination moves the cell pointer until the cell contents change from empty to filled or filled to empty.

8 To select a cell range using the mouse:
CLICK: cell C6 and hold down the left mouse button
DRAG: the mouse pointer to E8 (and then release the button)
Notice that the column letters and row numbers in the frame area appear bold for the selected cell range, as shown in Figure 2.1.

Figure 2.1

Selecting a cell range

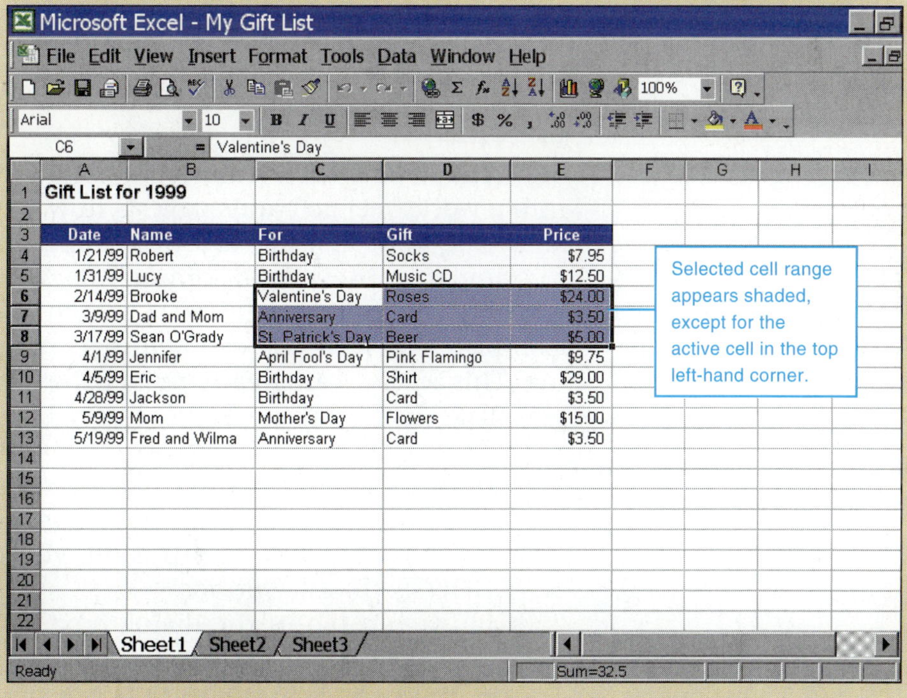

	A	B	C	D	E
1	Gift List for 1999				
2					
3	Date	Name	For	Gift	Price
4	1/21/99	Robert	Birthday	Socks	$7.95
5	1/31/99	Lucy	Birthday	Music CD	$12.50
6	2/14/99	Brooke	Valentine's Day	Roses	$24.00
7	3/9/99	Dad and Mom	Anniversary	Card	$3.50
8	3/17/99	Sean O'Grady	St. Patrick's Day	Beer	$5.00
9	4/1/99	Jennifer	April Fool's Day	Pink Flamingo	$9.75
10	4/5/99	Eric	Birthday	Shirt	$29.00
11	4/28/99	Jackson	Birthday	Card	$3.50
12	5/9/99	Mom	Mother's Day	Flowers	$15.00
13	5/19/99	Fred and Wilma	Anniversary	Card	$3.50

9 There is an easier method for selecting cell ranges for novice mouse users. To demonstrate, let's select the cell range from B10 to D13:
CLICK: cell B10
PRESS: (SHIFT) and hold it down
CLICK: cell D13
The range between the two cells should now appear highlighted. (*Note:* Remember to release the (SHIFT) key after the last selection is made.)

10 You can also select multiple cell ranges on a worksheet. To begin:
DRAG: from cell A6 to cell E6
PRESS: (CTRL) and hold it down
DRAG: from cell A9 to cell E9
You should see two separate cell ranges highlighted on the worksheet.

11 To select a third cell range:
PRESS: (CTRL) and hold it down
DRAG: from cell A12 to cell E12
(*Note:* Release the (CTRL) key after the last selection is made.)

12 To move the cell pointer to cell A1:
PRESS: (CTRL) + (HOME)

2.1.2 Entering Data Using AutoComplete

FEATURE
The **AutoComplete** feature second-guesses what you are typing into a worksheet cell and suggests how to complete the entry. After analyzing your first few keystrokes and scanning the same column for similar entries, AutoComplete tacks on the remaining letters when it thinks it has found a match. You can accept the Auto-Complete entry, or you can ignore its suggestion and continue typing. This feature can greatly reduce the number of repetitive entries you make in a worksheet.

METHOD
By default, the AutoComplete feature is turned on. If, however, you view its helpfulness as an intrusion, you can turn it off. To do so:
1. CHOOSE: Tools, Options
2. CLICK: *Edit* tab in the dialog box
3. SELECT: *Enable AutoComplete for cell values* check box to toggle AutoComplete on and off

PRACTICE

You will now practice using Excel's AutoComplete feature to enter data.

Setup: Ensure that the "My Gift List" workbook is displayed.

1 SELECT: cell A14

2 To add a new entry to the worksheet:
TYPE: 6/2/99
PRESS: ➡
TYPE: Anda
PRESS: ➡

3 You will now enter the word "Birthday" into cell C14. After typing the first letter, Excel notices that there is only one other entry in the column that begins with the letter "B" and, thus, makes the assumption that this is the word you want to enter. To demonstrate:
TYPE: B
Notice that Excel completes the word "Birthday" automatically.

4 To accept the completed word:
PRESS: ➡

5 For the remaining cells in the row:
TYPE: Shoes
PRESS: ➡
TYPE: $19.95
PRESS: ENTER
PRESS: HOME
Your cell pointer should now appear in cell A15.

6 Let's add another entry to the worksheet. Do the following:
TYPE: 6/5/99
PRESS: ➡
TYPE: Trevor and Ann
PRESS: ➡

7 You can use Excel's AutoComplete feature to display a sorted list of all the unique entries in a column. To illustrate:
RIGHT-CLICK: cell C15 to display its shortcut menu
CHOOSE: Pick From List
AutoComplete generates the list and then displays its results in a pop-up list box, as shown in Figure 2.2.

Figure 2.2

Entering data using the
AutoComplete pick list

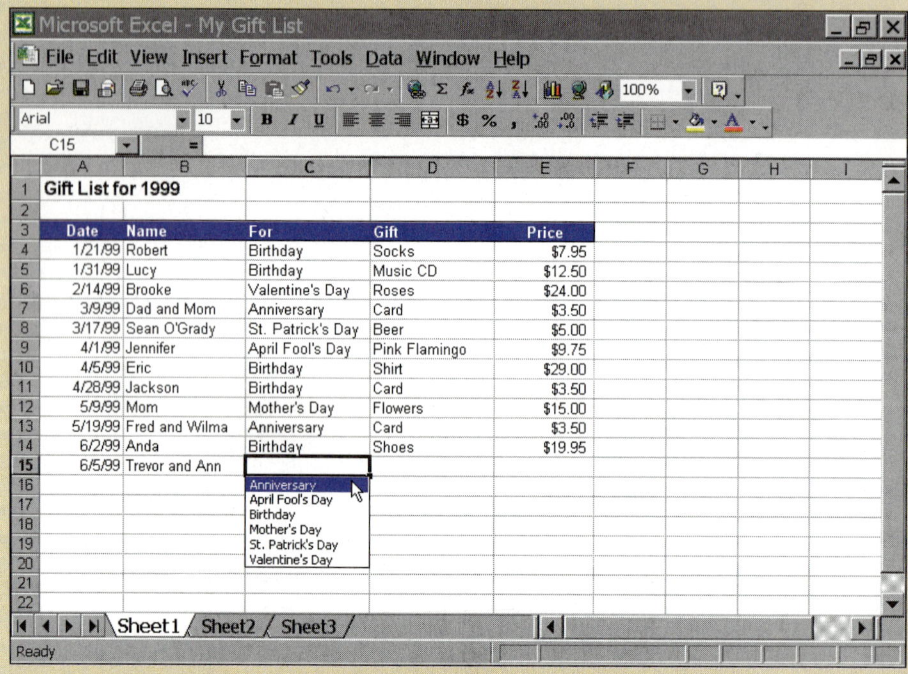

8 To make a selection:
CLICK: Anniversary in the pick list
(*Hint:* As a shortcut, press ⟨ALT⟩ + ⟨↓⟩ in a cell to display a column's pick list.)

9 To complete the row:
CLICK: cell D15
TYPE: **Picture Frame**
PRESS: ⟨→⟩
TYPE: **$15.00**
PRESS: ⟨ENTER⟩

10 Save the workbook and keep it open for use in the next lesson.
(*Hint:* The fastest methods for saving a workbook include clicking the Save button (⊞) or pressing ⟨CTRL⟩ + **s**.)

EXCEL

2.1.3   Using AutoCalculate and AutoSum

FEATURE

The **AutoCalculate** feature allows you to select a range of values
and view their sum in the Status bar. This feature is useful for
checking the result of a calculation without having to store its
value in the worksheet. If, on the other hand, you need to store a
result, click the **AutoSum** button (Σ) on the Standard toolbar.
Excel reviews the surrounding cells, guesses at the range you want
to sum, and then places a SUM function (described later in this
book) into the current or active cell.

METHOD

- To use the AutoCalculate feature:
  SELECT: the range of values that you want to sum
- To use the AutoSum feature:
  SELECT: the cell where you want the result to appear
  CLICK: AutoSum button (Σ)

PRACTICE

Using the same worksheet, you will now practice viewing Auto-
Calculate results and entering an addition formula using AutoSum.

Setup: Ensure that you have completed the previous lessons in this
module and that the "My Gift List" workbook is displayed.

1 Let's say you want to know how much money to set aside for
gifts in April. To find the answer, do the following:
SELECT: cell range from E9 to E11
Notice that only the April values are selected in the "Price"
column.

2 Review the Status bar information. Notice that "Sum=$42.25"
now appears near the right-hand side of the Status bar.

3 Let's perform another calculation:
SELECT: cell E4
PRESS: SHIFT and hold it down
PRESS: CTRL + ↓
All of the cells under the "Price" column heading should now
appear selected. Assuming that you completed the previous les-
sons, the Status bar will now display "Sum=$148.65," as shown
in Figure 2.3.

Figure 2.3

Adding values using
AutoCalculate

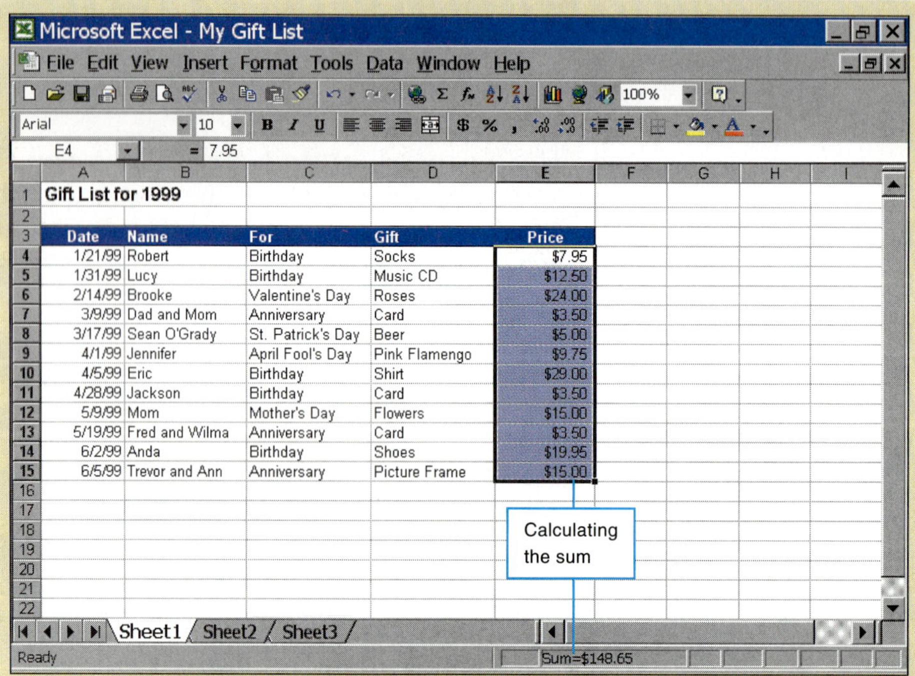

4   SELECT: cell D16

5   Let's enter a text label for the next calculation:
TYPE: **Total Cost**
PRESS: ➡

6   The quickest way to sum a row or column of values is using the
AutoSum button (Σ) on the Standard toolbar. To demonstrate:
CLICK: AutoSum button (Σ) once
A built-in function called SUM is entered into the cell, along
with the range that Excel assumes you want to sum. Notice that
this cell range is also highlighted by a dashed marquee.

7   To accept the highlighted cells as the desired range:
CLICK: AutoSum button (Σ) again
The result, $148.65, now appears in cell E16. (*Note:* You could
just as easily have pressed **ENTER** to accept the AutoSum entry.)

8   Perhaps you made a mistake in one of the column entries. To
correct the mistake, do the following:
SELECT: cell E14
TYPE: **$119.95**
PRESS: **ENTER**
Notice that the AutoSum result in cell E16 now reads $248.65.

9   Save the workbook by clicking the Save button (▣).

2.1.4 Inserting and Deleting Cells

FEATURE
You can insert a cell or cell range in the middle of existing data by moving the data that is there into the cells immediately below or to the right of the current selection. Likewise, you can delete a cell or cell range and close up the gap that is normally left when you clear the contents of a range.

METHOD
To insert a cell or cell range:
1. SELECT: the desired cell or cell range
2. CHOOSE: Insert, Cells
3. SELECT: *Shift cells right* or *Shift cells down* option button
4. CLICK: OK command button

To delete a cell or cell range:
1. SELECT: the desired cell or cell range
2. CHOOSE: Edit, Delete
3. SELECT: *Shift cells left* or *Shift cells up* option button
4. CLICK: OK command button

PRACTICE
You will now practice inserting and deleting cells.

Setup: Ensure that the "My Gift List" workbook is displayed.

1 Let's insert a new item into the worksheet list. To begin:
SELECT: cell range from A9 to E9

2 To insert a new range of cells:
CHOOSE: Insert, Cells
Your screen should now appear similar to Figure 2.4.

Figure 2.4

Inserting a range of cells

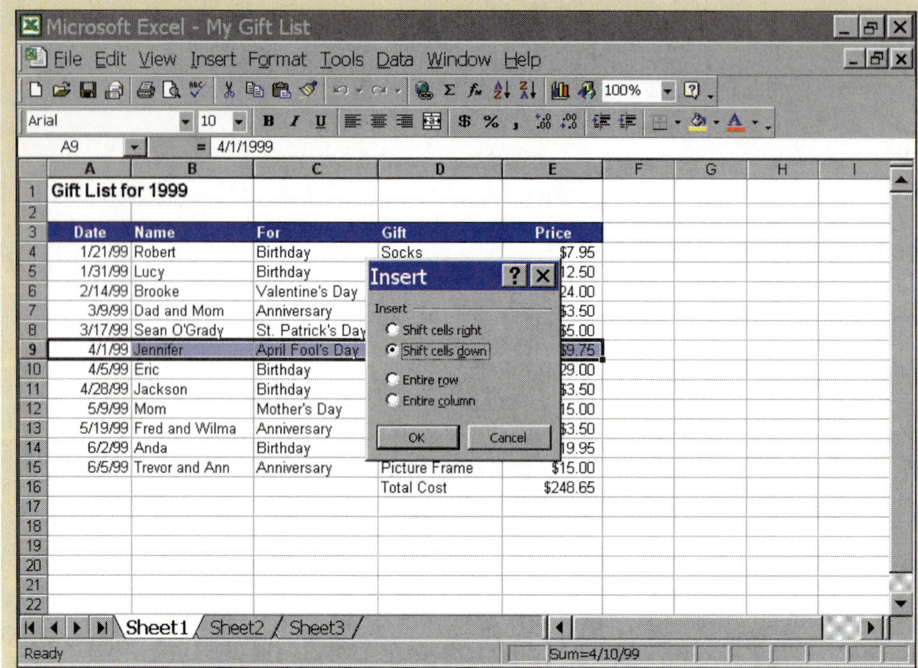

3 To complete the procedure, ensure that the *Shift cells down* option is selected and then do the following:
CLICK: OK command button
The existing data is pushed down to make space for the new cells.

4 Keep the cell range from A9 to E9 selected and enter a new item:
TYPE: **3/31/99**
PRESS: **ENTER**
Notice that the cell pointer moves to the next cell in the selected range.

5 To complete the row item with an Anniversary entry:
TYPE: **Tim and Starr**
PRESS: **ENTER**
TYPE: **An**
PRESS: **ENTER**
TYPE: **Mirror**
PRESS: **ENTER**
TYPE: **$37.00**
PRESS: **ENTER**
Notice that the cell pointer wraps around to the beginning of the selected range and that the "Total Cost" value in cell E17 is updated.

6 Now let's remove an item from the list:
SELECT: cell range from A12 to E12

7 To delete the selected cells:
CHOOSE: Edit, Delete
The Delete dialog box appears similar to the Insert dialog box shown in Figure 2.3.

8 To complete the procedure, ensure that the *Shift cells up* option is selected and then do the following:
CLICK: OK command button
The remaining cells slide up one row to close the gap and the "Total Cost" value in cell E16 is updated to $282.15.

9 PRESS: CTRL + HOME to move to cell A1

10 Save and then close the workbook.

2.1 Self Check   Which of the "Auto" features enables you to sum a range of values and display the result in the Status bar?

2.2 Copying and Moving Data

Excel provides tools for copying, moving, and pasting data. Like the "Auto" features, these tools can help you reduce the number of repetitive entries you are required to make. For example, once you enter a formula to sum one column of values, you can duplicate that formula to sum the adjacent columns. There are three methods for copying and moving data. First, you can cut or copy a single piece of data from any application and store it on the **Windows Clipboard.** Then, you can paste the data into any other worksheet, workbook, or application. Second, you can use the new **Office Clipboard** to collect up to 12 items and then paste the stored data singularly or as a group into any other Office 2000 application. Lastly, you can use **drag and drop** to copy and move cell information short distances using the mouse. In this module, you practice duplicating cell contents and extending data and formulas in a worksheet range.

2.2.1 Using the Clipboards

FEATURE

You use the Windows and Office Clipboards to copy and move information within Excel and among other applications. The Windows Clipboard can store a single item of data from any application, while the Office Clipboard can store up to 12 items. (*Note:* The last item that you cut or copy to the Office Clipboard will appear as the one item stored on the Windows Clipboard.) When working in an Office 2000 application, such as Excel, you display the Office Clipboard toolbar by choosing the View, Toolbars, Clipboard command.

METHOD

Task Description	Menu Command	Toolbar Button	Keyboard Shortcut
Move data from the worksheet to the Clipboard	Edit, Cut	✄	CTRL + X
Place a copy of the selected data on the Clipboard	Edit, Copy		CTRL + C
Insert data stored on the Clipboard into the worksheet	Edit, Paste		CTRL + V

PRACTICE

Using the Clipboards, you will now practice copying data in a worksheet. The steps for moving data are identical to copying, except you use the Cut command instead of Copy.

Setup: Ensure that no workbooks are displayed in the application window.

1 Open the data file named EXC220.

2 Save the file as "Sales Forecast" to your personal storage location.

3 Let's sum the product values for entry into the Total row:
SELECT: cell range from B6 to D6
CLICK: AutoSum button (Σ)
The results appear immediately in the selected range.

4 You will now use the Copy command to duplicate data in the worksheet. To demonstrate:
SELECT: cell range from A2 to D6
Notice that all the data is selected, except for the title in cell A1.

5 To copy the range selection to both Clipboards:
CLICK: Copy button (📋) on the Standard toolbar
(*Note:* The range that you want to copy appears surrounded by a dashed marquee.)

6 You must now select the top left-hand corner of the location where you want to place the copied data. Do the following:
SELECT: cell A9

7 To complete the copy operation:
CLICK: Paste button (📋)
The Paste button (📋) places the contents of the Windows Clipboard into the selected cell. The data, however, remains on both Clipboards.

8 Let's continue pasting the copied data into your worksheet:
SELECT: cell A16
CLICK: Paste button (📋)
A second copy appears beneath the original data.

9 To demonstrate using the Office Clipboard toolbar:
SELECT: cell A1
CHOOSE: View, Toolbars, Clipboard
Your screen should now appear similar to Figure 2.5. (*Hint:* Unlike the Windows Clipboard, remember that the Office Clipboard can store up to 12 items and then paste them all at the same time.)

Figure 2.5

Displaying the Office
Clipboard toolbar

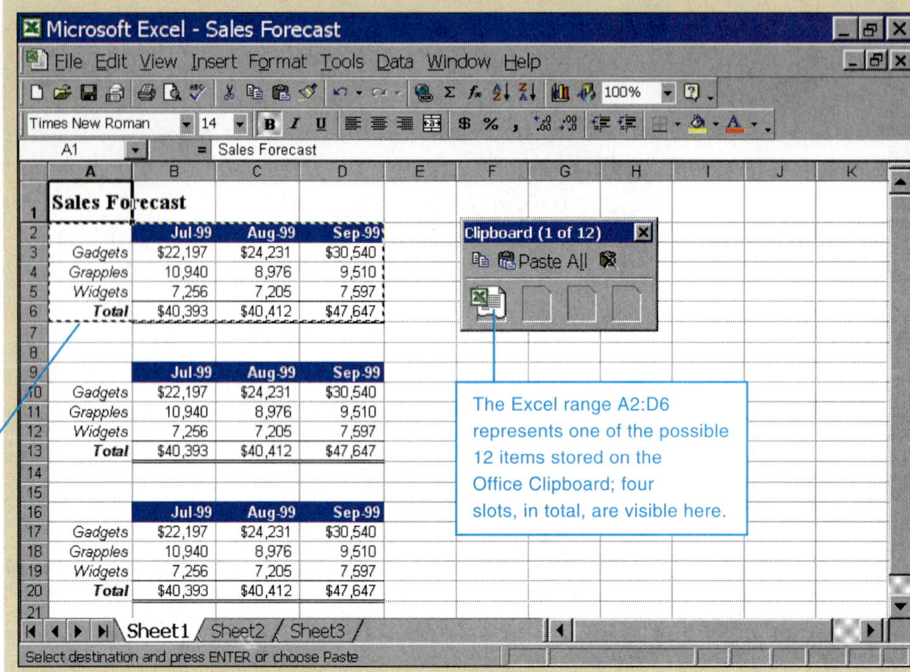

A dashed marquee
appears around the
range that has been
copied to the
Clipboard.

The Excel range A2:D6
represents one of the possible
12 items stored on the
Office Clipboard; four
slots, in total, are visible here.

10 To clear the contents of the Office Clipboard:
CLICK: Clear Clipboard button (⊠) on the Clipboard toolbar
Notice that the dashed marquee around the range also
disappears.

11 To add data items to the Office Clipboard:
SELECT: cell A3
CLICK: Copy button (🖺) on the Clipboard or Standard toolbars
SELECT: cell B3
CLICK: Copy button (🖺)
SELECT: cell C3
CLICK: Copy button (🖺)
SELECT: cell D3
CLICK: Copy button (🖺)
Depending on your screen resolution, your Office Clipboard may
expand to display an additional row of placeholders.

12 Position the mouse pointer over one of the data icons (🖼) in
the toolbar. A ToolTip will appear displaying the value stored in
the slot. Drag the mouse pointer over the other icons to see their
values. The data elements are stored in the order that they were
collected. You can paste a single item by selecting a target cell
and then clicking an icon in the toolbar. You can also paste all
of the items into a column format, as demonstrated in the next
step.

13 To paste all of the collected data elements into the worksheet:
SELECT: cell F9
CLICK: Paste All button (Paste All)
(*Note:* You may need to move the Office Clipboard
window by dragging its Title bar before you can
select cell F9.) The contents of the Office Clipboard
are pasted into a single column in the worksheet;
each data element is placed into its own row, as
shown here.

14 Let's prepare for another copy operation:
CLICK: Clear Clipboard button ( )

15 In this step, you want to collect, reorder, and then paste informa-
tion from Rows 3 through 5. The key to this step is to collect the
data in the order that you want to paste it later. For example:
SELECT: cell range A5 through D5
PRESS: ENTER + c
SELECT: cell range A3 through D3
PRESS: ENTER + c
SELECT: cell range A4 through D4
PRESS: ENTER + c
You should now see three occupied slots on the Clipboard
toolbar.

16 Let's paste the results over top of an existing data area in the
worksheet. Do the following:
SELECT: A10
CLICK: Paste All button (Paste All)
Notice that you need only select the top left-hand corner of the
desired target range. Your screen should now appear similar to
Figure 2.6.

17 CLICK: Close button (X) on the Office Clipboard toolbar

18 Save the workbook and keep it open for use in the next lesson.

Figure 2.6

Collecting and pasting
multiple items

You can use the Office
Clipboard toolbar to
change the layout of
data in the worksheet.

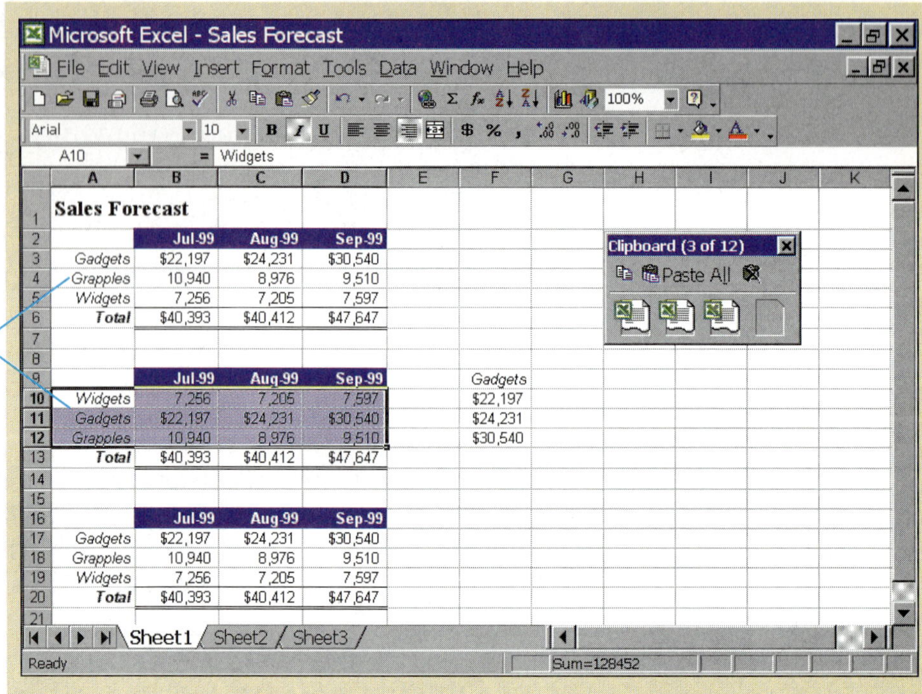

2.2.2   Using Drag and Drop

FEATURE

You can use the mouse (and bypass the Clipboards altogether) to
drag and drop data from one location in your worksheet to
another. Although you cannot perform multiple pastes, the drag
and drop method provides the easiest and fastest way to copy and
move cell information short distances.

METHOD

1. SELECT: the cell range that you want to copy or move
2. Position the mouse pointer over any border of the cell range,
   until a white arrow pointer appears.
3. If you want to perform a copy operation, hold down the
   CTRL key.
4. DRAG: the cell range by the border to the target destination
5. Release the mouse button and, if necessary, the CTRL key.

PRACTICE

Using a mouse, you will now practice dragging and dropping a cell
range in the worksheet.

Setup: Ensure that you have completed the previous lesson and that
the "Sales Forecast" workbook is displayed.

1 Let's practice moving the data that was copied to column F in the previous lesson. Do the following:
SELECT: cell range from F9 to F12

2 Position the mouse pointer over a border of the selected cell range until a white diagonal arrow appears.

3 CLICK: left mouse button and hold it down
DRAG: mouse pointer upwards until the ToolTip displays "F2:F5"
Your screen should now appear similar to Figure 2.7.

4 Release the mouse button to complete the drag and drop operation.

Figure 2.7

Using drag and drop to move cell data

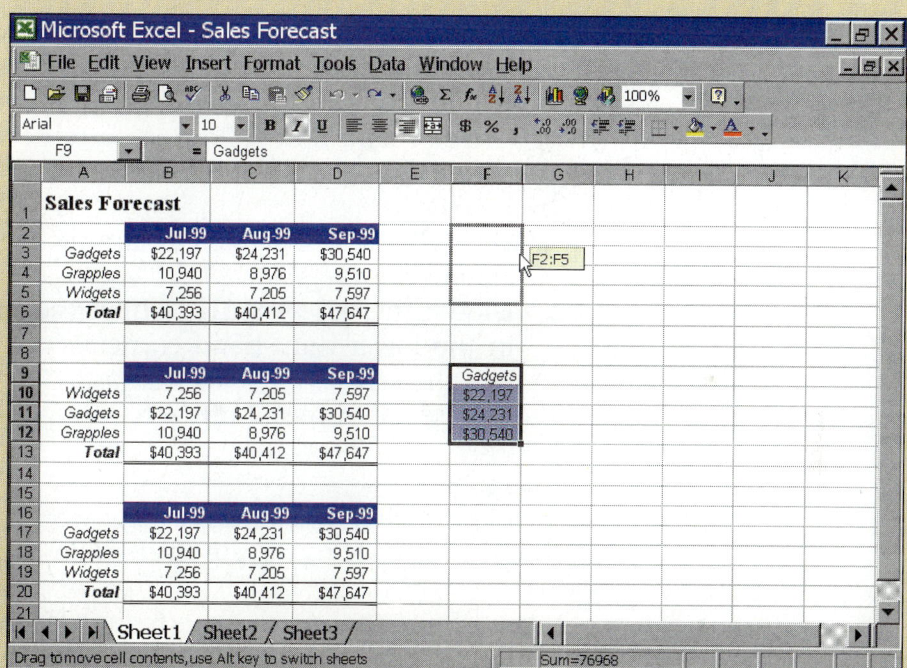

5 To copy a cell range using drag and drop:
SELECT: cell range from D9 to D13

6 Position the mouse pointer over a border of the cell range until a white diagonal arrow appears. Then, do the following:
PRESS: CTRL and hold it down
You should notice a plus sign is added to the mouse pointer.

7 CLICK: left mouse button and hold it down
DRAG: mouse pointer right to E9:E13

8 Release the mouse button and CTRL key to complete the copy operation. Notice that there are now two "Sep-99" columns.

SELECT: cell E9
TYPE: **Oct-99**
PRESS: `ENTER`
In one simple drag and drop operation, you successfully created
a new data column with the same formatting specifications as
the other monthly columns in the table.

10   Save and then close the workbook.

2.2.3 Creating a Series Using AutoFill

FEATURE

Excel's **AutoFill** feature allows you to enter a data series into a
worksheet. Whether a mathematical progression of values (1, 2,
3,...) or a row of date headings (Jan, Feb, Mar,...), a **series** is a
sequence of data that follows a pattern.

METHOD

1. SELECT: the cell range containing the data you want to
    extend
2. DRAG: the **fill handle,** which is a black square that appears
    in the lower right-hand corner of the cell range to extrapo-
    late the series
3. Release the mouse button to complete the operation.

PRACTICE

In this exercise, you create a new workbook and then extend the
contents of cells using the fill handle and the AutoFill feature.

Setup: Ensure that no workbooks appear in the application window.

1   To display a new workbook:
CLICK: New button (□)

2   Let's enter some source data from which you will create a series:
SELECT: cell A3
TYPE: **Jan**
PRESS: ⬇
TYPE: **Period 1**
PRESS: ⬇
TYPE: **Quarter 1**
PRESS: `ENTER`
Each of these entries will become the starting point for creating a
series that extends across their respective rows.

3 To extend the first entry in row 3:
SELECT: cell A3

4 Position the mouse pointer over the small black square (the fill handle) in the bottom right-hand corner of the cell pointer. The mouse pointer will change to a black cross when positioned correctly. (*Hint:* Figure 2.8 identifies the fill handle and mouse pointer.)

Figure 2.8

Using a cell's fill handle

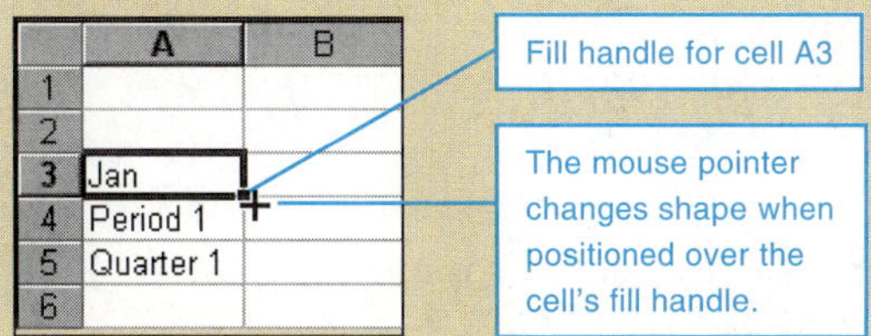

5 CLICK: left mouse button and hold it down
DRAG: the mouse pointer to column F, until the ToolTip displays "Jun"

6 Release the mouse button to complete the AutoFill operation.

7 Let's extend the next two rows:
SELECT: cell A4
DRAG: fill handle for cell A4 to column F
SELECT: cell A5
DRAG: fill handle for cell A5 to column F
(*Note:* Always release the mouse button after dragging to the desired location.) In the above example, notice that Excel recognizes the word Quarter; it resumes at Quarter 1 after entering Quarter 4.

8 You can also extend a date series using the fill handle:
SELECT: cell A7
TYPE: **Sep-99**
PRESS: ➡
TYPE: **Dec-99**
PRESS: ENTER

9 To extend the range using the same increment, you select both cells and then drag the range's fill handle. Do the following:
SELECT: cell range from A7 to B7
DRAG: fill handle for the range to column F
The quarterly values to Dec-00 appear.

10 You can also extract a nonlinear series from a range of values:
SELECT: cell A9
TYPE: **12**
PRESS: ➡
TYPE: **15**
PRESS: ➡
TYPE: **17**
PRESS: ENTER
Notice that there isn't a static incrementing value in this example.

11 To continue this range of values:
SELECT: cell range from A9 to C9
DRAG: fill handle for the range to column F
Excel calculates a "best guess" for the next few values. Your screen should now appear similar to Figure 2.9.

12 Save the workbook as "My Series" and then close the workbook.

Figure 2.9

Creating data series using the AutoFill feature

	A	B	C	D	E	F	G
1							
2							
3	Jan	Feb	Mar	Apr	May	Jun	
4	Period 1	Period 2	Period 3	Period 4	Period 5	Period 6	
5	Quarter 1	Quarter 2	Quarter 3	Quarter 4	Quarter 1	Quarter 2	
6							
7	Sep-99	Dec-99	Mar-00	Jun-00	Sep-00	Dec-00	
8							
9	12	15	17	19.66667	22.16667	24.66667	
10							
11							

2.2.4   Extending a Cell's Contents

FEATURE
You use the Edit, Fill commands to extend a formula across a row or down a column. These commands allow you to copy a cell's contents to its adjacent cells in a single step. If you prefer using the mouse, you can also extend a cell's contents using its fill handle.

METHOD
1. SELECT: the desired cell range, ensuring that the data you want to copy is located in the top left-hand corner
2. CHOOSE: Edit, Fill, Right (or Left) to copy across a row
    CHOOSE: Edit, Fill, Down (or Up) to copy down (or up) a column

PRACTICE

In this exercise, you open a cash flow worksheet and then copy and extend the formulas that are stored therein.

Setup: Ensure that no workbooks appear in the application window.

1 Open the data file named EXC224.

2 Save the file as "Filling Cells" to your personal storage location.

3 To extend the date headings using the AutoFill feature:
SELECT: cell B1
DRAG: fill handle for cell B1 to column E
When you release the mouse button, the formatted date headings are entered into the columns.

4 In this worksheet, the beginning balance for a new month is the ending balance from the previous month. To enter this formula into column C:
SELECT: cell C2
CLICK: Bold button ([B]) to apply boldface to the cell
TYPE: =b11
PRESS: ENTER

5 To copy and extend this formula to the right:
SELECT: cell range from C2 to E2
Notice that the top left-hand cell in the selected range contains the formula (and formatting) that you want to copy.

6 CHOOSE: Edit, Fill, Right
For the moment, only zeroes will appear in the cells.

7 To extend the formulas for multiple ranges:
SELECT: cell range from B6 to E6
PRESS: CTRL and hold it down
SELECT: cell range from B10 to E10
SELECT: cell range from B11 to E11
When all the ranges are highlighted, release the CTRL key.

8 To fill each row with their respective formulas stored in column B:
CHOOSE: Edit, Fill, Right
Your worksheet should now appear similar to Figure 2.10.

Figure 2.10

Filling ranges with formulas
stored in the leftmost column

	A	B	C	D	E	F
1	Cash Flow	Sep-99	Oct-99	Nov-99	Dec-99	
2	Beg Balance	125,349	106,093	106,093	106,093	
3	*Add:*					
4	Cash Sales	45,000				
5	Receivables	15,234				
6	Total	60,234	0	0	0	
7	*Subtract:*					
8	Cash Exp	27,490				
9	Payables	52,000				
10	Total	79,490	0	0	0	
11	End Balance	106,093	106,093	106,093	106,093	
12						

9   On your own, enter sample values into the worksheet and witness how the formulas recalculate the totals.

10   Save and then close the workbook.

2.2 Self Check   Which method would you use to copy several nonadjacent worksheet values for placement into a single column?

2.3   Modifying Rows and Columns

By adjusting the row heights and column widths in a worksheet, you can enhance its appearance for both viewing and printing—similarly to how a textbook employs white space or a document uses double-spacing to make the text easier to read. You can also reorganize or modify the structure of a worksheet by inserting and deleting rows and columns. This module shows you how to manipulate the appearance and structure of a worksheet.

2.3.1   Changing Column Widths

FEATURE

You can increase and decrease the width of your worksheet columns to allow for varying lengths of text labels, numbers, and dates. To speed the process, you can select and change more than one column width at a time. Excel can even calculate the best or **AutoFit** width for a column based on its existing entries. The maximum width for a column is 255 characters.

METHOD

- To change a column's width using the mouse:
  DRAG: its right borderline in the frame area
- To change a column's width using the menu:
  SELECT: a cell in the column that you want to format
  CHOOSE: Format, Column, Width
  TYPE: *the desired width*
- To change a column's width to its best fit:
  DOUBLE-CLICK: its right borderline in the frame area, or
  CHOOSE: Format, Column, AutoFit Selection

PRACTICE

In this lesson, you open a workbook used to summarize the income earned by organizers of a craft fair. Then you practice changing the worksheet's column widths to better view the data stored therein.

Setup: Ensure that no workbooks are open in the application window.

1 Open the data file named EXC230.

2 Save the file as "Craft Fair" to your personal storage location.

3 In columns D and E of the worksheet, you will notice that some cells contain a series of "#" symbols. These symbols inform you that the columns are not wide enough to display the contents. Let's adjust the width of column D using a command from the Menu bar:
SELECT: cell D1
Notice that you need not select the entire column to change its width; in fact, you can choose any cell within the column.

4 CHOOSE: Format, Column, Width
The Column Width dialog box appears, as shown here. Notice that 8.43 characters is the default column width.

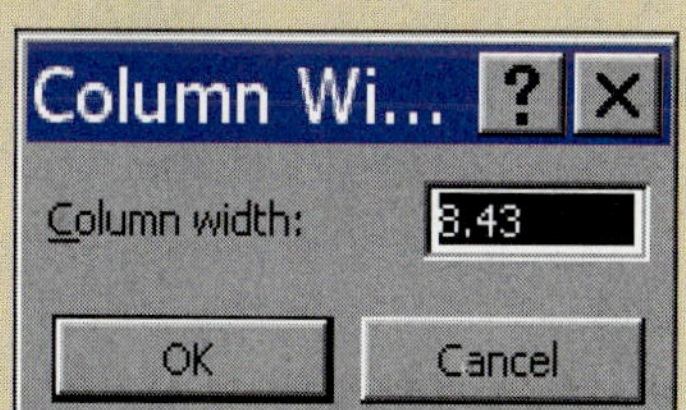

5 Enter the desired width as measured in characters:
TYPE: 12
PRESS: ENTER or CLICK: OK
All of the values stored in column D should now be visible.

6 Now let's adjust the width for column E. In the frame area, position the mouse pointer over the borderline between columns E and F. The mouse pointer changes shape when positioned correctly, as shown in Figure 2.11.

7 CLICK: the borderline and hold down the mouse button
DRAG: the mouse pointer to the right to increase the width to 12.00
Notice that the width (in characters and pixels) is displayed in a ToolTip. Your screen should now appear similar to Figure 2.11.

Figure 2.11

Changing a column's width

	A	B	C	D	E	F	G	H
1	KETTLE VALLEY CRAFT FAIR							
2	Profit and Loss Statement							
3	Year Ending December 2000							
4								
5				This Year	Last Year	$ Chg	% Chg	
6	INCOME							
7	Booth Rentals			254,054.00	########	73,445.00	41%	
8	Advertising			44,700.00	########	2,700.00	6%	
9	Donations			1,525.00	1,745.00	(220.00)	-13%	
10	Other Income			0.00	0.00	0.00	0%	
11	TOTAL INCOME			300,279.00	########	75,925.00	34%	
12								
13	COST OF SALES							
14	Equipment Rentals			125,412.00	########	36,434.00	41%	
15	Brochure Printing			34,900.00	########	2,785.00	9%	
16	Other Direct Costs			0.00	0.00	0.00	0%	
17	TOTAL COST OF SALES			160,312.00	########	39,219.00	32%	
18								

8 Remember to release the mouse button to finalize the new column width setting.

9 The AutoFit feature enables you to find the best width for a column based on its existing entries. To adjust column A, let's select the entire column as the basis for the width calculation. Do the following:
SELECT: column A
(*Hint:* This instruction tells you to move the mouse pointer over the "A" in the column frame area and click once. When done properly, the entire column will appear highlighted.)

10 CHOOSE: Format, Column, AutoFit Selection
Notice that the width has been adjusted so that it can comfortably hold the longest entry in the column.

2.3.2 Changing Row Heights

FEATURE

You can change the height of any worksheet row to customize the borders and line spacing in a worksheet. What's more, a row's height is adjusted automatically when you increase or decrease the font size of information appearing in the row. A row's height is measured in points, where 72 points is equal to one inch. The larger the font size that you select for a given cell, the larger its row height.

METHOD

- To change a row's height using the mouse:
  DRAG: its bottom borderline in the frame area
- To change a row's height using the menu:
  SELECT: a cell in the row that you want to format
  CHOOSE: Format, Row, Height
  TYPE: *the desired height* in points
- To change a row's height to its best fit:
  DOUBLE-CLICK: its bottom borderline in the frame area, or
  CHOOSE: Format, Row, AutoFit

PRACTICE

You will now change some row heights in a worksheet to improve the spacing between data.

Setup: Ensure that you have completed the previous lesson and that the "Craft Fair" workbook is displayed.

1 SELECT: cell A1

2 In the next two steps, you will change the line spacing for the entire worksheet. As with most formatting commands, you must first select the object for which you want to apply formatting. In this case, you need to select the entire worksheet. To begin:
CLICK: Select All button (□), as shown below

	A
1	KETTLE VALLEY CRAFT FAIR
2	Profit and Loss Statement
3	Year Ending December 2000

3 With the entire worksheet highlighted:
CHOOSE: Format, Row, Height
The following dialog box appears.

4 In the *Row height* text box, enter the desired height as measured in points:
TYPE: **20**
PRESS: [ENTER] or CLICK: OK
Notice that the rows are enlarged, providing more white space.

5 To remove the selection highlighting:
CLICK: cell A1

6 Let's change the height of row 4 using the mouse. To do so, position the mouse pointer over the borderline between rows 4 and 5. Then:
CLICK: the borderline and hold down the mouse button
DRAG: the mouse pointer up to decrease the height to 9.00 points
Similar to changing the column width, the mouse pointer changes and a yellow ToolTip appears with the current measurement.

7 Release the mouse button to finalize the new setting.

8 Let's practice adjusting a row to its best height:
SELECT: row 5
(*Hint:* This instruction tells you to move the mouse pointer over the "5" in the row frame area and click once. When done properly, the entire row will appear highlighted.)

9 CHOOSE: Format, Row, AutoFit
The row height is adjusted automatically.

10 Save the workbook and keep it open for use in the next lesson.

2.3.3 Inserting and Deleting Rows and Columns

FEATURE
You insert and delete rows and columns to affect the structure of a worksheet. But in doing so, you must be careful not to change other areas in your worksheet unintentionally. Deleting column B, for example, removes all of the data in the entire column, not only the cells that are currently visible on your screen.

METHOD
- To insert or delete a row:
  RIGHT-CLICK: a *row number* in the frame area
  CHOOSE: Insert or Delete
- To insert or delete a column:
  RIGHT-CLICK: a *column letter* in the frame area
  CHOOSE: Insert or Delete

PRACTICE
In this lesson, you will practice inserting and deleting rows and columns.

Setup: Ensure that you have completed the previous lessons and that the "Craft Fair" workbook is displayed.

1 After adjusting the width for column A earlier in the module, you may have noticed that columns B and C do not contain any data. Before deleting rows or columns, however, it is always wise to check your assumptions. To do so:
CLICK: cell B1
PRESS: CTRL + ↓
The cell pointer scoots down to row 65536. If there were data in the column, the cell pointer would have stopped at the cell containing the data.

2 To check whether there is any data in column C:
PRESS: →
PRESS: CTRL + ↑
The cell pointer scoots back up to row 1, unencumbered by any cells containing data.

3 Now that you are sure that these columns are indeed empty, let's delete them from the worksheet. To begin, select both of the columns:
CLICK: column B in the frame area
DRAG: the mouse pointer right to also highlight column C
Release the mouse button after the two columns appear highlighted.

4 To delete these two columns:
RIGHT-CLICK: column C in the frame area
Notice that you need only right-click one of the selected column letters. Your screen should now appear similar to Figure 2.12.

Figure 2.12

Displaying the right-click
menu for selected columns

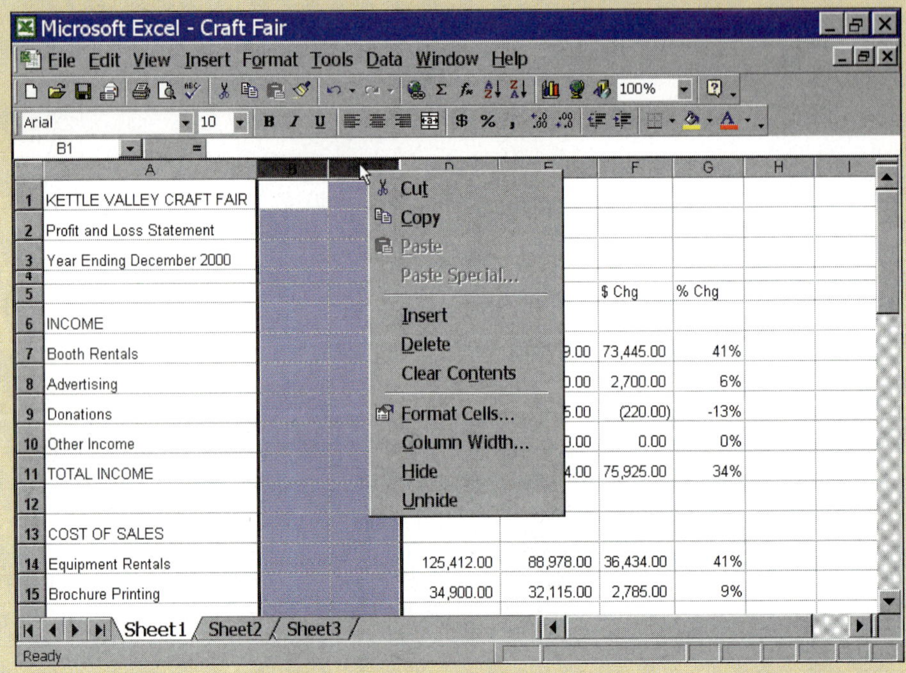

5 From the right-click menu:
CHOOSE: Delete
The column selection remains highlighted in case you want to
apply additional formatting commands.

6 To insert a row:
RIGHT-CLICK: row 8 in the frame area
CHOOSE Insert
A new row is inserted at row 8; pushing down the existing rows.

7 To enter some new information:
SELECT: cell A8
TYPE: Food Pavilion
PRESS: →
TYPE: 55800
PRESS: →
TYPE: 43750
PRESS: ENTER

8 To copy the formulas for calculating the annual increase:
SELECT: cell range D7 to E8
CHOOSE: Edit, Fill, Down
The results, 12,050.00 and 28%, now appear in row 8.

2.3.4 Hiding and Unhiding Rows and Columns

FEATURE

Rather than deleting a row or column, you can modify a worksheet so that not all of the data is displayed. For example, you may want to hide rows and columns that contain sensitive data, such as salaries or commissions. You can even hide detailed information temporarily that you do not want included in a particular report.

METHOD

To hide a row or column:
1. RIGHT-CLICK: the desired row or column
2. CHOOSE: Hide

To unhide a row or column:
1. SELECT: the rows or columns on either side of the hidden row or column
2. RIGHT-CLICK: the selected rows or columns
3. CHOOSE: Unhide

PRACTICE

In this lesson, you practice hiding and unhiding worksheet information.

Setup: Ensure that you have completed the previous lessons and that the "Craft Fair" workbook is displayed.

1 Let's hide columns D and E from displaying. Do the following:
CLICK: column D in the frame area
DRAG: the mouse pointer right to also highlight column E

2 To hide the selected columns:
RIGHT-CLICK: column E in the frame area
CHOOSE: Hide
Notice that the column frame area now shows A, B, C, and then F.

3 To hide several rows in the worksheet:
SELECT: rows 7 through 11 in the frame area
RIGHT-CLICK: row 7 in the frame area
CHOOSE: Hide
PRESS: CTRL + HOME to move the cell pointer
The row frame area now displays a gap between row 6 and row 12. Your screen should now appear similar to Figure 2.13.

Figure 2.13

Hiding columns and rows

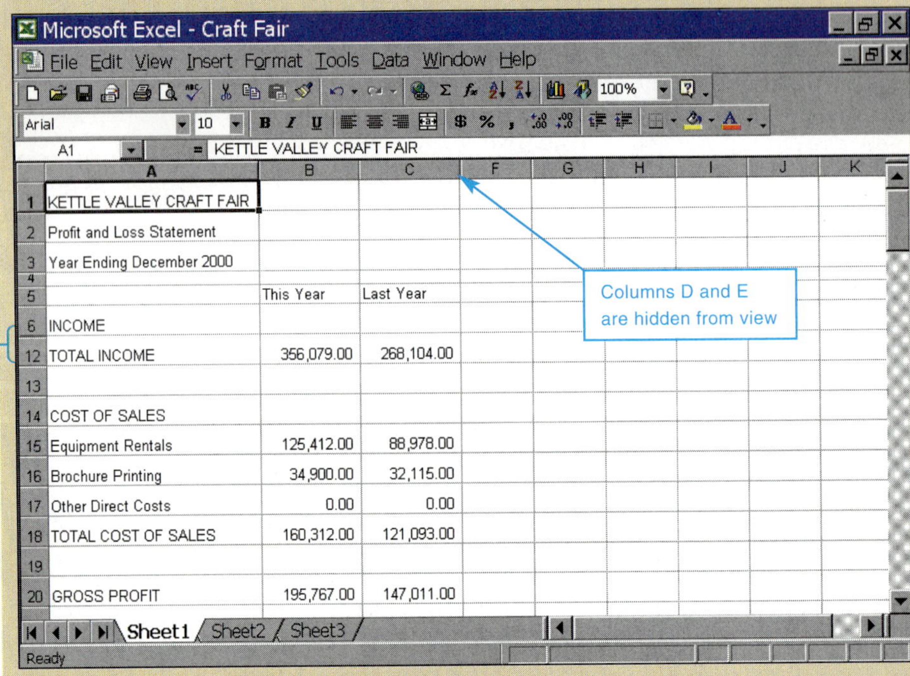

4 To unhide columns D and E, you must select the columns on either side. For example:
CLICK: column C in the frame area
DRAG: the mouse pointer right to also highlight column F

5 Let's use the Menu bar to unhide the columns:
CHOOSE: Format, Column, Unhide
The columns reappear on the worksheet.

6 To unhide the rows:
SELECT: rows 6 through 12
CHOOSE: Format, Row, Unhide
The rows reappear on the worksheet.

7 Save and then close the workbook.

8 Exit Microsoft Excel.

2.3 Self Check   Why must you be careful when deleting rows or columns?

2.4 Chapter Review

This chapter introduced you to some common procedures for modifying the contents and structure of a worksheet. In the first module, you entered data and formulas using Excel's special "Auto" features, including AutoComplete and AutoSum. Then you learned how to use the Windows and Office Clipboards and Excel's drag and drop features for moving, copying, and pasting data. You also practiced using the AutoFill feature by dragging a cell range's fill handle to extend a data series. As for modifying a worksheet's structure, you inserted and deleted cells, rows, and columns. And lastly, you practiced hiding, unhiding, and changing the height and width of rows and columns.

2.4.1 Command Summary

Many of the commands and procedures appearing in this chapter are summarized in the following table.

Skill Set	To Perform this Task . . .	Do the Following . . .
Using Functions	Entering the SUM function using the AutoSum button	SELECT: a cell to place the result CLICK: AutoSum button (Σ)
	Displaying the sum result of a calculation using AutoCalculate	SELECT: a cell range and view the result in the Status bar
Working with Cells	Insert a cell or cell range	SELECT: the desired cell range CHOOSE: Insert, Cells
	Delete a cell or cell range	SELECT: the desired cell range CHOOSE: Edit, Delete
	Insert data using AutoComplete	RIGHT-CLICK: the desired cell CHOOSE: Pick From List SELECT: the desired data
	Copy or move data using the toolbar	SELECT: the desired cell or range CLICK: Copy or Cut SELECT: the target cell or range CLICK: Paste button
	Move data using drag and drop	SELECT: the desired cell or range DRAG: the selection by its border

Continued

Skill Set	To Perform this Task . . .	Do the Following . . .
	Copy data using drag and drop	SELECT: the desired cell or range PRESS: CTRL and hold it down DRAG: the selection by its border
	Display the Office Clipboard	CHOOSE: View, Toolbars, Clipboard
	Clear the Office Clipboard	CLICK: Clear Clipboard button
	Create a series using the fill handle	SELECT: the desired range DRAG: the fill handle
	Copy a formula across a row or down a column	SELECT: the range to fill; with the formula in the top left-hand corner CHOOSE: Edit, Fill, Right (or Down)
Formatting Worksheets	Change a cell's column width	CHOOSE: Format, Column, Width TYPE: *width* in characters
	Change a cell's row height	CHOOSE: Format, Row, Height TYPE: *height* in points
Modifying Worksheets	Insert and delete columns	RIGHT-CLICK: a column's frame area CHOOSE: Insert or Delete
	Insert and delete rows	RIGHT-CLICK: a row's frame area CHOOSE: Insert or Delete
	Hide a row or column	RIGHT-CLICK: in the frame area CHOOSE: Hide
	Unhide a row or column	SELECT: rows or columns on either side of the hidden row or column RIGHT-CLICK: the frame selection CHOOSE: Unhide

2.4.2 Key Terms

This section specifies page references for the key terms identified in this chapter. For a complete list of definitions, refer to the Glossary provided in the Appendix.

AutoCalculate, *p. 59*

AutoComplete, *p. 56*

AutoFill, *p. 70*

AutoFit, *p. 74*

AutoSum, *p. 59*

cell range, *p. 53*

drag and drop, *p. 63*

fill handle, *p. 70*

Office Clipboard, *p. 63*

series, *p. 70*

Windows Clipboard, *p. 63*

2.5 Review Questions

2.5.1 Short Answer

1. What visible feature differentiates the active cell in a selected cell range?
2. How do you select more than one cell range in a worksheet?
3. Where does Excel's AutoComplete feature get the values for displaying in a pick list?
4. What are the two choices for moving existing data when you insert a new cell or cell range?
5. Name the two types of Clipboards and explain how they differ.
6. What is the primary difference between using the Clipboards and using the drag and drop method to copy information?
7. What is the fastest way to place five year's worth of quarterly headings at the top of your worksheet (i.e., Jan-00, Mar-00, Jun-00,…)?
8. What does "########" in a cell indicate?
9. What is meant by a "best fit" or "AutoFit" column width?
10. In what circumstances might you hide a row or column?

2.5.2 True/False

1. _____ You use ⟨ALT⟩ to select a range of cells using the keyboard.
2. _____ Excel's AutoComplete feature allows you to sum a range of values and place the result into a worksheet cell.
3. _____ You use the Edit, Clear command to delete the contents of a cell and the Edit, Delete command to delete the actual cell.
4. _____ You can collect up to 12 items for pasting using the Office Clipboard.
5. _____ You can collect up to four items for pasting using the Windows Clipboard.
6. _____ When you drag and drop using the ⟨CTRL⟩ key, a plus sign appears indicating that you are using the copy feature.
7. _____ To copy and extend a formula to adjacent cells, you can use either the fill handle or the Edit, Fill, Right command.
8. _____ When you insert a column, the existing column is pushed left.
9. _____ When you insert a row, the existing row is pushed down.
10. _____ You unhide rows and columns using the Window, Unhide command.

2.5.3 Multiple Choice

1. You hold down the following key to select multiple cell ranges using the mouse.
   a. ⟨ALT⟩
   b. ⟨CTRL⟩
   c. ⟨SHIFT⟩
   d. ⟨PRTSCR⟩

2. This feature allows you to view the sum of a range of values without entering a formula into a worksheet cell.
   a. AutoCalculate
   b. AutoComplete
   c. AutoTotal
   d. AutoValue

3. The AutoSum feature enters this function into a cell to sum a
    range of values:
    a. ADD
    b. SUM
    c. TOTAL
    d. VALUE

4. If you want to delete cells from the worksheet, you select the
    desired range and then choose the following command:
    a. Edit, Clear, All
    b. Edit, Clear, Cells
    c. Edit, Cells, Delete
    d. Edit, Delete

5. To perform a drag and drop operation, you position the
    mouse pointer over the selected cell or cell range until it
    changes to this shape.
    a.
    b.
    c.
    d.

6. What menu command allows you to copy a formula in the
    active cell to a range of adjacent cells in a row?
    a. Edit, Fill, Down
    b. Edit, Fill, Right
    c. Edit, Copy, Right
    d. Edit, Extend, Fill

7. To select an entire column for editing, inserting, or deleting:
    a. PRESS: ALT + ↓ with the cell pointer in the column
    b. DOUBLE-CLICK: a cell within the column
    c. CLICK: the column letter in the frame area
    d. CHOOSE: Edit, Select Column

8. The height of a row is typically measured using these units.
    a. Characters
    b. Fonts
    c. Picas
    d. Points

9. To change a column's width using the mouse, you position
    the mouse pointer into the column frame area until it changes
    to this shape.
    a.
    b.
    c.
    d.

10. Row 5 is hidden on your worksheet. To unhide the row, you must make this selection before issuing the appropriate menu command.
    a. rows 4 and 6
    b. rows 1 through 4
    c. row 4
    d. row 6

2.6 Hands-On Projects

2.6.1 Grandview College: Course List

In this exercise, you practice using Excel's "Auto" features to enter information and calculate results.

1. Load Microsoft Excel.
2. Open the data file named EXC261.
3. Save the workbook as "Course List" to your personal storage location.
4. To complete this worksheet, you must enter some additional information for "Intermediate French." To begin:
    SELECT: cell B9
    TYPE: L
    PRESS: ENTER
    Notice that the word "Languages" is inserted automatically.
5. To enter some data for the "Writer's Workshop," do the following:
    RIGHT-CLICK: cell B10
    CHOOSE: Pick From List
    CLICK: English in the pick list
6. To use AutoComplete with the keyboard:
    SELECT: cell C10
    PRESS: ALT + ↓
    PRESS: ↓ four more times to highlight "Molina"
    PRESS: ENTER
7. Now let's use the AutoCalculate feature to sum the total number of hours without placing an entry into the worksheet. Do the following:
    SELECT: cell range from D5 to D10
    Notice that the Status bar now displays 169.

8. You will now enter a total formula for the Hours column:
   SELECT: cell D12
   CLICK: AutoSum button (Σ)
   CLICK: AutoSum button (Σ) a second time to accept the cell range
   The answer, 169, now appears in the cell.
9. On your own, place a total formula in cell E12 for the Credits column.
10. Save and then close the workbook.

2.6.2 Fast Forward Video: Top Five Rentals

You will now practice copying and moving data using Excel's AutoFill feature, drag and drop, and the Windows and Office Clipboards.

1. Open the data file named EXC262.
2. Save the workbook as "Top Five" to your personal storage location.
3. Let's use the AutoFill feature to extend the heading to column C:
   SELECT: cell B1
   DRAG: fill handle for cell B1 to column C
   Notice that the text entry becomes "Week-2" and that the formatting is also copied.
4. On your own, extend the column heading for Week-2 in row 8.
5. You will now extend the row labels for "Videos" in column A. Do the following:
   SELECT: cell range from A2 to A3
   DRAG: fill handle for the selected cell range to row 6
6. On your own, extend the row labels for "Games" in column A.
7. Using the Windows Clipboard, copy the first two videos from Week-1 (Rocky: the Next Generation and Lethal Instinct) to the same positions in Week-2:
   SELECT: cell range from B2 to B3
   CLICK: Copy button () on the Standard toolbar
   SELECT: cell C2
   CLICK: Paste button ()
   PRESS: ESC to remove the dashed marquee
8. Using drag and drop, copy the number 3 video of Week-1 (Rent: the Movie) to the number 5 position of Week-2:
   SELECT: cell B4

9. Position the mouse pointer over the border of the selected cell so that a white diagonal arrow appears. Then, do the following:
    PRESS: CTRL and hold it down
    DRAG: mouse pointer to cell C6
10. Release the mouse button and then the CTRL key to complete the copy operation.
11. Using drag and drop, copy the cell range B5:B6 (X-Files 2 and Wild and Crazy Guys) to cells C4:C5.
12. You will use the Office Clipboard to modify the Games order from Week-1 to Week-2. First, display the Office Clipboard toolbar and clear its existing contents:
    CHOOSE: View, Toolbars, Clipboard
    CLICK: Clear Clipboard button (▨) on the Clipboard toolbar
13. Now, add the Games to the Office Clipboard:
    SELECT: cell B12
    CLICK: Copy button (▨) on the Clipboard or Standard toolbars
    SELECT: cell B9
    CLICK: Copy button (▨)
    SELECT: cell B10
    CLICK: Copy button (▨)
    SELECT: cell B13
    CLICK: Copy button (▨)
    SELECT: cell B11
    CLICK: Copy button (▨)
14. Now, paste all of the data elements into the Week-2 column:
    SELECT: cell C9
    CLICK: Paste All button (▨ Paste All)
    Your screen should now appear similar to Figure 2.14.
15. Lastly, remove the range selection highlighting and close the Office Clipboard toolbar:
    PRESS: CTRL + HOME
    CLICK: Close button on the Office Clipboard toolbar
16. Save and then close the "Top Five" workbook.

Figure 2.14

Pasting data from
the Office Clipboard

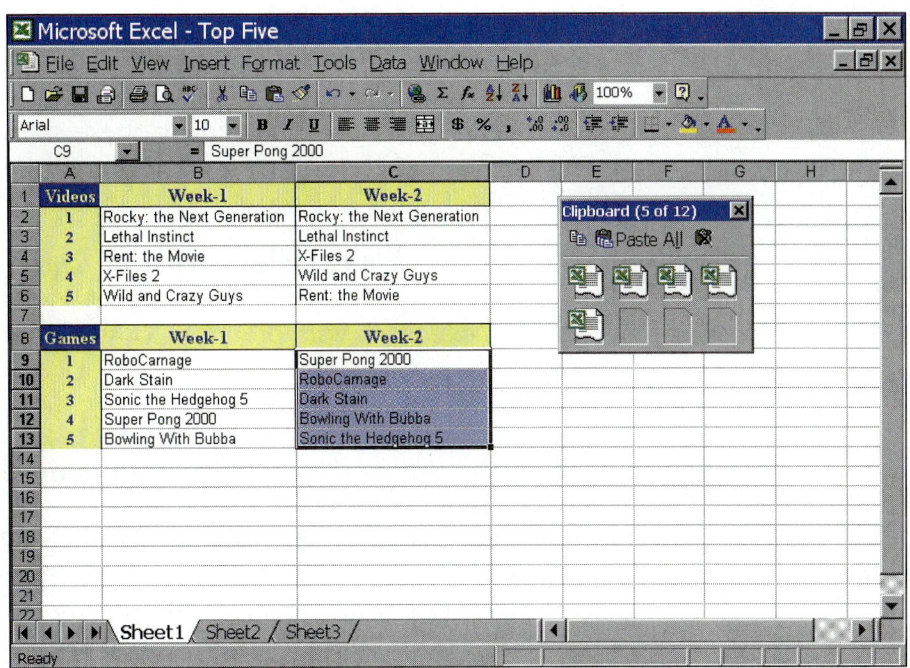

2.6.3 Sun Valley Frozen Foods: Sales Force

In this exercise, you practice modifying an existing worksheet that is
used to track sales representatives for Sun Valley Frozen Foods.

1. Open the data file named EXC263.
2. Save the workbook as "Sales Force" to your personal storage
    location.
3. You may have noticed that the title in cell A1 is difficult to
    read. Adjust the height for row 1 to its "best fit" or "AutoFit"
    height.
4. The sales representatives' names are truncated by the "Loca-
    tion" entries in column B. Therefore, adjust the width of col-
    umn A to ensure that all the names are visible.
5. Change the column width for columns B through D to 8
    characters.
6. Change the column width for columns E through G to 10
    characters.
7. Change the height of rows 2 through 15 to 15.00.
8. In cell F4, enter a commission rate of 5%.
9. In cell G4, multiple the commission rate (F) by the
    Revenue (E).
10. Copy the entries in cells F4 and G4 down the column to
    row 15.
11. Remove the Route information by deleting column C.
12. Remove the information for Bruce Towne by deleting the cell
    range A8 to F8 and then closing up the gap.

13. Hide the two end columns used in calculating and displaying a sales rep's commission.
14. Without placing a formula on the worksheet, calculate the total Revenue collected by these sales reps. What is this value?
15. Save and then close the workbook.

2.6.4 Lakeside Realty: Sales Projections

In this exercise, you practice copying data and modifying a worksheet.

1. Open the data file named EXC264.
2. Save the workbook as "Sales Volume" to your personal storage location.
3. Increase the width of column A to 12 characters.
4. Use the AutoSum button to sum the values for columns B through D and display the results in row 9.
5. To extend the table to project values for the years 2000, 2001, and 2002, select the cell range from B4 to D9.
6. Drag the fill handle of the selected range to column G. When you release the mouse button, the range is filled with projected results. These results are based on the trends calculated from the selected columns of data. Notice that you did not enter any formulas into the worksheet, other than using AutoSum to provide a totals row.
7. Use the Office Clipboard to collect and sort data from the worksheet and then paste the results into the area below the table. Specifically, replicate the result shown in Figure 2.15.

Figure 2.15

Using the Office Clipboard to organize data

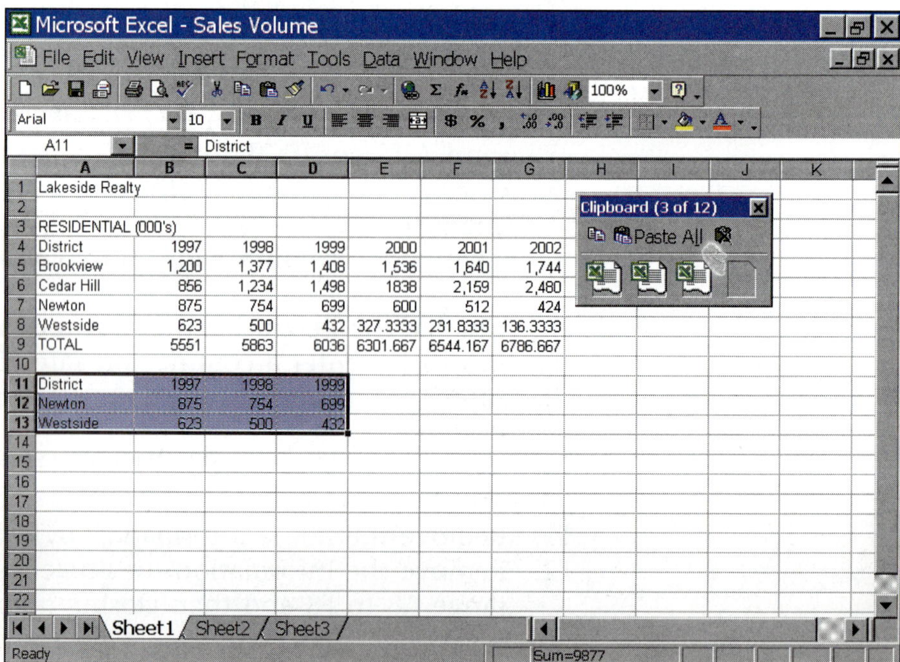

	A	B	C	D	E	F	G	H	I	J	K
1	Lakeside Realty										
2											
3	RESIDENTIAL (000's)										
4	District	1997	1998	1999	2000	2001	2002				
5	Brookview	1,200	1,377	1,408	1,536	1,640	1,744				
6	Cedar Hill	856	1,234	1,498	1838	2,159	2,480				
7	Newton	875	754	699	600	512	424				
8	Westside	623	500	432	327.3333	231.8333	136.3333				
9	TOTAL	5551	5863	6036	6301.667	6544.167	6786.667				
10											
11	District	1997	1998	1999							
12	Newton	875	754	699							
13	Westside	623	500	432							
14											

Ready   Sum=9877

8. Clear the Clipboard contents and then close the Clipboard toolbar.
9. Hide rows 4 through 8.
10. Save and then close the workbook.

2.6.5   On Your Own: Blue Zone Personnel

A friend of yours has just accepted a position at Blue Zone Personnel. In addition to her general administrative duties, she must help the accountant prepare monthly income statements. Since she seemed quite nervous about the new position, you offered to help her develop an Excel worksheet. You open the EXC265 workbook that she has been using and save it as "Blue Zone" to her personal storage location.

After adjusting the column widths, you review the structure of the worksheet. To begin, you insert a row above EXPENSES and label it Total Revenue. Then, you use the AutoSum feature to sum the revenues for September and October. Continuing in this manner, you adjust and insert rows, data, and formulas so that the worksheet appears similar to Figure 2.16. Then, you save and close the workbook.

Figure 2.16

Modifying a worksheet's structure and appearance

	A	B	C	D
1	Blue Zone Personnel			
2				
3	REVENUE	Sep-99	Oct-99	
4	Programming	12,400	13,100	
5	Service Calls	450	540	
6	Technical Support	225	330	
7	Total Revenue	13,075	13,970	
8	EXPENSES			
9	Advertising	200	250	
10	Bank Charges	25	25	
11	Depreciation	2,400	2,400	
12	Payroll Costs	10,000	10,000	
13	Telephone	275	275	
14	Total Expenses	12900	12950	
15	PROFIT	175	1,020	
16				

2.6.6 On Your Own: Running Diary

It's May and you're finally getting around to that New Year's resolution of getting into shape. To motivate yourself, you decide to create a running diary using Microsoft Excel. Open the data file named EXC266 and then save it as "My Running Diary" to your personal storage location.

Given your current statistics, you'd like to project how long it will take you to reach 10 miles. To do so, you select the cell range from B4 through B12. Then drag the fill handle for the range downward until the ToolTip displays a value over 10. You then press CTRL + HOME to return to the top of the worksheet. To make it easier to count the number of runs, you insert a new column A and then number each run in the column using the fill handle. *How many runs will it take you to reach 10 miles?* You then use Excel's AutoCalculate feature to determine how many total miles you have run as of May 23rd. *How many miles have you run thus far?* Impressed with your computer knowledge, your running partner asks you to track her running statistics also. Rather than create a new worksheet, you copy and paste the column headings beside your own, so that they begin in column H. Lastly, you save and close the workbook and then exit Excel.

2.7 Case Problems: Granby Insurance Agency

Scott Allenby, the business manager for the Granby Insurance Agency, is responsible for generating monthly profitability reports. One of the key business areas for Granby involves a long-standing agreement with a local car dealer to manage their financing, insurance, and after-market sales. Upon reviewing some of the past data from the dealership, Scott identifies an opportunity to use Microsoft Excel for generating their reports.

In the following case problems, assume the role of Scott and perform the same steps that he identifies. You may want to re-read the chapter opening before proceeding.

1. Scott decides to focus his attention on one report that is generated for the car dealership at the end of each month. He calls a good friend, whom he knows has several months experience using Excel, and describes what he needs over the phone. He then sends him a fax of the actual report to help clarify the discussion. The next day, Scott receives a diskette from his friend which contains a workbook called EXC271. He opens the workbook and then saves it as PROFIT to his personal storage location.

The PROFIT report, which is the car dealer's own abbreviation for a Performance Review of Finance and Insurance Totals, summarizes the number of new and used cars that are sold in a given month, including the number of financing, insurance, warranty, and rust protection packages. After reviewing the worksheet, Scott decides to make a few additions and modifications.

- In cell A1, edit the title to read "Profitability Review of Finance and Insurance Totals."
- In cells G3 and H3, enter the headings "Total Cars" and "Revenue," respectively.
- In cell G5, enter a formula that adds the number of new car sales to the number of used car sales.
- In cell H5, enter a formula that adds the revenue for new car sales to the revenue for used car sales.
- Using the fill handle, copy the formulas in cells G5 and H5 down their respective columns to row 9.
- Using the AutoSum feature, sum the values in columns C through H and place the results in row 10.

Save the workbook and keep it open for use in the next problem.

2. Wednesday morning does not start out well for Scott. The owner of the dealership calls to request that Granby Insurance no longer track the sale of "Rust Protection" packages. He also asks Scott to hide the "Used Car" columns in the report. Fortunately, Scott remembers how to remove and hide cells, rows, and columns. He also feels that this is a great opportunity to adjust some of the worksheet's column widths and row heights. Specifically, Scott performs the following steps:

- Select the "best fit" or "AutoFit" width for column A. Notice that the width is adjusted to handle the length of the title in cell A1.
- Specify a column width of 18 characters for column A.
- Specify a column width of 9 characters for columns C through H.
- Specify a row height of 7.50 points for row 4.
- Ensure that column B is empty. Then delete the entire column.
- Select the cell range (A8:G8) for Rust Protection. Then choose the Edit, Delete command to remove the cells from the worksheet and shift the remaining cells upward.
- Select columns D and E. Then hide the columns from displaying.

Your screen should now appear similar to Figure 2.17. Save the workbook and keep it open for use in the next problem.

Figure 2.17

Manipulating columns and rows in a worksheet

	A	B	C	F	G	H
1	Profitability Review of Finance and Insurance Totals					
2						
3	Product Category	New Cars	Revenue	Total Cars	Revenue	
4						
5	Retail Sales	20	492,000	35	630,000	
6	Life Ins. Policies	4	1,250	6	3,750	
7	Option Packages	5	2,150	5	2,150	
8	Ext. Warranties	1	375	2	715	
9	Totals	30	495775	48	636615	
10						

3. Scott decides that it would be helpful to develop a projection for next month's PROFIT report. Rather than create a new worksheet, he unhides columns D and E and then copies the data from cells A3 through G9 to the Windows Clipboard. He moves the cell pointer to cell A12 and then pastes the data. In order to start with a clean slate, Scott selects cells B14 through G17 and erases the cell contents in the range. Then he selects cell B14 and enters a formula that shows an increase of 20% over the value stored in cell B5. In other words, he multiplies the value in cell B5 by 1.2. Lastly, Scott copies the formula to the remaining cells in the range. The workbook appears similar to Figure 2.18. To ensure that the projection area works properly, Scott changes some of the values in the top table area. Satisfied that the bottom table area updates automatically, he saves and closes the workbook.

Figure 2.18

Creating a projection based on an existing range of cells

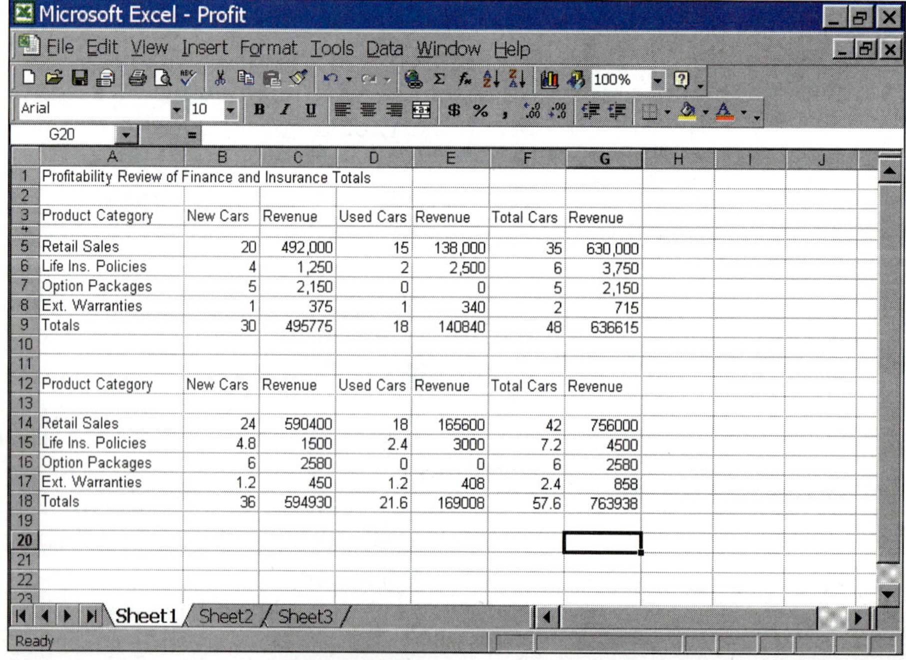

Microsoft Excel - Profit

File Edit View Insert Format Tools Data Window Help

Arial   10   G20

	A	B	C	D	E	F	G	H	I	J
1	Profitability Review of Finance and Insurance Totals									
2										
3	Product Category	New Cars	Revenue	Used Cars	Revenue	Total Cars	Revenue			
4										
5	Retail Sales	20	492,000	15	138,000	35	630,000			
6	Life Ins. Policies	4	1,250	2	2,500	6	3,750			
7	Option Packages	5	2,150	0	0	5	2,150			
8	Ext. Warranties	1	375	1	340	2	715			
9	Totals	30	495775	18	140840	48	636615			
10										
11										
12	Product Category	New Cars	Revenue	Used Cars	Revenue	Total Cars	Revenue			
13										
14	Retail Sales	24	590400	18	165600	42	756000			
15	Life Ins. Policies	4.8	1500	2.4	3000	7.2	4500			
16	Option Packages	6	2580	0	0	6	2580			
17	Ext. Warranties	1.2	450	1.2	408	2.4	858			
18	Totals	36	594930	21.6	169008	57.6	763938			
19										
20										
21										
22										
23										

Sheet1 / Sheet2 / Sheet3 /

Ready

4. Scott opens a second workbook that he receives from his friend called EXC274. He then saves the workbook as "Car Buyers" to his personal storage location. This particular workbook stores customer information from each sale made in the month.

Scott reviews the worksheet and decides to make a few changes. First, he inserts a new column A and then enters 1 into cell A4 and 2 into cell A5. Using the mouse, he selects both cells and then drags the range's fill handle downward to continue numbering the customers. *What is the number of the last customer, Heidi Buehre?* He then moves to cell E12 and displays the Auto-Complete pick list. *What vehicles are listed in the pick list and in what order do they appear?* To remove the pick list, Scott presses the ESC key. Lastly, Scott uses Excel's AutoCalculate feature to sum the purchase price of all vehicles sold in January without having to enter a formula into the worksheet. *What is the total value of vehicles purchased?*

Ready to go home for the day, Scott saves and then closes the workbook. Then he exits Microsoft Excel.

Notes

MICROSOFT EXCEL 2000
Formatting and Printing

CHAPTER
THREE

Chapter Outline

Learning Objectives

After reading this chapter, you will be able to:

- Format cell entries to appear boldface or italic and with different typefaces and font sizes

- Format numeric and date values

- Format cells to appear with borders, shading, and color

- Preview and print a worksheet

- Publish a worksheet to the World Wide Web

- Define page layout options, such as margins, headers, and footers, for printing your worksheets

EXCEL

Case Study

Marvin's Music

Marvin's Music is an independently owned sidewalk store that is located in the downtown core of Randall, Virginia. Established in 1974, Marvin's has successfully sold record albums, 8-track tapes, cassettes, and audio CDs. And, just recently, they began stocking movie videos and DVDs. For the past 25 years, Marvin's most prominent business strategy has been a commitment to stocking a large selection of music that appeals to a broad audience. They have always taken pride in their large inventory and in providing personalized customer service.

Stacey Marvin, the store's owner and general manager, is concerned for her business. She recently read in the newspaper that a large discount superstore is planning to move into the area. In a meeting with Justin Lee, her senior sales associate, she discussed some possible advertising ideas for combating the new competitor. For the past 18 months, Justin has been acting as Stacey's right hand. He handles much of the purchasing and receiving duties and is the primary contact person for Marvin's suppliers. Justin is also familiar with using the custom accounting software and Microsoft Excel, both of which are loaded on the office's personal computer.

In this chapter, you and Justin learn more about working with Excel worksheets. First, you learn how to format a worksheet to make it appear more attractive and easier to read. After previewing and printing a worksheet, you learn to save it as an HTML document for publishing to a Web site. Lastly, you customize several layout options, such as margins and headers, for more effective printing.

3.1 Enhancing a Worksheet's Appearance

Most people realize how important it is to create worksheets that are easy to read and pleasing to the eye. Clearly, a visually attractive worksheet will convey information better than an unformatted one. With Excel's formatting capabilities, you can enhance your worksheets for publishing online or to print. In addition to choosing from a variety of fonts, styles, and cell alignments, you can specify decimal places and add currency and percentage symbols to values. The combination of these features enables you to produce professional-looking spreadsheet reports and presentations.

3.1.1 Applying Fonts, Font Styles, and Colors

FEATURE

Applying **fonts** to titles, headings, and other worksheet cells is often the most effective means for drawing a reader's attention to specific areas in your worksheet. You can also specify font styles, like boldface and italic, adjust font sizes, and select colors. Do not feel obliged, however, to use every font that is available to you in a single worksheet. Above all, your worksheets must be easy to read—too many fonts, styles, and colors are distracting. As a rule, limit your font selection for a single worksheet to two or three **typefaces**, such as Times New Roman and Arial.

METHOD

To apply character formatting, select the desired cell range and then:

- CLICK: Font list box (Arial)
- CLICK: Font Size list box (10)
- CLICK: Bold button (B)
- CLICK: Italic button (I)
- CLICK: Underline button (U)
- CLICK: Font Color button (A)

To display the *Font* formatting options:

1. SELECT: cell range to format
2. CHOOSE: Format, Cells
3. CLICK: *Font* tab in the Format Cells dialog box
4. SELECT: the desired font, font style, size, color, and effects

PRACTICE

In this lesson, you open and format a workbook that tracks a mutual fund portfolio.

Setup: Ensure that Excel is loaded.

1 Open the data file named EXC310.

2 Save the file as "My Portfolio" to your personal storage location.

3 Your first step is to select the cell range to format. Do the following to begin formatting the column labels:
SELECT: cell range from A3 to G3

4   Let's make these labels bold and appear with underlining:
CLICK: Bold button (B)
CLICK: Underline button (U)

5   Now you will format the title labels in cells A1 and A2. To begin:
SELECT: cell range from A1 to A2

6   To change the typeface used in the cells:
CLICK: down arrow attached to the Font list box (Arial)
Your screen should now appear similar but not identical to Figure 3.1.

Figure 3.1

Selecting a typeface from
the Font list box

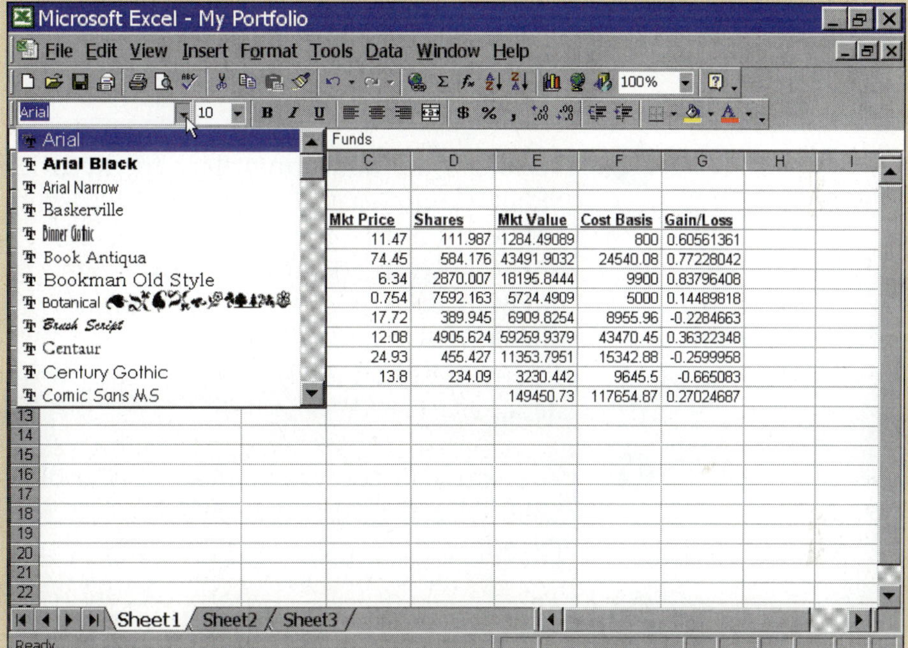

7   Using the scroll bars attached to the drop-down list box:
SELECT: Times New Roman

8   To increase the font size:
CLICK: down arrow attached to the Font Size list box (10)
SELECT: 14
The cells now appear formatted using a 14-point, Times New
Roman typeface; the row heights have also been adjusted auto-
matically.

9   You can also use the Format Cells dialog box to apply formatting
to the selected cell range. Do the following:
SELECT: cell A1
CHOOSE: Format, Cells
CLICK: *Font* tab
Your screen should now appear similar to Figure 3.2.

Figure 3.2

Format Cells dialog
box: *Font* tab

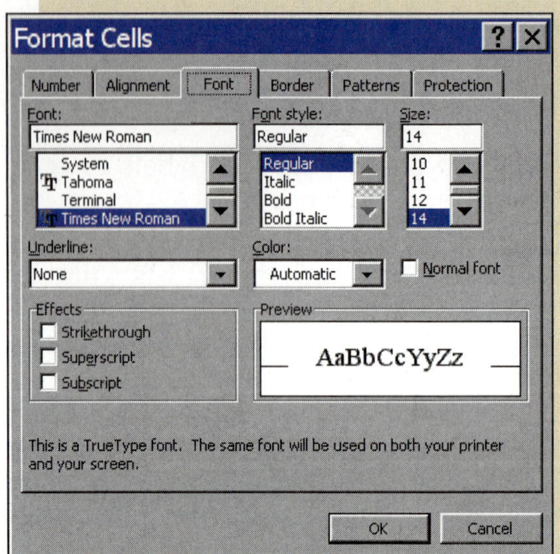

10 To add some additional flare to the title:
SELECT: *any typeface* from the *Font* list box
SELECT: Bold in the *Font style* list box
SELECT: 16 in the *Size* list box
SELECT: Blue from the *Color* drop-down list box
CLICK: OK
The title in cell A1 should now stand out from the rest of the
data.

11 You can also use shortcut keys to apply formatting:
SELECT: cell range from A12 to G12
PRESS: CTRL + b to apply boldface

12 Save the workbook and keep it open for use in the next lesson.

3.1.2 Formatting Numbers and Dates

FEATURE
Numeric formats improve the appearance and readability of numbers in a worksheet by inserting dollar signs, commas, percentage
symbols, and decimal places. Although a formatted number or date
appears differently on the worksheet, the value that is stored and
displayed in the Formula bar does not change. Excel stores date
and time entries as values and, therefore, allows you to customize
their display as you do numbers.

METHOD

To apply number formatting, select the desired cell range and then:

- CLICK: Currency Style button ($)
- CLICK: Percent Style button (%)
- CLICK: Comma Style button (,)
- CLICK: Increase Decimal button
- CLICK: Decrease Decimal button

To display the *Number* formatting options:
1. SELECT: cell range to format
2. CHOOSE: Format, Cells
3. CLICK: *Number* tab
4. SELECT: a number or date format from the *Category* list box
5. SELECT: formatting options for the selected category

PRACTICE

You will now apply number, currency, percentage, decimal place, and date formatting to the worksheet.

Setup: Ensure that you have completed the previous lesson and that the "My Portfolio" workbook is displayed.

1 Columns B and G in the worksheet contain data that is best represented using a percent number format. First, column B displays the proportional share of an investment compared to the total portfolio. Column G calculates the gain or loss performance. To display these calculated results as percentages, do the following:
SELECT: cell range from B4 to B11
PRESS: CTRL and hold it down
SELECT: cell range from G4 to G12

2 Release the CTRL key after the last range is selected. Notice that these two ranges are highlighted independently—ready for formatting. (*Hint*: You will no longer be reminded to release the CTRL key when dragging the cell pointer over a range.)

3 To apply a percent style:
CLICK: Percent Style button (%)

4 To display the percentages with two decimal places:
CLICK: Increase Decimal button twice

5 Let's apply some further number formatting:
SELECT: cell range from C4 to F11
CHOOSE: Format, Cells
CLICK: *Number* tab

6 In the Format Cells dialog box that appears:
SELECT: Number in the *Category* list box
SELECT: 2 in the *Decimal places* text box
SELECT: *Use 1000 Separator (,)* check box
SELECT: Black (1,234.10) in the *Negative numbers* list box
Your screen should now appear similar to Figure 3.3.

Figure 3.3

Format Cells dialog

box: *Number* tab

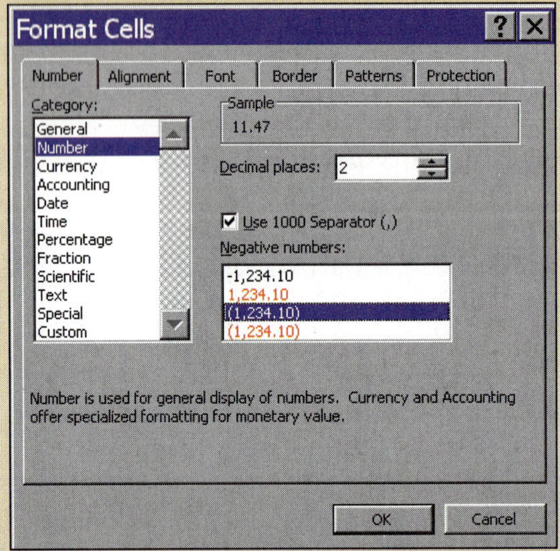

7 To apply the formatting options:
CLICK: OK

8 To increase the decimal places in the Shares column:
SELECT: cell range from D4 to D11
CLICK: Increase Decimal button (⬚)

9 To format the summary values using the Currency style:
SELECT: cell range from E12 to F12
CLICK: Currency Style button (⬚)

10 Depending on your system, the columns may not be wide enough to display the formatted values. With the two cells still selected:
CHOOSE: Format, Column, AutoFit Selection
You should now see all the data appearing in the column.

11 Let's develop a notes area:
SELECT: cell A14
TYPE: Notes
PRESS: ⬇

12 To enter the first note or comment:
TYPE: 31-Aug-99
PRESS: ➡
TYPE: The market rebounded from a low of 9,200 in June.
PRESS: ENTER

13 SELECT: cell A15
In the Formula bar, notice that the date reads 8/31/1999.

14 To format the date to appear differently on the worksheet:
CHOOSE: Format, Cells
Notice that "Date" is already selected in the *Category* list box and that the current date format appears highlighted in the *Type* list box.

15 To apply a new format, you select one of the listed versions:
SELECT: "March 14, 1998" in the *Type* list box
CLICK: OK command button
(*Note*: The *Type* list box displays the date formats for March 14, 1998. Keep in mind that you are selecting a display format and not a date value to insert into the worksheet.) Your screen should now appear similar to Figure 3.4.

Figure 3.4

Applying number and date formats

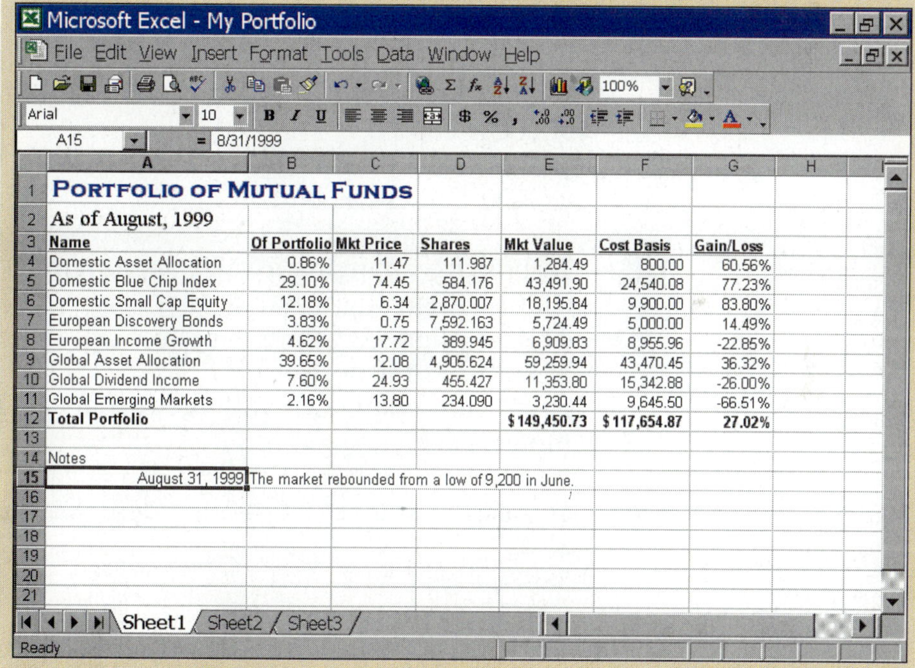

3.1.3 Aligning and Merging Cells

FEATURE

You can change the **cell alignment** for any type of data entered into a worksheet. By default, Excel aligns text against the left edge of a cell and values against the right edge. Not only can you change these default alignments, you can also merge or combine data across cells.

METHOD

To align and merge data, select the desired cell range and then:
- CLICK: Align Left button (⊞)
- CLICK: Center button (⊞)
- CLICK: Align Right button (⊞)
- CLICK: Merge and Center button (⊞)

To display the *Alignment* formatting options:
1. SELECT: cell range to format
2. CHOOSE: Format, Cells
3. CLICK: *Alignment* tab
4. SELECT: to align or merge cells

PRACTICE

You will now practice aligning cell information and merging cells.

Setup: Ensure that you have completed the previous lessons in the module and that the "My Portfolio" workbook is displayed.

1 You align the contents of a cell using buttons on the Formatting toolbar. Let's manipulate the "Notes" title in cell A14:
SELECT: cell A14
CLICK: Bold button (⊞)
CLICK: Underline button (⊞)

2 To practice changing a cell's alignment:
CLICK: Align Right button (⊞)
CLICK: Align Left button (⊞)
CLICK: Center button (⊞)
Notice the change in alignment that takes place with each mouse click.

3 You can change the cell alignment for number and date values also:
SELECT: cell A15
CLICK: Center button (⊞)
The date appears centered under the column heading for "Notes."

4 A little more interesting is the ability to merge cells together and center the contents. Do the following:
SELECT: cell range from A1 to G1
CLICK: Merge and Center button (⊞)
Notice that the title is now centered over the table area. (*Note*: The merged cell is considered cell A1. The next cell in the row is cell H1.)

5 Let's merge and center the subtitle in cell A2 using the dialog box:
SELECT: cell range from A2 to G2
CHOOSE: Format, Cells
CLICK: *Alignment* tab
Your screen should now appear similar to Figure 3.5.

Figure 3.5

Format Cells dialog box: *Alignment* tab

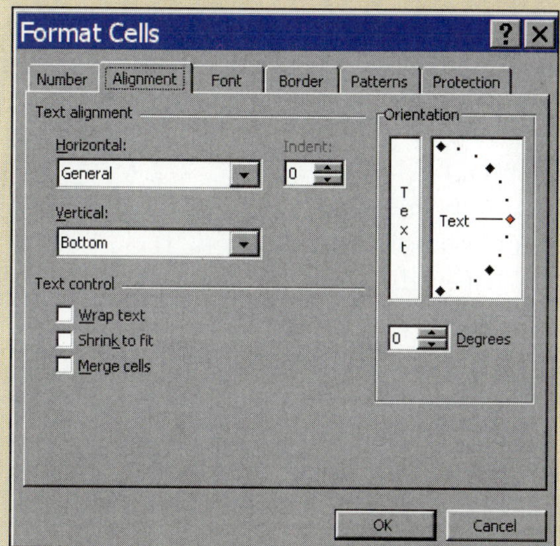

6 In the Format Cells dialog box:
SELECT: Center from the *Horizontal* drop-down list box
SELECT: *Merge cells* check box
CLICK: OK command button

7 Let's practice splitting up a merged cell without using the Undo command:
SELECT: cell A2 (which now covers the area to G2)
CHOOSE: Format, Cells
The last tab that was selected in the dialog box (*Alignment*) is displayed automatically.

8 To remove the merged cell:
SELECT: *Merge cells* check box so that no "✔" appears
CLICK: OK command button
The entry remains centered, but only between column A's borders.

9 Save the workbook and keep it open for use in the next lesson.

3.1.4   Adding Borders and Shading

FEATURE

As with the other formatting options, you use borders, patterns, shading, and colors to enhance a worksheet's readability. The gridlines that appear in the worksheet window are nonprinting lines, provided only to help you line up information. Borders can be used to place printed gridlines on a worksheet and to separate data into logical sections. These formatting options also enable you to create professional-looking invoice forms, memos, and tables.

METHOD

To apply borders or coloring, select the desired cell range and then:
- CLICK: Borders button (▦)
- CLICK: Fill Color button (▦)

To display the Border and Patterns formatting options:
1.   SELECT: cell range to format
2.   CHOOSE: Format, Cells
3.   CLICK: *Border* or *Patterns* tab
4.   SELECT: borders or pattern, shading, and fill color options

PRACTICE

In this exercise, you further format the worksheet by applying borders and fill coloring to selected cell ranges.

Setup: Ensure that you have completed the previous lessons in the module and that the "My Portfolio" workbook is displayed.

1   In order to better see the borders that you will apply in this lesson, let's remove the **gridlines** from the worksheet display:
CHOOSE: Tools, Options
CLICK: *View* tab
SELECT: *Gridlines* check box, so that no check mark appears
CLICK: OK

2   Now let's apply some borders:
SELECT: cell range from A12 to G12
CLICK: down arrow attached to the Borders button (▦)
A drop-down list of border options appears, as shown on the next page.

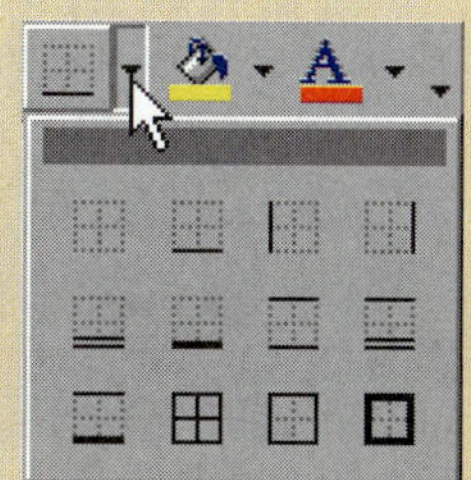

3 From the drop-down list that appears:
SELECT: Top and Double Bottom Border button (▦)
CLICK: cell A1 to remove the highlighting
A nice border now separates the data from the summary information. You may have noticed that clicking the Underline button (▯) underlines only the words in a cell, while applying borders underlines the entire cell.

4 Let's apply a new fill color (sometimes called *shading*) to empha-
size the title in cell A1:
CLICK: down arrow attached to the Fill Color button (▨)
A drop-down list of colors appears, as shown below.

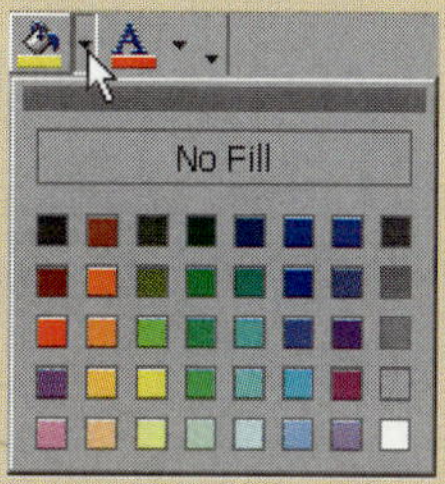

5 SELECT: a dark blue color from the drop-down list
The title should now appear on a colored background.

6 To see the title, you need to adjust the text color:
CLICK: down arrow attached to the Font Color button (▟)
SELECT: white from the drop-down list
Your screen should now appear similar to Figure 3.6.

Figure 3.6

Applying borders and colors to a worksheet

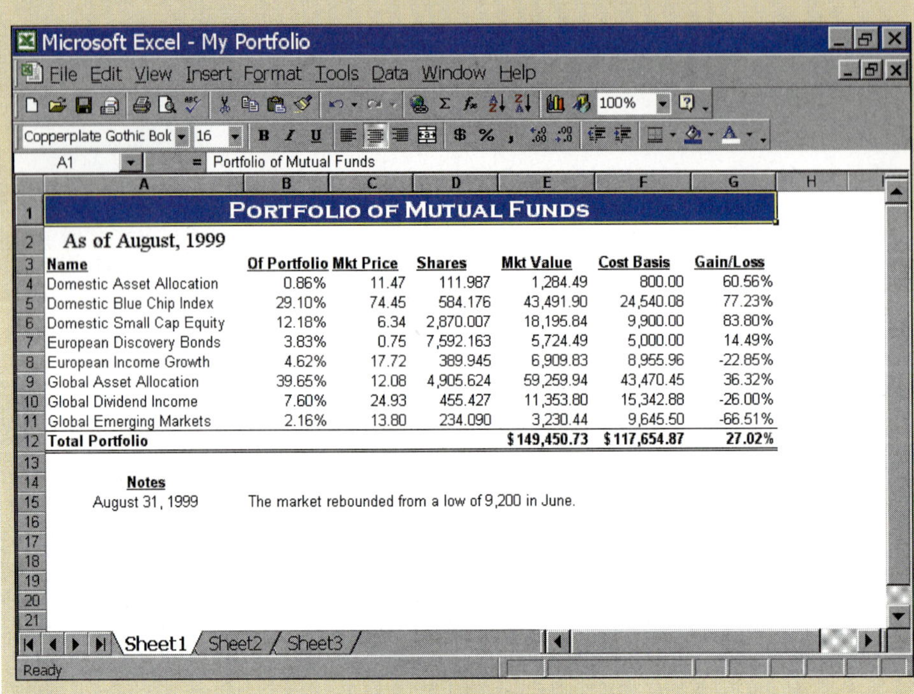

7 To turn the worksheet gridlines back on:
CHOOSE: Tools, Options
CLICK: *View* tab
SELECT: *Gridlines* check box, so that a "✔" appears
CLICK: OK

8 On your own, apply a border underline and a light gray shading (fill color) to the cell range A2 to G2. You can see how a subtle use of color can produce a truly professional-looking worksheet.

9 Save and then close the workbook.

3.1 Self Check   What is the basic difference between using the Underline button (▣) and the Borders button (▣)?

3.2 Applying and Removing Formatting

Excel 2000 provides a wealth of formatting commands for improving the appearance of a worksheet, its individual cells, and the contents within those cells. In addition to selecting formatting options individually, you can use the Format Painter button (▣) and the Edit, Paste Special command to copy formatting characteristics. These tools, along with Excel's AutoFormat feature, can help you apply formatting commands to a worksheet consistently and more efficiently. In this module, you work with these tools as well as learn how to remove formatting characteristics from a worksheet.

3.2.1 Using Format Painter

FEATURE

You use the **Format Painter** feature to copy formatting styles and attributes from one area in your worksheet to another. Not only does this feature speed formatting procedures, it ensures formatting consistency among cells in your worksheet.

METHOD

To copy formatting from one cell range to another:
1. SELECT: the cell range whose formatting you want to copy
2. CLICK: Format Painter button (⬚) on the Standard toolbar
3. SELECT: the cell range that you want to format

PRACTICE

You will now use Format Painter to copy formatting from one area of a worksheet to another.

Setup: Ensure that no workbooks are open in the application window.

1   Open the data file named EXC320.

2   Save the file as "ABC Retailers" to your personal storage location.

3   You will now apply formatting commands to the first journal entry in the worksheet. Then, once the formatting is completed, you will copy the set of formatting options to the other journal entries. To begin:
SELECT: cell A5

4   To change the date formatting:
CHOOSE: Format, Cells
CLICK: *Number* tab
SELECT: Date in the *Category* list box
SELECT: 3/14/1998 in the *Type* list box
CLICK: OK command button
The cell entry now appears as 10/10/1999.

5 To emphasize the account numbers and explanation:
SELECT: cell range from C5 to C6
CLICK: Bold button (**B**)
SELECT: cell B7
CLICK: Italic button (*I*)
SELECT: Green from the Font Color button (**A**)

6 To show the values in the Amount column as currency:
SELECT: cell range from D5 to E6
CLICK: Currency Style button
CLICK: Decrease Decimal button twice
The journal entry now appears formatted. (*Hint*: If necessary, increase the width of columns D and E to display the currency values.)

7 Using Format Painter, you will copy the formatting from this journal entry to another journal entry in the worksheet. Do the following:
SELECT: cell range from A5 to E7

8 To copy the formatting attributes:
CLICK: Format Painter button on the Standard toolbar
Notice that a dashed marquee appears around the selected range.

9 To apply the formatting to the next journal entry:
CLICK: cell A9
Notice that you need only click the top left-hand cell in the target range. Your screen should now appear similar to Figure 3.7.

Figure 3.7

Applying a formatting coat
using Format Painter

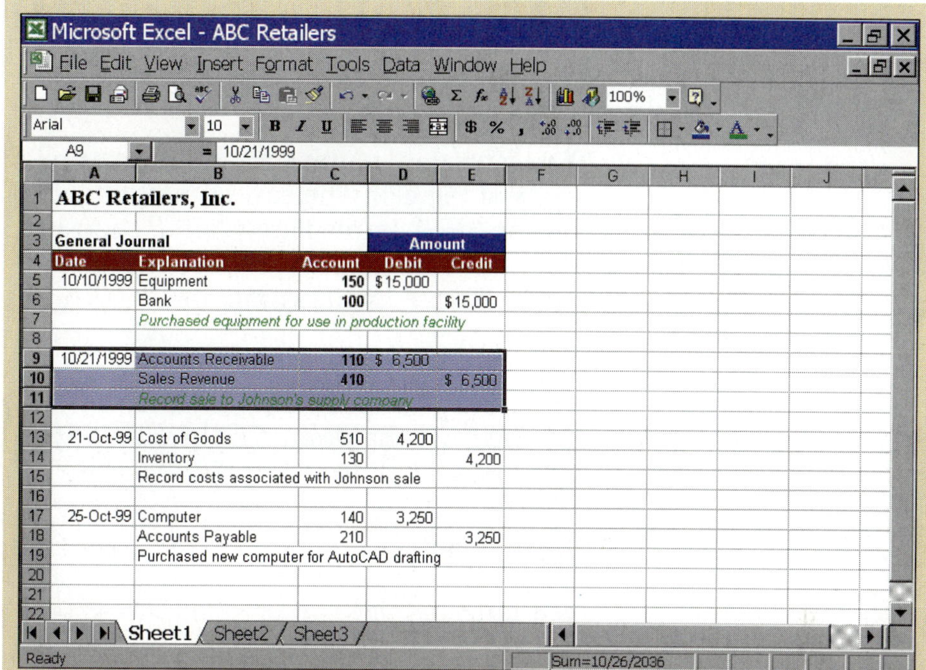

10   You can apply more than one coat using Format Painter. To demonstrate, ensure that the cell range A9 through E11 remains highlighted and then do the following:
DOUBLE-CLICK: Format Painter button (⌧)
Double-clicking the toolbar button will make the button stay active even after you apply the first coat to a target cell range.

11   With the Format Painter button (⌧) toggled on, you can apply multiple formatting coats. Do the following:
CLICK: cell A13
CLICK: cell A17
The remaining journal entries have been formatted.

12   To toggle this feature off:
CLICK: Format Painter button (⌧)

13   To better view your handiwork, do the following:
PRESS: CTRL + HOME

14   Save the workbook and keep it open for use in the next lesson.

3.2.2 Removing Formatting Attributes

FEATURE
You can safely remove a cell's formatting without affecting the contents of the cell. The easiest method, of course, is to click the Undo button (⟲) immediately after choosing a formatting command. You can also remove formatting characteristics by choosing the Edit, Clear, Formats command.

METHOD
To remove all formatting from a cell range:
1. SELECT: the desired cell range
2. CHOOSE: Edit, Clear, Formats

PRACTICE
You will now practice removing formatting characteristics from a cell range.

Setup: Ensure that you have completed the previous lessons in the module and that the "ABC Retailers" workbook is displayed.

1 Let's demonstrate the effects of entering data into a formatted cell. In this example, you will attempt to enter a value into a cell that is formatted to display a date. Do the following:
SELECT: cell A17
TYPE: 1000
PRESS: ENTER
The cell displays 9/26/1902.

2 You will now remove the formatting from this cell:
SELECT: cell A17
CHOOSE: Edit, Clear, Formats
The cell now displays the correct value, 1000.

3 The Edit, Clear, Formats command removes all formatting from a cell or cell range. To remove a single formatting characteristic, you can simply modify that characteristic. You will now remove the green color from the journal entry's explanatory note. To do so:
SELECT: cell B19
CLICK: down arrow attached to the Font Color button (A⏷)
SELECT: Automatic from the drop-down list
The text retains the italic formatting but changes to the default black color.

4 To remove all of the formatting characteristics for the last two journal entries, do the following:
SELECT: cell range from A13 to E19
CHOOSE: Edit, Clear, Formats
Notice that the date in cell A13 is actually stored as a value, 36454. In the next lesson, you will reapply formatting to the journal entries.

3.2.3   Using the Paste Special Command

FEATURE
The Edit, Paste Special command allows you to copy portions or characteristics of a cell or cell range to another area. Some of these characteristics include cell values, formulas, comments, and formats. Like the Format Painter feature, this command is useful for copying formatting options from one cell range to another.

METHOD
To copy and paste formatting characteristics:
1.   SELECT: the cell whose formatting you want to copy
2.   CLICK: Copy button (⧉)
3.   SELECT: the cells where you want to apply the formatting
4.   CHOOSE: Edit, Paste Special
5.   SELECT: *Formats* option button
6.   CLICK: OK command button

PRACTICE
In this exercise, you practice copying and pasting formatting characteristics using the Edit, Paste Special command.

Setup: Ensure that you have completed the previous lessons in the module and that the "ABC Retailers" workbook is displayed.

1 In order to paste formatting characteristics, you must first copy them to the Clipboard. Do the following:
SELECT: cell range from A9 to E11
CLICK: Copy button (⧉)
A dashed marquee appears around the selected range.

2 To display the Paste Special dialog box:
SELECT: cell A13
CHOOSE: Edit, Paste Special
The dialog box shown in Figure 3.8 is displayed. (*Note*: There are several intermediate and advanced features accessible from this dialog box. For now, you need only focus on the *Formats* option button.)

Figure 3.8

The Paste Special
dialog box

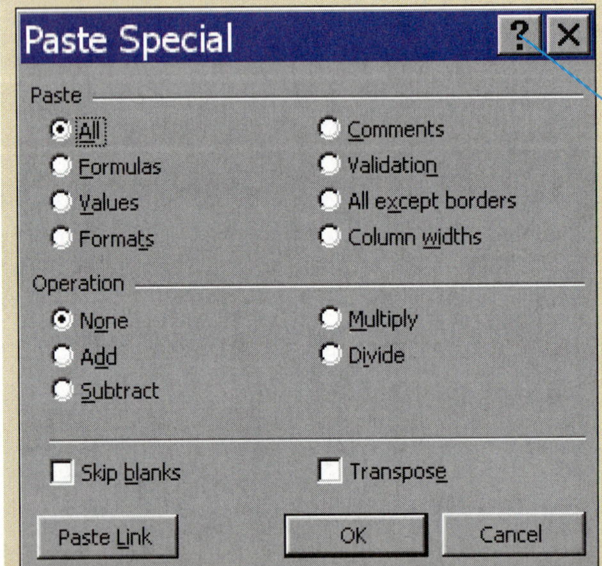

To find out more about the features of this dialog box, click the question mark button and then click on one of the option buttons. A brief ToolTip will appear. Click again to remove the ToolTip.

3 To paste the formatting:
SELECT: *Formats* option button
CLICK: OK
The formatting is applied.

4 To format the last journal entry:
SELECT: cell A17
CHOOSE: Edit, Paste Special
SELECT: *Formats* option button
CLICK: OK

5 Save and then close the workbook.

3.2.4 Using the AutoFormat Command

FEATURE
Rather than spend time selecting formatting options, you can use the **AutoFormat** feature to quickly apply an entire group of formatting commands to a cell range. The AutoFormat command works best when your worksheet data is organized using a table layout, with labels running down the left column and across the top row. After you specify one of the predefined table formats, Excel proceeds to apply fonts, number formats, alignments, borders, shading, and colors to the selected range. It is an excellent way to ensure consistent formatting across worksheets.

METHOD
1. SELECT: cell range to format
2. CHOOSE: Format, AutoFormat
3. SELECT: an option from the *Table format* list box

PRACTICE
You will now apply a predefined table format to a portfolio tracking worksheet.

Setup: Ensure that no workbooks are open in the application window.

1 Open the data file named EXC324.

2 Save the workbook as "Sandy's" to your personal storage location.

3 To apply an AutoFormat style to specific cells in a worksheet, select the cell range that you want to format. Do the following:
SELECT: cell range from A3 to F10
(*Hint*: As long as the table layout does not contain blank rows or columns, you can simply place the cell pointer within the table.)

4 To display the AutoFormat options:
CHOOSE: Format, AutoFormat
The AutoFormat dialog box appears as shown in Figure 3.9.

Figure 3.9

AutoFormat dialog box

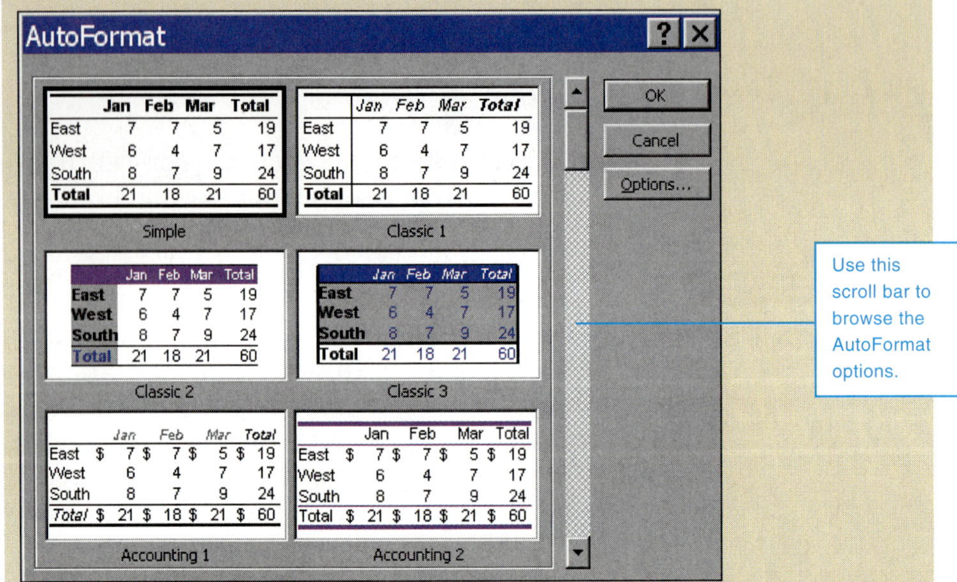

5 After scrolling the list in the AutoFormat dialog box, do the following:
SELECT: Colorful 2 option
CLICK: OK

6 To remove the cell highlighting:
CLICK: any cell outside of the highlighted range
Your worksheet should now appear similar to Figure 3.10.

Figure 3.10

Applying an AutoFormat

	A	B	C	D	E	F	G
1	**Sandy's Appliance Department**						
2							
3		*Qtr 1*	*Qtr 2*	*Qtr 3*	*Qtr 4*	*Total*	
4	*Dishwasher*	5,764	6,409	6,390	7,255	25,818	
5	*Dryer*	8,331	12,259	10,668	10,871	42,129	
6	*Microwave*	2,980	3,310	1,872	2,390	10,552	
7	*Refrigerator*	35,400	42,810	46,230	35,788	160,228	
8	*Stove/Range*	24,767	28,105	27,492	21,560	101,924	
9	*Washer*	12,890	16,881	12,452	13,700	55,923	
10	*Total*	90,132	109,774	105,104	91,564	396,574	
11							
12							

7 On your own, place the cell pointer within the table area and then apply some of the other AutoFormat options, such as Classic 2.

8 Save and then close the workbook.

3.2 Self Check　How might you ensure formatting consistency among related worksheets and workbooks?

3.3　Printing and Web Publishing

This module focuses on outputting your worksheet creations. Most commonly, you will print a worksheet for inclusion into a report or other such document. However, the Internet is a strong publishing medium unto itself. With the proper access, anyone can become an author and publisher. This lesson introduces you to previewing and printing workbooks using traditional tools, but also publishing workbooks electronically on the World Wide Web.

For those of you new to the online world, the **Internet** is a vast collection of computer networks that spans the entire planet. This worldwide infrastructure is made up of many smaller networks connected by standard telephone lines, fiber optics, cable, and satellites. The term **Intranet** refers to a private and usually secure local or wide area network that uses Internet technologies to share information. To access the Internet, you need a network or modem connection that links your computer to your account on the university's network or an Independent Service Provider (ISP).

Once you are connected to the Internet, you can use Web browser software, such as Microsoft Internet Explorer or Netscape Navigator, to access the **World Wide Web**. The Web provides a visual interface for the Internet and lets you search for information by simply clicking on highlighted words and images, known as **hyperlinks**. When you click a link, you are telling your computer's Web browser to retrieve a page from a Web site and display it on your screen. Not only can you publish your workbooks on the Web, you can incorporate hyperlinks directly within a worksheet to facilitate navigating between documents.

3.3.1 Previewing and Printing a Worksheet

FEATURE

Before sending a worksheet to the printer, you can preview it using a full-page display that will resemble the printed version. In this Preview display mode, you can move through the workbook pages, zoom in and out on desired areas, and modify page layout options, such as margins. When satisfied with its appearance, you can send it to the printer directly.

METHOD

- To preview a workbook:
  CLICK: Print Preview button (🔍), or
  CHOOSE: File, Print Preview
- To print a workbook:
  CLICK: Print button (🖨), or
  CHOOSE: File, Print

PRACTICE

You will now open a relatively large workbook, preview it on the screen, and then send it to the printer.

Setup: Ensure that no workbooks are displayed in the application window.

1 Open the data file named EXC330.

2 Save the workbook as "Published" to your personal storage location.

3 To preview how the workbook will appear when printed:
CLICK: Print Preview button (🔍)
Your screen should now appear similar to Figure 3.11.

Figure 3.11

Previewing a workbook

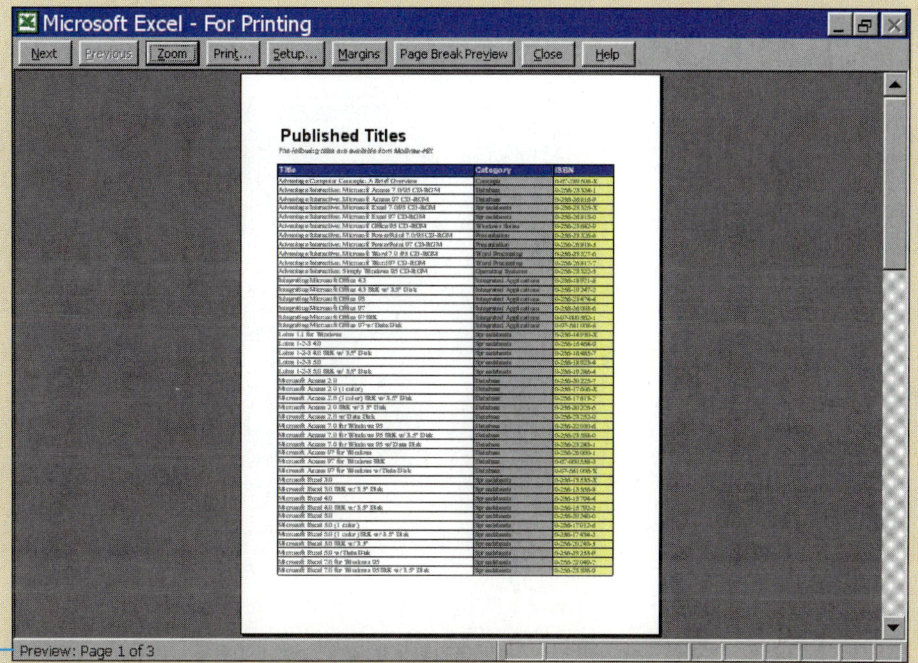

Identifies that you are in Preview mode and viewing "Page 1 of 3" total pages

4 To display the next page:
CLICK: Next button in the toolbar

5 To return to the first page:
CLICK: Previous button

6 To zoom in on the worksheet, move the magnifying glass mouse pointer over the worksheet area and then click once.

7 To zoom out on the display, click the mouse pointer once again.

8 On your own, practice zooming in and out on different areas of the page. You can also use the scroll bars to position the window.

10 Assuming that you are satisfied with the worksheet:
CLICK: Print button
The dialog box displayed in Figure 3.12 appears. You can use this dialog box to specify what to print and how many copies to produce. (*Note*: The quickest method for sending the current worksheet to the printer is to click the Print button (🖨) on the Standard toolbar.)

Figure 3.12

Print dialog box

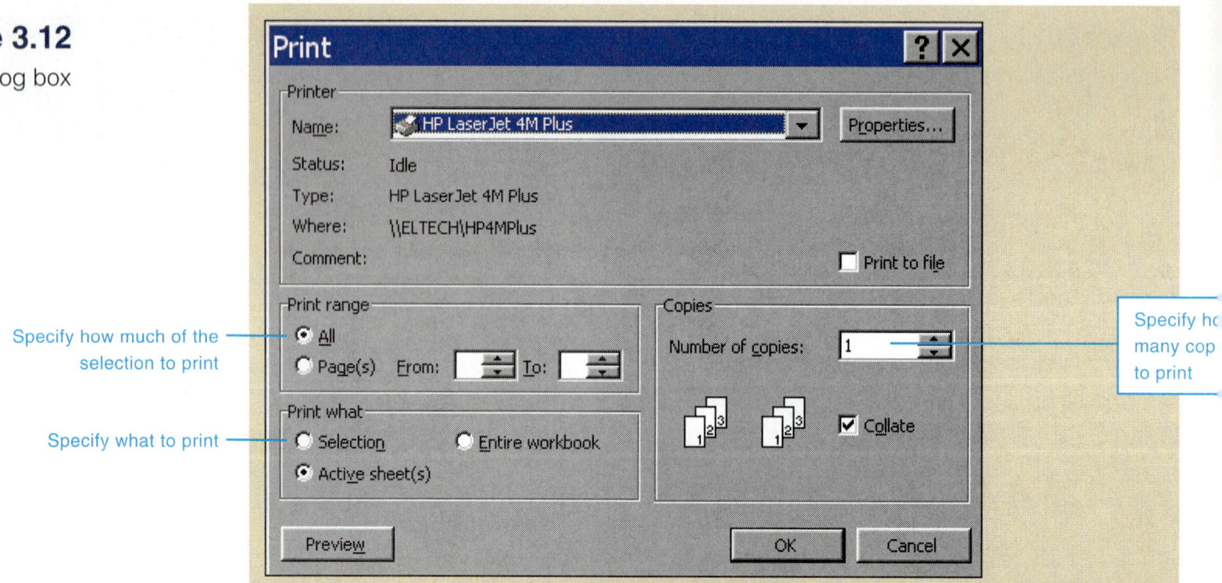

10 If you do not have access to a printer, click the Cancel button and proceed to the next lesson. If you have a printer connected to your computer and want to print out the worksheet, do the following:

CLICK: OK

After a few moments, the worksheet will appear at the printer.

3.3.2 Previewing and Publishing to the Web

FEATURE

Excel makes it easy to convert a workbook for display on the World Wide Web. The process involves saving the workbook in **HTML** (Hypertext Markup Language) format for publishing to a Web server. You can choose to publish a single worksheet or an entire workbook, complete with graphics and hyperlink objects. Once saved using the proper format, you may upload the files to your company's intranet or to a Web server.

METHOD

- To save a worksheet as a Web page:
  CHOOSE: File, Save as Web Page
- To view a worksheet as a Web page:
  CHOOSE: File, Web Page Preview

PRACTICE

You will now practice saving and viewing a worksheet as an HTML Web document.

Setup: Ensure that you have completed the previous lesson and that the "Published" workbook is displayed.

1 To save the current worksheet as a Web page:
CHOOSE: File, Save as Web Page
The Save As dialog box appears with some additional options, as shown in Figure 3.13. Notice that "Web Page" appears as the file type in the *Save as type* drop-down list box.

Figure 3.13

Save As dialog box
for a Web page

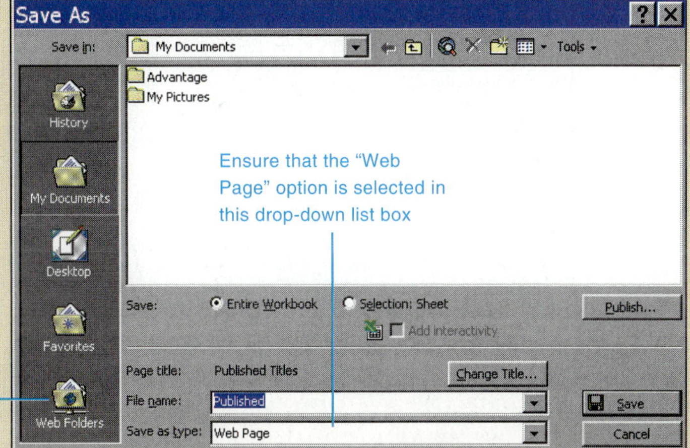

Save the Web page directly to a Web server on the Internet

2 Using the *Save in* drop-down list box or the Places bar:
SELECT: *your storage location*, if not already selected
(*Note*: To publish or post your workbook Web page to an intranet or to the Internet, you can click the Web Folders button () in the Places bar and then select a server location.)

3 To proceed with the conversion to HTML:
CLICK: Save command button
The workbook document is saved as "Published.htm" to your personal storage location.

4 To preview how the workbook will appear in a Web browser:
CHOOSE: File, Web Page Preview
After a few moments, the workbook appears displayed in a Web browser window. Figure 3.14 shows the document displayed using Internet Explorer.

Figure 3.14

Viewing a worksheet
as a Web page

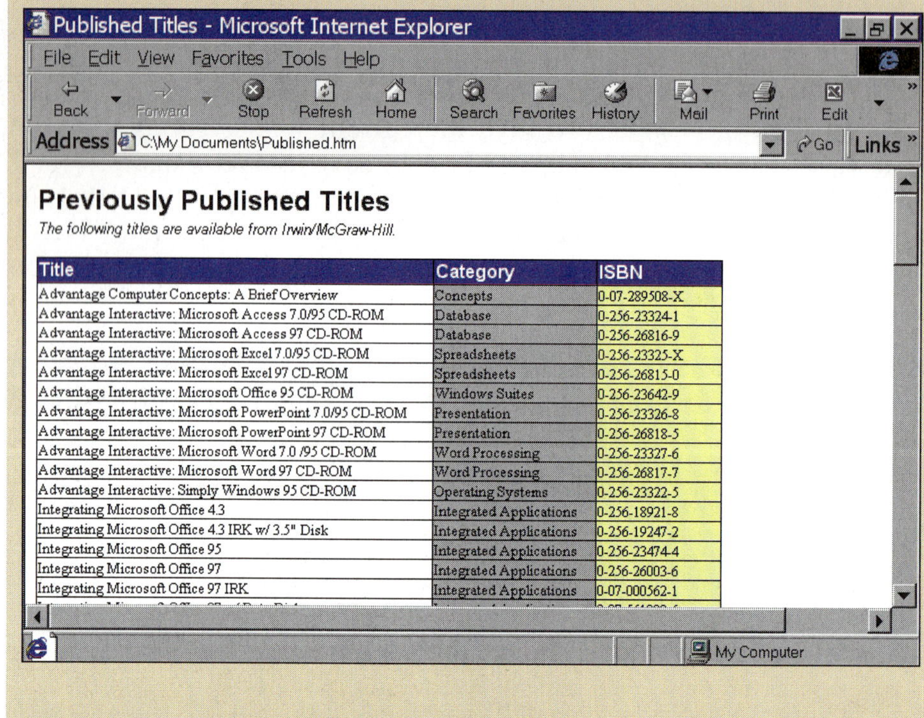

Published Titles - Microsoft Internet Explorer

File Edit View Favorites Tools Help

Address C:\My Documents\Published.htm

Previously Published Titles

The following titles are available from Irwin/McGraw-Hill.

Title	Category	ISBN
Advantage Computer Concepts: A Brief Overview	Concepts	0-07-289508-X
Advantage Interactive: Microsoft Access 7.0/95 CD-ROM	Database	0-256-23324-1
Advantage Interactive: Microsoft Access 97 CD-ROM	Database	0-256-26816-9
Advantage Interactive: Microsoft Excel 7.0/95 CD-ROM	Spreadsheets	0-256-23325-X
Advantage Interactive: Microsoft Excel 97 CD-ROM	Spreadsheets	0-256-26815-0
Advantage Interactive: Microsoft Office 95 CD-ROM	Windows Suites	0-256-23642-9
Advantage Interactive: Microsoft PowerPoint 7.0/95 CD-ROM	Presentation	0-256-23326-8
Advantage Interactive: Microsoft PowerPoint 97 CD-ROM	Presentation	0-256-26818-5
Advantage Interactive: Microsoft Word 7.0 /95 CD-ROM	Word Processing	0-256-23327-6
Advantage Interactive: Microsoft Word 97 CD-ROM	Word Processing	0-256-26817-7
Advantage Interactive: Simply Windows 95 CD-ROM	Operating Systems	0-256-23322-5
Integrating Microsoft Office 4.3	Integrated Applications	0-256-18921-8
Integrating Microsoft Office 4.3 IRK w/ 3.5" Disk	Integrated Applications	0-256-19247-2
Integrating Microsoft Office 95	Integrated Applications	0-256-23474-4
Integrating Microsoft Office 97	Integrated Applications	0-256-26003-6
Integrating Microsoft Office 97 IRK	Integrated Applications	0-07-000562-1

My Computer

5 To close the Web browser window:
CLICK: its Close button (⊠)

6 Close the "Published" workbook without saving the changes.

3.3 Self Check   How does the Print Preview display mode differ from the Web Page
Preview display mode?

3.4 Customizing Print Options

To assume control over how your workbooks will appear when
printed, you define page layout settings using the File, Page Setup
command. In the dialog box that appears, you may specify **margins,
headers, footers,** and whether gridlines or row and column headings should appear on the final printed output. To make the process
more manageable, Excel organizes the page layout settings under four
tabs (*Page, Margins, Header/Footer,* and *Sheet*) in the Page Setup dialog
box. The features and settings accessible from these tabs are discussed
in the following lessons.

3.4.1 Adjusting Page and Margin Settings

FEATURE
You use the *Page* tab in the Page Setup dialog box to specify the paper size, print scale, and print orientation (for example, portrait or landscape) for a workbook. The *Margins* tab allows you to select the top, bottom, left, and right page margins, and to center the worksheet both horizontally and vertically on a page. You can also manipulate the page margins while viewing a worksheet in Print Preview mode.

METHOD
1.   CHOOSE: File, Page Setup
2.   CLICK: *Page* and *Margins* tabs
3.   SELECT: the desired page layout options

PRACTICE
In this lesson, you open and print a workbook that summarizes a company's amortization expense.

Setup: Ensure that no workbooks are open in the application window.

1 Open the data file named EXC340.

2 Save the file as "CCA Schedule" to your personal storage location.

3 To begin, let's display the worksheet using Print Preview mode:
CLICK: Print Preview button (🔍)

4 Practice zooming in and out on the worksheet using the Zoom command button and the magnifying glass mouse pointer.

5 To view the second page of the printout:
CLICK: Next command button
Notice that the worksheet does not fit for printing on a single page.

6 To exit from Print Preview mode:
CLICK: Close button

7 Let's adjust some page layout settings. Do the following:
CHOOSE: File, Page Setup
CLICK: *Page* tab
Your screen should now appear similar to Figure 3.15.

Figure 3.15

Page Setup dialog

box: *Page* tab

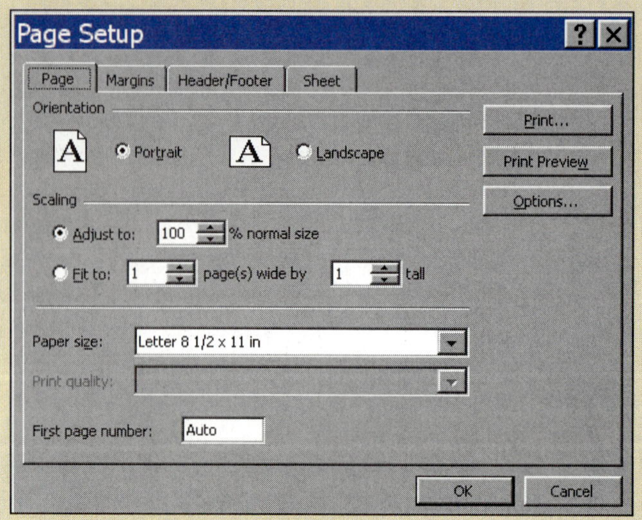

8 In the *Orientation* area:
SELECT: *Landscape* option button

9 To center the worksheet between the left and right margins:
CLICK: *Margins* tab

10 In the *Center on page* area:
SELECT: *Horizontally* check box
CLICK: Print Preview command button
You should now see the entire worksheet appear on a single
printed page and centered between the margins.

3.4.2 Inserting Headers and Footers

FEATURE

You can place descriptive information, such as the current date, in
the header and footer of a page. The contents of a header or footer
repeat automatically for each page that is printed. Some suggestions include using these areas for displaying your name, copyright
information, the words "confidential" or "first draft," or page numbering. You may simply want to place the workbook's filename in
the header so that you can easily find it again on your hard disk.

METHOD

1. CHOOSE: File, Page Setup
2. CLICK: *Headers/Footers* tab
3. SELECT: a predefined header or footer, or
     CLICK: Custom Header button to design a new header, or
     CLICK: Custom Footer button to design a new footer

PRACTICE

You will now add a custom header and footer to the worksheet.

Setup: Ensure that you have completed the previous lesson and that the "CCA Schedule" workbook is displayed in Print Preview mode.

1 To return to the Page Setup dialog box from Print Preview mode:
CLICK: Setup command button
The dialog box appears displaying the last tab that was selected.

2 To add headers and footers to the page:
CLICK: *Header/Footer* tab

3 First, select an existing footer for printing at the bottom of each page:
CLICK: down arrow attached to the *Footer* drop-down list
SELECT: "CCA Schedule, Page 1" option
Once selected, you should see the workbook's filename "CCA Schedule" appear centered in the footer preview area, and the words "Page 1" appear right-aligned.

4 To create a custom header:
CLICK: Custom Header command button
Figure 3.16 shows the Header dialog box and labels the buttons used for inserting information into the different sections.

Figure 3.16

Custom Header
dialog box

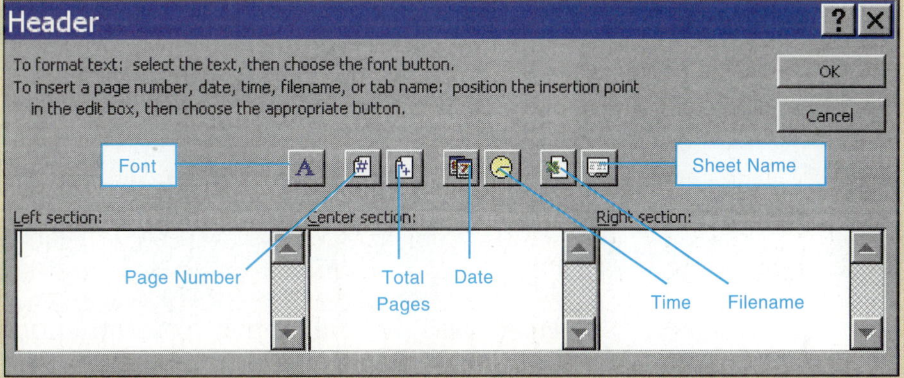

5 To create a header that prints the current date against the right margin:
CLICK: the mouse pointer in the *Right section* area
TYPE: **Printed on:**
PRESS: Space bar once
CLICK: Date button (⊡) as labeled in Figure 3.16
CLICK: OK
You will see the custom header appear in the preview area.

6 To return to Print Preview mode:
CLICK: OK
Your screen should now appear similar to Figure 3.17. Notice the header in the top right-hand corner and the footer along the bottom.

7 To exit from Print Preview mode:
CLICK: Close button

Figure 3.17

Previewing the CCA
Schedule worksheet

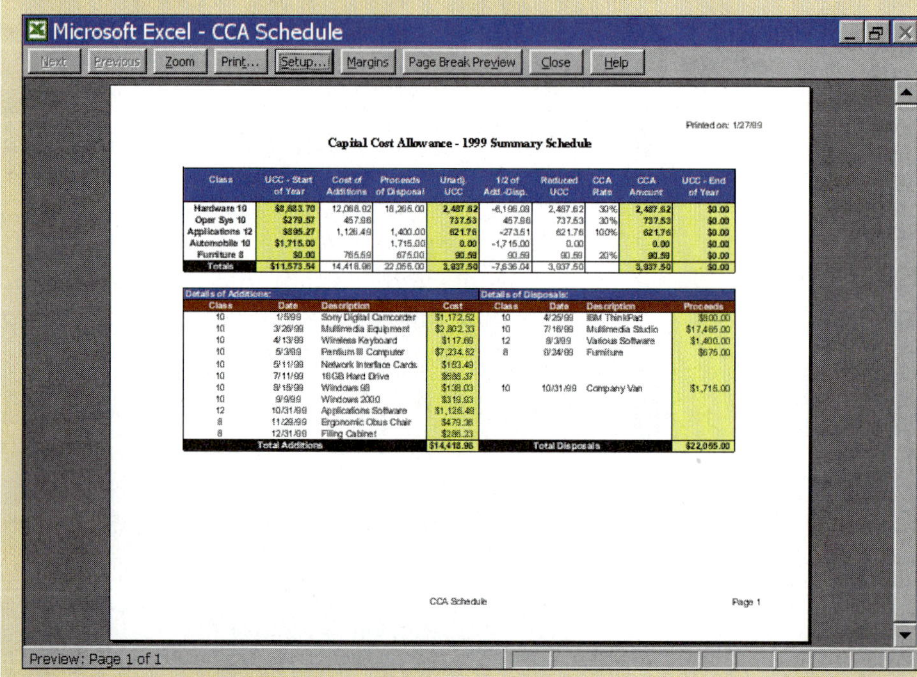

3.4.3 Selecting Worksheet Content to Print

FEATURE
From the Print dialog box, you can choose to print an entire workbook, a single worksheet, or a specified cell range. Alternatively, you can preselect a cell range to print by first specifying the print area. Other print options are available from the Page Setup dialog box, where you can choose to print the worksheet gridlines or row and column headings.

METHOD

To specify a print area:
1. SELECT: a cell range
2. CHOOSE: File, Print Area, Set Print Area

To select from the general print options:
1. CHOOSE: File, Print
2. SELECT: one of the following *Print what* option buttons—
    Selection, *Active Sheet(s)*, or *Entire Workbook*
3. SELECT: *Number of copies* to print

To specify whether to print gridlines or row and column headings:
1. CHOOSE: File, Page Setup
2. CLICK: *Sheet* tab
3. SELECT: *Gridlines* check box to toggle the printing of grid-
    lines
4. SELECT: *Row and column headings* check box to print the
    frame area

PRACTICE

In this lesson, you practice selecting print options and setting print
areas. Lastly, you have the opportunity to print the worksheet.

Setup: Ensure that you have completed the previous lesson and that
the "CCA Schedule" workbook is displayed.

1 You will often find the need to print specific ranges in a worksheet, rather than the entire workbook. This need is solved by
first setting a print area. To practice selecting a cell range for
printing:
SELECT: cell range from A1 (a merged cell) to J12
CHOOSE: File, Print Area, Set Print Area

2 Now that you have defined a specific cell range as the print area:
CLICK: Print Preview button ([image])
Notice that only the selected range is previewed for printing.

3 To return to the worksheet:
CLICK: Close command button

4 To return to printing the entire worksheet:
CHOOSE: File, Print Area, Clear Print Area
This command removes the print area definition.

5 Let's view some other print options:
CHOOSE: File, Page Setup
CLICK: *Sheet* tab
Your screen should now appear similar to Figure 3.18.

Figure 3.18

Page Setup dialog
box: *Sheet* tab

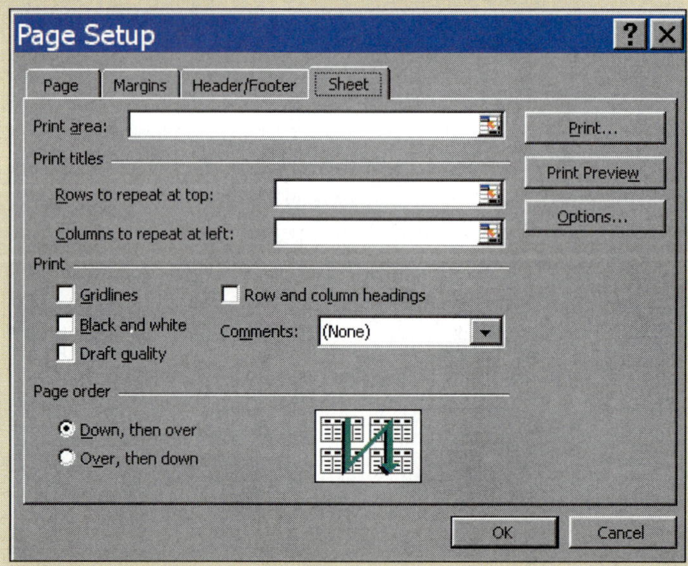

6 Sometimes printing the gridlines or row and column headings is useful for reviewing a worksheet for errors. To demonstrate:
SELECT: *Gridlines* check box in the *Print* area
SELECT: *Row and column headings* check box
CLICK: Print Preview
The printed worksheet now looks similar to the screen display, with the exception of the header and footer. (*Note*: All page setup options are saved along with the workbook file.)

7 If you have a printer connected to your computer, perform the following steps. Otherwise, proceed to the next step.
CLICK: Print command button
CLICK: OK, when the Print dialog box appears

8 If necessary, close the Print Preview window. Then save and close the "CCA Schedule" workbook.

9 Exit Microsoft Excel.

3.4 Self Check How would you create a custom footer that displayed your name against the left page border and your company's name against the right page border?

3.5 Chapter Review

The majority of this chapter described common methods for enhancing the appearance of your worksheets. You were introduced to several of Excel's formatting capabilities and commands. Specifically, you applied fonts, number formats, cell alignments, borders, colors, and predefined table formats to a worksheet. You also learned how to print and electronically publish your worksheets for printing and display on the World Wide Web. Lastly, you were introduced to several of Excel's page layout options for controlling and customizing how a worksheet prints.

3.5.1 Command Summary

Many of the commands and procedures appearing in this chapter are summarized in the following table.

Skill Set	To Perform This Task . . .	Do the Following . . .
Formatting Worksheets	Apply font typefaces, font sizes, and font styles	CHOOSE: Format, Cells CLICK: *Font* tab
	Apply number formats	CHOOSE: Format, Cells CLICK: *Number* tab
	Increase and decrease decimal places	CLICK: Increase Decimal button (⬚) CLICK: Decrease Decimal button (⬚)
	Modify a cell's alignment	CHOOSE: Format, Cells CLICK: *Alignment* tab
	Merge a range of cells	CHOOSE: Format, Cells CLICK: *Alignment* tab SELECT: *Merge cells* check box

Continued

Skill Set	To Perform This Task . . .	Do the Following . . .
	Add borders, patterns, and shading	CHOOSE: Format, Cells CLICK: *Border* or *Patterns* tab
	Copy formatting from one range to another using the toolbar	SELECT: the desired range CLICK: Format Painter button (⬧) SELECT: the target range
	Copy formatting from one range to another using the Clipboard	SELECT: the desired range CLICK: Copy button (⬧) SELECT: the target range CHOOSE: Edit, Paste Special SELECT: *Formats* option button
	Clear formatting that appears in a range	SELECT: the desired range CHOOSE: Edit, Clear, Formats
	Use AutoFormats	CHOOSE: Format, AutoFormat SELECT: *a predefined format*
Page Setup and Printing	Preview a worksheet	CLICK: Preview button (⬧), or CHOOSE: File, Print Preview
	Print a worksheet	CLICK: Print button (⬧), or CHOOSE: File, Print
	Preview worksheet as a Web page	CHOOSE: File, Web Page Preview
	Print the selected cell range, active worksheet, or the entire workbook	CHOOSE: File, Print SELECT: *the desired option button*
	Set the worksheet area to print workbook	SELECT: the desired range CHOOSE: File, Print Area, Set Print Area
	Clear the selected print area	CHOOSE: File, Print Area, Clear Print Area
	Specify page orientation and paper size	CHOOSE: File, Page Setup CLICK: *Page* tab
	Specify print margins and placement on a page	CHOOSE: File, Page Setup CLICK: *Margins* tab

Continued

Skill Set	To Perform This Task . . .	Do the Following . . .
	Define headers and footers for printing	CHOOSE: File, Page Setup CLICK: *Header/Footer* tab
	Print the screen	PRESS: PRTSCR key
Managing Files	Save worksheet as an HTML document	CHOOSE: File, Save as Web Page

3.5.2 Key Terms

This section specifies page references for the key terms identified in this chapter. For a complete list of definitions, refer to the Glossary provided in the Appendix.

AutoFormat, *p. 119*

cell alignment, *p. 107*

fonts, *p. 102*

footers, *p. 126*

Format Painter, *p. 113*

gridlines, *p. 110*

headers, *p. 126*

HTML, *p. 124*

hyperlinks, *p. 121*

Internet, *p. 121*

Intranet, *p. 121*

margins, *p. 126*

typefaces, *p. 102*

World Wide Web, *p. 121*

3.6   Review Questions

3.6.1 Short Answer

1. Why should you limit the number of typefaces used in a worksheet?
2. Name two methods for specifying decimal places in a worksheet.
3. How do you split a merged cell?
4. How do you apply multiple coats using the Format Painter tool?
5. Name two color settings that you can change in a worksheet.

6. How do you turn off gridlines from displaying in a worksheet?
7. How do you turn on gridlines for printing on a worksheet?
8. What should you do prior to sending a worksheet to the printer?
9. Name the tabs in the Page Setup dialog box.
10. How do you create a Web document from a standard Excel worksheet?

3.6.2   True/False

1. _____ The **B** button stands for bold. The **U** button stands for underline. The **I** button stands for incline.
2. _____ You use the *Number* tab in the Format Cells dialog box to select date and time formatting options.
3. _____ Whenever you merge cells, the contents must also be centered.
4. _____ You can remove formatting from a cell range by choosing the Edit, Clear, Special command.
5. _____ The AutoFormat command works best when your data is organized using a table layout.
6. _____ You can zoom in and out on a worksheet using Print Preview mode.
7. _____ You can view a worksheet as it would appear in a Web browser, prior to saving it as a Web page.
8. _____ The two page orientation options are *Picture* and *Landscape.*
9. _____ You can access the Page Setup dialog box directly from Print Preview mode.
10. _____ To convert a worksheet for display on the World Wide Web, you save the workbook into HTML format.

3.6.3 Multiple Choice

1. To change the text color of a cell entry:
   a. CLICK: Fill Color button ( )
   b. CLICK: Font Color button ( )
   c. CLICK: Text Color button ( )
   d. You cannot change the text color of a cell entry.

2. Excel stores date and time entries as:
   a. formats
   b. formulas
   c. labels
   d. values

3. To merge a range of cells, you select the *Merge cells* check box on this tab of the Format Cells dialog box:
   a. *Number* tab
   b. *Alignment* tab
   c. *Margins* tab
   d. *Merge* tab

4. To remove a cell's formatting, you can:
   a. CHOOSE: Edit, Clear, Formats
   b. CHOOSE: Edit, Formats, Clear
   c. CHOOSE: Format, Cells, Clear
   d. CHOOSE: Format, Clear

5. To copy a cell's formatting characteristics to another cell, you can:
   a. Use the AutoFormat feature
   b. Use the AutoPainter feature
   c. Use the Format Painter feature
   d. Use the Edit, Paste Formats command

6. To select one of Excel's prebuilt table formats:
   a. CHOOSE: Format, AutoTable
   b. CHOOSE: Format, TableFormat
   c. CHOOSE: Format, AutoFormat
   d. CHOOSE: Format, Table

7. To produce gridlines on your printed worksheet:
   a. SELECT: *Gridlines* check box in the Page Setup dialog box
   b. CLICK: Gridline button ( ) on the Formatting toolbar
   c. CLICK: Underline button ( ) on the Formatting toolbar
   d. Both a and b above

8. To identify a specific cell range on the worksheet for printing:
   a. CHOOSE: File, Print Range
   b. CHOOSE: File, Print Area, Set Print Area
   c. CHOOSE: File, Set Print Area
   d. CHOOSE: File, Set Print Range

9. To print data at the top of each page, you create the following:
   a. footer
   b. footnote
   c. headline
   d. header

10. To save the current worksheet as a Web page:
    a. CLICK: Save button ()
    b. CHOOSE: File, Save as Web Page
    c. CHOOSE: File, Save as HTML
    d. CHOOSE: File, Publish to Web

3.7 Hands-On Projects

3.7.1 Grandview College: Bookstore Inventory

In this exercise, you practice using Excel's formatting commands to enhance the appearance of a monthly bookstore report.

1. Load Microsoft Excel.
2. Open the data file named EXC371.
3. Save the workbook as "Bookstore" to your personal storage location.
4. Let's start by formatting the worksheet's title:
   SELECT: cell A1
   CHOOSE: Format, Cells
   CLICK: *Font* tab in the dialog box
5. In the Format Cells dialog box, make the following selections:
   SELECT: Times New Roman in the *Font* list box
   SELECT: Bold Italic in the *Font style* list box
   SELECT: 16 in the *Size* list box
   SELECT: Dark Red in the *Color* drop-down list box
   Notice that the *Preview* area in the dialog box displays all of your choices.

6. To accept the dialog box selections:
    CLICK: OK
7. Let's center the title across the width of the worksheet:
    SELECT: cell range from A1 to G1
    CLICK: Merge and Center button (▦)
8. To apply percentage formatting:
    SELECT: cell range from D4 to D9
    CLICK: Percent Style button (%)
    CLICK: Increase Decimal button (⊞) twice
9. To apply currency formatting:
    SELECT: cell range from C4 to C10
    CLICK: Currency Style button ($)
    (*Hint*: You include cell C10 in the range so that you can later copy this column's formatting to other ranges in the worksheet.)
10. Let's copy this column's formatting to the other columns. With the range still selected, do the following:
    DOUBLE-CLICK: Format Painter button (▨)
    CLICK: cell E4 to apply one formatting coat
    CLICK: cell G4 to apply another formatting coat
    CLICK: Format Painter button (▨) to toggle the feature off
    (*Note*: Don't bother changing the column widths just yet.)
11. Now apply an AutoFormat to the data area:
    SELECT: cell range from A3 to G10
    CHOOSE: Format, AutoFormat

12. In the AutoFormat dialog box:
    SELECT: Classic 2
    CLICK: OK
13. To better see the results of the formatting:
    CLICK: cell A1
    A much nicer looking report!
14. Save and then close the workbook.

3.7.2 Fast Forward Video: Sales Analysis

You will now practice enhancing the layout of an existing worksheet by adjusting rows and columns and by formatting its text labels, numbers, and headings.

1. Open the data file named EXC372.
2. Save the workbook as "Video Sales" to your personal storage location.
3. To begin, adjust the width of column C to 5 characters:
   SELECT: cell C1
   CHOOSE: Format, Column, Width
   TYPE: **5**
   CLICK: OK
4. Now, delete row 3 using the following steps:
   RIGHT-CLICK: row 3 in the frame area
   CHOOSE: Delete
5. To format the headings:
   SELECT: cell A4
   PRESS: CTRL and hold it down
   CLICK: cell A9
   CLICK: Bold button (B)
   Remember to release the CTRL when you are finished.
6. To format the "Total Sales" label with boldface and italic:
   SELECT: cell A14
   CLICK: Bold button (B)
   CLICK: Italic button (I)
7. To format the two column headings:
   SELECT: cell range from D3 to E3
   PRESS: CTRL+b to apply boldface
   PRESS: CTRL+u to underline the contents
8. To format the values in the Amount column:
   CLICK: cell D5
   PRESS: SHIFT and hold it down
   CLICK: cell D14
   All of the cells between these two should now appear highlighted.
9. To apply currency formatting:
   CLICK: Currency Style button ($)
10. To apply percent formatting to the values in the adjacent column:
    SELECT: cell range from E5 to E12
    CLICK: Percent Style button (%)
    CLICK: Increase Decimal button twice

11. To format all of the category labels at the same time:
SELECT: cell range from B5 to B8
PRESS: CTRL and hold it down
SELECT: cell range from B10 to B12 by dragging with the mouse
There should now be two highlighted ranges on the worksheet.

12. To italicize the data and align it to the right:
CLICK: Italic button (*I*)
CLICK: Align Right button (≣)

13. Finally, let's format the titles in rows 1 and 2. Do the following:
SELECT: cell range from A1 to A2
CLICK: Bold button (**B**)
CLICK: down arrow attached to the Font list box (Arial ▾)
SELECT: Times New Roman
CLICK: down arrow attached to the Font Size list box (10 ▾)
SELECT: 14

14. To center the titles across the active area:
SELECT: cell range from A1 to E1
CLICK: Merge and Center button (▦)
SELECT: cell range from A2 to E2
CLICK: Merge and Center button (▦)
Your worksheet should now appear similar to Figure 3.19.

15. Save and then close the workbook.

Figure 3.19

Formatting the Sales
Analysis worksheet

	A	B	C	D	E	F
1		**Fast Forward Video**				
2		**Sales Analysis**				
3				**Amount**	**Pct of Total**	
4	**Rentals**					
5		*New Releases*		$1,071.35	43.79%	
6		*Weekly Movies*		$ 826.00	33.76%	
7		*Games*		$ 549.10	22.44%	
8		*Total Rentals*		$2,446.45	84.63%	
9	**Retail Sales**					
10		*Videos*		$ 132.50	29.83%	
11		*Snacks*		$ 311.65	70.17%	
12		*Total Retail*		$ 444.15	15.37%	
13						
14	**Total Sales**			$2,890.60		
15						

3.7.3 Sun Valley Frozen Foods: Inventory Projections

Incorporating some skills learned in Chapter 2, you will now practice modifying a worksheet and applying formatting commands.

1. Open the workbook named EXC373.
2. Save the workbook as "Sun Seasonal" to your personal storage location.
3. Adjust the width of column A to 18 characters.
4. Delete column B.
5. Adjust columns B through E to their best-fit widths.
6. Format the headings in row 1 to appear boldface and centered in their respective columns.
7. Format the "Total" label in cell A7 to appear boldface and italic.
8. Insert two rows at the top of the worksheet for entering a title. (*Hint*: Rather than performing the Insert command twice to insert two rows, you can select rows 1 and 2 first and then perform the command once.)
9. Enter a title for the worksheet:
    SELECT: cell A1
    TYPE: **Seasonal Inventory Projections**
    PRESS: (ENTER)
10. Merge and center the title in cell A1 between columns A and E.
11. Format the title to appear with a larger and more unique font. Also, apply a dark blue color to the font text on a light yellow background fill. Then, surround the merged cell with a Thick Box border.
12. To bring out the Total row, apply a Top and Double Bottom border to cells A9 through E9. With the cell range highlighted, assign a light gray background fill color.

13. To remove the highlighting:
    CLICK: cell A1
14. Save and then close the workbook.

3.7.4 Lakeside Realty: Listing Summary

In this exercise, you use the AutoFormat command and modify the page layout in an existing workbook.

1. Open the workbook named EXC374.
2. Save the workbook as "Listing Summary" to your personal storage location.
3. Apply the "Classic 3" AutoFormat style to the cell range from A3 to K10.

4. PRESS: (HOME) to remove the highlighting
5. Format the worksheet title in cell A1 to make it stand out from the table information.
6. Use the Page Setup dialog box to change the page orientation to *Landscape*.
7. Use the Page Setup dialog box to center the worksheet horizontally on the page.
8. Add a footer that prints the workbook's filename aligned left and the page number aligned right.
9. Add a header that shows the company name, "Lakeside Realty," aligned left and the current date aligned right.
10. Preview the worksheet. Your screen should now appear similar to Figure 3.20.

Figure 3.20

Previewing a

formatted worksheet

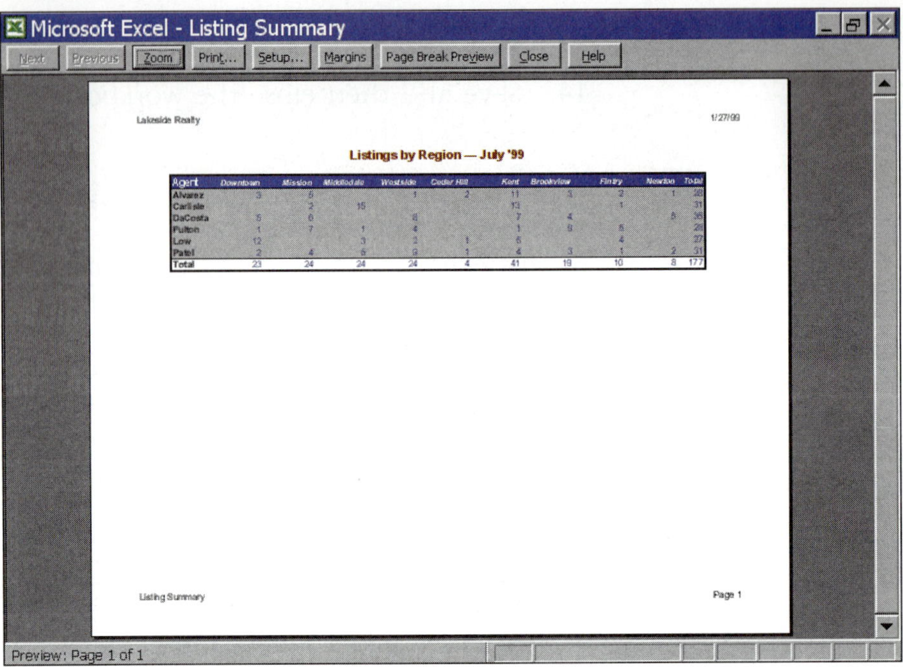

11.   Print a copy of the worksheet.
12.   Save and then close the workbook.

3.7.5   On Your Own: Financial Data Table

To practice formatting and manipulating data, open the workbook named EXC375. Then make a copy of the file by saving the workbook as "Financial Data" to your personal storage location. On your own, resize all of the columns to ensure that the data is visible. Insert a new row at the beginning of the worksheet and enter the worksheet title "United Consolidated Group." Using fonts, colors, alignment, and background fills, format the titles in rows 1 and 2 to stand out from the rest of the data.

Format the data in columns B through D with currency formatting and two decimal places, except for the date headings. Format the data in column E with percent formatting and two decimal places. Center and apply boldface to the column headings in row 3. Then apply boldface and italics to the cell range from A4 to A9. Before proceeding, adjust the column widths and row heights as required. When satisfied, preview and print the worksheet. Lastly, save and then close the workbook.

3.7.6 On Your Own: Personal Expense Comparison

To practice working with formatting and page layout options, use Excel to create a monthly expense comparison worksheet. After displaying a blank workbook, enter the following column headings in a single row: **Expense**, **January**, **February**, and **Change**. Then enter the following expense categories in a single column under the "Expense" heading.

- Rent/Mortgage
- Food
- Clothing
- Transportation
- Utilities
- Education
- Entertainment

For both the January and February columns, enter some reasonable data. Add the label "Total" below the last expense category and then use AutoSum to calculate totals for the monthly columns. Create formulas to calculate the difference for each expense category. Lastly, use the AutoFormat "Accounting 2" option to format the worksheet.

For printing purposes, add a custom footer that prints the current date, your name, and the page number at the bottom of each page. When you are finished, save the workbook as "My Expenses" to your personal storage location. Preview and print the worksheet, and then close the workbook and exit Excel.

3.8 Case Problems: Marvin's Music

Marvin's Music store is facing increased competitive pressures with the recent announcement that a discount superstore chain is moving into the area. Stacy Marvin realizes that in order to stay competitive, she needs to be able to track and analyze her inventory costs, stock levels, and sales trends quickly and accurately. Fortunately, her senior sales associate, Justin Lee, has explained how he can use Excel to create worksheets that will make these tasks easier.

In the following case problems, assume the role of Justin and perform the same steps that he identifies. You may want to re-read the chapter opening before proceeding.

1. Stacey asks Justin to prepare a worksheet that will summarize Marvin's current stock levels. He begins by launching Microsoft Excel so that a new blank workbook is displayed. As shown in Figure 3.21, he enters the worksheet title, row and column labels, and inventory values for each category.

Figure 3.21

Creating an inventory worksheet

	A	B	C	D	E
1	Inventory by Category				
2		CDs	Tapes	Total	
3	Pop	18500	6500		
4	Rock	23600	15350		
5	Dance	19000	9200		
6	Country	15420	8670		
7	Easy Listening	11330	3200		
8	Classical	5680	1340		
9	Soundtracks	4200	1030		
10	Total				
11					

Using the AutoSum feature, Justin has Excel calculate totals for both the row and column values. He then selects the cell range from A2 to D10 and applies the "Classic 2" AutoFormat style. Not yet satisfied, he merges and centers the title between columns A and D, and then applies formatting to make it appear consistent with the rest of the worksheet. Justin saves the workbook as "MM Inventory1" to his *personal storage location* and then prints a copy to show to Stacey.

2. After reviewing the worksheet, Stacey asks Justin to make the following adjustments:

- Insert a new row for "World Music" at row 9, enter 4100 for CDs and 3500 for Tapes, and ensure the totals are updated.
- Adjust the width of column A to 15 characters and then change the height of row 1 to 24 points.
- Make the values appear with dollar signs and commas, but with no decimal places.
- Adjust the width of columns B, C, and D to be larger than they presently appear and ensure that they are all the same width.

When Justin finishes customizing the worksheet to appear similar to Figure 3.22, he saves the workbook as "MM Inventory2" to the same location.

Figure 3.22

Customizing the
inventory worksheet

	A	B	C	D	E
1	**Inventory by Category**				
2		CDs	Tapes	Total	
3	Pop	$18,500	$6,500	$25,000	
4	Rock	$23,600	$15,350	$38,950	
5	Dance	$19,000	$9,200	$28,200	
6	Country	$15,420	$8,670	$24,090	
7	Easy Listening	$11,330	$3,200	$14,530	
8	Classical	$5,680	$1,340	$7,020	
9	World Music	$4,100	$3,500	$7,600	
10	Soundtracks	$4,200	$1,030	$5,230	
11	Total	$101,830	$48,790	$150,620	
12					

3.   The next day, Stacey assigns Justin the task of completing the company's Advertising Schedule worksheet that she started a few days earlier. Justin opens the workbook named EXC383 and then saves it as "MM Ad Schedule" to his *personal storage location*. According to the sticky notes attached to Stacey's printout of the worksheet, Justin needs to enter the following three new promotions:

Back-to-School—1 newspaper ad on August 27th for $500
Rocktober Blitz—6 radio spots on October 11th for $2900
Christmas—3 TV ads starting Dec 1st for $9000

Using the toolbar, Justin formats the worksheet by applying the Currency style to the "Cost" column and then decreases the decimal places shown to 0. He adjusts the width of column F to show all of the information displayed. Then he uses the Format Cells dialog box to change the date values to appear using a "dd-mmm-yy" format. Again, he adjusts the column width as necessary.

Noticing that Stacey placed an extra column between the "Theme" and "Date" columns, Justin deletes column B and then resizes column A to display using its best-fit width. He also selects a new typeface and font size for the column headings, and modifies the alignment of the titles. Justin prints, saves, and then closes the workbook.

4.   Having completed his work for Stacey, Justin opens one of his pet worksheet projects named EXC384. This workbook contains a sales transaction analysis that summarizes information from the store's point-of-sale equipment. He immediately saves the workbook as "MM Daily Sales" to his *personal storage location*.

To speed the formatting process, Justin uses the AutoFormat feature to apply a combination of table formatting attributes to the worksheet. Then, to distinguish the cells containing the times of day from the rest of the worksheet area, Justin applies a dark red fill color to the background of row 1 and makes the font color white. Next he increases the width for all of the columns to give the worksheet a more spacious look. At the top of the worksheet, Justin inserts a new row and then enters the title "Sales Transactions by Time Period." He merges and centers the title over the columns and then applies formatting to make the title stand out from the data.

To prepare for printing, Justin adds a custom header that places the company name at the center of the page. He then adds a custom footer that contains the words "Prepared by *your name*" on the right, the date in the center, and the page number on the right-hand side. Next, he adjusts the page setup so the worksheet is centered horizontally on the page. Justin then saves the workbook as a Web page and views it using his Web browser. Satisfied that he's put in a full day, Justin saves and closes the workbook. Then he exits Microsoft Excel.

MICROSOFT EXCEL 2000
Analyzing Your Data

CHAPTER
FOUR

Chapter Outline

Learning Objectives

After reading this chapter, you will be able to:

- Create, modify, remove, and apply range names

- Understand absolute and relative cell addresses

- Use natural language formulas in a worksheet

- Use mathematical and statistical functions, such as SUM, AVERAGE, COUNT, MIN, and MAX

- Use date functions, such as NOW and TODAY

- Embed, move, and size a chart on a worksheet

- Preview and print a chart

Case Study

Interior Hockey Association

The Interior Hockey Association consists of eight junior hockey teams in as many communities. The IHA is run by a small group of dedicated volunteers who handle everything from coaching to administration. An ex-player himself, Brad Stafford has volunteered for the organization for the past four years. In addition to fundraising, Brad is responsible for keeping records and tracking results for all of the teams in the league.

Shortly after the end of the season, the IHA publishes a newsletter that provides various statistics and other pertinent information about the season. In the past, this newsletter required weeks of performing manual calculations, followed by days of typing results into a word processor. Having enrolled in an Excel course last month, Brad now realizes that worksheets and charts can help him to complete his upcoming tasks.

In this chapter, you and Brad learn about using ranges and functions in Excel worksheets. First, you use named ranges to create formula expressions that are easier to understand. Then you practice using Excel's built-in functions to perform calculations. Lastly, you learn how to plot and print your worksheet data in a chart.

4.1 Working with Named Ranges

In its simplest form, a cell range is a single cell, such as B4. Still, the term *cell range* is more commonly used to describe a "from here to there" area on a worksheet. A range can also cover a three-dimensional area, crossing more than one worksheet within a workbook. In a new workbook, Excel provides three worksheets named *Sheet1, Sheet2,* and *Sheet3*. It may help you to think of a worksheet as a tear-off page on a notepad—the notepad representing the workbook. You access the worksheets in a workbook by clicking on the tabs appearing along the bottom of the document window.

A **range name** is a nickname given to a group of cells that can later be used in constructing formulas. For example, the formula expression `=Revenue-Expenses` is far easier to understand than `=C5-C6`. Working with cell references from more than one worksheet adds another level of complexity. For example, if the value for Revenue is stored on Sheet1 and the value for Expenses is stored on Sheet2, the formula would read `=Sheet1!C5-Sheet2!C6`. Notice that the worksheet name is separated from the cell address using an exclamation point (!). By default, range names already contain this information, making them far easier to remember than these cryptic expressions.

In this module, you learn how to name ranges and how to work with different types of cell references.

4.1.1 Naming Cell Ranges

FEATURE
By naming parts of a worksheet, you make it (and the formulas contained therein) much easier to read and construct. There are two ways to name cell ranges. First, click in the Name box, located at the far left of the Formula bar, and then type a unique name with no spaces. Second, use a menu command to create names automatically from the row and column headings appearing in a worksheet.

METHOD
To name a cell range using the Name box:
1.   SELECT: the desired range
2.   CLICK: in the Name box
3.   TYPE: *a range name*

To name a cell range using the Menu bar:
1.   SELECT: the desired range, including the row and column headings
2.   CHOOSE: Insert, Name, Create

PRACTICE
You will now name cell ranges appearing in an existing worksheet using the two methods described above.

Setup: Ensure that Excel is loaded

1 Open the data file named EXC410.

2 Save the workbook as "Salaries" to your personal storage location.

3 To increase Matthew's salary by the growth factor appearing in cell B3, perform the following steps:
SELECT: cell C6
TYPE: =b6*(1+b3)
PRESS: **ENTER**
The answer, 41400, appears in cell C6. In order for another user to understand this calculation, they would need to track down each cell address in the formula.

4 A better approach is to name the cells that you often refer to in formulas. Let's name the cell containing the growth factor before entering a formula to increase Jennifer's salary:
SELECT: cell B3
CLICK: in the Name box with the I-beam mouse pointer
TYPE: Growth (as shown below)

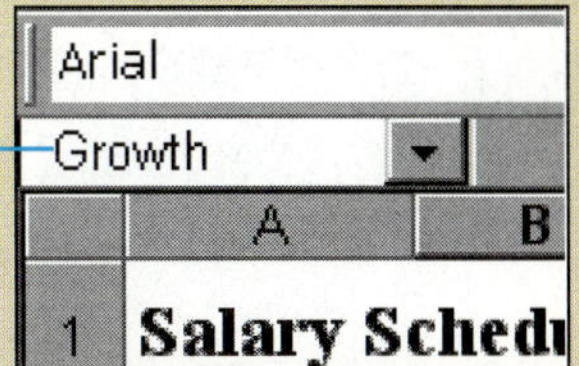

Type the desired range name in the Name box

5 PRESS: ENTER
You have now created a named range called "Growth" that you can use in place of the cell address when entering formulas.

6 To use the range name:
SELECT: cell C7
TYPE: =b7*(1+Growth)
PRESS: ENTER
The answer, 53820, appears. A new user reading this formula would now be able to decipher its objective.

7 You can also use range names to navigate within your worksheet:
CLICK: down arrow attached to the Name box
SELECT: Growth in the drop-down list that appears
The cell pointer moves immediately to cell B3.

8 Now update the growth factor:
TYPE: 5%
PRESS: ENTER
The worksheet cells containing formulas are updated.

9 Another method for creating range names uses the existing heading labels in your worksheet. You can use this method effectively when the data is organized in a table layout. To demonstrate:
SELECT: cell range from A5 to D9
Notice that the selected range includes the fiscal years across the top row and the employee names down the leftmost column.

10 To specify that the heading labels be used in naming the ranges:
CHOOSE: Insert, Name, Create

11 In the Create Name dialog box, ensure that the *Top row* and *Left column* check boxes appear selected as shown in Figure 4.1.

Figure 4.1

Creating range names
from worksheet values

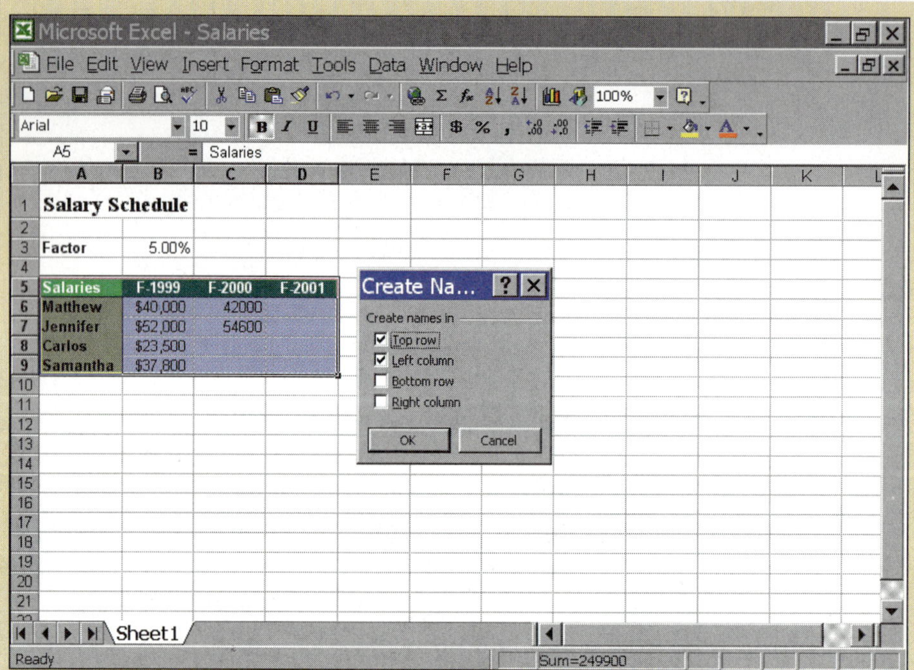

12 To complete the operation:
CLICK: OK

13 Now let's practice selecting named ranges:
CLICK: down arrow attached to the Name box
Many range names now appear in the drop-down list.

14 To move the cell pointer to one of the row ranges:
CLICK: Jennifer in the drop-down list
The cell range from B7 to D7 appears selected.

15 To display one of the column ranges:
CLICK: down arrow attached to the Name box
CLICK: F_2001 in the drop-down list
(*Note:* The label "F-2001" is used as the column heading instead
of the value 2001, since Excel can only create range names from
labels. You must also beware of conflicts with cell addresses. For
example, the range name F2001 is unacceptable because it refers
to a cell address.)

16 Lastly, let's select the entire data area in the table:
CLICK: down arrow attached to the Name box
CLICK: Salaries in the drop-down list

17 PRESS: CTRL + HOME to remove the highlighting

18 Save the workbook and keep it open for use in the next lesson.

4.1.2 Managing Range Names

FEATURE

Once created, you can easily modify and delete range names using the Define Name dialog box. Another useful feature is the ability to paste a list of the existing range names into your worksheet. Refer to this list when you are building formula expressions or when you need to jump to a particular spot in the worksheet.

METHOD

To display the Define Name dialog box:
- CHOOSE: Insert, Name, Define

To paste range names into the worksheet:
- CHOOSE: Insert, Name, Paste

PRACTICE

You will now practice deleting and pasting range names.

Setup: Ensure that you have completed the previous lesson and that the "Salaries" workbook is displayed.

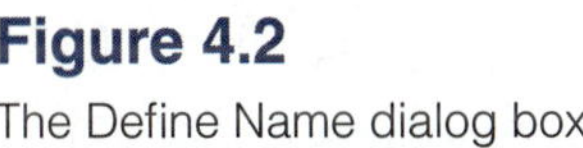

You manipulate range names using the Define Name dialog box. To illustrate, let's delete the yearly range names that were created in the last lesson. Do the following:
CHOOSE: Insert, Name, Define
The dialog box in Figure 4.2 should now appear on the screen.

Figure 4.2

The Define Name dialog box

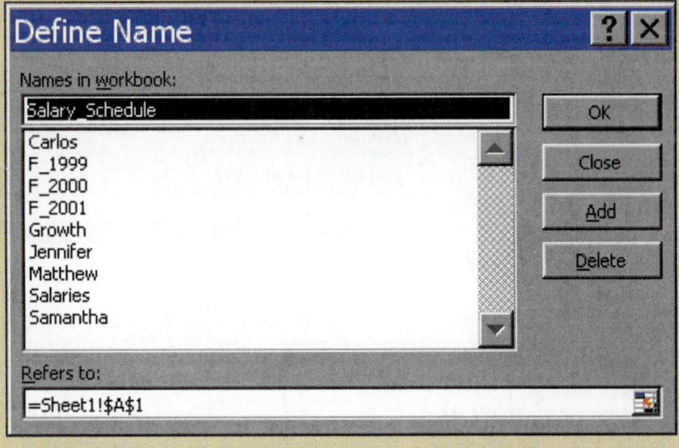

2 To remove the "F_1999" range name:
SELECT: F_1999 in the *Names in workbook* list box
Notice that the range address "=Sheet1!$B$6:$B$9" appears in the *Refer to* text box. (*Note:* If necessary, you can edit the cell references appearing in this text box. The significance of dollar signs in the range address is discussed in the next lesson.)

3 CLICK: Delete command button

4 To remove the remaining yearly range names:
SELECT: F_2000 from the list box
CLICK: Delete command button
SELECT: F_2001 from the list box
CLICK: Delete command button

5 To dismiss the dialog box:
CLICK: Close command button

6 To help you document and double-check the cell references in a worksheet, Excel enables you to paste a list of the existing named ranges into the worksheet. To demonstrate this technique:
SELECT: cell A12
CHOOSE: Insert, Name, Paste
CLICK: Paste List command button

7 To remove the highlighting:
PRESS: CTRL + HOME
Your screen should now appear similar to Figure 4.3.

8 Save the workbook and keep it open for use in the next lesson.

Figure 4.3

Pasting a list of range names into the worksheet

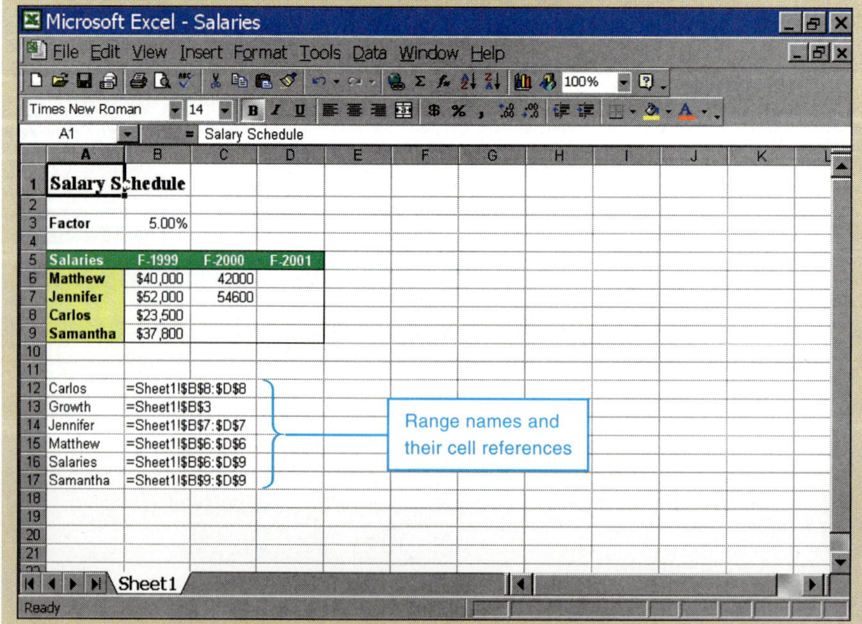

4.1.3   Using References in Formulas

FEATURE

There are two types of cell references that you can enter into formulas: *relative* and *absolute*. The difference between the two types becomes especially important when you start copying and moving formulas in your worksheet. A **relative cell address** in a formula adjusts itself automatically when copied, since the cell reference is relative to where it sits in the worksheet. An **absolute cell address** always refers to an exact cell location.

METHOD

The formulas that you have entered so far have all used relative cell references—Excel's default method. To specify an absolute reference, you precede each column letter and row number in a cell address with a dollar sign. For example, to make cell B5 an absolute cell reference, you type $B$5. A **mixed cell address,** on the other hand, locks only a portion of a cell address by placing the dollar sign ($) before either the address's column letter or row number, such as B$5. Sometimes it helps to vocalize the word "absolutely" as you read a cell address, whereby $B$5 would be read as "absolutely column B and absolutely row 5."

PRACTICE

In this lesson, you practice using relative and absolute cell addressing in performing simple copy and paste operations.

Setup: Ensure that you have completed the previous lesson and that the "Salaries" workbook is displayed.

1 Let's begin by reviewing the formula in cell C6:
SELECT: cell C6
Review the expression "=B6*(1+B3)" in the Formula bar. You can vocalize this formula as "take the value appearing to my left and then multiply it by 1 plus the value appearing three rows up and one column to the left." Notice that you need a point of reference for this formula to make any sense, which is the location of the cell pointer in cell C6.

2 Let's copy the formula in cell C6 to cell D6:
CLICK: Copy button (⌧) on the Standard toolbar
SELECT: cell D6
CLICK: Paste button (⌧)
PRESS: ESC to remove the dashed marquee
The result, 42000, appears in cell D6. This, however, is not the desired result. The value has not been incremented by the growth factor.

3 In the Formula bar, notice that the formula "=C6*(1+C3)" no longer performs the correct calculation. Copying and pasting has modified the cell addresses by automatically adjusting the column letters.

4 If you want to ensure that Excel does not change a cell address during a copy operation, you need to make it absolute:
PRESS: (DELETE)
SELECT: cell C6

5 Position the I-beam mouse pointer over the cell address B3 in the Formula bar and then click the left mouse button once.

6 To change the growth factor reference into an absolute address, you type dollar signs in front of the column letter and row number. Or, you can do the following:
PRESS: (F4) ABS key (ABS stands for absolute)
Notice that B3 now appears as $B$3, as shown below.

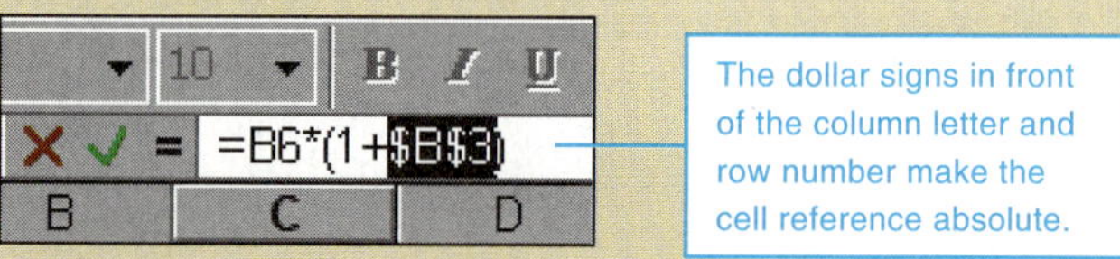

7 Continue pressing (F4) to see how Excel cycles through possible combinations of relative, absolute, and mixed cell addressing.

8 Before proceeding, ensure that $B$3 appears in the Formula bar and then press (ENTER).

9 Copy and paste the formula into cell D6 again. The correct result, 44100, now appears in the cell.

10 Remember that you used a range name in constructing the formula for cell C7. On your own, copy the formula in cell C7 to cell D7. Notice that the formula calculates correctly because range names, such as Growth, are defined using absolute cell addresses.

11 To continue:
PRESS: (ESC) to remove the marquee
PRESS: (CTRL)+(HOME)

12 Save and then close the worksheet.

4.1.4 Entering Natural Language Formulas

FEATURE
Another alternative to using cell references is to enter a special type of expression called a **natural language formula.** Similar to using range names, a natural language formula allows you to build a formula using the row and column labels from the active worksheet. In order for natural language formulas to work effectively, the worksheet should be organized using a table format with distinctly labeled rows and columns.

METHOD
1. SELECT: the cell where you want the result to appear
2. TYPE: = (an equal sign)
3. TYPE: *an expression*, using row and column labels
4. PRESS: ENTER

PRACTICE
You will now use natural language formulas to calculate an expression in a worksheet.

Setup: Ensure that no workbooks are open in the application window.

1 Open the data file named EXC414.

2 Save the workbook as "Natural" to your personal storage location.

3 Before you begin, you'll need to review some configuration settings:
CHOOSE: Tools, Options
CLICK: *Calculation* tab
This tab, as shown in Figure 4.4, enables you to specify calculation options and dictate whether Excel recognizes labels in formulas.

Figure 4.4

Options dialog box:
Calculation tab

Select this option to have Excel recalculate the formulas in your worksheet whenever you change a value.

Ensure that this check box is selected before attempting to enter a natural language formula.

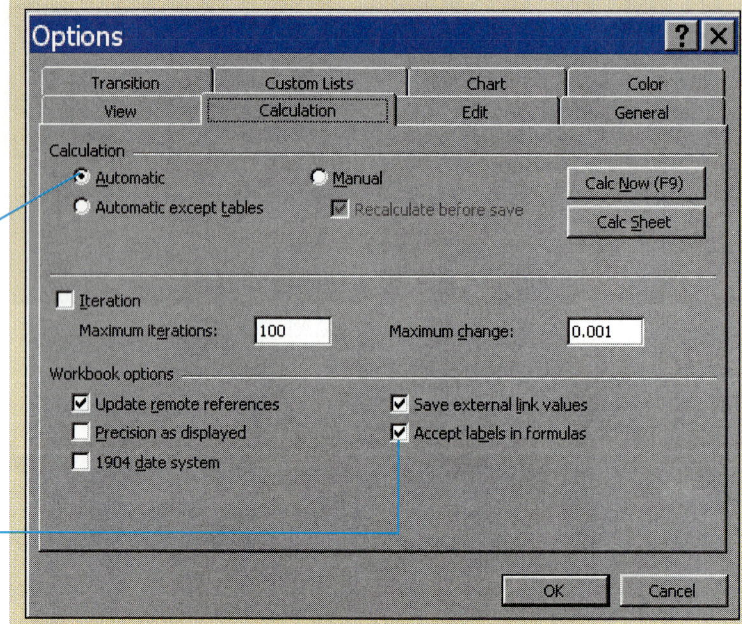

4 On the *Calculation* tab of the Options dialog box:
SELECT: *Automatic* option button
SELECT: *Accept labels in formulas* check box so that a "✔" appears
CLICK: OK command button

5 To calculate the profit for Q1 using a natural language formula:
SELECT: cell B6
TYPE: =Revenue-Expenses
PRESS: ➡
The result, 32500, appears in the cell. (*CAUTION:* You cannot mix labels with cell references in a natural language formula. For example, the formula =Revenue-B5 does not compute.)

6 To proceed, enter the same natural language formula into cells C6, D6, and E6. Notice that Excel calculates the results correctly.

7 Save and then close the workbook.

4.1 Self Check   Why is "AD1999" an unacceptable name for a cell range?

4.2 Using Built-In Functions

This module introduces you to Excel's built-in **functions.** Don't let the word *function* conjure up visions of your last calculus class; functions are shortcuts that you use in place of entering lengthy and complicated formulas. Functions are incredible time-savers that can increase your productivity in creating worksheets.

There are several methods for entering a function into a worksheet cell. To begin with, you can type a function name, preceded by an equal sign (=), and then enter its **arguments** (labels, values, or cell references). Many functions are quite complex, however, and all require that you remember the precise order, called **syntax,** in which to enter arguments. An easier method is to select a function from the Paste Function dialog box shown in Figure 4.5. You access this dialog box by choosing the Insert, Function command or by clicking the Paste Function button (f_x). In addition to organizing Excel's functions into tidy categories (further described in Table 4.1), the Paste Function dialog box lets you view a function's syntax, along with a brief description.

Figure 4.5

Paste Function
dialog box

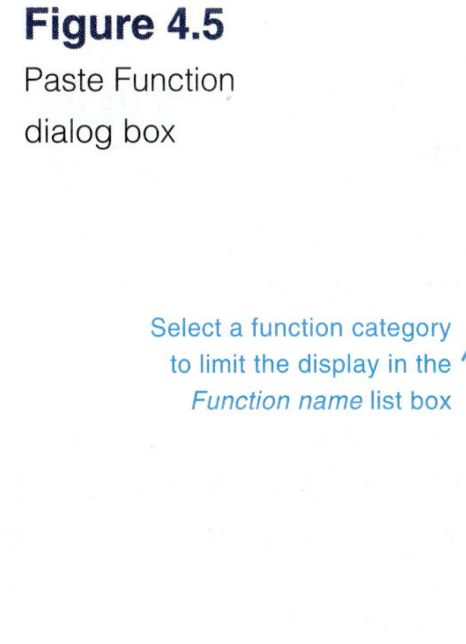
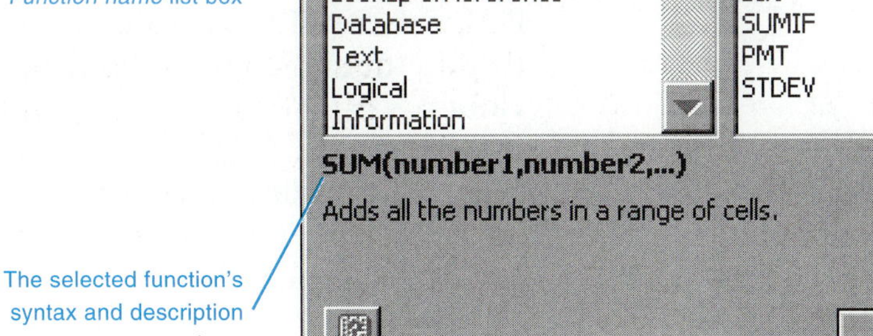

Select a function category
to limit the display in the
Function name list box

Select a function
name to display its
syntax and a brief
description below

The selected function's
syntax and description
appear here

Table 4.1

Function Categories

Category	Description
Financial	Determine loan payments, present and future values, depreciation schedules, and rates of return
Date & Time	Perform date and time calculations; input the current date and/or time into a cell
Math & Trig	Sum a range of values; perform trigonometric calculations; determine absolute and rounded values
Statistical	Determine the average, median, minimum, and maximum values for a range; calculate statistical measures, like variance and standard deviation
Lookup & Reference	Look up and select values from a range; return the active cell's column letter and row number
Database	Perform mathematical and statistical calculations on worksheet values in a table or list format
Text	Manipulate, compare, format, and extract textual information; convert values to text (and vice versa)
Logical	Perform conditional calculations using IF statements; compare and evaluate values
Information	Return information about the current environment; perform error-checking and troubleshooting

4.2.1 Adding Values (SUM)

FEATURE

You use the SUM function to add together the values appearing in a range of cells. SUM is the most frequently used function in Excel, saving you from having to enter long addition formulas such as =A1+A2+A3 . . . +A99. The AutoSum button (∑) inserts the SUM function into a worksheet cell automatically, guessing at the range argument to use.

METHOD

=SUM(range)

PRACTICE

You will now practice entering the SUM function.

Setup: Ensure that no workbooks appear in the application window.

1 Open the data file named EXC420.

2 Save the workbook as "Functions" to your personal storage location. Your screen should now appear similar to Figure 4.6.

Figure 4.6

The "Functions" workbook

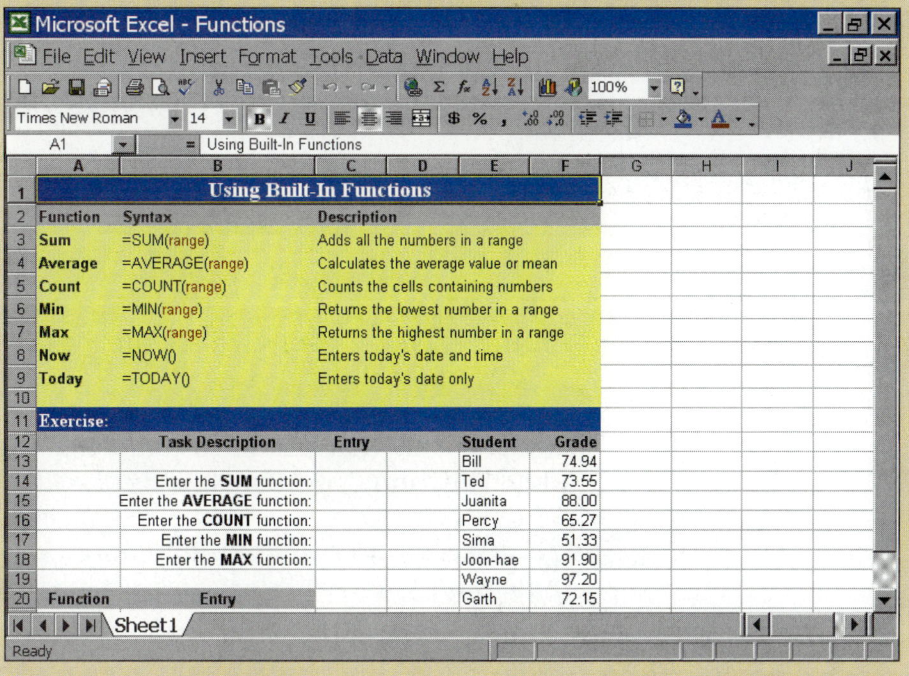

	A	B	C	D	E	F
1		Using Built-In Functions				
2	Function	Syntax	Description			
3	Sum	=SUM(range)	Adds all the numbers in a range			
4	Average	=AVERAGE(range)	Calculates the average value or mean			
5	Count	=COUNT(range)	Counts the cells containing numbers			
6	Min	=MIN(range)	Returns the lowest number in a range			
7	Max	=MAX(range)	Returns the highest number in a range			
8	Now	=NOW()	Enters today's date and time			
9	Today	=TODAY()	Enters today's date only			
10						
11	Exercise:					
12		Task Description	Entry		Student	Grade
13					Bill	74.94
14		Enter the **SUM** function:			Ted	73.55
15		Enter the **AVERAGE** function:			Juanita	88.00
16		Enter the **COUNT** function:			Percy	65.27
17		Enter the **MIN** function:			Sima	51.33
18		Enter the **MAX** function:			Joon-hae	91.90
19					Wayne	97.20
20	Function	Entry			Garth	72.15

Sheet1

Ready

3 Let's total the grade values in column F. Do the following:
SELECT: cell C14

4 To enter the SUM function:
TYPE: `=sum(f13:f22)`
PRESS: ENTER
The result, 761.51, appears in the cell. (*Note:* You can enter a function's name and arguments using either lowercase or uppercase letters. Ensure that there are no blank spaces entered mistakenly.)

5 Let's change Percy's grade:
SELECT: cell F16

6 To enter the revised grade:
TYPE: `75.27`
PRESS: ENTER
The new SUM result displays 771.51 in cell C14.

7 Save the workbook and keep it open for use in the next lesson.

4.2.2 Calculating Averages (AVERAGE)

FEATURE
You use the AVERAGE function to compute the average value (sometimes called the arithmetic mean) for a range of cells. This function adds together all of the numeric values in a range and then divides the sum by the number of cells used in the calculation.

METHOD
`=AVERAGE(range)`

PRACTICE
In this exercise, you calculate the average value for a named range in a worksheet.

Setup: Ensure that you have completed the previous lesson and that the "Functions" workbook is displayed.

1 To make it easier to enter functions, you can name the cell ranges on your worksheet. Let's name the range that contains the grade values:
SELECT: cell range from E12 to F22
Notice that you include the column headings, Student and Grade, in the selection.

2 CHOOSE: Insert, Name, Create

3 In the Create Name dialog box:
SELECT: *Top row* check box, if not already selected
SELECT: *Left column* check box, if not already selected
CLICK: OK command button

4 To view the range names that have been created:
CLICK: down arrow attached to the Name box
Your screen should now appear similar to Figure 4.7.

Figure 4.7

Viewing a worksheet's
range names

The Name Box displays
the range names created
from the worksheet
selection

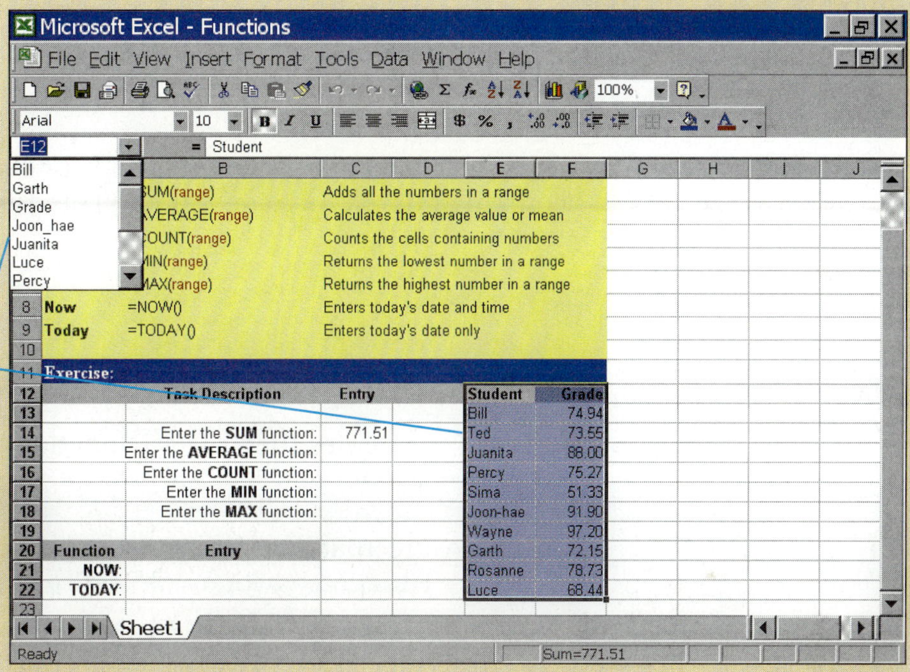

5 In the drop-down list box that appears:
CLICK: Garth
Your cell pointer should now be positioned in cell F20. Notice
also that the Name box displays the name "Garth."

6 To select the entire "Grade" range:
CLICK: down arrow attached to the Name box
CLICK: Grade in the drop-down list
The cell range from F13 to F22 is selected.

7 Let's use the range name to calculate the average grade:
SELECT: cell C15
TYPE: =average(grade)
PRESS: ENTER
The result, 77.151, appears in the cell.

8 To determine the average of a list of nonadjacent values, separate the items in the list using commas. To illustrate:
SELECT: cell D15
TYPE: `=average(Bill,Ted,Sima,Rosanne)`
PRESS: `ENTER`
The result, 69.6375, appears as the average of only these students' grades.

4.2.3 Counting Values (COUNT)

FEATURE
The COUNT function counts the number of cells in a range that contain numeric or date values. This function ignores cells containing text labels.

METHOD
`=COUNT(range)`

PRACTICE
You will now enter the COUNT function in the "Functions" workbook.

Setup: Ensure that you have completed the previous lessons and that the "Functions" workbook is displayed.

1 Move the cell pointer to where you want the result to appear:
SELECT: cell C16

2 You will now use the mouse to help you count the number of entries in a range. To begin:
TYPE: `=count(`

3 Using the mouse, position the cell pointer over cell F13. Then:
CLICK: cell F13 and hold down the left mouse button
DRAG: mouse pointer to cell F22
Notice that as you drag the mouse pointer, the range is entered into the function as an argument. When you reach cell F22, the argument displays the range name "Grade."

4 Release the mouse button.

5 To complete the function entry:
TYPE: `)`
PRESS: `ENTER`
The result, 10, appears in cell C16.

6 Save the workbook and keep it open for use in the next lesson.

4.2.4   Analyzing Values (MIN and MAX)

FEATURE
You use the MIN and MAX functions to determine the minimum (lowest) and maximum (highest) values in a range of cells.

METHOD
`=MIN(`*range*`)`
`=MAX(`*range*`)`

PRACTICE
In this lesson, you practice using the **Formula Palette** to calculate the minimum and maximum grades in a range. The Formula Palette provides a helpful dialog box for selecting and entering function arguments in the correct order.

Setup: Ensure that you have completed the previous lessons in this module and that the "Functions" workbook is displayed.

1 To calculate the lowest grade achieved:
SELECT: cell C17
TYPE: `=min(grade)`
PRESS: ➡
The result, 51.33, appears.

2 To find the lowest grade achieved among three students:
TYPE: `=min(Wayne,Garth,Luce)`
PRESS: [ENTER]
The result, 68.44, appears.

3 You will now use Excel's Formula Palette to calculate the maximum value in a range. Do the following:
SELECT: cell C18
TYPE: `=max(`
Ensure that you include the open parentheses "(" at the end of the function name.

4 To display the Formula Palette:
CLICK: Edit Formula button (=) in the Formula bar
The Formula Palette appears under the Formula bar, as shown in Figure 4.8. (*Note:* You can ignore the Assistant character that may appear on your screen. He, she, or it will go away after you complete the next few steps.)

Figure 4.8

Formula Palette:

Entering the MAX function

You use the Formula Palette when you need assistance entering a function.

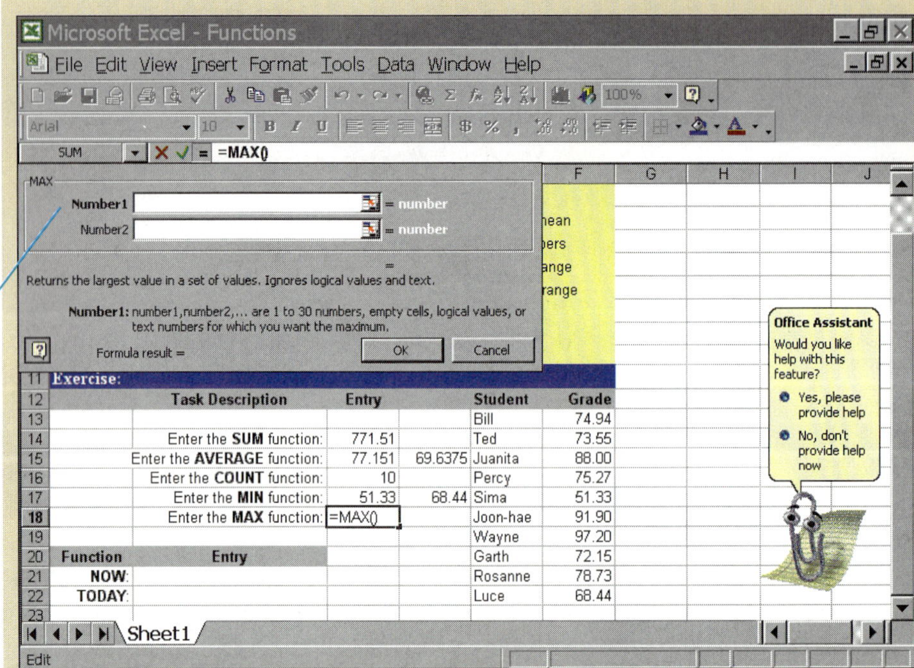

5 In the *Number1* argument text box:
TYPE: grade
Notice that the actual cell contents appear at the right of the text box and that the result is calculated immediately and shown below.

6 To complete the entry:
CLICK: OK command button

7 To find the maximum grade achieved among three students:
SELECT: cell D18
TYPE: =max(
CLICK: Edit Formula button ([=])

8 In the Formula Palette:
TYPE: Juanita
PRESS: TAB
TYPE: Ted
PRESS: TAB
TYPE: Luce
Notice that the Formula bar displays the function as you build it in the Formula Palette.

9 To complete the entry:
CLICK: OK command button
The result, 88, appears in the cell.

10 Save the workbook and keep it open for use in the next lesson.

4.2.5 Calculating Dates (NOW and TODAY)

FEATURE

You use the NOW and TODAY functions to display the current date and time. The NOW function returns the current date and time as provided by your computer's internal clock. The TODAY function provides the current date only. Neither of these functions require any arguments.

METHOD

=NOW()
=TODAY()

PRACTICE

In this exercise, you insert the NOW and TODAY functions into the worksheet.

Setup: Ensure that you have completed the previous lessons in this module and that the "Functions" workbook is displayed.

1 To insert the current date and time into the worksheet, do the following:
SELECT: cell B21
TYPE: =now()
PRESS: ENTER
The date is displayed using the "mm/dd/yy" format (depending on your default settings), while the time is typically displayed using the "hh:mm" 24-hour clock format.

2 To display only the time in the cell, you must format the entry:
SELECT: cell B21
CHOOSE: Format, Cells
CLICK: *Number* tab

3 You must now select a time format:
SELECT: Time in the *Category* list box
SELECT: 1:30:55 PM in the *Type* list box
CLICK: OK command button

4 To recalculate the NOW function:
PRESS: F9 CALC key
You should see the cell value change to the current time. (*Hint:* You can use ENTER to recalculate all formulas and functions in a worksheet.)

5 To enter the current date only:
SELECT: B22
TYPE: `=today()`
PRESS: ENTER
The current date should now appear in the worksheet.

6 On your own, format the current date to display using the "14-Mar-98" format option.

7 Save and then close the workbook.

4.2 Self Check   When might you use the Formula Palette or Paste Function dialog box to enter a function into the worksheet?

4.3 Creating an Embedded Chart

Since the earliest versions of spreadsheet software, users have been able to display their numerical data using graphs and charts. While acceptable for in-house business presentations and school projects, these graphics often lacked the depth and quality required by professional users. Until now! You can confidently use Excel to produce visually stunning worksheets and charts that are suitable for electronic business presentations, color print masters, Internet Web pages, and 35mm slide shows.

There are many types of charts available for presenting your worksheet data to engineers, statisticians, business professionals, and other audiences. Some popular business charts—line chart, column chart, pie chart, and XY scatter plot diagram—are described below.

- ***Line Charts***   When you need to plot trends or show changes over a period of time, the **line chart** is the perfect tool. The angles of the line reflect the degree of variation, and the distance of the line from the horizontal axis represents the amount of the variation. An example of a line chart appears in Figure 4.9, along with some basic terminology.

EXCEL

Figure 4.9

A line chart

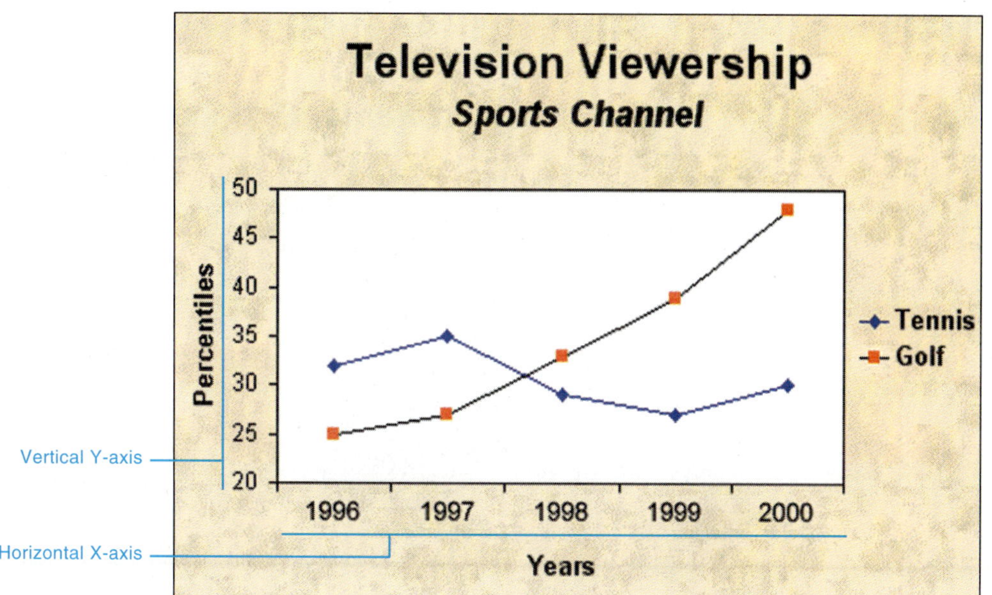

- ***Bar or Column Charts***   When the purpose of the chart is to compare one data element with another data element, a **column chart** is the appropriate form to use. A column chart (Figure 4.10) shows variations over a period of time, similarly to a line chart. A **bar chart** also uses rectangular images, but they run horizontally rather than vertically.

Figure 4.10

A column chart

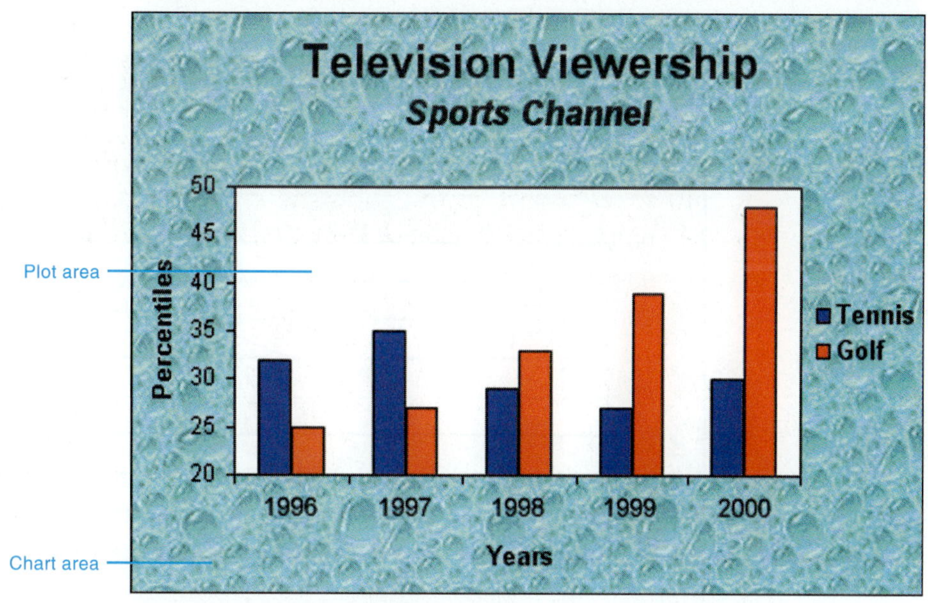

- ***Pie Charts***   A **pie chart** shows the proportions of individual components compared to the total. Similar to a real pie (the baked variety), a pie chart is divided into slices or wedges. (In Excel, you can even pull out the slices from the rest of the pie.) An example of a pie chart appears in Figure 4.11.

Figure 4.11

A pie chart

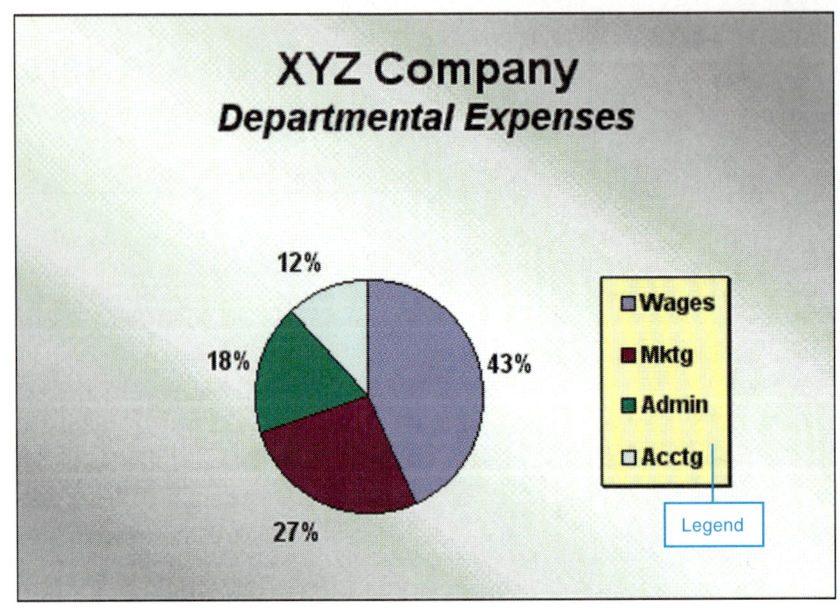

- ***Scatter Plot Charts***   **XY charts,** which are commonly referred to as *scatter plot diagrams,* show how one or more data elements relate to another data element. Although they look much like line charts, XY charts show the correlation between elements and include a numeric scale along both the X and Y axes. The XY chart in Figure 4.12 shows that worker productivity diminishes as stress levels increase.

Figure 4.12

An XY chart

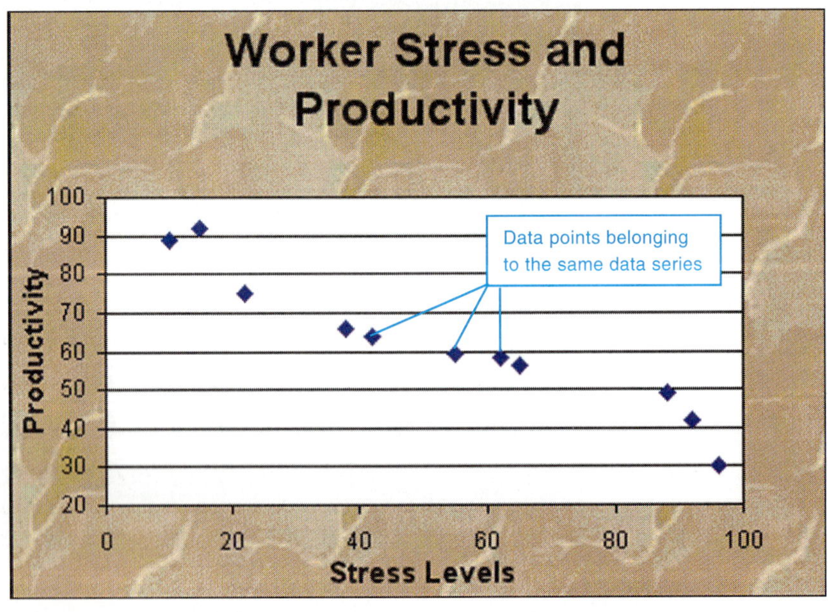

There are two methods for creating a chart in Excel, differing primarily in the way the chart is stored and printed. First, you can create a new chart as a separate sheet in a workbook. This method works well for printing full-page charts and for creating computer-based presentations or electronic slide shows. Second, you can create an **embedded chart** that is stored on the worksheet. Embed a chart when you want to view or print the chart alongside the worksheet data. Whichever method you choose, use the step-by-step features in Excel's **Chart Wizard** to construct a chart from existing worksheet data.

In this module, you learn how to create and print an embedded chart.

4.3.1 Creating a Chart Using the Chart Wizard

FEATURE

You create a chart by selecting a range of cells to plot and then launching the Chart Wizard. The wizard examines the selected range and then displays its dialog box. You make selections, such as choosing a chart type, and then proceed through the steps to embed the chart on the worksheet. An embedded chart is actually placed over—not entered into—a cell range. Once embedded, you can move, size, and delete the chart.

METHOD

1.   SELECT: the cell range to plot in a chart
2.   CLICK: Chart Wizard button (⊞)
3.   Complete the steps in the Chart Wizard.

PRACTICE

You will now create and embed a new chart onto a worksheet.

1   Open the data file named EXC430.

2   Save the workbook as "Cruising" to your personal storage location.

3   Let's plot the worksheet's demographic data. To begin, select both the headings and the data:
SELECT: cell range from A2 to D5

4   To start the Chart Wizard:
CLICK: Chart Wizard button (⊞) on the Standard toolbar
Your screen should now appear similar to Figure 4.13. (*Note:* If the Assistant appears, right-click it and choose the Hide command.)

Figure 4.13

Chart Wizard: Step 1 of 4

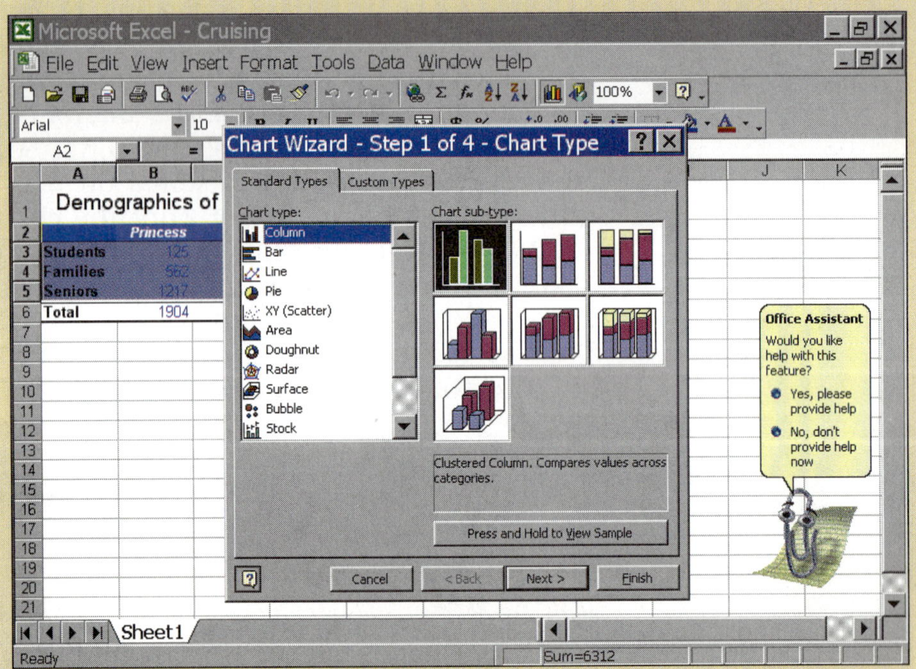

5 To see a sample of how Excel will plot this data:
CLICK: "Press and Hold to View Sample" command button
(*Note:* You must hold down the left mouse button to see the
chart inside the *Sample* preview window. When finished viewing,
release the mouse button.)

6 Let's select a different chart sub-type that amalgamates (adds
together) the two data series in a column. Do the following:
SELECT: Stacked Column in the *Chart sub-type* area
When you click on a chart sub-type, the chart's name and
description appear above the "Press and Hold to View Sample"
command button.)

7 Once again, preview a sample of the chart:
CLICK: "Press and Hold to View Sample" command button

8 To continue creating the chart:
CLICK: Next › to proceed to Step 2 of 4
CLICK: Next › to proceed to Step 3 of 4

9 In Step 3 of 4 of the Chart Wizard:
TYPE: **Cruise Lines** into the *Category (X) axis* text box
TYPE: **Passengers** into the *Value (Y) axis* text box
(*Hint:* Click the I-beam mouse pointer into a text box and then
type the appropriate text. You can also press TAB to move forward through the text boxes.) Notice that the preview area is
immediately updated to display the new titles, as shown in Figure 4.14.

Figure 4.14

Chart Wizard:

Step 3 of 4

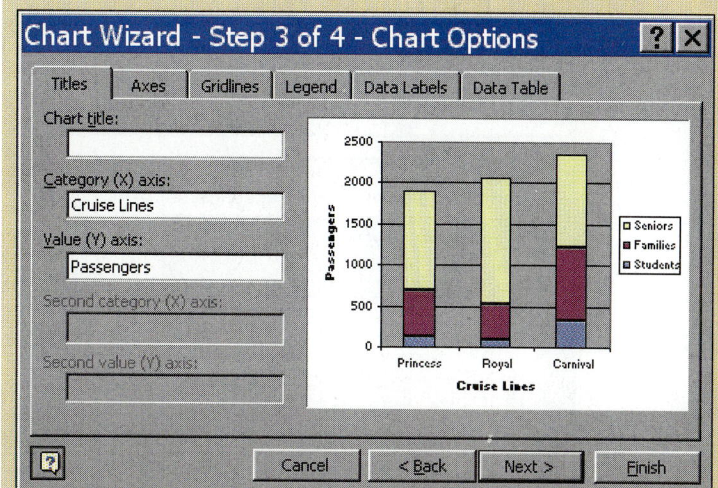

10 To proceed to the final step:
CLICK: Next >

11 In Step 4 of 4, you specify where you want to store the chart. To
create an embedded chart:
SELECT: *As object in* option button, if it is not already selected
Notice that the current worksheet's name, Sheet1, already appears
in the drop-down list box next to the option button.

12 To complete the Chart Wizard:
CLICK: Finish
The embedded chart appears in the application window. (*Note:*
You may also see Excel's Chart toolbar appear.)

13 The black selection handles that surround the chart indicate that
it is currently selected. Using the mouse, you can size the
embedded chart by dragging these handles. On your own, practice sizing the chart.

14 You can also move the chart by dragging the object using the
mouse. Position the white mouse arrow over a blank portion of
the chart's background area. Then, drag the chart into position.
Practice moving and sizing the chart to appear similar to Figure
4.15.

Figure 4.15

Moving and sizing an
embedded chart object

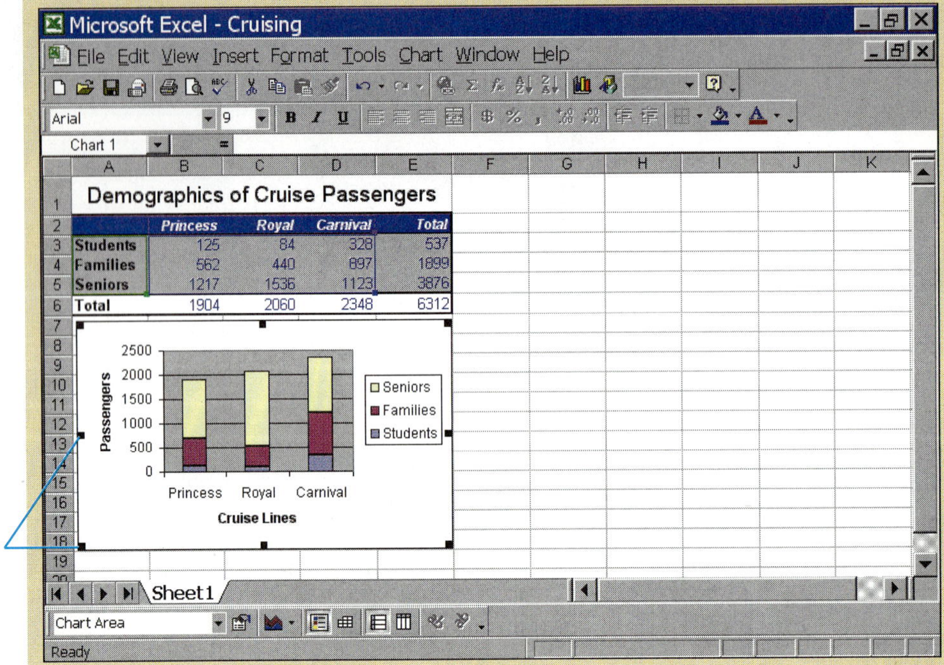

Selection or
sizing handles

15 To return focus to the worksheet:
CLICK: any visible cell in the worksheet area, such as cell F1
Notice that the Chart toolbar and the selection boxes around the
chart both disappear.

16 The embedded chart is dynamically linked to the information
stored in the worksheet. To demonstrate, let's update the "Carni-
val" column in the embedded chart:
SELECT: cell D5
TYPE: 123
PRESS: ENTER
The chart is updated immediately to reflect the new data.

17 To undo the last change:
CLICK: Undo button ( )

18 Save the workbook and keep it open for use in the next lesson.

4.3.2 Previewing and Printing an Embedded Chart

FEATURE

One of the primary reasons for embedding a chart on a worksheet is to view and print it alongside its worksheet data. You must ensure that the print area (or range), however, includes the entire chart object. And, as before, remember to preview your worksheet and chart prior to printing.

METHOD

1. SELECT: a cell range that includes the chart
2. CHOOSE: File, Print Area, Set Print Area
3. CHOOSE: File, Print or
    CHOOSE: File, Print Preview

PRACTICE

In this lesson, you preview and print an embedded chart along with its worksheet data.

Setup: Ensure that you have completed the previous lesson and that the "Cruising" workbook is displayed.

1 To print the worksheet and embedded chart on the same page:
SELECT: cell range from A1 to F20
(*Note:* Depending on the size and placement of your chart object, you may need to increase or decrease this print range. Make sure that the entire object is covered in the highlighted range.)

2 CHOOSE: File, Print Area, Set Print Area

3 To preview the worksheet and chart:
CLICK: Print Preview button

4 To zoom in on the preview window:
CLICK: Zoom command button

5 On your own, scroll the preview window to appear similar to Figure 4.16. Notice that the chart is printed immediately and seamlessly below the worksheet data.

Figure 4.16
Previewing an embedded chart

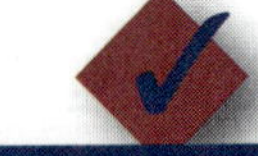

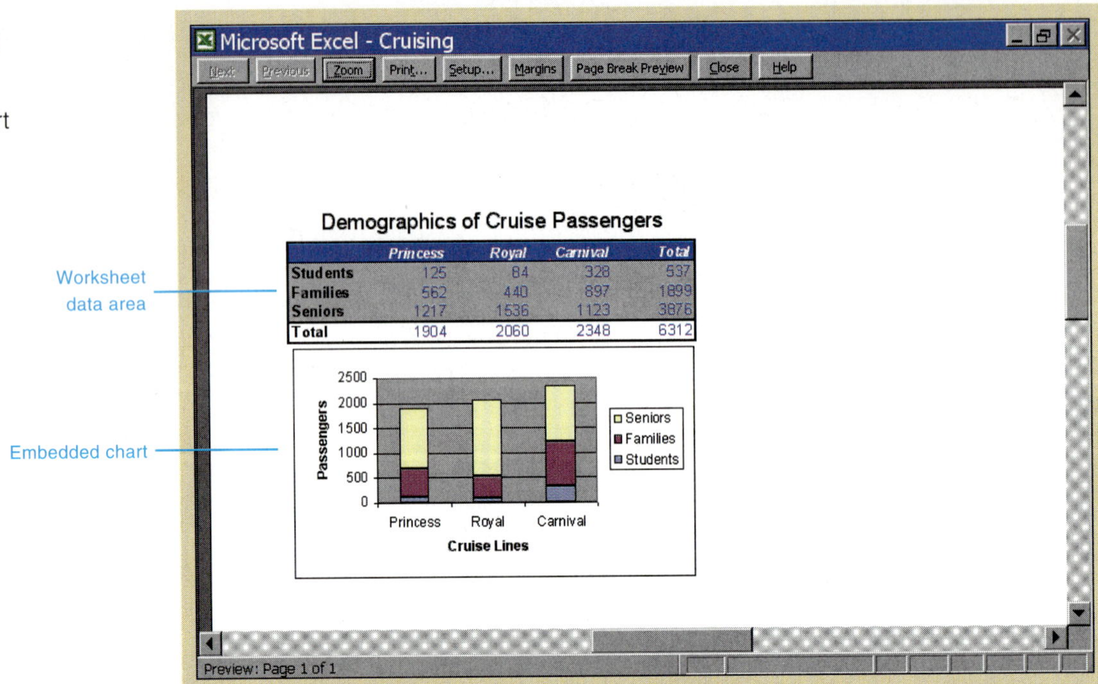
Microsoft Excel - Cruising
Next
Previous
Zoom
Print...
Setup...
Margins
Page Break Preview
Close
Help
Demographics of Cruise Passengers
Princess Royal Carnival Total
Students 125 84 328 537
Families 562 440 897 1899
Seniors 1217 1536 1123 3876
Total 1904 2060 2348 6312
2500
2000
1500
1000
500
0
Passengers
Princess Royal Carnival
Cruise Lines
Seniors
Families
Students
Preview: Page 1 of 1
Worksheet data area
Embedded chart

6. To print the chart from the Preview window:
   CLICK: Print command button

7. If you don't have access to a printer, click the Cancel command button and proceed to the next step. If you have a printer attached to your computer and want to print this chart, do the following :
   CLICK: OK command button

8. To remove the highlighting from the worksheet area:
   CLICK: cell A1

9. Save and then close the workbook.

10. Exit Microsoft Excel.

4.3 Self Check What must you do when selecting the print range for a worksheet that contains an embedded chart?

4.4 Chapter Review

This chapter introduced you to some powerful tools for analyzing and summarizing data. You learned how to name cells and ranges and how to use these names in constructing expressions and navigating the worksheet. The first module also discussed the differences between absolute and relative cell addresses. An absolute cell address appears with dollar signs ($), which serve to anchor an address to an exact location on the worksheet. The second module focused on Excel's built-in functions. These functions, such as SUM and AVERAGE, are used as shortcuts to performing complex or lengthy calculations. Remember to use the Formula Palette and Paste Function feature when you need assistance entering the arguments for a function. In the last module, you learned to create an embedded chart using the Chart Wizard and to position and print the chart alongside its worksheet data.

4.4.1 Command Summary

Many of the commands and procedures appearing in this chapter are summarized in the following table.

Skill Set	To Perform This Task . . .	Do the Following . . .
Working with Named Ranges	Name a cell range	SELECT: the desired range CLICK: in the Name box TYPE: *a range name*
	Create range names from labels appearing on the worksheet	SELECT: the desired range CHOOSE: Insert, Name, Create
	Modify and delete range names	CHOOSE: Insert, Name, Define
	Paste a list of range names onto the worksheet	CHOOSE: Insert, Name, Paste
Working with Formulas	Modify and use cell references (absolute, relative, and mixed)	SELECT: the desired cell CLICK: in the cell address in the Formula bar PRESS: F4 to apply reference type
	Recalculate formulas in a worksheet	PRESS: F9 CALC key

Continued

Skill Set	To Perform This Task . . .	Do the Following . . .
Using Functions	Use the Formula Palette to enter a function and its arguments	CLICK: Edit Formula button (=)
	Insert a function using the Paste Function dialog box	CLICK: Paste Function button (f_x) SELECT: a category and function

	Use basic functions:
	• Sum a range of values
	• Average a range of values
	• Count the numeric and date values in a range
	• Find the lowest value in a range
	• Find the highest value in a range
		
		`=SUM(range)`
		`=AVERAGE(range)`
		
		`=COUNT(range)`
		`=MIN(range)`
		`=MAX(range)`

	Use date functions:
	• Enter the current date and time
	• Enter today's date
		
		`=NOW()`
		`=TODAY()`

Using Charts and Objects	Use the Chart Wizard to create a chart	SELECT: the cell range to plot CLICK: Chart Wizard button
	Preview and print an embedded chart	SELECT: the desired range CHOOSE: File, Print Area, Set Print Area CLICK: Print Preview or Print

4.4.2 Key Terms

This section specifies page references for the key terms identified in this chapter. For a complete list of definitions, refer to the Glossary provided in the Appendix.

absolute cell address, *p. 157*

arguments, *p. 161*

barchart, *p. 171*

Chart Wizard, *p. 173*

column chart, *p. 171*

embedded chart, *p. 173*

Formula Palette, *p. 167*

functions, *p. 161*

line chart, *p. 170*

mixed cell address, *p. 157*

natural language formula, *p. 159*

pie chart, *p. 171*

range name, *p. 151*

relative cell address, *p. 157*

scatter plot charts, *p. 172*

syntax, *p. 161*

XY charts, *p. 172*

4.5 Review Questions

4.5.1 Short Answer

1. Why would you want to name a range of cells?
2. How do you place a list of range names into the worksheet?
3. Name the two primary types of cell references and explain how they differ.
4. In order for natural language formulas to work effectively, how should the worksheet be organized?
5. Which function would you use to extract the highest value from a range named "salary?" How would you enter the function?
6. Which function would you use to place only the current time in your worksheet? What else might you want to do?
7. What is the name of the dialog box that you can use to select functions from categories? How do you access this dialog box?

8. What is the name of the dialog box that can help you to enter a function's arguments correctly? How do you access this dialog box?
9. Describe the four steps in creating a chart using the Chart Wizard.
10. What are the black boxes called that surround an embedded chart? What are they used for?

4.5.2 True/False

1. _____ Range names that you create use absolute cell references.
2. _____ Cell addresses that you enter into formulas use, by default, relative cell references.
3. _____ The "&s" in the cell reference &D&5 indicate an absolute cell reference.
4. _____ You cannot mix labels, such as "Revenue," with cell references in a natural language formula.
5. _____ You enter a function using parentheses instead of the equal sign.
6. _____ The SUM function appears in the Statistical function category of the Paste Function dialog box.
7. _____ You must use the Formula Palette to enter the COUNT function.
8. _____ The TODAY function updates the computer's internal clock to the current date and time.
9. _____ A pie chart shows the proportions of individual components compared to the total.
10. _____ You can move and size an embedded chart once it is placed on the worksheet.

4.5.3 Multiple Choice

1. What menu command allows you to create range names using the labels that already appear in the worksheet?
   a. Edit, Name, Create
   b. Range, Name, Create
   c. Insert, Name, Create
   d. Insert, Name, Define

2. Which of the following symbols precedes an absolute cell reference?
   a. $
   b. @
   c. &
   d. #

3. Which key do you press to change a cell address to being absolute, relative, or mixed?
   a. `F2`
   b. `F3`
   c. `F4`
   d. `F9`

4. Which key do you press to recalculate or update a worksheet?
   a. `F2`
   b. `F3`
   c. `F4`
   d. `F9`

5. Which is the correct expression for adding the values stored in the cell range from A1 to A20?
   a. `=ADD(A1+A20)`
   b. `=SUM(A1:A20)`
   c. `=SUM(A1+A20)`
   d. `=AutoSUM(A1,A20)`

6. Which is the correct expression for determining the average of a range named "Units"?
   a. `=AVG(Units)`
   b. `=UNITS(Average)`
   c. `=AVERAGE(Units)`
   d. `=SUM(Units/Average)`

7. What does the COUNT function actually count?
   a. All of the cells in a range
   b. All of the cells containing data in a range
   c. Only those cells containing text and numbers
   d. Only those cells containing numeric or date values

8. Which button do you click to display the Formula Palette?
   a. 
   b.
   c.
   d.

9. What is the name of the step-by-step charting tool provided by Excel?
   a. Chart Master
   b. Chart Wizard
   c. Plot Master
   d. Plot Wizard

10. A chart may be created as a separate chart sheet or as an embedded object. In which step of the Chart Wizard do you specify how a chart is created and stored?
    a. Step 1
    b. Step 2
    c. Step 3
    d. Step 4

4.6 Hands-On Projects

4.6.1 Grandview College: Enrollment Statistics

In this exercise, you practice creating and working with named cell ranges and constructing formulas using absolute and relative cell addresses.

1. Open the data file named EXC461.
2. Save the workbook as "Enrollment" to your personal storage location.
3. You will now name a cell range on the worksheet. To begin:
   SELECT: cell B8
   CLICK: in the Name box
   TYPE: **Total**
   PRESS: ENTER
   You have successfully named this cell "Total."
4. To create a set of range names using existing worksheet labels:
   SELECT: cell range from A2 to B7
   CHOOSE: Insert, Name, Create
   CLICK: OK command button

5. To view the list of range names that you just created:
   SELECT: cell E2
   CHOOSE: Insert, Name, Paste
   CLICK: Paste List command button
   SELECT: cell A1 to remove the highlighting
   (*Note:* The list is pasted in alphabetical order.)
6. To enter a formula using named cell ranges:
   SELECT: cell B10
   TYPE: =
   CLICK: cell B3
   TYPE: +
   CLICK: cell B7
   Notice that the expression "`=Continuing_Ed+Vocational`"
   appears in the Formula bar.
7. To complete the formula entry:
   PRESS: ENTER
8. On your own, enter a formula in cell B11 that totals the rest
   of the departments not included in the previous step.
9. Let's calculate the enrollment percentage for each department.
   Starting in cell C2, you will enter a formula that can be later
   used for copying. To do so, you need to specify an absolute
   cell reference for the Total value and a relative cell reference
   for the Arts value. To illustrate:
   SELECT: cell C2
   TYPE: `=b2/total`
   PRESS: ENTER
   (*Note:* A range name provides an absolute cell reference. Therefore, you cannot use the range name "Arts" in the formula
   expression.)
10. To copy the formula to the remaining departments:
    SELECT: cell C2
    DRAG: the fill handle for cell C2 to cell C8
    (*Hint:* The fill handle for a cell or cell range is the small black
    box in the bottom right-hand corner of the range selection.)
11. On your own, select the cells in the range C2:C8 and view the
    contents in the Formula bar. Notice that the relative cell refer-
    ences (B2, B3,… B8) adjust automatically. The range name
    "Total" remained absolute.
12. Save and then close the "Enrollment" workbook.

4.6.2 Fast Forward Video: Rental Category Chart

You will now practice creating a chart using Excel's Chart Wizard.

1. Open the data file named EXC462.
2. Save the workbook as "Video Chart" to your personal storage location.
3. To begin, select the cell range that contains the data for plotting:
   SELECT: cell range A3 to G5
   Notice that you did not include the "Total" row or "Total" column.
4. Launch the Chart Wizard:
   CLICK: Chart Wizard button (▨) on the Standard toolbar
5. To display the two categories, New Release and Weekly, side by side:
   SELECT: Column as the *Chart type*
   SELECT: Clustered Column as the *Chart sub-type*
   CLICK: Next › to proceed to Step 2 of 4
   CLICK: Next › to proceed to Step 3 of 4
6. On the *Titles* tab of Step 3 in the Chart Wizard:
   TYPE: **Income by Category** into the *Chart title* text box
   TYPE: **Movie Category** into the *Category (X)* axis text box
   TYPE: **Rental Income** into the *Value (Y)* axis text box
   CLICK: Next ›
7. To embed the chart in the worksheet:
   SELECT: *As object* in option button, if it is not already selected
   CLICK: Finish
   The chart object appears in the middle of the application window.
8. To move the embedded chart, position the mouse pointer on an empty portion of the chart's background. Then do the following:
   DRAG: the chart below the data area
9. To size the embedded chart, position the mouse pointer over the selection handle in the bottom right-hand corner. Then:
   DRAG: the selection handle down and to the right to enlarge the chart

10. On your own, finalize the size and placement of the embedded chart so that it appears similar to Figure 4.17.

Figure 4.17

Sizing and moving an embedded chart

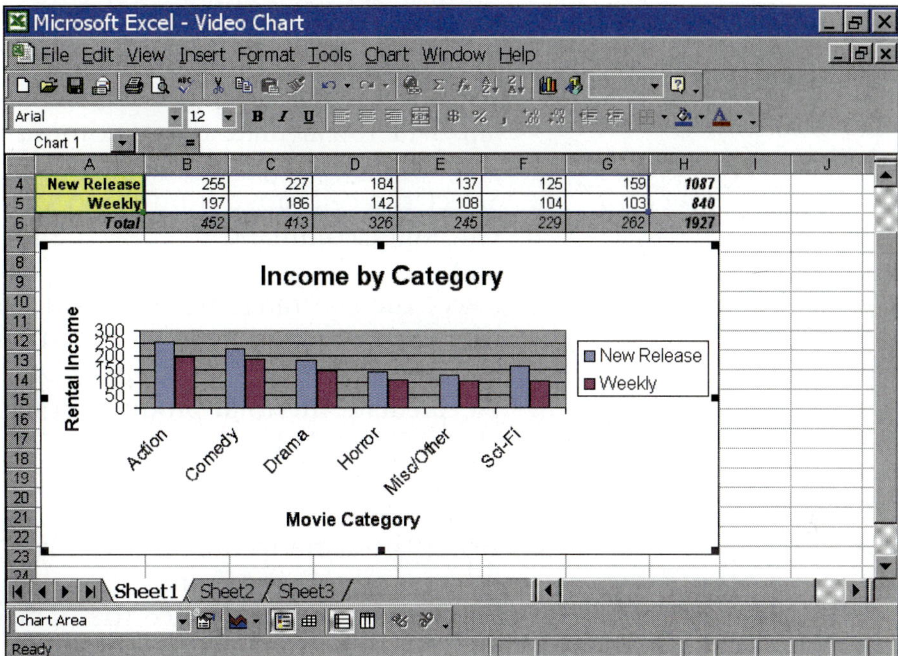

11. You've just received word that some information in the worksheet has been entered incorrectly. Study the Misc/Other category columns on the chart. Now, update the worksheet:
    SELECT: cell F4
    TYPE: **104**
    PRESS: ⬇
    TYPE: **175**
    PRESS: ENTER
    Notice that the chart has been updated to reflect the new values.
12. Save and then close the "Video Chart" workbook.

4.6.3 Sun Valley Frozen Foods: Daily Production

You will now practice using some of Excel's built-in functions in an existing worksheet. You will also use the AutoFill feature to create a series and then the Fill command to copy formulas.

1. Open the data file named EXC463.
2. Save the workbook as "Sun Daily" in your personal storage location.

3. Use the fill handle to complete a series listing the days of the week (Monday through Friday) in cells A3 to A7.

4. In cell B9, enter the following function to calculate the mini-mum production amount for corn:
    TYPE: `=min(b3:b7)`
    PRESS: ENTER

5. Using the same approach as before, enter formulas in cells B10 and B11 to calculate the maximum and average production for corn.

6. Select the cell range from B9 to E11 and then use the Edit, Fill, Right command to copy the formulas to columns C, D, and E.

7. Select the cell range from A2 to E7 and then use the Insert, Name, Create command to assign range names using the exist-ing labels.

8. To calculate the total production for Corn:
    SELECT: cell B13
    TYPE: `=sum(corn)`
    PRESS: ENTER

9. Using the same technique, calculate the totals for the Peas, Beans, and Other columns. (*Note:* You cannot use the Edit, Fill, Right command since the named range "Corn" uses an absolute cell reference.)

10. Save and then close the "Sun Daily" workbook.

4.6.4   Lakeside Realty: Mortgage Rate Chart

In this exercise, you create an embedded chart and then print it alongside the worksheet data.

1. Open the data file named EXC464.

2. Save the workbook as "Mortgage Chart" to your personal stor-age location.

3. Select the cell range from A2 to G8.

4. Launch the Chart Wizard.

5. In the *Chart type* and *Chart sub-type* list boxes, select a line chart with markers displayed at each data value. Then proceed to the third step.

6. In step 3 of the Chart Wizard, add the title "Average Mortgage Rates" to appear at the top of the chart. Then proceed to the next step.
7. Save the chart as an object in Sheet1 and then click the Finish command button.
8. Size and move the embedded chart so that it covers the range from cell A13 to G27.
9. Update July's six-month rate to 6.00 in the worksheet.
10. Set the print area to cover the range from A1 to H28.
11. Preview and then print the selected print area.
12. Save and then close the "Mortgage Chart" workbook.

4.6.5 On Your Own: Auto Fuel Comparison

This exercise lets you practice naming ranges and entering functions. To begin, open the EXC465 workbook and then save it as "Auto Fuel" to your personal storage location.

To begin, let's create some range names. Assign the name "Capacity" to the cell range B2:B7. Assign the name "City" to the cell range C2:C7. Assign the name "Hwy" to the cell range D2:D7. Paste a list of the range names in column F. In row 8, calculate the average for each column using their respective range names and the AVERAGE function. For more practice, enter a function in cell B10 that returns a count of the number of numerical entries in the "Capacity" range. In cell C10, display the minimum miles per gallon city rating. In cell D10, display the maximum miles per gallon highway rating.

When you are finished, save and then close the "Auto Fuel" workbook.

4.6.6 On Your Own: Personal Expense Chart

For additional practice creating charts, open the EXC466 data file. Before continuing, save the workbook as "Expense Chart" to your personal storage location. Then complete the worksheet by inputting your monthly expenses into the appropriate cells.

Using the Chart Wizard, create a pie chart of these expenses. Do not add a title to the chart and save it as an embedded object in the worksheet. Once it appears on the worksheet, size the chart so that the information is easily read. Lastly, position the chart to the right of the worksheet data. Print the worksheet data and the chart on the same page. Remember to use the Set Print Area command and Print Preview to ensure that your settings are correct. When you are satisfied with the results, send the worksheet and embedded chart to the printer.

Save and then close the "Expense Chart" workbook. Then, exit Excel.

4.7   Case Problems: Interior Hockey Association

The Interior Hockey Association is a junior hockey league that is just finishing its current season. As one of the many volunteers that keep the IHA going, Brad Stafford has the task of summarizing various statistics for inclusion into the season-end newsletter. Brad has recently learned how to use ranges and functions in Excel and now wants to use them to produce worksheets that can be incorporated into the newsletter.

In the following case problems, assume the role of Brad and perform the same steps that he identifies. You may want to re-read the chapter opening before proceeding.

1. It's 8:00 P.M. on a Sunday evening when Brad decides to sit down at his home computer and spend some time working on the IHA newsletter. After loading Excel, he opens the EXC471 workbook that he has been using to project next year's attendance levels. Brad wants to communicate the fine growth in attendance that the IHA has been experiencing. Before continuing, he saves the workbook as "IHA Attendance" to his personal storage location.

    Having learned about range names, Brad's first step is to use the Name box and apply a range name of "Factor" to cell C12. Then, he selects the cell range A2:B10 and uses the Insert, Name, Create command to create range names from the selection's row and column labels. To verify that the range names are correct, Brad selects cell E1 in the worksheet and then pastes a list of all existing named ranges.

    Brad remembers that to calculate next year's attendance using a growth factor formula, he will have to use both relative and absolute cell addresses. Otherwise, when he performs a copy operation, the formula's cell addresses will be adjusted automatically. Brad wants to ensure that the formulas always use the value in cell C12 as the growth factor. Fortunately, Brad also remembers that a named range is, by default, an absolute reference. Therefore, using a relative cell address and the "Factor" range name, he can complete his task. To begin, he enters the formula **=b3*(1+Factor)** into cell C3. Notice that Brad typed "b3" and not "Bristol" into the cell. (*Hint:* The range name "Bristol" refers to the absolute cell address $B$3 and not the relative cell address that is required for this calculation.) This formula calculates next year's projected attendance for Bristol.

Brad uses Excel's AutoFill feature to extend the formula in cell C3 for the rest of the teams. Finally, he uses the Format Painter to copy the formatting from column B to the new results in column C. Brad saves and then closes the workbook.

2. Brad Stafford is constructing a worksheet that shows the team standings at the end of the IHA's regular season play. To review the worksheet, he opens the EXC472 file and then saves it as "IHA Standings" to his personal storage location.

   With the teams already in the proper order, Brad wants to chart their results. He selects the cell range B2:C10 and then launches the Chart Wizard. In the first step, Brad selects a "Clustered bar with a 3-D visual effect" chart. Then he clicks the Finish command button. When the embedded chart appears in the application window, Brad sizes it so that all the team names are visible on the vertical axis. He then moves the chart below row 14, as shown in Figure 4.18.

Figure 4.18

Analyzing data using an embedded chart

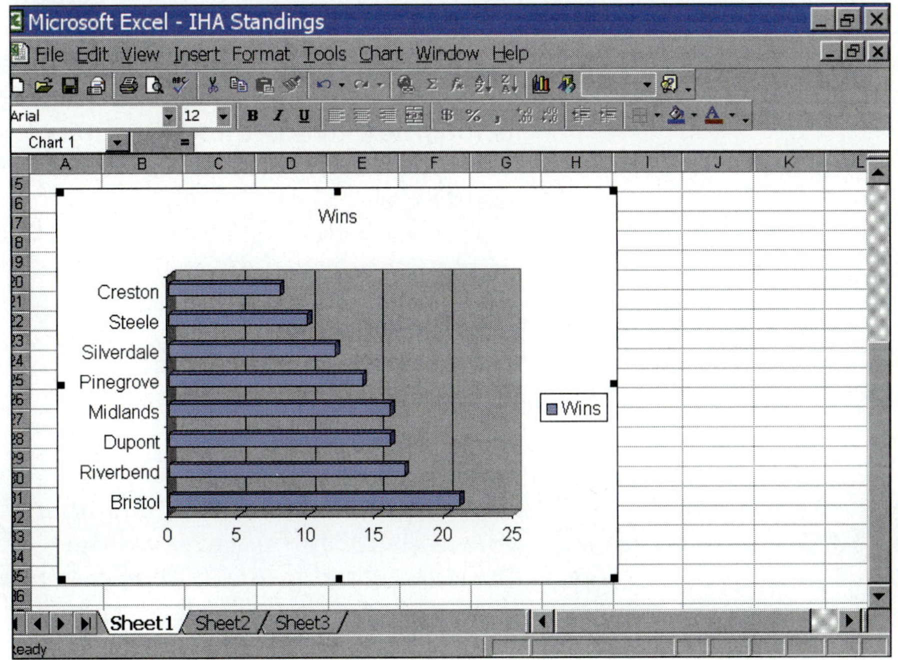

Continuing his work, Brad enters a formula into cell C12 that averages the values in that column. He uses the Fill, Right command to extend the formula across to column F. Lastly, Brad saves, prints, and then closes the workbook.

3.   With the deadline for the season-end newsletter fast approaching, Brad is determined to finish the Team Goal Statistics worksheet. He opens the EXC473 data file and then saves it as "Goal Table" to his personal storage location.

   After double-checking to make sure that the formulas in column D are correct, Brad copies the formula from cell D3 to the cell range D14:D21. He then enters SUM functions into cells C11 and C22 that sum the goals for Offense and Defense, respectively. In column G, Brad uses Excel's built-in functions to find the highest, lowest, and average number of goals for both Offense and Defense. He names the two data ranges and then enters the functions into the appropriate cells. When he is finished, Brad saves and then closes the workbook.

4.   The final worksheet that Brad needs to compile is for the "Scoring by Periods" statistics. He opens the EXC474 data file and saves it as "IHA Scoring" in his personal storage location.

   Using one of Excel's built-in functions, Brad calculates and displays the total goals scored by the first team in column F. After entering the function, he uses AutoFill to extend the formula to the rest of the teams. Next, he uses the appropriate function in row 11 to calculate the average for the first period. He formats the result to display using a single decimal place and then extends the formula to cover columns C through F.

   Brad completes the worksheet using the MIN and MAX functions to calculate the high and low scores for each period. As before, he extends these functions to cover the remaining columns. Lastly, Brad saves and closes the workbook and then exits Excel.

MICROSOFT EXCEL 2000
Presenting Your Data
CHAPTER
FIVE

Chapter Outline

Learning Objectives

After reading this chapter, you will be able to:

- Indent, rotate, wrap, and shrink a cell entry

- Create and apply number formats and styles to maintain consistency and to speed worksheet formatting

- Use drawing tools to create and format lines and shapes for enhancing a worksheet's appearance

- Insert WordArt objects, clip art, and other embedded objects into a worksheet

- Create, modify, and format chart sheets and elements

Case Study

Ponderosa Canyon

Ponderosa Canyon is a small western city with a frontier heritage. By encouraging its downtown storefronts to adopt a western theme and by holding several frontier-oriented events, the Ponderosa Canyon business community has succeeded in developing and promoting a thriving tourist destination. The two most popular events, sponsored by local business people, are the annual Cattle Drive and the Gold Rush Fair.

Ponderosa Canyon's Chamber of Commerce is busily working on an information package to further promote the area's attractions. Specifically, an internal committee has appointed Wendy Manuel, owner of the Prairie Schooner Gift Shop, to take charge of developing the promotional package. After many discussions with other business owners, Wendy feels that a strong visual presentation will provide the most impact. She also wants to highlight some census data that is stored in an Excel worksheet.

In this chapter, you and Wendy learn how to present your worksheet data more effectively by formatting text, applying styles, and working with graphics. In addition to inserting AutoShapes, WordArt, and Clip Art into a worksheet, you practice customizing, formatting, and printing charts.

5.1 Formatting Cells

Microsoft Excel 2000 provides a wealth of formatting options for improving the appearance of a worksheet, its individual cells, and the contents within those cells. While the more popular formatting commands such as changing a cell's font and fill color have already been described in previous chapters, this module introduces additional features that will help round out your formatting toolkit. As with many software features, sometimes knowing what the software can do is as important as remembering how to do it. In this module, you learn how to manipulate text within a cell. You also apply formatting options using the AutoFormat command and implement conditional formatting in a cell range.

5.1.1 Indenting and Rotating Text

FEATURE

As you might indent a paragraph in Microsoft Word to make it stand out from the rest of the document, you can indent a text label, date, or numeric value within a cell. Indenting has the effect of aligning a cell's contents to the left border and then moving the entire entry one or more character spaces to the right. Apart from indenting, you can format a cell by rotating its contents to display on an angle. With longer entries, for example, you may choose to rotate a cell's orientation rather than increase a column's width. Note, however, that you cannot indent and rotate a cell entry at the same time.

METHOD

Using the Menu bar:

1. CHOOSE: Format, Cells
2. CLICK: *Alignment* tab
3. SELECT: a value in the *Indent* spin box to indent the cell contents, or
    SELECT: a value in the *Degrees* spin box to rotate the cell contents
4. CLICK: OK command button

Using the Formatting toolbar:

* CLICK: Increase Indent (▤)
* CLICK: Decrease Indent (▤)

PRACTICE

You now practice indenting and rotating text in an existing worksheet.

Setup: Ensure that Excel is loaded.

1 Open the data file named EXC510.

2 Save the workbook as "Wobbly Inventory" to your personal storage location.

3 In the Product column (A), indenting the product names will set them apart from their categories. To do so:
SELECT: cell range from A7 to A14

4 To indent the selection two character spaces to the right:
CLICK: Increase Indent button (▤) twice

5 To indent the other categories' product entries:
SELECT: cell range from A16 to A19
PRESS: CTRL and hold it down
SELECT: cell range from A21 to A25
Two cell ranges should now be highlighted on the worksheet.
(*Note:* Remember to release the CTRL key after selecting the last range.)

6 Let's use the Format Cells dialog box to indent the selection:
CHOOSE: Format, Cells
CLICK: *Alignment* tab

7 By clicking the up arrow attached to the spin control:
SELECT: 2 in the *Indent* spin box
Your screen should now appear similar to Figure 5.1.

Figure 5.1

Indenting the contents
of the selected range

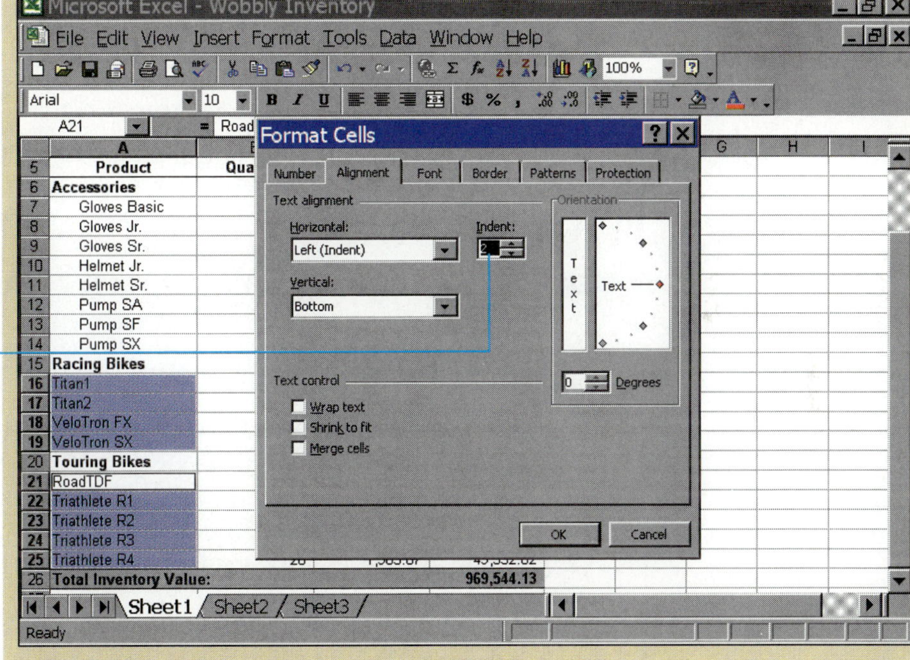

Specify the number of character spaces to indent to the right.

8 To accept the dialog box and continue:
CLICK: OK command button
The cell entries in the selected ranges should now appear indented.

9 To demonstrate how you can rotate the contents of a cell range:
SELECT: cell range from A5 to D5

10 To jazz up the selected column headings:
CHOOSE: Format, Cells
Notice that the *Alignment* tab is already selected since it was the tab displayed when you last closed the dialog box.

11 You set the rotation for text by clicking and dragging in the *Orientation* area of the dialog box. You can also specify a positive value in the *Degrees* spin box to angle text from bottom left to upper right. A negative value angles text from upper left to bottom right. By clicking the up arrow attached to the spin control:
SELECT: 30 in the *Degrees* spin box
The *Orientation* area should now appear similar to the graphic shown at the right.

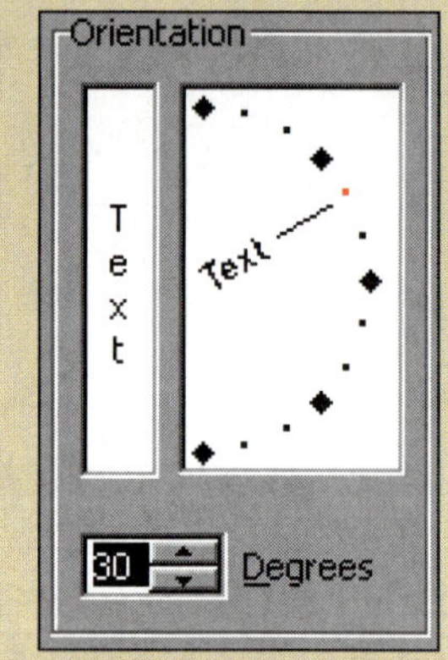

12 To accept the dialog box and continue:
CLICK: OK command button

13 With the cell range still selected:
CLICK: Align Left button (▤)
PRESS: CTRL + HOME to remove the highlighting
Notice that the row height is increased automatically to display the angled headings.

14 Save the workbook and keep it open for use in the next lesson.

5.1.2   Aligning, Wrapping, and Shrinking Text

FEATURE

In addition to indenting and rotating text, you can align a cell's contents vertically between a row's top and bottom borders, wrap a longer text entry within a cell, and shrink an entry to fit within a column. These formatting features, along with aligning and merging cells, are especially useful for enhancing titles, headings, and larger blocks of text.

METHOD

1. CHOOSE: Format, Cells
2. CLICK: *Alignment* tab
3. SELECT: an option from the *Vertical* drop-down list box in the *Text alignment* area, or
   SELECT: *Wrap text* check box in the *Text control* area, or
   SELECT: *Shrink to fit* check box in the *Text control* area
4. CLICK: OK command button

PRACTICE

You now practice aligning cell values, wrapping a short sentence within a cell, and shrinking a range of headings to fit in their respective columns.

EXCEL

Setup: Ensure that you've completed the previous lesson and that the "Wobbly Inventory" workbook is displayed.

1 After increasing the height of a row, you can align its entries to appear centered vertically between the top and bottom borders. To illustrate:
SELECT: cell range from A4 to D4
CHOOSE: Format, Row, Height

2 In the Row Height dialog box:
TYPE: **20**
CLICK: OK command button
Notice that the existing entries in the row align, by default, to the bottom border.

3 To center the row entries vertically:
CHOOSE: Format, Cells

4 On the *Alignment* tab of the Format Cells dialog box (Figure 5.2):
SELECT: Center from the *Vertical* drop-down list box
CLICK: OK command button

Figure 5.2

Format Cells dialog box: *Alignment* tab

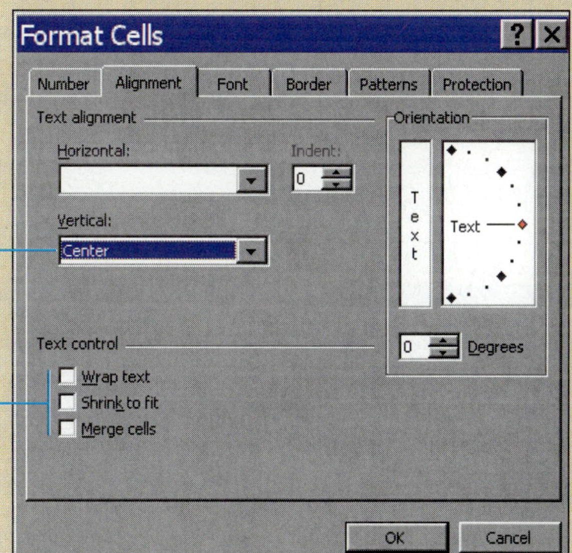

Changes how text is vertically aligned within a cell or cell range.

Changes how text is positioned and displayed within a cell or cell range.

5 To format the appearance of a sentence or paragraph that appears in a single cell, do the following:
SELECT: cell range from A28 to D28
Notice that the text entry is stored entirely in the leftmost cell (A28) of the selected range.

6 You will now merge the selected cells to form a single cell and then wrap the entry to appear between its column borders. To do so:
CHOOSE: Format, Cells
SELECT: *Wrap text* check box so that a "✔" appears
SELECT: *Merge cells* check box so that a "✔" appears
CLICK: OK command button

7 To increase the height of the row:
CHOOSE: Format, Row, Height
TYPE: **40**
CLICK: OK command button
All of the text in the cell entry should now be visible.

8 To shrink an entry to fit within its cell borders:
SELECT: cell A26
CHOOSE: Format, Cells
SELECT: *Shrink to fit* check box so that a "✔" appears
CLICK: OK command button

9 Let's adjust the column width to view the dynamic nature of this formatting option:
CHOOSE: Format, Column, Width
TYPE: **15**
CLICK: OK command button
Notice that the entry in cell A26 shrinks even further and that the sentence in cell A28 wraps anew in the merged cell range. Your screen should appear similar to Figure 5.3.

10 Save the workbook and keep it open for use in the next lesson.

Figure 5.3

Manipulating text entries in a worksheet

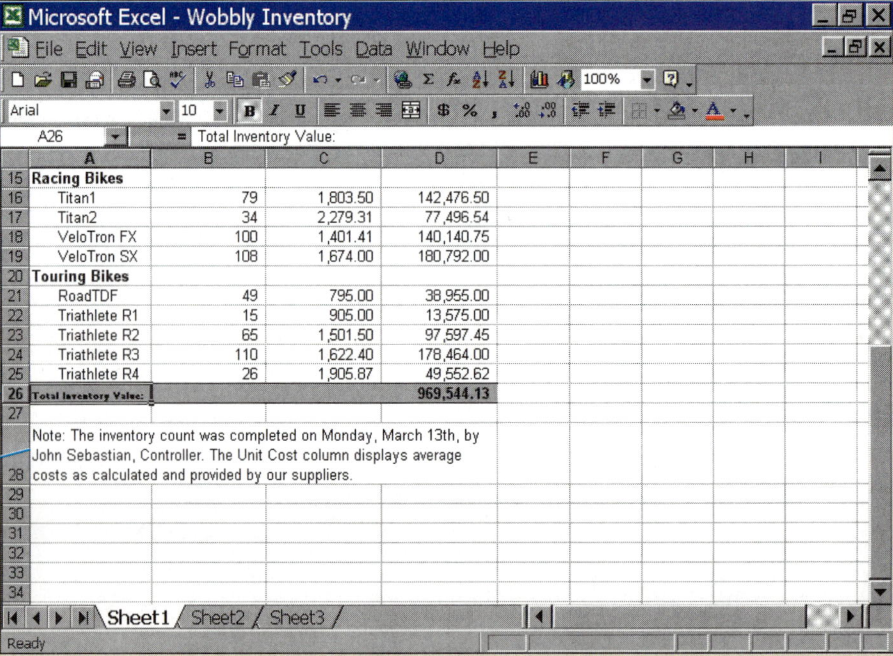

	A	B	C	D
15	**Racing Bikes**			
16	Titan1	79	1,803.50	142,476.50
17	Titan2	34	2,279.31	77,496.54
18	VeloTron FX	100	1,401.41	140,140.75
19	VeloTron SX	108	1,674.00	180,792.00
20	**Touring Bikes**			
21	RoadTDF	49	795.00	38,955.00
22	Triathlete R1	15	905.00	13,575.00
23	Triathlete R2	65	1,501.50	97,597.45
24	Triathlete R3	110	1,622.40	178,464.00
25	Triathlete R4	26	1,905.87	49,552.62
26	Total Inventory Value:			969,544.13
27				
28	Note: The inventory count was completed on Monday, March 13th, by John Sebastian, Controller. The Unit Cost column displays average costs as calculated and provided by our suppliers.			

Sheet1 / Sheet2 / Sheet3 /
Ready

5.1.3 Selecting AutoFormat Options

FEATURE

The AutoFormat command lets you select a predefined table format for a cell range, complete with numeric formats, alignments, borders, shading, and colors. By default, all of the formatting elements for the chosen AutoFormat option are applied to the worksheet selection. If this is not the desired behavior, Excel also allows you to limit the application of formatting to a selection of elements. You may, for example, want to format a range using an AutoFormat's color and font selections without adjusting the existing column widths.

METHOD

1. SELECT: cell range to format
2. CHOOSE: Format, AutoFormat
3. CLICK: Options command button
4. SELECT: an option from the *Table format* list box
5. SELECT: the desired options in the *Formats to apply* area
6. CLICK: OK command button

PRACTICE

Let's practice using the AutoFormat command to apply selected formatting options to a cell range.

Setup: Ensure that you've completed the previous lesson and that the "Wobbly Inventory" worksheet is displayed.

1 Before choosing the AutoFormat command, it's wise to select and confirm the cell range that you want formatted on the worksheet. If you do not preselect a range, Excel must guess the desired area, as demonstrated in the following step:
SELECT: cell A4
CHOOSE: Format, AutoFormat
Notice that the table area in the worksheet is selected behind the AutoFormat dialog box. (*Hint:* To better view the selected area, move the AutoFormat dialog box out of the way by dragging its Title bar.)

2 Each table format includes six formatting elements: *Number, Font, Alignment, Border, Patterns,* and *Width/Height.* You can specify which portions of an AutoFormat style that you want to apply to the selected range. To make your selections:
CLICK: Options command button
Your dialog box should now appear similar to Figure 5.4.

Figure 5.4

AutoFormat dialog box

Select a table format to apply in this list area.

Select the formatting elements to apply.

3 To apply only the *Font* and *Patterns* selections:
CLICK: *Number* check box so that no "✔" appears
CLICK: *Border* check box so that no "✔" appears
CLICK: *Alignment* check box so that no "✔" appears
CLICK: *Width/Height* check box so that no "✔" appears
Notice that the table previews in the list area are updated dynamically.

4 To complete the AutoFormat selection and continue:
SELECT: List 2
CLICK: OK command button
Notice that the worksheet is formatted using font selections and colors, but that the indentation and number formatting remains the same.

5 Close the workbook without saving the changes.

5.1 Self Check   What are the two ways that you can indent a cell entry?

5.2 Using Number Formats and Styles

Excel provides several built-in number formats and styles for improving the readability and display of your worksheet data. Number formats change the appearance of values by adding standard symbols, such as dollar signs, commas, and percentage symbols. Styles, which are most commonly associated with word processing, ensure formatting consistency and reduce repetitive procedures. Similar in function to an AutoFormat option, a **style** is a set of formatting characteristics that has been assigned a name. In addition to applying these formatting options, you learn how to create and define your own custom formats and styles in this module.

5.2.1 Using Number Formats

FEATURE

To enter a formatted number (for example, 87.5%) into a worksheet, type the number along with the desired symbols. To apply formatting to an existing value, choose a format from the *Number* tab in the Format Cells dialog box. Regardless of how a value is displayed, Excel stores values (numbers and dates) internally in their raw or unformatted form. In other words, the value appearing in a worksheet cell is not necessarily the value used by Excel in performing a calculation. Take, for example, two values, 2.3 and 2.4, that are stored in cells A1 and A2. These values are then formatted to display without decimal places, leaving the number 2 displayed in each cell. In cell A3, you enter the formula "=A1+A2" and then format the cell similarly. You will find that Excel correctly calculates 2.3+2.4 to equal 4.7, and then rounds the answer to display 5 in cell A3. So now, due to number formatting, your worksheet displays 2+2=5. Be aware of this formatting paradox when evaluating a worksheet's results!

METHOD

To view a cell's actual value:

1. SELECT: the desired cell
2. View the value that appears in the Formula bar.

To remove a cell's formatting characteristics:

1. SELECT: the desired cell
2. CHOOSE: Edit, Clear, Formats

PRACTICE

You now practice applying and removing number and date formatting.

Setup: Ensure that no workbooks appear in the application window.

1 To display a new workbook:
CLICK: New button (🗅) on the Standard toolbar

2 Enter the following data, starting in cell A1, exactly as shown:
TYPE: 1000
PRESS: ⬇
TYPE: $5,000.00
PRESS: ⬇
TYPE: 5/10/00
PRESS: ENTER
Excel treats the value in cell A1 as containing data only. In cell A2, Excel stores data (5000) and formatting (Currency number format with two decimal places). Likewise, cell A3 stores a serial date value (36656) and formatting (Date format using m/d/y).

3 To view the actual value in a cell:
SELECT: cell A2 and then look in the Formula bar
Notice that the $5,000.00 entry appears as 5000 in the Formula bar.

4 The **cell layer** in a worksheet holds both the data and formatting (number formats, borders, and font attributes) for a particular cell address. Each of these elements can be changed without affecting the other. For example, you can apply formatting to a cell without affecting its contents. It's also important to understand that a cell without data is not necessarily the same as an empty cell. To illustrate:
SELECT: cell range from A1 to A3
PRESS: DELETE
Notice that the worksheet once again appears empty.

5 Let's see how empty the worksheet really is though. Do the following:
TYPE: 12345
PRESS: ⬇
TYPE: 12345
PRESS: ⬇
TYPE: 12345
PRESS: ENTER
Your worksheet should now appear similar to Figure 5.5. Notice that pressing DELETE removes only the contents of the selected cell range and not its formatting.

Figure 5.5

Entering data into formatted cells

	A	B	C	D	E	F
1	12345					
2	$12,345.00					
3	10/18/33					
4						
5						
6						
7						

6   To remove the formatting information that is stored in the cell layer:
SELECT: cell range from A1 to A3
CHOOSE: Edit, Clear, Formats
Notice that the value "12345" appears in all of the cells.

7   Close the workbook without saving the changes.

In Addition	Excel stores dates as serial values equal to the number of days that have
Understanding How Excel Stores Dates and Times	elapsed since January 1, 1900. For example, Excel stores the date January 1, 2000 as 36526. Times (hours, minutes, and seconds) are stored as decimal fractions equal to a portion of a day. Because dates and times are values, they can be used in performing calculations.

In Addition	In the process of converting formatted dates into serial values, Excel applies
Excel and the Millennium Issue	some general rules. For entries using a two-digit year of 00 to 29 (e.g., 3/31/05), Excel converts the year to 2000 to 2029. For year entries using 30 to 99, Excel converts the year to 1930 to 1999. You can avoid these conversion issues altogether by always using a four-digit year when entering dates, such as 3/31/2005 or 31-Mar-2005.

5.2.2 Creating a Custom Number Format

FEATURE

If one of Excel's built-in number or date formats is not suitable, you can select from a variety of formatting codes to create your own **custom format.** All number formats, built-in and custom, consist of four sections separated by semicolons. If you were to apply the number format shown at the top of the next page, for example, a positive, negative, or zero value entered into the formatted cell would appear with two decimal places, while any text entry would display "N/A." Note that the "N/A" will not appear in the Formula bar since it is part of the number formatting construct and not part of the cell contents.

$$\#,\#\#0.00;[Red](\#,\#00.00);0.00;\text{“N/A”}$$

Display format for positive values	Display format for negative values	Display format when zero	Display format for text entries

METHOD

1. CHOOSE: Format, Cells
2. CLICK: *Number* tab
3. SELECT: Custom in the *Category* list box
4. TYPE: *desired format codes* (Table 5.1) in the *Type* text box
5. CLICK: OK command button

PRACTICE

Let's practice creating a custom date format.

Setup: Ensure that no workbooks appear in the application window.

1 Open the data file named EXC520.

2 Save the workbook as "Marsden" to your personal storage location.

3 In column A, the date values under the heading "Period" are displayed in a typical "month/day/year" fashion. Since this worksheet contains operating results limited to May, 2000, you can remove the month and year from the display format. Do the following:
SELECT: cell range from A5 to A15
CHOOSE: Format, Cells
CLICK: *Number* tab in the dialog box

4 The currently selected format appears, "Date" in the *Category* list box and "3/14/98" in the *Type* list box. To change the display to appear with the day of the week and then the day number, you need to apply a custom format. To create the new format:
SELECT: Custom in the *Category* list box

5 To remove the contents of the *Type* list box:
DOUBLE-CLICK: "m/d/yy" in the *Type* list box
PRESS: `DELETE`

6 To enter the desired format:
TYPE: **ddd, d**
CLICK: OK command button
The selected cells in the worksheet should now appear formatted. (*Hint:* Refer to Table 5.1 for a listing of commonly used custom format codes.)

Table 5.1

Format codes

Code	Description
#	Digit placeholder; displays a number, if available
0	Digit placeholder; displays a number or, if no number is available, a zero
?	Alignment placeholder; adds a space to align the decimal point; displays fractions
,	Comma; displays a comma as the thousands separator (or as a multiple of a thousand)
@	Entered in the text portion of a format, concatenates the format with the cell's text entry
[color]	Color indicator; assigns a color to a display format
d and dd	Day; displays as 1-31 and 01-31
ddd and dddd	Day; displays as Sun-Sat and Sunday-Saturday
m and mm	Month; displays as 1-12 and 01-12
mmm and mmmm	Month; displays as Jan-Dec and January-December
yy and yyyy	Year; displays as 00-99 and 1900-9999
h, m, and s	Similar to date codes; "h" for hours, "m" for minutes, and "s" for seconds. Use "AM/PM" for a 12-hour clock.

7 A custom number format is always saved with the workbook. To view the new format:

CHOOSE: Format, Cells

Your worksheet should now appear similar to Figure 5.6.

Figure 5.6

Creating a custom format

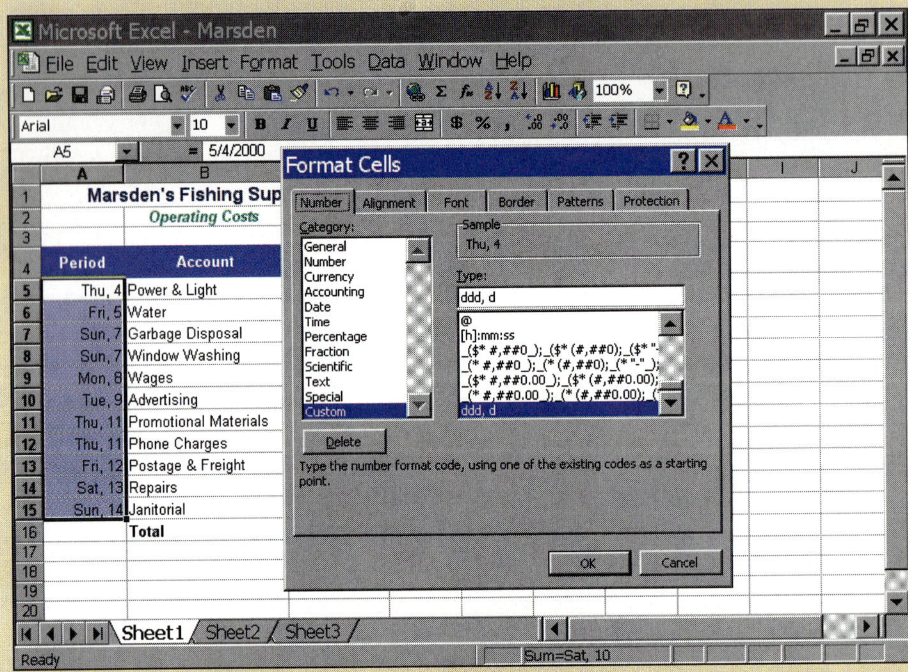

(8) Some additional custom formats that you can create are provided in Table 5.2. For now, remove the dialog box without making a selection:
CLICK: Cancel command button

(9) Save the workbook and keep it open for use in the next lesson.

Table 5.2

Examples of
custom formats

Custom Format	Value Entered	Value Displayed
$#,##0.00	1234.5678	$1,234.57
0.000%	.07925469	7.925%
# ?/?	5.25	5¼
(###) ###-####	6307894000	(630) 789-4000
;;;"Part # "@	xyz123	Part # xyz123

5.2.3 Applying and Modifying Styles

FEATURE

Using styles to enhance cells ensures that you are formatting your workbooks consistently and efficiently. Also, when you change the formatting specifications stored in a style, all cells based on that style are updated automatically. Consequently, it is much easier to make sweeping changes to a worksheet's appearance when styles are used throughout. Excel provides five predefined or built-in styles (Comma, Comma [0], Currency, Currency [0], and Percent) for number formatting and one default style called Normal. You apply a style to a selected cell range using the Style dialog box or by clicking the Formatting toolbar buttons ($, %, or ,).

METHOD

1. SELECT: the desired cell range
2. CHOOSE: Format, Style
3. SELECT: an option from the *Style name* drop-down list box
4. CLICK: OK command button

PRACTICE

You now practice applying and modifying styles.

Setup: Ensure that you've completed the previous lesson and that the "Marsden" workbook is displayed.

1 To begin, remove the cell formatting for the Cost values in column C:
SELECT: cell range from C5 to C16
CHOOSE: Edit, Clear, Formats
Notice that the raw and unformatted values now appear in the column.

2 With the range still highlighted, let's apply an existing style to the Cost values using the menu:
CHOOSE: Format, Style
The dialog box shown in Figure 5.7 appears.

Figure 5.7

Style dialog box

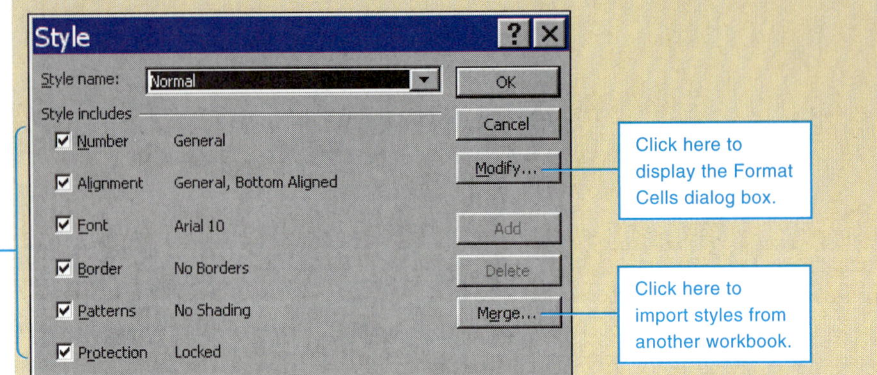

3 To choose an existing style that displays no decimal places:
SELECT: Currency [0] from the *Style name* drop-down list box
Notice that the only selected formatting option for this style is the *Number* check box.

4 To apply the style and continue:
CLICK: OK command button
The column values are formatted.

5 Let's apply the Currency style (not Currency [0]) to the range:
CLICK: Currency Style button ($)

6 You will now modify the style so that the dollar sign displays next to the number, rather than left-aligned to the cell border. To begin:
CHOOSE: Format, Style
CLICK: Modify command button
The Format Cells dialog box appears.

7 To adjust the positioning of the dollar sign:
SELECT: Currency from the *Category* list box
SELECT: 2 in the *Decimal places* spin box, if not already selected
SELECT: red-colored ($1,234.10) in the *Negative numbers* list box
CLICK: OK command button

8 To apply the modified style and continue:
CLICK: OK command button
For this workbook only, this is the new formatting specification for the Currency style. Any cells in this workbook that have been previously formatted using the Currency style will be updated automatically.

9 To demonstrate the style:
CLICK: Comma Style button (,)
CLICK: Currency Style button ($)
Notice that the Currency style no longer uses the Accounting number format.

10 Save the workbook and keep it open for use in the next lesson.

5.2.4   Creating and Removing Styles

FEATURE
To increase your formatting productivity, Excel allows you to create and name your own styles. You can specify up to six formatting elements for each style, including *Number, Alignment, Font, Border, Patterns,* and *Protection.* You do not, however, need to use all six elements. As with custom number formats, custom styles are stored within the workbook in which they are created.

METHOD
1.   SELECT: a cell on which to base the formatting specification
2.   CHOOSE: Format, Style
3.   TYPE: *new style name* in the *Style name* drop-down list box
4.   CLICK: Add command button

PRACTICE
Let's practice creating and removing styles in the Marsden workbook.

Setup: Ensure that you've completed the previous lesson and that the "Marsden" workbook is displayed.

1 To create a new style based on the appearance of an existing cell, select the desired cell and then display the Style dialog box:
SELECT: cell C4
CHOOSE: Format, Style

2 Enter a name for the new style:
TYPE: ColumnHead
(*CAUTION:* Do not press **ENTER** after typing this entry.)

3 Notice that the Style dialog box inherits and displays the formatting attributes of the currently selected cell, as shown in Figure 5.8. The frame border for the *Styles Includes* area also displays "By Example." Let's remove some of the formatting elements that you will not use:
CLICK: *Number* check box to remove the "✔"
CLICK: *Protection* check box to remove the "✔"
(*Hint:* At this point, you can modify any of the formatting attributes by clicking the Modify command button. Make your changes using the Format Cells dialog box and click the OK command button to return.)

Figure 5.8

Defining a new style

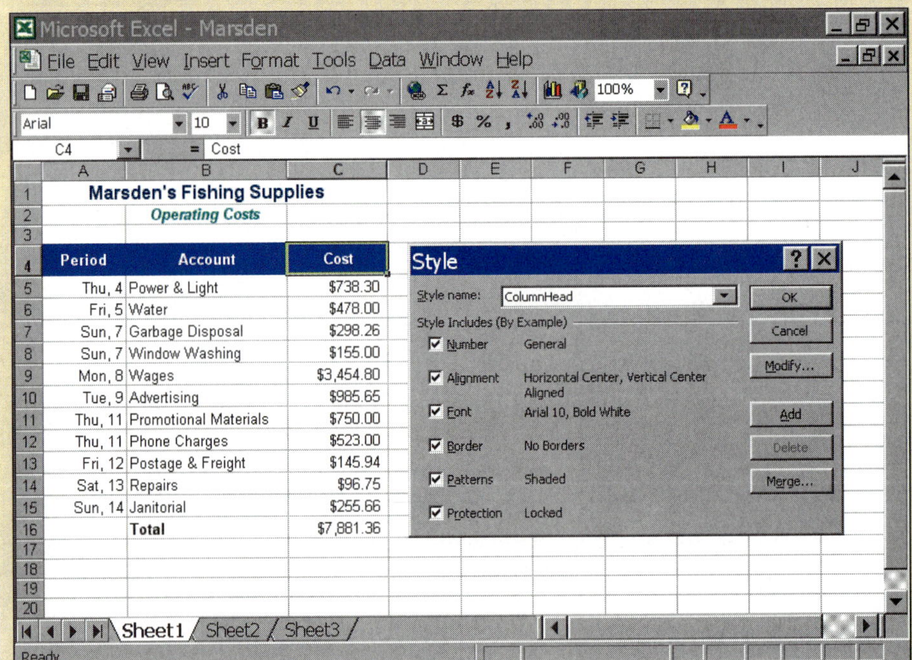

4 To add the style to the workbook:
CLICK: Add command button
CLICK: OK command button

5 To apply the new style:
SELECT: cell D4
CHOOSE: Format, Style
SELECT: ColumnHead from the *Style name* drop-down list box
CLICK: OK command button
The style has now been applied to the cell.

6 TYPE: **Paid**
PRESS: ENTER
The entry should appear formatted as the other column headings.

7 To remove a style:
CHOOSE: Format, Style
SELECT: ColumnHead from the *Style name* drop-down list box
CLICK: Delete command button
CLICK: OK command button
Notice that the style formatting is removed from cells C4 and D4.

8 Close the workbook without saving the changes.

5.2 Self Check How would you change the default font for an entire workbook to be 12-point, Times New Roman?

5.3 Working with Draw Objects

Think of your worksheet as a single piece of paper comprised of two layers. On the first layer, called the *cell layer,* you enter labels, values, and formulas into a worksheet grid of rows and columns. The second layer, known as the **draw layer,** exists as an invisible surface floating above (and mostly independent of) the worksheet cells. This transparent layer holds **objects,** such as lines, arrows, clip art images, and embedded charts. You can size, move, and delete objects on the draw layer without affecting the data stored in the underlying cells.

While you can format a worksheet in many different ways, you should practice restraint and follow these basic visual design principles.

- **Simplicity**   Do not clutter your worksheet with too many graphics. If you incorporate too many draw objects, the worksheet data becomes muddled and difficult to understand. As a rule of thumb, include only those graphics that help clarify or draw the reader's attention to specific worksheet information.
- **Unity**   Although white space is important, too much space between worksheet data and graphic objects can destroy the unity of your visual presentation. The graphics that you use must clearly relate to the data.
- **Emphasis**   Use emphasis sparingly and correctly. Emphasis is used to draw one's attention to certain areas or trends through highlighting. You typically highlight data by adding draw objects, such as arrows, or by using colors, patterns, and textures. Too much highlighting tends to confuse and frustrate the reader.

- ***Balance***   Balance and symmetry make your worksheets visually attractive and enjoyable to read. A worksheet must appear balanced—both as a unit and in the context of the printed page. Changing the position of draw objects, emphasizing headings, and changing the thickness of lines and borders can all affect balance.

In this module, you learn how to insert and manipulate graphic objects on the draw layer of a worksheet.

5.3.1 Inserting Objects on the Draw Layer

FEATURE
You place lines, arrows, rectangles, ovals, and other shapes (collectively known as **AutoShapes**) onto the draw layer of a worksheet. AutoShapes can serve to draw the viewer's attention to specific areas or to simply enhance a worksheet's visual appearance. While working on the draw layer, you may find it useful to increase and decrease the zoom setting, as you would in previewing a page to print.

METHOD
1. CLICK: an object button on the Drawing toolbar
2. CLICK: in the worksheet to insert the object
3. DRAG: the object's selection handles to size the object
4. DRAG: the center of the object to move it

PRACTICE
You now insert and manipulate AutoShape objects on the worksheet's draw layer.

Setup: Ensure that no workbooks appear in the application window.

1 Open the data file named EXC530.

2 Save the workbook as "KCTO Ch5" to your personal storage location.

3 In order to add graphics to the draw layer, you first display the Drawing toolbar:
CLICK: Drawing button (▣) on the Standard toolbar
(*Note:* If the Drawing toolbar does not appear docked along the bottom of the window, drag the toolbar into position by its Title bar.)

4 When working on the draw layer, it's sometimes easier to zoom in and out on specific areas of the worksheet. To practice zooming:
SELECT: cell range from A1 to G1
CHOOSE: View, Zoom

5 In the Zoom dialog box:
SELECT: *Fit selection* option button
CLICK: OK command button
The columns from A through G should now be visible.

6 To display some additional columns using the Standard toolbar:
SELECT: cell range from A1 to K1
CLICK: down arrow attached to the Zoom button (100% ▾)
CLICK: Selection in the drop-down menu, as shown in Figure 5.9

Figure 5.9

Zooming in and out on a worksheet

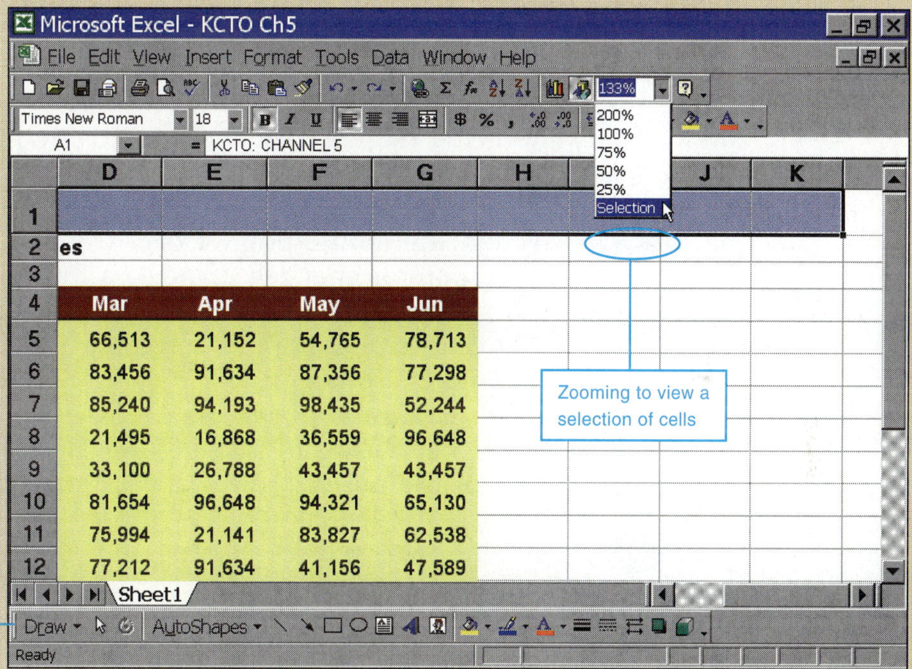

	D	E	F	G
4	Mar	Apr	May	Jun
5	66,513	21,152	54,765	78,713
6	83,456	91,634	87,356	77,298
7	85,240	94,193	98,435	52,244
8	21,495	16,868	36,559	96,648
9	33,100	26,788	43,457	43,457
10	81,654	96,648	94,321	65,130
11	75,994	21,141	83,827	62,538
12	77,212	91,634	41,156	47,589

7 To add impact, let's place an explosion graphic containing the words "Great Results!" in the top right-hand corner of the worksheet:
CLICK: AutoShapes button (AutoShapes ▾) on the Drawing toolbar
CHOOSE: Stars and Banners

8 On the Stars and Banners sub-menu:
CHOOSE: Explosion 1 (▨)
The pop-up menu disappears and your mouse pointer changes into a small cross hair as you move it over the worksheet cells.

9 There are two methods for placing an object onto the draw layer. For most objects, you simply click the cross-hair mouse pointer anywhere on the worksheet to create a default-sized graphic. For more precision, you drag the mouse pointer and size the object as you place it. Let's insert a default-sized Explosion graphic object:
CLICK: in the middle of cell H2
(*Note:* Although cell H2 is used as a reference point in the above step, the object is not attached or *anchored* to the cell in any way.)

10 The Explosion object appears surrounded by eight white boxes, as shown to the right. These boxes are called **sizing handles** and only appear when the object is selected. You use these handles to modify the height and width of the object using the mouse. To deselect the AutoShape object: 
CLICK: cell D1 (*or any other cell*)
The sizing handles disappear when the graphic is no longer selected.

11 Position the mouse pointer over the Explosion object until the mouse pointer changes shape to a four-pronged cross and arrow. To move a graphic, drag the object's border using this mouse pointer. To size a graphic, select the object and then drag its sizing handles. To begin:
CLICK: Explosion object once
Notice that the sizing handles are displayed. You will also see the name of the object, AutoShape 1, appear in the Name box.

12 On your own, practice moving and sizing the Explosion object. Before proceeding, your screen should appear similar to Figure 5.10.

Figure 5.10

Moving and sizing an
AutoShape graphic object

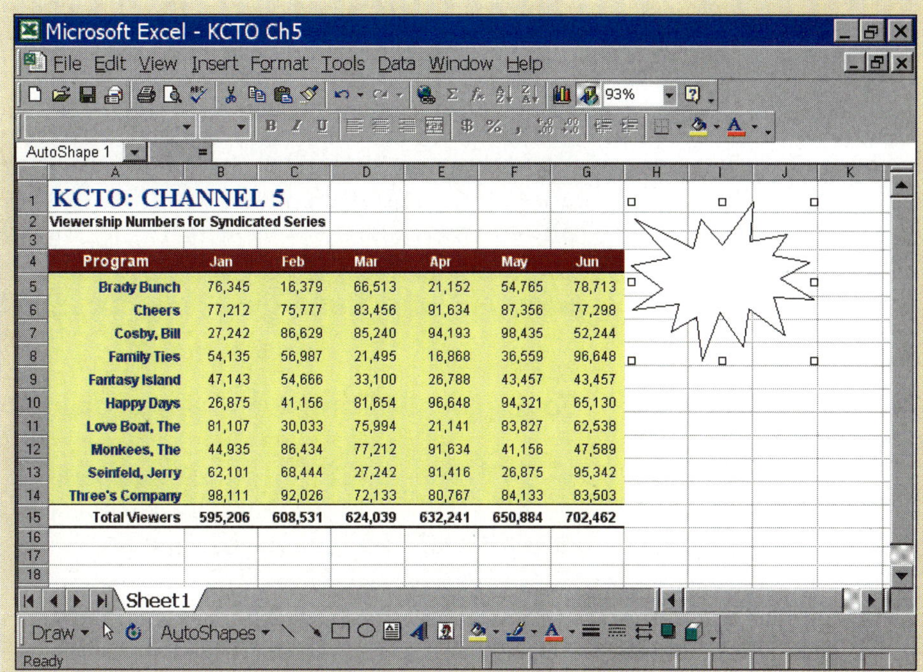

13 To display text within the Explosion object:
RIGHT-CLICK: Explosion object
CHOOSE: Add Text
You should now see a flashing I-beam cursor inside of the object.

14 On the Formatting toolbar, set the display format for the text:
SELECT: 14 points from the Font Size button (10 ▾)
CLICK: Center button (▤)
CLICK: Bold button (B)
(*Note:* You can also apply formatting after you have typed the
text.)

15 You are now ready to enter some text:
TYPE: Great
PRESS: ENTER
TYPE: Results!
CLICK: cell D1 to remove the selection
The Explosion object now displays the comment.

16 If necessary, adjust the size of the Explosion object so that all of
the text is visible. (*Hint:* When you move the mouse over the
text portion of an object, the pointer changes shape to an
I-beam. To start editing the text, you click once on the text portion. To select the object, position the mouse pointer over one of
its borders and then click once.)

17 Save the workbook and keep it open for use in the next lesson.

5.3.2   Manipulating Draw Objects

FEATURE

Besides sizing an object, you can enhance an AutoShape's appearance and visibility by selecting line styles and fill colors. You can also move and copy objects using standard drag and drop techniques or the Clipboard. To remove an object from the draw layer, select the object and then press the DELETE key.

METHOD

To display the Format AutoShape dialog box:

- DOUBLE-CLICK: an AutoShape object, or
- RIGHT-CLICK: an AutoShape object
  CHOOSE: Format AutoShape

PRACTICE

You now practice inserting, copying, and removing draw objects. You also apply formatting to objects using toolbar and menu commands.

Setup: Ensure that you have completed the previous lesson and that the "KCTO Ch5" workbook is displayed.

1   Using the toolbar, let's format the "Great Results!" Explosion object by selecting a new background fill color:
SELECT: Explosion object by clicking once on its border
CLICK: down arrow attached to the Fill Color button (⬛▾)
SELECT: Blue from the color palette

2   To make the object's text easier to read, drag the I-beam mouse pointer over the text "Great Results!" until the two words appear highlighted. Then, change the text color:
CLICK: down arrow attached to the Font Color button (⬛▾)
SELECT: White from the color palette

3   To remove the text highlighting:
CLICK: cell D1

4   Let's use some more draw objects to highlight information on the worksheet. Do the following:
CLICK: Oval button (⬭) on the Drawing toolbar

EXCEL

5 Rather than clicking on the worksheet to place a default-sized oval, position the mouse pointer above and to the left of the value in cell G13. Then, click the mouse button and drag the cross-hair pointer to the bottom right-hand corner of the cell. When finished dragging the pointer, release the mouse button. You should now see a white oval appear over top of the cell.

6 To change the oval's formatting characteristics:
RIGHT-CLICK: Oval object
CHOOSE: Format AutoShape
The Format AutoShape dialog box appears, as shown in Figure 5.11. (*Hint:* You can also double-click on the border of an object to display the dialog box in Figure 5.11.)

Figure 5.11

Format AutoShape dialog
box: *Colors* and *Lines* tab

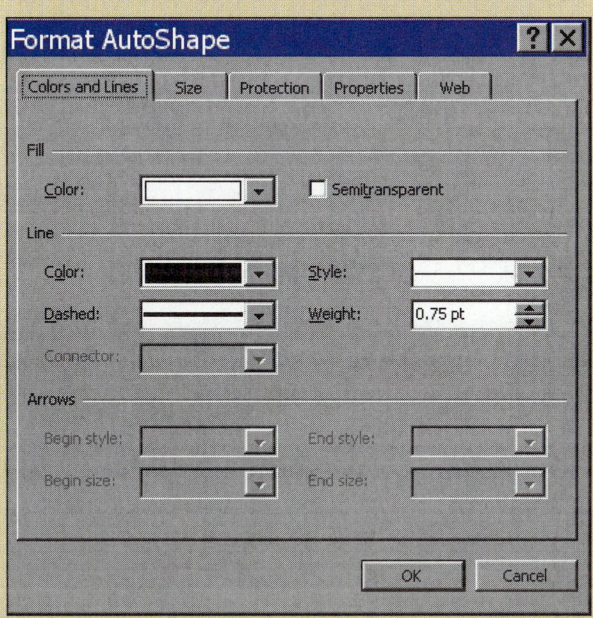

7 In the *Fill* area of the dialog box:
SELECT: "No Fill" from the *Color* drop-down list box

8 In the *Line* area of the dialog box:
SELECT: Red from the *Color* drop-down list box
SELECT: 2¼ pt from the *Style* drop-down list box

9 Before closing this dialog box:
CLICK: *Size* tab to view options for sizing and rotating the object
CLICK: *Protection* tab to view the object's "locked" status
CLICK: *Properties* tab to view options for positioning and printing
CLICK: *Web* tab to specify the text property of a Web graphic
CLICK: *Colors and Lines* tab to return to the first tab
CLICK: OK command button

10 Let's add an arrow to the worksheet to direct the reader's attention:
CLICK: Arrow button (⬉) on the Drawing toolbar
DRAG: from the bottom of the Explosion object to the top right-hand corner of the Oval object (and then release the mouse button)
(*Note:* When inserting an arrow, notice that the arrowhead points in the same direction that you dragged toward.)

11 To format this arrow using the Drawing toolbar:
CLICK: Line Style button (▤)
SELECT: 1½ pt from the pop-up menu
SELECT: cell D1 to remove the sizing handles
The arrow line appears darker and more distinguishable. Your worksheet should now appear similar to Figure 5.12.

Figure 5.12

Placing and formatting draw objects

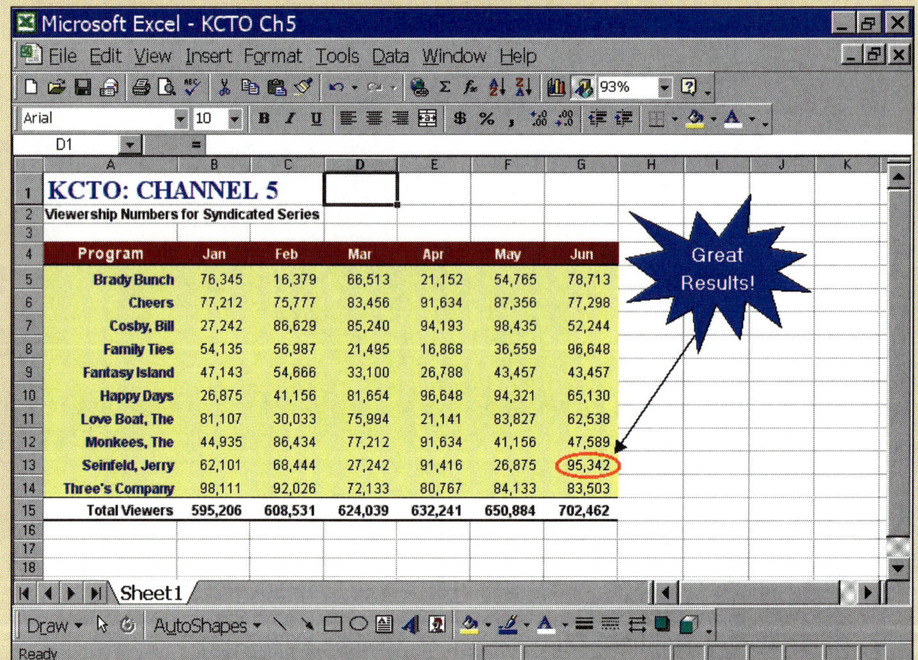

Program	Jan	Feb	Mar	Apr	May	Jun
Brady Bunch	76,345	16,379	66,513	21,152	54,765	78,713
Cheers	77,212	75,777	83,456	91,634	87,356	77,298
Cosby, Bill	27,242	86,629	85,240	94,193	98,435	52,244
Family Ties	54,135	56,987	21,495	16,868	36,559	96,648
Fantasy Island	47,143	54,666	33,100	26,788	43,457	43,457
Happy Days	26,875	41,156	81,654	96,648	94,321	65,130
Love Boat, The	81,107	30,033	75,994	21,141	83,827	62,538
Monkees, The	44,935	86,434	77,212	91,634	41,156	47,589
Seinfeld, Jerry	62,101	68,444	27,242	91,416	26,875	95,342
Three's Company	98,111	92,026	72,133	80,767	84,133	83,503
Total Viewers	595,206	608,531	624,039	632,241	650,884	702,462

12 In addition to sizing and moving objects, you can also copy and delete objects that you place onto a worksheet. You will now place a copy of the red Oval object over cell G8. To do so, position the mouse pointer over the border of the red Oval object until the mouse pointer changes. Then, do the following to copy the object:
PRESS: ⌜CTRL⌟ and hold it down
CLICK: the left mouse button and hold it down
DRAG: the red Oval object over cell G8

13 Release the mouse button when the new object is positioned correctly. Then, release the `CTRL` key to complete the operation. You should now see a second red Oval object appear on the worksheet.

14 To delete the Oval 2 object appearing over cell G8, ensure that it is selected and then do the following:
PRESS: `DELETE`

15 Save the workbook and keep it open for use in the next lesson.

In Addition Ordering the Display of Objects on the Draw Layer	The last object that you add to the draw layer is displayed in front of or overlapping all other objects. To change the display order of an object, right-click the object and choose the Order command. You can then manipulate the object using the Send to Back, Send Backward, Bring to Front, or Bring Forward commands. Layering objects becomes especially important when you also add WordArt, clip art, and charts to the worksheet's draw layer.

5.3.3 Applying Shadows and 3-D Effects

FEATURE

Excel provides two special formatting commands for enhancing draw objects. First, you can make a graphic appear with a shadowed background. Second, you can extrude a graphic into a three-dimensional object. Each of these enhancements provide you with several ways to jazz up and customize the look of AutoShape objects in your worksheets.

METHOD

To apply Shadow or 3-D Effects, select an object and then:

- CLICK: Shadow button (■) on the Drawing toolbar, or
- CLICK: 3-D button (■) on the Drawing toolbar

PRACTICE

You now practice applying special effects to the Explosion object in the KCTO Ch5 worksheet.

Setup: Ensure that you have completed the previous lesson and that the "KCTO Ch5" workbook is displayed.

1 To begin, select the object that you want to format:
SELECT: Explosion object
Ensure that the object is surrounded by its sizing handles.

2 To apply a shadowed background:
CLICK: Shadow button (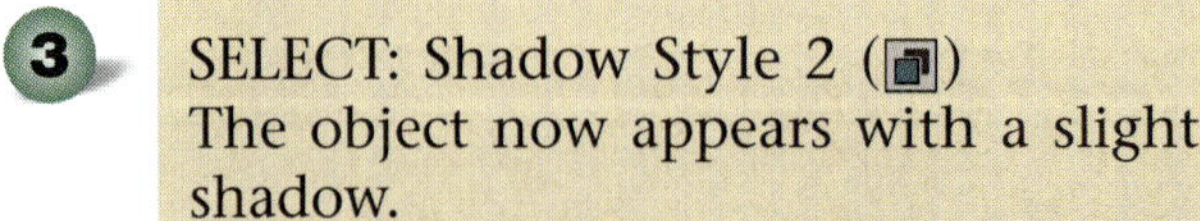) on the Drawing toolbar
The pop-up menu shown at the right will appear. When you move the mouse pointer over a menu option, you will see the button's name displayed in a ToolTip.

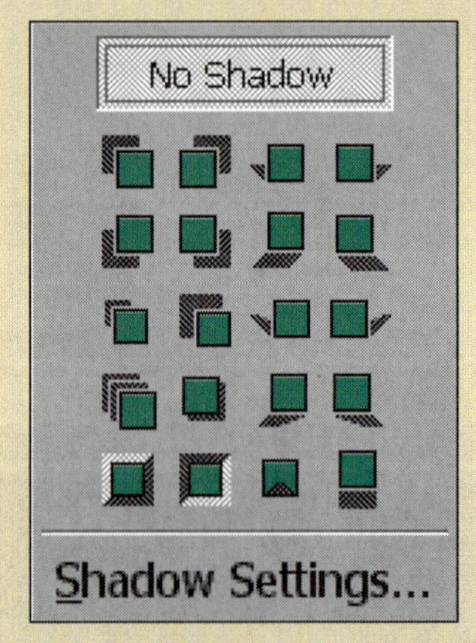

3 SELECT: Shadow Style 2 (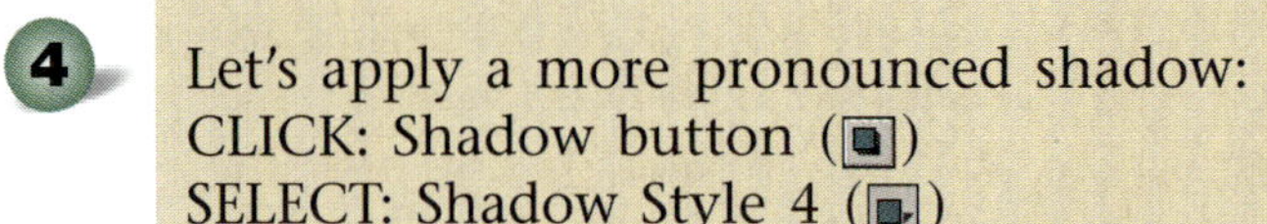)
The object now appears with a slight shadow.

4 Let's apply a more pronounced shadow:
CLICK: Shadow button (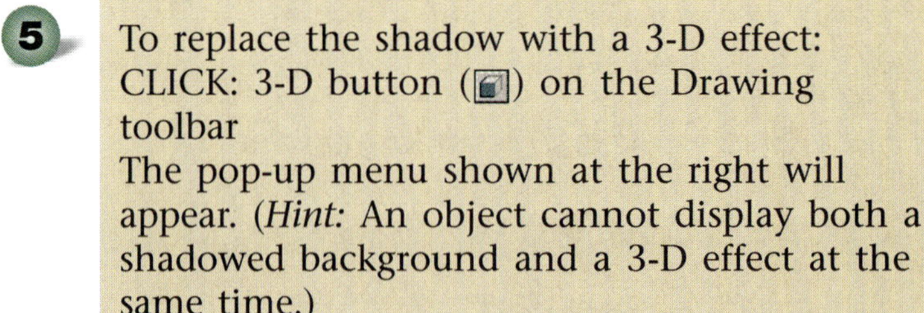)
SELECT: Shadow Style 4 ()

5 To replace the shadow with a 3-D effect:
CLICK: 3-D button () on the Drawing toolbar
The pop-up menu shown at the right will appear. (*Hint:* An object cannot display both a shadowed background and a 3-D effect at the same time.)

6 SELECT: 3-D Style 15 ()
(*Note:* This 3-D style is obviously overwhelming for this worksheet and is used for demonstrative purposes only. Remember to think about *simplicity*, *emphasis*, *unity*, and *balance* when inserting and formatting graphics.)

7 To select a more subtle 3-D style:
CLICK: 3-D button ()
SELECT: 3-D Style 1 ()

8 Save and then close the workbook.

5.3 Self Check How would you place a "STOP" sign on a worksheet using the techniques described in this module?

5.4 Working with Other Media

Besides lines, ovals, and other AutoShapes, Excel allows you to insert WordArt objects, clip art images, digital photographs, sounds, and other media elements into your worksheets. Imagine, for a moment, attaching a sound clip to a cell that explains how its result is calculated; or, in an inventory worksheet, providing an item's picture beside its numerical data. Used in this manner, media helps reduce ambiguity and enhances a worksheet's appearance and ease-of-use. Used incorrectly, however, media can jumble the message you are trying to convey and quickly distract the user. In this module, you learn how to jazz up your worksheets using common media elements.

5.4.1 Inserting WordArt

FEATURE

WordArt is a shared application provided in Microsoft Office that you use to insert text objects formatted with special effects. WordArt objects grab your reader's attention by emphasizing text beyond basic formatting techniques. WordArt is used primarily for worksheet headings and titles.

METHOD

1. CHOOSE: Insert, Picture, WordArt, or
   CLICK: Insert WordArt button (🔳) on the Drawing toolbar
2. SELECT: a style from the WordArt Gallery dialog box
3. TYPE: *your text* into the Edit WordArt Text dialog box

PRACTICE

In this lesson, you use WordArt to create a worksheet title heading

Setup: Ensure that no workbooks appear in the application window.

1 Open the data file named EXC540.

2 Save the workbook as "KCTO Media" to your personal storage location. Although similar to the workbook used in the previous module, this worksheet provides some extra white space at the top for inserting media elements.

3 To insert a WordArt object:
CLICK: Insert WordArt button (🔳) on the Drawing toolbar
The WordArt Gallery dialog box, shown in Figure 5.13, will appear.

Figure 5.13

WordArt Gallery dialog box

4 SELECT: *any WordArt style*
CLICK: OK command button
(*Hint:* Select a horizontal text style that provides a colorful 3-D style.)

5 In the Edit WordArt Text dialog box:
TYPE: KCTO Channel 5
CLICK: OK command button
The WordArt object appears, along with the WordArt toolbar, on the draw layer. (*Hint:* Ensure that you keep your text concise—do not enter long sentences for display using WordArt.)

6 To position the title at the top of the worksheet:
DRAG: WordArt object to row 1

7 On your own, size and position the WordArt object as you would any graphic object. (*Hint:* Refer to Figure 5.15 for an example.)

8 Save the workbook and keep it open for use in the next lesson.

5.4.2 Inserting Clip Art

FEATURE

The Microsoft **Clip Gallery,** another shared application, enables you to insert pictures, sound, animation, and video into your worksheets. The Gallery contains many images sorted into a variety of categories.

METHOD

1. CHOOSE: Insert, Picture, Clip Art, or
   CLICK: Insert Clip Art button () on the Drawing toolbar
2. CLICK: *Clip Art* tab
3. SELECT: an image from the list box
4. CLICK: Insert command button

PRACTICE

Let's add one of the standard clip art images to the worksheet.

Setup: Ensure that you've completed the previous lesson and that the "KCTO Media" worksheet is displayed.

To begin, you must display the Clip Gallery dialog box:
SELECT: cell G1
CLICK: Insert Clip Art button (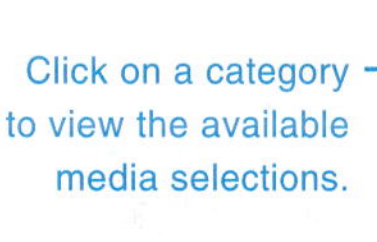) on the Drawing toolbar
You should now see the dialog box shown in Figure 5.14.

Figure 5.14

Microsoft Clip Gallery
dialog box

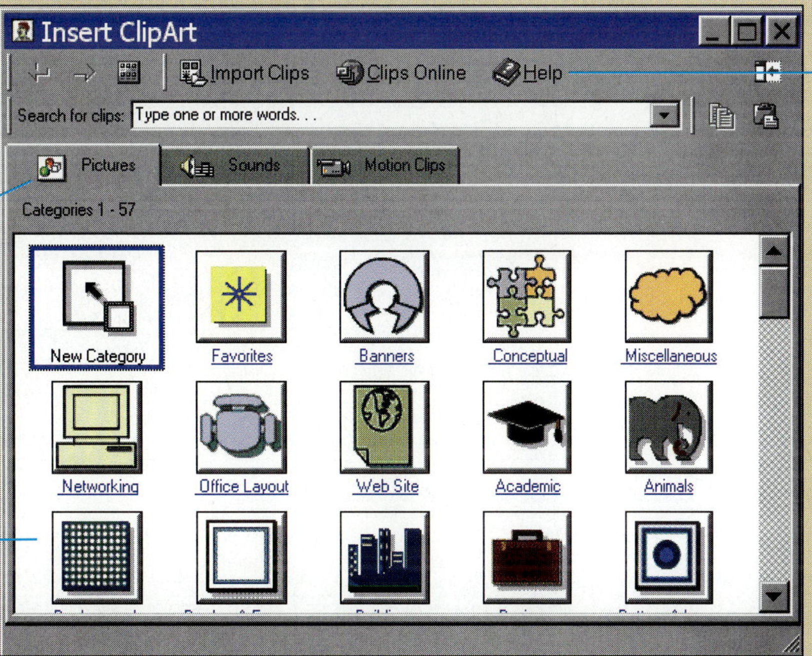

Click on a tab to select the desired media type.

Use the toolbar to import media clips from your disk storage locations and from the World Wide Web.

Click on a category to view the available media selections.

2 To view some clip art images:
SELECT: *Pictures* tab, if it isn't already selected
CLICK: Academic category icon
You should now see some clip art related to academia.

3 To return to the categories listing:
CLICK: Back button (⬅) in the toolbar

4 To select an image that relates to television:
CLICK: Entertainment category icon
CLICK: Motion Pictures clip
A pop-up toolbar menu appears, as shown to the right.

5 To insert the clip into the worksheet:
CLICK: Insert Clip button (⬛)

6 To close the Clip Gallery dialog box
CLICK: its Close button (✕)
You should now see the clip art image on the worksheet and the Picture toolbar displayed in the window.

7 On your own, move and size the clip art image to appear similar to Figure 5.15. When ready to proceed:
SELECT: cell A2

8 Save the workbook and keep it open for use in the next lesson.

Figure 5.15

Inserting WordArt objects and clip art images

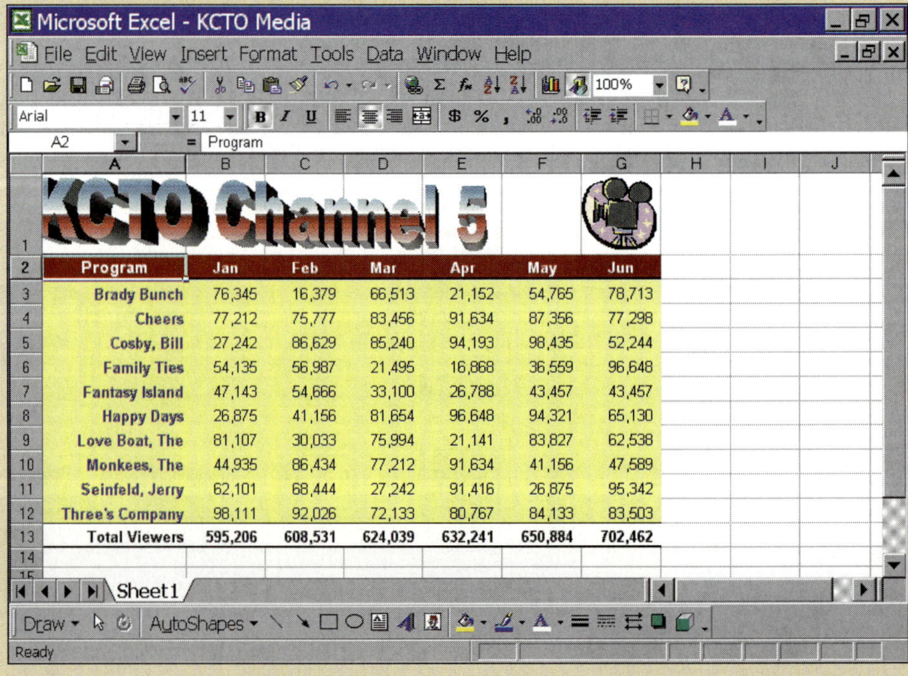

	A	B	C	D	E	F	G	H	I	J
2	Program	Jan	Feb	Mar	Apr	May	Jun			
3	Brady Bunch	76,345	16,379	66,513	21,152	54,765	78,713			
4	Cheers	77,212	75,777	83,456	91,634	87,356	77,298			
5	Cosby, Bill	27,242	86,629	85,240	94,193	98,435	52,244			
6	Family Ties	54,135	56,987	21,495	16,868	36,559	96,648			
7	Fantasy Island	47,143	54,666	33,100	26,788	43,457	43,457			
8	Happy Days	26,875	41,156	81,654	96,648	94,321	65,130			
9	Love Boat, The	81,107	30,033	75,994	21,141	83,827	62,538			
10	Monkees, The	44,935	86,434	77,212	91,634	41,156	47,589			
11	Seinfeld, Jerry	62,101	68,444	27,242	91,416	26,875	95,342			
12	Three's Company	98,111	92,026	72,133	80,767	84,133	83,503			
13	Total Viewers	595,206	608,531	624,039	632,241	650,884	702,462			

In Addition
Inserting Graphic Files
and Photographs

In addition to clip art images, you can add other graphic files to your worksheets. A computer **graphic file** is usually created by an illustrator. However, you can easily create your own graphic files using a **scanner**. A scanner is a hardware device that converts photographs and other paper-based material into computer images.

5.4.3 Displaying a Background Bitmap

FEATURE

You can apply a textured background to your worksheet by selecting a bitmap for display. The bitmap is tiled (repeated ad infinitum) across the entire worksheet area. This feature is especially useful for displaying a light watermark containing the words "DRAFT" or "CONFIDENTIAL," or for specifying a company's logo as the background for a page. However, you should note that a background bitmap can increase a workbook's file size dramatically. Also, because you cannot print a background image, this feature should only be used to enhance a worksheet for on-screen viewing.

METHOD

1. CHOOSE: Format, Sheet
2. CHOOSE: Background
3. SELECT: a *background bitmap*

PRACTICE

In this lesson, you tile the worksheet's background with graphic images that have been created for you.

Setup: Ensure that you've completed the previous lesson and that the "KCTO Media" worksheet is displayed.

1 To select a bitmap for display as the background:
CHOOSE: Format, Sheet, Background

2 In the Sheet Background dialog box:
CLICK: down arrow attached to the Views button (▦▾) on the toolbar
CHOOSE: Preview

3 Using the *Look in* drop-down list, navigate to the folder containing the student data files and then do the following:
SELECT: EXC543a from the file list area
You should see a preview of the image appear in the right-hand pane of the dialog box window.

4 To select this image as the worksheet background:
CLICK: Insert command button
The worksheet window will appear covered by the selected graphic.

5 Let's choose a more subtle background:
CHOOSE: Format, Sheet, Delete Background
CHOOSE: Format, Sheet, Background
(*Note:* You must remove the existing background image prior to selecting a new bitmap for display.)

6 To select a new graphic:
SELECT: EXC543b from the file list area
CLICK: Insert command button

7 To remove the Drawing toolbar from the display:
RIGHT-CLICK: any button on the Drawing toolbar
CHOOSE: Drawing
The toolbar disappears from the application window.

8 Save and then close the workbook.

5.4 Self Check What are the three media types that you can insert into a worksheet using the Microsoft Clip Gallery dialog box?

5.5 Creating a Chart Sheet

Although the Chart Wizard does a satisfactory job of creating a chart, you will want to explore Excel's customizing and formatting options for more demanding jobs. For instance, you can easily change a chart's appearance by applying a new chart type. You can also update a chart by adding and deleting data series in its plot area. In this module, you create a separate chart sheet and then perform some basic editing tasks.

EXCEL

5.5.1 Plotting Your Worksheet Data

FEATURE
When your data doesn't fall neatly into a table layout, you must manually select the individual ranges that you want to plot. One of the key points to remember is that the selected ranges should be the same shape and size (for example, they must contain the same number of data elements). Using this method, you can also select the headings and labels that you want to include as the legend for the data series and as the titles for the axes.

METHOD
1. SELECT: the first cell range to plot
2. PRESS: CTRL and hold it down
3. SELECT: the additional ranges to plot in the chart
4. RELEASE: CTRL
5. CHOOSE: Insert, Chart or
    CLICK: Chart Wizard button (📊)
6. Complete the steps in the Chart Wizard.

PRACTICE
You now create a chart from a worksheet that uses a number of nonadjacent rows and columns to store survey information.

Setup: Ensure that no workbooks are open in the application window.

1 Open the data file named EXC550.

2 Save the workbook as "Local Survey" to your personal storage location.

3 Your objective is to create a pie chart that displays the proportion of total jobs represented by each sector. To begin, locate the 2000 "Jobs" data in row 10 and then do the following:
SELECT: cell range from B10 to F10

4 To select the sector names for display as the legend:
PRESS: CTRL and hold it down
SELECT: cell range from B3 to F3
Notice that you included cell B3 in the selection, since the Chart Wizard prefers that all ranges be an identical shape. (*Note:* Remember to release the CTRL key when you have finished selecting ranges.)

5 To start the Chart Wizard:
CLICK: Chart Wizard button (📊)

6 In Step 1 of 4 in the Chart Wizard:
SELECT: Pie in the *Chart type* list box
SELECT: "Pie with a 3-D visual effect" in the *Chart sub-type* area

7 Preview the chart using the "Click and Hold to View Sample" command button and then:
CLICK: Next > to proceed
Your screen should now appear similar to Figure 5.16. Notice that each sector is shown as a wedge of the pie. The larger the wedge, the larger the proportional share of the total that that sector comprises.

Figure 5.16

Chart Wizard: Step 2 of 4

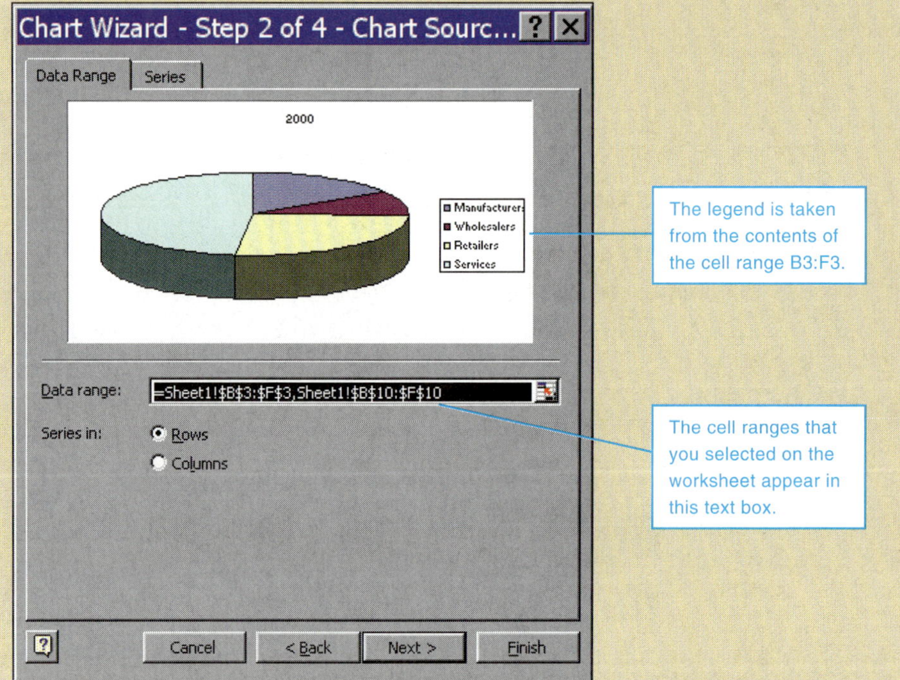

The legend is taken from the contents of the cell range B3:F3.

The cell ranges that you selected on the worksheet appear in this text box.

8 To finish creating the pie chart:
CLICK: Next > to proceed to Step 3 of 4
CLICK: Next > to proceed to Step 4 of 4

9 To store the pie chart in a separate chart sheet:
SELECT: *As new sheet* option button
TYPE: Jobs Chart
CLICK: Finish
The chart appears in the application window. Notice the chart and sheet tabs that appear along the bottom of the window.

10 Save the workbook and keep it open for use in the next lesson.

5.5.2　Applying Chart Types

FEATURE

Using the Chart Wizard, you can specify an initial chart type for plotting your data. There are many different chart types and sub-types from which to choose. And, you can change the current chart type at any time to provide a different view of your data. Table 5.3 describes the 14 standard chart types that are available in Excel's gallery. (*Note:* There are also 20 additional custom chart types.)

METHOD

1.   CHOOSE: Chart, Chart Type
2.   SELECT: a type from the *Chart type* list box
3.   SELECT: a sub-type from the *Chart sub-type* area
4.   CLICK: OK command button

PRACTICE

Let's change the chart type of the recently created pie chart.

Table 5.3

Standard
chart types

Chart Type	Description
Area	Compares the amount or magnitude of change in data elements over a period of time.
Bar	Compares data elements by value or time.
Bubble	Plots the relationship between different sets of data; like an XY chart, but includes a third variable whose value is shown by the size of the bubble.
Column	Compares data elements over a period of time.
Cylinder, Cone, and Pyramid	A bar or column chart that uses a cylinder, cone, or pyramid shape in place of a rectangle.
Doughnut	Shows the proportion of individual elements when compared to a total.
Line	Shows trends in data over equal intervals of time.
Pie	Shows the proportion of each individual element when compared to the total.

Continued

Table 5.3

Continued

Chart Type	Description
Radar	Shows each category as an axis or spoke from the center point, with lines connecting values in the same series.
Stock	A high-low-close chart shows value ranges with a finite value, typically used for quoting stocks.
Surface	Shows various combinations between two sets of data.
XY (Scatter Plot)	Plots the relationships between different sets of data, usually for scientific numerical analysis.

Setup: Ensure that you've completed the previous lesson and that the *Jobs Chart* sheet is displayed in the "Local Survey" workbook.

1 Let's view the available chart types:
CHOOSE: Chart, Chart Type
The Chart Type dialog box, which is identical to Step 1 of the Chart Wizard dialog box, appears on the screen.

2 To display a horizontal 3-D bar chart:
SELECT: Bar in the *Chart type* list box
SELECT: "Clustered bar with a 3-D visual effect" in the *Chart subtype* area
CLICK: OK command button

3 To ensure that you are viewing as much of the chart as possible:
CHOOSE: Selection from the Zoom button (100%)

4 On your own, apply some of the other chart types. When you are ready to proceed, perform steps 2 and 3 prior to moving to the next lesson.

5 Save the workbook and keep it open for use in the next lesson.

5.5.3 Adding and Deleting Data Series

FEATURE

Imagine that you have created a chart only to find that you forgot to include an important set of data. Rather than creating a completely new chart using the Chart Wizard, you can add and delete data series in an existing chart. If you are working in a separate chart sheet, you use the Menu bar or the Copy and Paste commands to add a new data series.

METHOD

To add a new data series:

1. CHOOSE: Chart, Add Data
2. SELECT: the cell range in the worksheet

To delete an existing data series:

1. RIGHT-CLICK: the data series in the plot area
2. CHOOSE: Clear

PRACTICE

In this lesson, you practice adding a comparative data series for the year 2001 to the *Jobs Chart* sheet.

Setup: Ensure that you've completed the previous lesson and that the *Jobs Chart* sheet is displayed in the "Local Survey" workbook.

1 To add a new data series to the horizontal bar chart:
CHOOSE: Chart, Add Data
A dialog box appears allowing you to enter the desired cell range.

2 Let's collapse the Add Data dialog box in order to make it easier to see the worksheet data that we need to select:
CLICK: Dialog Collapse button (⬛) for the *Range* text box
The dialog box withdraws so that only its text box appears.

3 To display the worksheet data:
CLICK: *Sheet1* tab at the bottom of the worksheet window

4 With the worksheet displayed in the application window:
SELECT: cell range from B11 to F11 using the mouse
Notice that the absolute addresses of the cell range appear in the dialog box, as shown below.

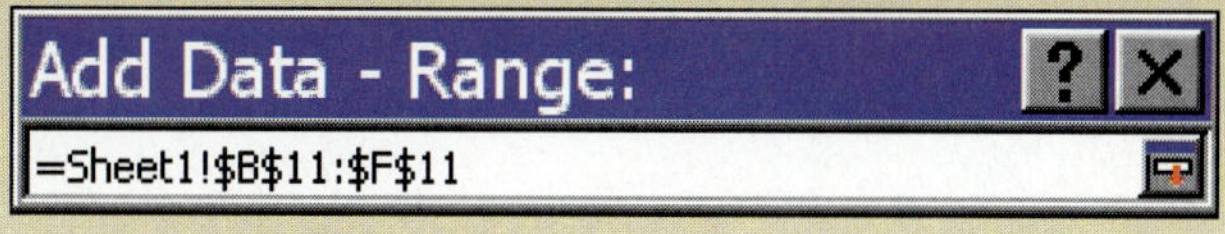

5   To expand the Add Data dialog box:
CLICK: Dialog Expand button ( )

6   To complete the process:
CLICK: OK command button
The *Jobs Chart* sheet is immediately displayed, as shown in Figure
5.17, showing the new data series as another horizontal bar.
(*Note:* If you make a mistake and need to delete a data series
from a chart, you right-click the series and then choose the Clear
command.)

7   Save and then close the workbook.

Figure 5.17

Adding a data series
to a chart sheet

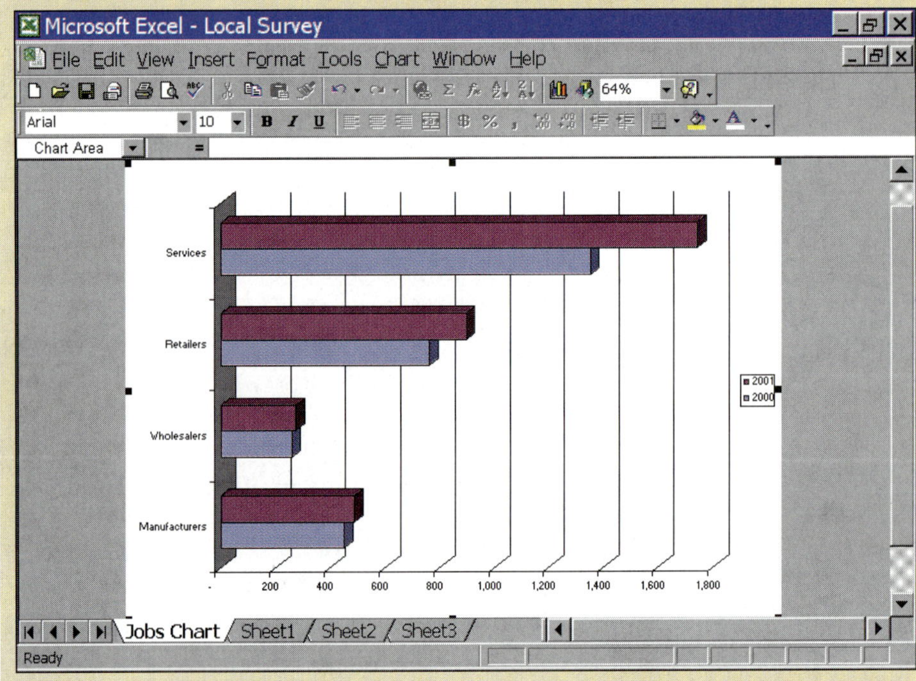

5.6　Customizing Charts

Customizing a chart involves adding titles, legends, and annotations. You can also use arrows and AutoShapes to emphasize certain aspects of the chart. Formatting a chart refers to setting the display options for each chart element. For example, if you are working on a color monitor, Excel differentiates each data series in a chart by assigning them different colors. When you print the chart to a noncolor printer, however, the various colors appear as shades of gray. Therefore, you may need to format the columns to display patterns instead of colors. Additionally, modifying font typefaces and sizes can improve a chart's readability.

As you may have noticed, Excel modifies the work area when a chart sheet is active. Additional menu commands and the Chart toolbar appear for formatting and manipulating the parts of a chart. Take a few moments to study the parts of a chart labeled in Figure 5.18 and described in Table 5.4.

Figure 5.18

Parts of a chart

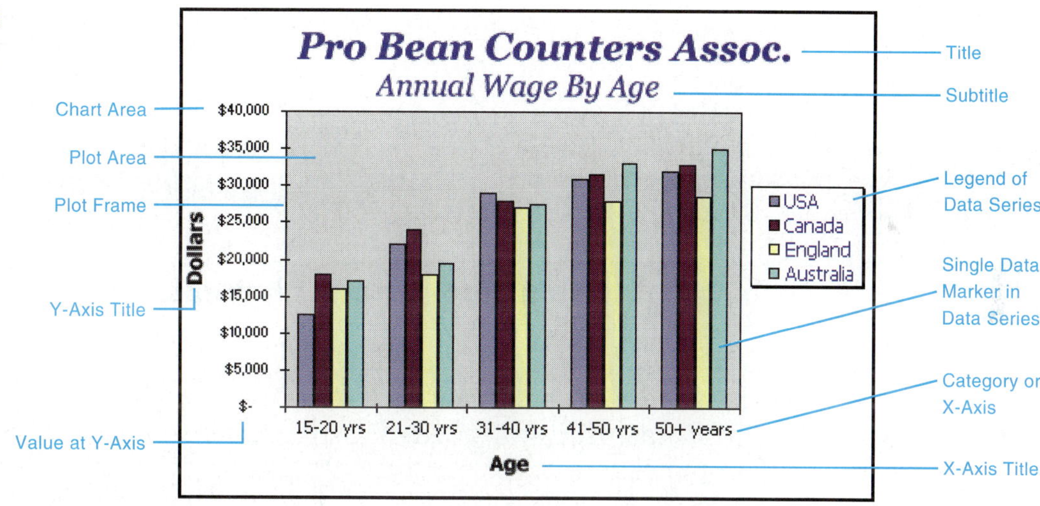

Table 5.4	*Chart Element*	*Description*
Parts of a chart	Chart and Chart Frame	The area inside a chart, including the **plot area**, titles, **legend**, and other objects.
	Plot Area and Plot Frame	The area for plotting values from the worksheet. The plot area contains the axes and data series.
	Axes (X and Y) and Axes Titles	Most charts have a horizontal category **X-axis** and a vertical value **Y-axis** for plotting values.
	Data Marker	A single dot, bar, or symbol that represents one number from the worksheet.
	Data Series	A series of related values from the worksheet. A data series consists of related data markers.
	Legend	A key for deciphering the different data series and markers appearing in the plot area.

5.6.1 Formatting Chart Elements

FEATURE

To differentiate your charts from the masses, you may want to employ some of Excel's formatting tools. Similarly to formatting a worksheet, you specify font typefaces and style attributes, text and fill colors, and even rotate text on angles.

METHOD

To display the Format dialog box for a chart element:

- DOUBLE-CLICK: a chart element, or
- RIGHT-CLICK: a chart element
  CHOOSE: Format command

PRACTICE

You now practice formatting an existing chart. The workbook displays a quarterly summary of the hospital beds required in a small community.

EXCEL

Setup: Ensure that no workbooks are open in the application window.

1 Open the data file named EXC560.

2 Save the workbook as "Haven County" to your personal storage location.

3 To display the chart sheet:
CLICK: *Chart* tab
A 3-D column chart has been created using the Chart Wizard. Each quarter is displayed along the horizontal or X-axis and the number of beds is displayed on the vertical or Y-axis. A simple legend is also provided to differentiate the three data series that are plotted.

4 Ensure that the Chart toolbar appears in the application window. (*Hint:* If the Chart toolbar is not visible, right-click an existing toolbar and choose Chart from the menu.) You may dock the toolbar against one of the borders or float the toolbar, as shown in Figure 5.19. If your screen does not look similar to Figure 5.19, click the Selection option from the Zoom button ([100%▼]) on the Standard toolbar.

Figure 5.19

The *Chart* sheet for Haven County

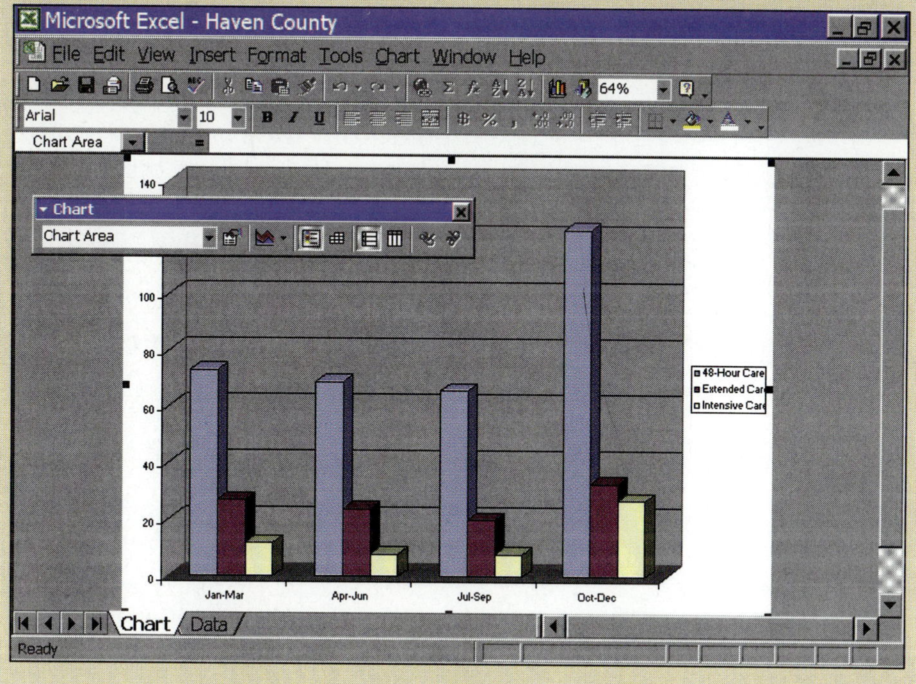

5 Let's format the legend so that it stands apart from the other chart elements. Position the mouse pointer over the legend and then:
RIGHT-CLICK: the legend
CHOOSE: Format Legend
A dialog box appears with a variety of formatting options.

6 To reposition the legend in the chart area:
CLICK: *Placement* tab
SELECT: *Bottom* option button
CLICK: OK command button
The legend will now appear along the bottom of the chart.

7 To continue formatting the legend:
DOUBLE-CLICK: the legend
The Format Legend dialog box displays immediately.

8 Let's return the legend to its original position:
SELECT: *Right* option button

9 To change the legend's background color and appearance:
CLICK: *Patterns* tab
SELECT: *Shadow* check box in the *Border* area
SELECT: a pale yellow color in the *Area* area

10 To change the legend's typeface and font size:
CLICK: *Font* tab
SELECT: Times New Roman from the *Font* list box
SELECT: Bold from the *Font style* list box
SELECT: 12 from the *Size* list box

11 To complete the legend formatting:
CLICK: OK command button

12 You can move and size certain chart objects using the mouse. On your own, position the mouse pointer over one of the black selection boxes surrounding the legend. Then, drag the box in order to size the legend. For all of the text to be visible, the legend may need to overlap the plot area. Release the mouse button when you are finished.

13 To format a data series, double-click one of its columns:
DOUBLE-CLICK: the 48-Hour Care column for Apr-Jun
Notice that the Format Data Series dialog box (Figure 5.20) that appears is similar to the Format Legend dialog box.

Figure 5.20

Format Data Series
dialog box

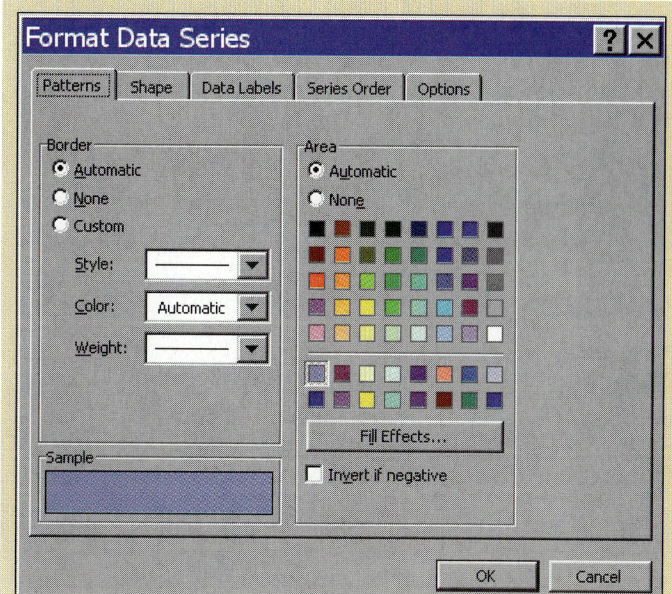

14 On your own, click on each tab in the Format Data Series dialog box. You use the *Shape* tab to control the column shape, the *Data Labels* tab to add labels and values to the chart, the *Series Order* tab to adjust the column ordering, and the *Options* tab to adjust a few additional display particulars. Return to the *Patterns* tab once you have finished.

15 Let's change the color of the data series:
SELECT: a green color from the *Area* area
CLICK: OK command button
Notice that the legend and the entire data series are modified.

16 Save the workbook and keep it open for use in the next lesson.

5.6.2 Adding and Deleting Chart Elements

FEATURE

You can easily add and delete elements, such as titles, headings, data labels, and legend text, for an existing chart. Titles are used to state the purpose of the chart and to explain the scales used for the axes. Data labels appear inside the plot area and display the actual values plotted by each data symbol. A legend provides a visual key for the data series plotted in the chart. Finally, you can display a data grid containing the actual values that you've plotted on the chart. To remove any element appearing in a chart, you right-click the element and then choose the Clear command.

METHOD
1. SELECT: the chart
2. CHOOSE: Chart, Chart Options

PRACTICE
You now practice adding titles and a data table to the chart.

Setup: Ensure that you've completed the previous lesson and that the "Haven County" workbook is displayed.

1
To add and delete chart elements:
CHOOSE: Chart, Chart Options

2
Let's add two titles to the chart:
CLICK: *Titles* tab, if it isn't already selected
TYPE: **Haven County Hospital** in the *Chart title* text box
TYPE: **Bed Count** in the *Value (Z) axis* text box
Notice that the preview area is updated to show the titles.

3
A data table displays a grid of the plotted values beneath the X-axis. To add a data table to the chart:
CLICK: *Data Table* tab
SELECT: *Show data table* check box
CLICK: OK command button
Your screen should now appear similar to Figure 5.21.

Figure 5.21

Adding titles and
a data table

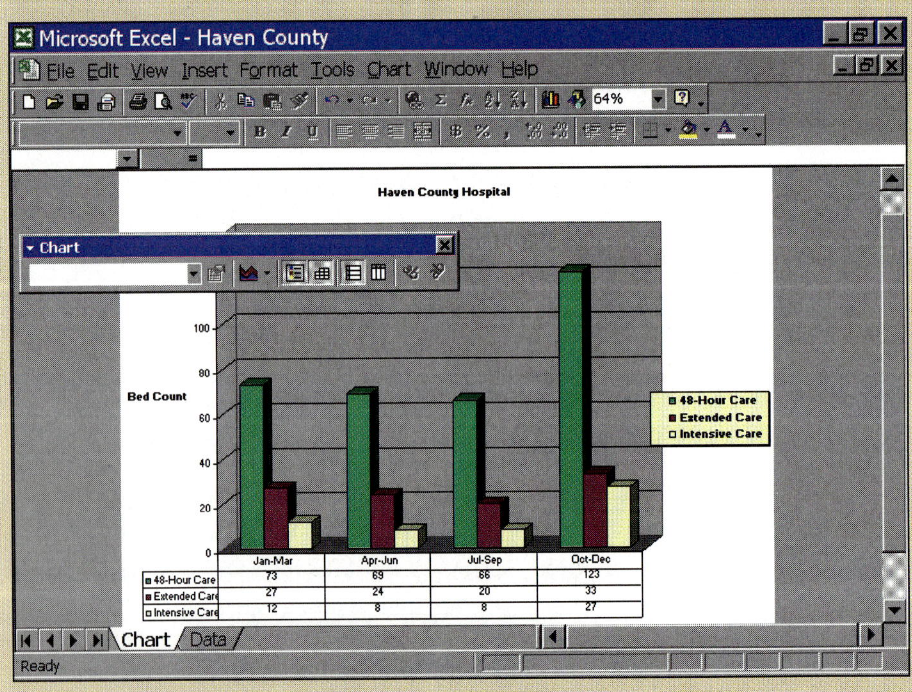

4 Let's remove the data table:
CLICK: Data Table button (▦) on the Chart toolbar
(*Note:* The button appears pressed in while the table is displayed.)

5 Save the workbook and keep it open for use in the next lesson.

In Addition
Manipulating Chart
Elements Using the
Chart Toolbar

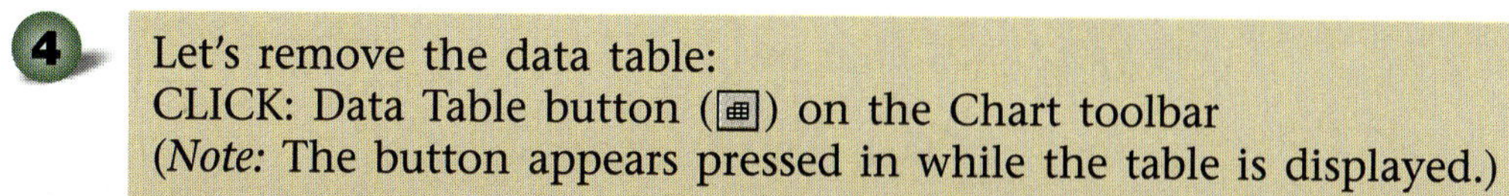

You can use the buttons on the Chart toolbar to select a chart element
(Category Axis ▾), display the Format dialog box (▦), change the chart type (▦▾),
display and hide the legend (▦), and rotate text (▦, ▦).

5.6.3 Adding Draw Objects to a Chart

FEATURE
Similar to adding draw objects to a worksheet, you can insert
arrows and other AutoShape graphics onto a chart sheet. In the
previous lesson, you attached text to specific regions on a chart,
such as titles and axes. By adding a text box, you can display free-
form text anywhere on a chart.

METHOD
1. CLICK: an object button on the Drawing toolbar
2. CLICK: on the chart sheet to insert the object
3. Size and move the object as desired.

PRACTICE
You now enhance the chart by adding a text box and an arrow.

Setup: Ensure that you've completed the previous lesson and that
the "Haven County" workbook is displayed.

1 To add draw objects to the chart:
CLICK: Drawing button (▦) on the Standard toolbar
SELECT: 100% from the Zoom button (100% ▾)

2 Using Figure 5.22 as your guide, scroll the window to view the
appropriate area of the chart. To add an arrow to the chart:
CLICK: Arrow button (▦) on the Drawing toolbar

3 You can use the keyboard to help you draw a straight arrow:
PRESS: (SHIFT) and hold it down

4 On your own, position the mouse pointer above the Jul-Sep columns and then drag the pointer toward the 48-Hour Care column for Oct-Dec. When satisfied, release the mouse button and the (SHIFT) key. A straight arrow will appear in the plot area. (*Hint:* If you make a mistake, select the object and then press (DELETE).)

5 To add a text box to the chart:
CLICK: Text Box button (▦) on the Drawing toolbar
CLICK: the I-beam mouse pointer above the Apr-Jun columns
TYPE: October Flooding
PRESS: (ENTER)
TYPE: and Cold Winter

6 Position the mouse pointer over one of the borders (not selection handles) of the text box and drag the box into place. (*Hint:* You can also format the text to appear with a different typeface and font size.)

7 To better view the chart:
CLICK: on the white chart area, outside of the plot area
Your screen should now appear similar to Figure 5.22.

8 Remove the Drawing toolbar from the application window.

9 Save the workbook and keep it open for use in the next lesson.

Figure 5.22

Adding draw objects
to a chart

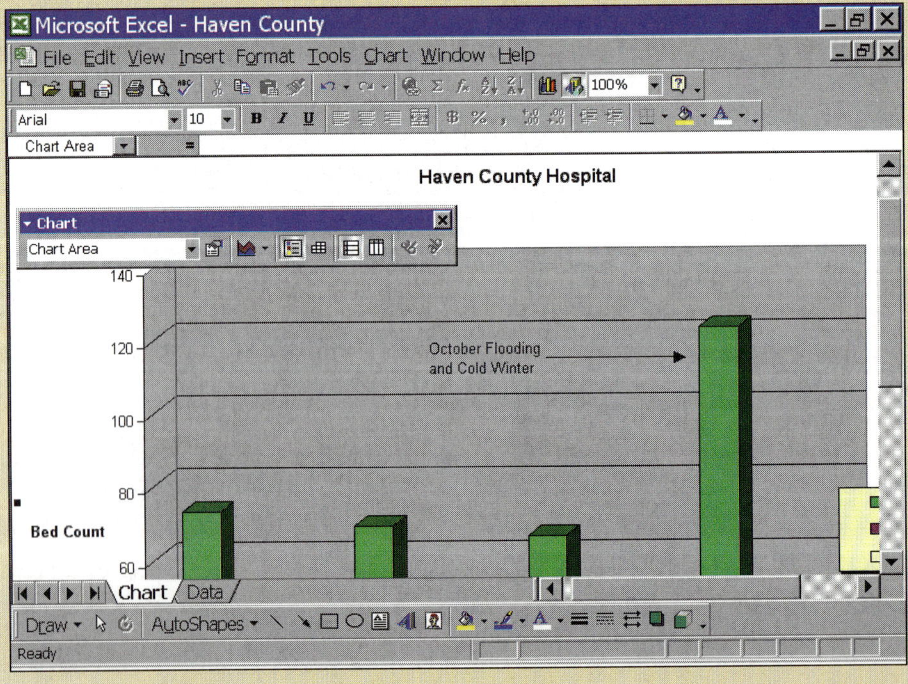

5.6.4 Printing a Separate Chart Sheet

FEATURE

For the most part, a chart sheet is printed using the same process you use in printing a worksheet. There are some subtle differences, however, in how you choose to fit the chart to the printed page. For example, using the Page Setup dialog box, you can specify that the chart be expanded to fit the full page or scaled proportionally. For review purposes, you may also choose to print the chart using draft quality or in black and white. In addition to saving ink, these print options take much less time to produce output than if you used your printer's best quality.

METHOD

To display the Page Setup dialog box for a chart sheet:

1.   CHOOSE: File, Page Setup
2.   CLICK: *Chart* tab in the dialog box

PRACTICE

You now practice printing a chart sheet.

Setup: Ensure that you've completed the previous lesson and that the "Haven County" workbook is displayed.

1 To specify page setup options for a chart:
CHOOSE: File, Page Setup
CLICK: *Chart* tab in the dialog box

2 In the *Printed chart size* area:
SELECT: *Scale to fit page* option button

3 To preview how the chart sheet will appear when printed:
CLICK: Print Preview command button
Your screen should appear similar to Figure 5.23.

Figure 5.23

Print previewing a chart sheet

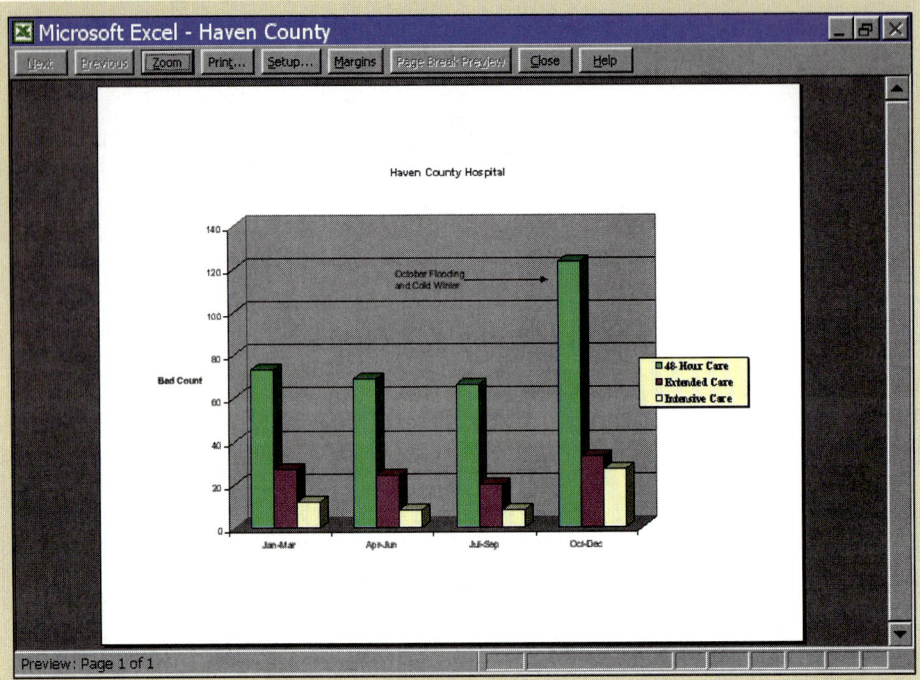

4 If you have a printer connected to your computer, click the Print command button in the toolbar area and then click the OK command button in the Print dialog box to continue. If you do not have a printer, click the Close command button in the Print Preview window.

5 Save and then close the workbook.

6 Exit Microsoft Excel.

In Addition Using Microsoft Data Map	Using a specialty charting tool called *Microsoft Map*, you can create a map to analyze your worksheet information geographically. This data map feature also enables you to quickly analyze trends relative to a region's demographic breakdown. For more information, refer to the Help system in Microsoft Excel.

5.6 Self Check   What might you do differently in formatting a chart for printing as opposed to formatting a chart for displaying online?

5.7 Chapter Review

Most people recognize the benefit of using formatting styles, graphics, and charts to improve the effectiveness of their presentations. Once the domain of desktop publishing and graphics software, Excel now enables you to indent, rotate, wrap, and shrink text entries, insert graphics and pictures, and plot data using a variety of chart formats. If used properly, a worksheet's formatting can help you direct the reader's attention and emphasize key areas. Yet, sometimes, a simple graphic representation of data is all that is needed, especially for conveying information from rows and columns of tiny numbers. For the same reason that road maps are easier to follow than written directions, a visual display is far more appealing and effective than numbers alone. Charts can help you summarize and present data, and predict or forecast trends. In this chapter, you learned several principles and commands for successfully formatting and incorporating graphics in a worksheet.

5.7.1 Command Summary

Many of the commands and procedures appearing in this chapter are summarized in the following table.

Skill Set	To Perform this Task . . .	Do the Following . . .
Formatting Worksheets	Indent and rotate text in a cell	CHOOSE: Format, Cells CLICK: *Alignment* tab
	Wrap, merge, and shrink text entries appearing in a cell(s)	CHOOSE: Format, Cells CLICK: *Alignment* tab
	Apply select formatting elements from an AutoFormat option	CHOOSE: Format, AutoFormat CLICK: Options command button
	Apply, modify, and remove styles	CHOOSE: Format, Style SELECT: *the desired style* CLICK: OK, Modify, or Delete
	Create a new style	SELECT: a cell with the desired formatting CHOOSE: Format, Style TYPE: *new style name* CLICK: Add command button

Continued

Skill Set	To Perform this Task . . .	Do the Following . . .
Formatting Worksheets *Continued*	Display a background bitmap	CHOOSE: Format, Sheet, Background SELECT: *a bitmap file*
Formatting Numbers	Apply number formats	CHOOSE: Format, Cells CLICK: *Number* tab SELECT: *the desired number format*
	Create custom number formats	CHOOSE: Format, Cells CLICK: *Number* tab SELECT: Custom in the *Category* list box TYPE: *custom number format*
Using Charts and Objects	Create and modify lines and AutoShape objects	CLICK: an object button on the Drawing toolbar CLICK: in the worksheet
	Size and move objects on the draw layer	DRAG: object's handles to size, and DRAG: object's borders to move
	Delete an object on the draw layer	SELECT: an object PRESS: `DELETE`
	Create and modify 3-D shapes and apply shadows to objects	SELECT: an object CLICK: 3-D button, or CLICK: Shadow button
	Format an AutoShape object	RIGHT-CLICK: an AutoShape object CHOOSE: Format command
	Insert a WordArt object	CLICK: Insert WordArt button, or CHOOSE: Insert, Picture, WordArt
	Insert a Clip Art object	CLICK: Insert Clip Art button, or CHOOSE: Insert, Picture, Clip Art
	Modify charts; changing the chart type	CHOOSE: Chart, Chart Type SELECT: *a type and sub-type*
	Modify charts; adding data series	CHOOSE: Chart, Add Data SELECT: *the additional range to plot*

Continued

Skill Set	To Perform this Task . . .	Do the Following . . .
Using Charts and Objects *Continued*	Modify charts; adding chart elements, such as titles	SELECT: the chart CHOOSE: Chart, Chart Options
	Format a chart element	RIGHT-CLICK: *a chart element* CHOOSE: Format command
	Change the page setup for charts	CHOOSE: File, Page Setup CLICK: *Chart* tab

5.7.2 Key Terms

This section specifies page references for the key terms identified in this chapter. For a complete list of definitions, refer to the Glossary provided at the end of this learning guide.

AutoShapes, *p. 214*

cell layer, *p. 204*

Clip Gallery, *p. 225*

custom format, *p. 205*

draw layer, *p. 213*

graphic file, *p. 227*

legend, *p. 236*

objects, *p. 213*

plot area, *p. 236*

scanner, *p. 227*

sizing handles, *p. 216*

style, *p. 203*

WordArt, *p. 223*

X-axis, *p. 236*

Y-axis, *p. 236*

5.8   Review Questions

5.8.1   Short Answer

1. Which six formatting elements are included in the AutoFormat feature?
2. What is the difference between a custom format and a style?
3. How would you change the function of a style button ($\$$, %, or ,) on the Formatting toolbar?
4. Name the four visual design principles described in this chapter.
5. Describe the two primary layers that exist in a worksheet.
6. How do you format a graphic draw object?
7. What two shared applications are used to insert graphic objects?
8. What are some placement options for a chart's legend?
9. How do you add an arrow to a chart?
10. How do you add free-form text to a chart?

5.8.2   True/False

1. —— Custom number formats can be used to enhance the display of date and time values.
2. —— You can create and apply styles to format values in a worksheet, but not text labels.
3. —— The lines, arrows, and other draw objects that you add to a worksheet are collectively known as *AutoShapes*.
4. —— You can only place text in the cell layer of a worksheet.
5. —— To size a graphic object, such as a circle or rectangle, you drag its selection or sizing handles.
6. —— Because a WordArt object usually replaces a worksheet title, it is stored in the cell layer of a worksheet.
7. —— If you forget to enter a chart title using the Chart Wizard, you can always add one later.
8. —— You double-click a chart element to display its Format dialog box.
9. —— You cannot print a chart unless it is embedded on a worksheet.
10. —— Excel provides special page setup options for printing a chart.

5.8.3 Multiple Choice

1. Which of the following statements about the AutoFormat command is *false?*
   a. You can format an area using fonts, shading, and border attributes.
   b. You can format an area by applying only column width and row height attributes.
   c. By your selecting one cell, the AutoFormat command can identify a surrounding table area for formatting.
   d. The AutoFormat command will not work on a worksheet area that already contains formatting.

2. When creating a custom number format, you place codes in the following order, separated by semicolons:
   a. positive; negative; text
   b. zero; positive; negative; text
   c. positive; negative; zero; text
   d. positive; zero; negative; text

3. Excel provides the following built-in styles, accessible from the Formatting toolbar:
   a. Comma, Percent, Currency
   b. Comma, Normal, Percent
   c. Comma [0], Percent, Accounting
   d. Number, Currency [2], Font

4. Which of the following is *not* one of the visual design principles mentioned in this chapter?
   a. Emphasis
   b. Unity
   c. Artistry
   d. Balance

5. Which of the following statements about graphic objects is *true?*
   a. Graphic objects float above the cell layer of a worksheet.
   b. Graphic objects float below the cell layer of a worksheet.
   c. Once inserted, you can size but not move a graphic object.
   d. You must select an object's color before placing it onto a worksheet.

6. To copy an AutoShape object using drag and drop, hold down this key as you drag the object using the mouse.
   a. ALT
   b. CTRL
   c. SHIFT
   d. HOME

7. Two special effects that you can apply to draw objects include:
    a. Shadow and Extrude
    b. Extrude and 3-D
    c. Implode and Explode
    d. Shadow and 3-D

8. Which of the following media tabs is *not* present in the Clip Gallery's Insert ClipArt dialog box?
    a. Animation
    b. Pictures
    c. Sounds
    d. Motion Clips

9. To add a new data series to an existing chart:
    a. DOUBLE-CLICK: the desired data series
    b. CHOOSE: Chart, Add Data
    c. CHOOSE: Chart, Chart Options
    d. You cannot add a data series to an existing chart.

10. When defining the page setup for a separate chart sheet, you will notice the addition of a new tab in the dialog box called:
    a. Draw
    b. Graph
    c. Chart
    d. Object

5.9   Hands-On Projects

5.9.1   Grandview College: Information Technology (IT) Courses

In this exercise, you practice inserting AutoShape objects onto the draw layer of an existing worksheet.

1. Open the data file named EXC591.
2. Save the workbook as "IT Courses" to your personal storage location.
3. If the Drawing toolbar is not already displayed, do the following:
    CLICK: Drawing button (   ) on the Standard toolbar
4. In order to emphasize a new course called "Advanced HTML," let's add an AutoShape object to the worksheet. Do the following:
    CLICK: AutoShapes button (AutoShapes ▾) on the Drawing toolbar
    CHOOSE: Stars and Banners

5. On the Stars and Banners cascading menu:
   CHOOSE: Vertical Scroll (⬚)
6. To place a default-sized graphic object on the draw layer:
   CLICK: in the middle of cell E2
7. To place a text comment in the Vertical Scroll object:
   RIGHT-CLICK: inside the Vertical Scroll object
   CHOOSE: Add Text
   CLICK: Center button (▤)
   TYPE: **New**
   PRESS: ENTER
   TYPE: **Course**
8. Using the sizing handles, make the Vertical
   Scroll object smaller as shown to the right.
   (*Hint:* Size the object to cover three rows in
   columns E and F.)

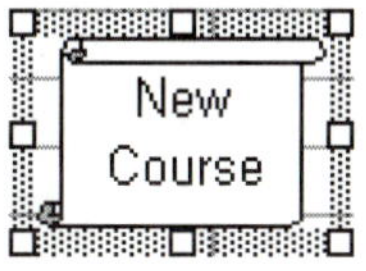

9. To apply a shadowed background to the Scroll object:
   CLICK: Shadow button (▣) on the Drawing toolbar
   SELECT: Shadow Style 6 (▣)
10. Let's zoom the window to display only the worksheet columns
    that we are interested in. Do the following:
    SELECT: cell range from A1 to F1
    CLICK: down arrow attached to the Zoom button (100% ▾)
    CLICK: Selection in the drop-down menu
11. Now add an Oval object to highlight a value in the "Waiting"
    column:
    CLICK: Oval button (◯) on the Drawing toolbar
    DRAG: the cross-hair pointer from the top left-hand corner of
    cell D5 to the bottom right-hand corner of the cell and then
    release the mouse button
12. To change the oval's formatting:
    DOUBLE-CLICK: in the middle of the Oval object
    The Format AutoShape dialog box is displayed.
13. In the *Fill* area of the dialog box:
    SELECT: "No Fill" from the Color drop-down list box
14. In the *Line* area of the dialog box:
    SELECT: a dark red from the *Color* drop-down list box
    SELECT: 1½ pt from the *Style* drop-down list box
    CLICK: OK command button
15. Lastly, add an arrow to point from the Scroll object to the
    Oval object:
    CLICK: Arrow button (◥) on the Drawing toolbar
    DRAG: from the Scroll object to the Oval object and then
    release the mouse button
    SELECT: cell A10 to remove the highlighting
    Your screen should now appear similar to Figure 5.24.
16. Save and then close the "IT Courses" workbook.

Figure 5.24

Adding AutoShape objects
to a worksheet

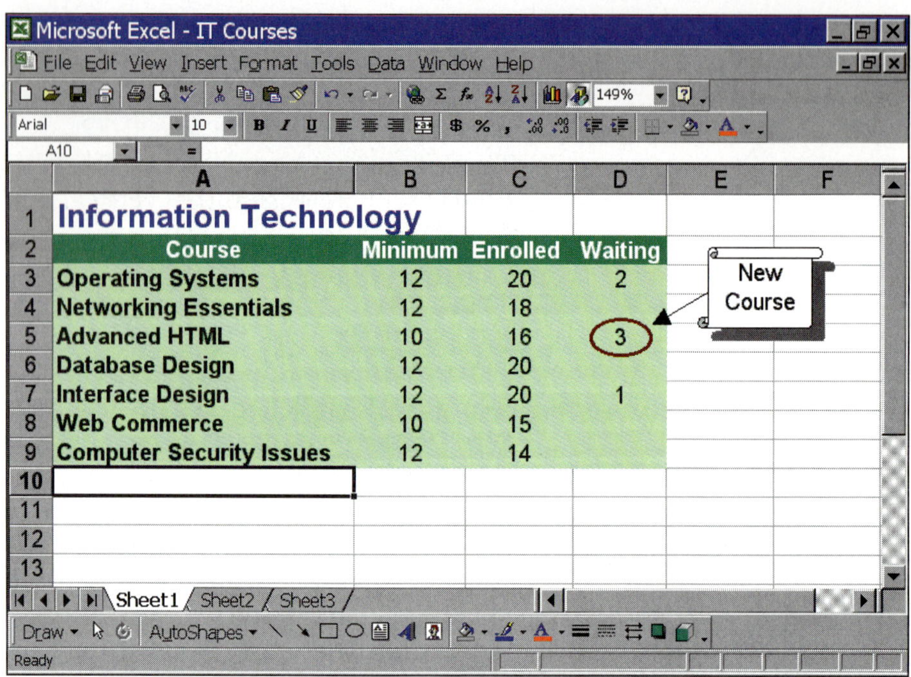

5.9.2   Fast Forward Video: New Releases

You will now practice manipulating and formatting text in a worksheet. In addition, you are given the opportunity to define a new formatting style.

1. Open the data file named EXC592.
2. Save the workbook as "New Releases" to your personal storage
    location.
3. Your objective in this exercise is to format the worksheet to
    display all of the text information without changing any col-
    umn widths. To begin, let's rotate the headings in row 4:
    SELECT: cell range from A4 to E4
4. CHOOSE: Format, Cells
    CLICK: *Alignment* tab
5. In the *Orientation* area of the dialog box:
    SELECT: 20 in the *Degrees* spin box
    CLICK: OK command button
6. To differentiate the category headings from the movie titles,
    you will now indent the titles. To begin, select the required
    cell ranges:
    SELECT: cell range from A6 to A8
    PRESS: CTRL and hold it down
    SELECT: cell range from A10 to A12
    SELECT: cell range from A14 to A15
    SELECT: cell range from A17 to A18
7. Release the CTRL key and then proceed:
    CLICK: Increase Indent button (⌦)
    All of the selected ranges should now appear indented.

EXCEL

8. With the ranges still selected, let's wrap the text in the cells:
   CHOOSE: Format, Cells
   SELECT: Wrap Text check box so that a "✔" appears
   CLICK: OK command button

9. To wrap the text in the Actors column:
   SELECT: cell range from C6 to C18
   CHOOSE: Format, Cells
   SELECT: Wrap Text check box so that a "✔" appears
   CLICK: OK command button

10. Because you may want to change their formatting characteristics later, you decide to highlight the category headings in column A using a style. Do the following:
    SELECT: cell A5
    CLICK: Bold button (B)
    SELECT: Dark Red color from the Fill Color button ()
    SELECT: White color from the Font Color button ()

11. Let's define a new style based on this newly formatted cell:
    CHOOSE: Format, Style
    TYPE: **Category**
    Notice that the *Style Includes* area now displays *(By Example)* and lists the formatting attributes for the selected cell.

12. Remove the formatting attributes that are not part of the style:
    CLICK: *Number* check box to remove the "✔"
    CLICK: *Protection* check box to remove the "✔"

13. To add the new style:
    CLICK: Add command button
    CLICK: OK command button

14. Let's apply the formatting to the remaining categories:
    SELECT: cell A9
    PRESS: CTRL and hold it down
    SELECT: cell A13
    SELECT: cell A16

15. Release the CTRL key and then proceed:
    CHOOSE: Format, Style
    SELECT: Category from the *Style name* drop-down list box
    CLICK: OK command button
    PRESS: CTRL + HOME to return to the top of the worksheet

16. Save and then close the workbook.

5.9.3 Sun Valley Frozen Foods: Department Expenses

In this exercise, you insert WordArt and Clip Art objects to enhance the attractiveness of a worksheet. You also use AutoShapes to direct the reader's attention to specific information.

1. Open the data file named EXC593.
2. Save the workbook as "Sun Expense" to your personal storage location.
3. In the next few steps, you improve the worksheet title using WordArt. To begin, delete the existing title that appears in cell A1.
4. Using the Insert WordArt button (![]) on the Drawing toolbar, add a worksheet title that includes the text "Sun Valley." You may select any style and formatting (font, font size, and font style) that you desire.
5. Adjust the height of row 1 and then size and move the WordArt object into position at the top of the worksheet.
6. Using the Insert Clip Art button (![]) on the Drawing toolbar, add a suitable graphic to appear beside the table of expenses.
7. Size and move the clip art graphic so that it is roughly the same height as the table of expenses.
8. Using the Oval button (![]) on the Drawing toolbar, draw an oval over the value appearing in cell B8. Then, format the object to display using no fill color and to have a bright blue 2-point line.
9. Insert an Explosion AutoShape object a few rows below cell B8 and include the text "Capital Expense."
10. Size and move the Explosion object to ensure that all of the text is visible. Then, format the object to appear with a short shadow.
11. Draw an arrow to point from the Explosion object to the Oval object. Then, select cell A3 to remove the sizing handles. Your screen should now appear similar to Figure 5.25.
12. Save and then close the "Sun Expense" workbook.

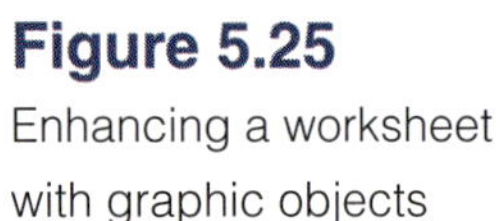

Figure 5.25

Enhancing a worksheet

with graphic objects

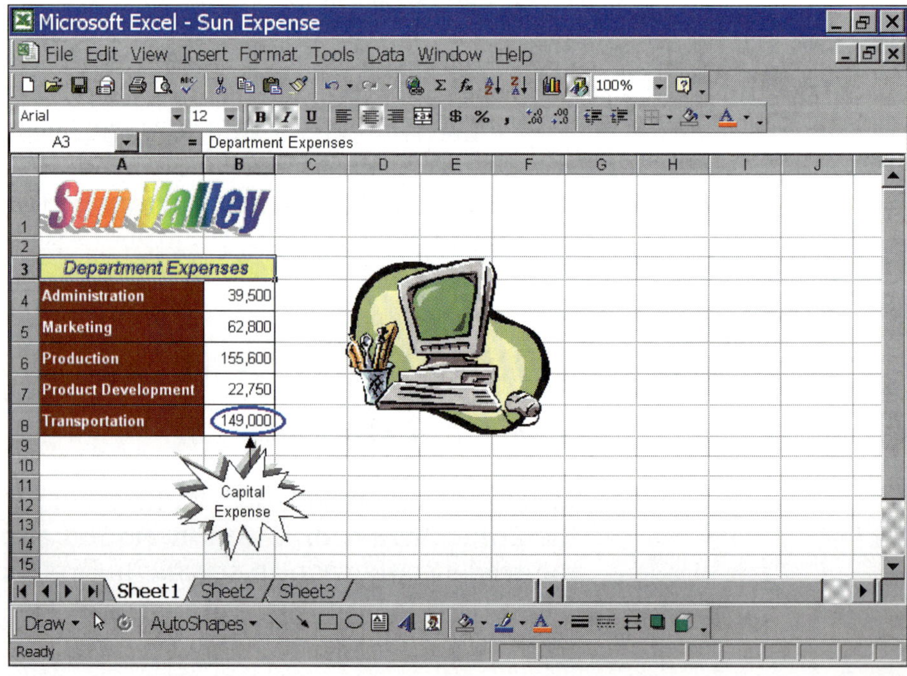

5.9.4 Lakeside Realty: Offer to Purchase Results

In addition to formatting numbers and dates in a worksheet, you practice creating custom number formats in this exercise.

1. Open the data file named EXC594.
2. Save the workbook as "Purchase Results" to your personal storage location.
3. Let's make the column headings in row 4 easier to read. To start, select the cell range from A4 to E4. Then, using the Format Cells dialog box, center horizontally and wrap the text appearing in the selected cells.
4. Apply a currency number format, with no decimal places, to the cell range from C5 to D10.
5. You will now create and apply a custom number format:
   SELECT: cell range from A5 to A15
   CHOOSE: Format, Cells
   CLICK: *Number* tab, if it is not already selected
6. In the *Category* list box:
   SELECT: Custom
   DOUBLE-CLICK: "General" in the *Type* text box
   PRESS: DELETE
7. To create a new number format that displays the realty office's initials in front of each contract number:
   TYPE: **LR-#####**
   CLICK: OK command button
   Notice that each contract now appears with the letters "LR-" in front.
8. Let's enter the next contract number:
   SELECT: cell A11
   TYPE: **14100**
   PRESS: ➡
   Notice that the entry displays as "LR-14100."
9. On your own, apply a custom format to the date range from E5 to E15 so that the date "5/7/00" in cell E5 appears as "Sun-07."
10. Save and then close the workbook.

5.9.5 On Your Own: 4-Wheel Rentals

In order to practice formatting text and numbers, you are now asked to open an existing workbook, make formatting changes and enhancements, create a style, insert a clip art image, save the workbook, and then send it to the printer. To begin, open the data file named EXC595 and then save it as "4WRentals" to your personal storage location.

Perform the following steps to enhance the worksheet:

- Replace the title in cell A1 with a WordArt object that is centered above the monthly columns.
- Apply a currency number format, with no decimal places, to the values appearing in rows 5 and 8.
- Apply a comma number format, with the thousands separator but no decimal places, to the values appearing in rows 6 and 7.
- Apply the "Classic 2" AutoFormat option to the worksheet's table area, but do not alter the existing number formats or width and height of columns and rows.
- Create a style named "Baseline" from the formatted contents of cell A8, but do not include the number or protection attributes. Then, apply the new style to the cell range B8 to G8.
- Insert a related clip art image to appear below the table area.

Save the workbook and then send it to the printer. When satisfied with the printed output, close the workbook.

5.9.6 On Your Own: Communications Survey

An associate has asked that you review and modify a departmental Excel chart. After opening the EXC596 data file, you review and save the friend's workbook as "Comm Survey" to your personal storage location. To display the chart, you click on the *Chart1* tab appearing at the bottom of the worksheet window. Immediately, you notice some features that you'd like to change. In particular, you perform the following steps:

- Change the chart type to a clustered column with a 3-D visual effect.
- Change the title to "Weekly Usage of Communications Technology."
- Format the title to appear in an 18-point font size, boldface, and italic.
- Move the legend to the bottom of the chart.
- Format the legend to appear in a larger font and with a shadow and fill color. (*Note:* You may have to size the legend to view its contents.)
- Make the "More Than 10" data series color lighter.

When you are finished, save and print the chart sheet. Then, close the "Comm Survey" workbook. If you are not proceeding to the case problems, exit Microsoft Excel.

5.10 Case Problems: Ponderosa Canyon

The Ponderosa Canyon Chamber of Commerce has made up its mind to invest in creating a professional information package for local and national distribution. A local business owner, Wendy Manuel, has been asked to lead the project and investigate ways of attracting both potential businesses and tourists. Having gathered some important statistics, Wendy is now in the process of summarizing and presenting her results using the graphical features of Excel.

In the following case problems, assume the role of Wendy and perform the same steps that she identifies. You may want to re-read the chapter opening before proceeding.

1. Wendy is taking her newfound responsibility very seriously. She has garnered input from small business owners and from members of several community service groups. With the help of a friend at the local college, she has also finished compiling a workbook of key statistics for the area. Now she wants to improve the appearance of the worksheet for inclusion in the information package.

    To begin, Wendy opens the EXC5X1 data file and then saves the workbook as "Fast Facts" to her personal storage location. For her initial objective, Wendy wants to insert a few labels on the worksheet. She clicks the AutoShapes button on the Drawing toolbar and then chooses the Callouts menu. After selecting and inserting the AutoShape object named "Rounded Rectangular Callout" to the right of the "Schools" area, Wendy types "Regional College" and watches as the callout expands automatically. She sizes and formats the object so that each word appears centered on its own line. Then, she drags the object's yellow selection handle to point its stem toward cell B12. Lastly, she applies formatting to emphasize the callout.

    On the same worksheet, Wendy uses WordArt to insert a title at the top of the page. After selecting a suitable style in the Word-Art Gallery dialog box, she enters the words "Fast Facts" and selects an interesting typeface and font size. Wendy finds that she must increase the height of row 1 in order to place the object neatly in the row. She also fine-tunes the title by sizing the WordArt object. Satisfied with the visual balance of the worksheet, Wendy saves and then closes the workbook.

2. Last year, the Tourist Information Center displayed a guest book and welcomed visitors to sign in and provide comments or suggestions. Using this guest book, Wendy was able to identify the number and origin of visitors. Having entered this

information into a worksheet, Wendy now wants to create a visual representation of the data using Excel's charting capabilities. She opens the EXC5X2 data file and then saves the workbook as "Visitors" to her personal storage location.

Wendy begins by selecting the cell range (A3:B7) containing the visitor information and then launches the Chart Wizard. After viewing several different chart types, Wendy decides on using the "Exploded Pie" style and proceeds through the wizard. She entitles the chart "Visitor Origins" and makes sure to create it as a new sheet.

Wendy feels that the chart needs to be beautified before including it with the other promotional material. She decides to apply some basic formatting. First, she specifies a Fill Color for the Chart area and then increases the title's font size to 36 points. She formats the legend by sizing it and then choosing the same fill color with no border lines. Stepping away from her monitor to view the chart from another perspective, Wendy decides to apply even further formatting to the legend. Once completed, the chart sheet appears similar to Figure 5.26. Wendy saves and then closes the "Visitors" workbook.

Figure 5.26

Creating an exploded

pie chart

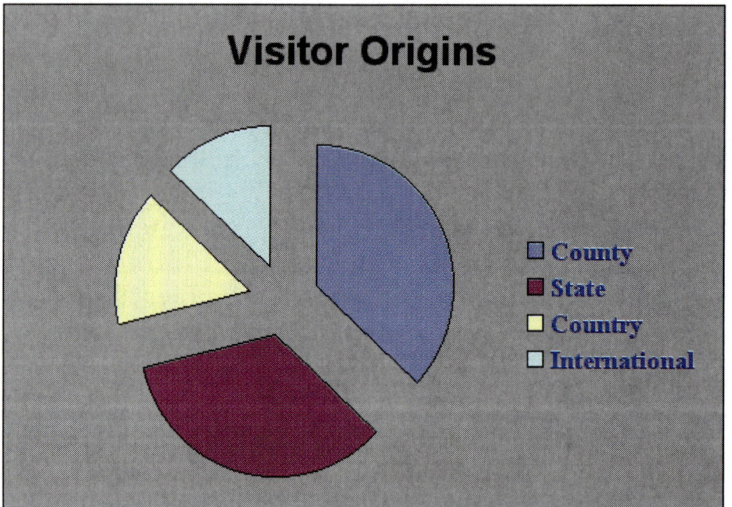

3. After she comes back from lunch, Wendy notices that a new diskette has been placed on her desk. The diskette label reads "Market Occupancy Levels" and the attached note tells her that it is from the Tourism Information Center. She opens the EXC5X3 workbook that is stored on the diskette and then saves it as "Occupancy" to her personal storage location. After reviewing the table of numbers, Wendy selects the data range and launches the Chart Wizard. She decides to use a line chart to show how the occupancy levels progressed over the season

for each category. She accepts all the Chart Wizard's suggested defaults for the first three steps, but chooses to store the chart on a separate chart sheet.

Although the line chart is practical, Wendy believes that a stacked column chart will better display the cumulative occupancies for the entire region. After changing the chart's type, she moves the legend to the bottom of the chart and then selects the plot area by clicking on its gray background. She reduces the height of the plot area by grabbing the center sizing handle at the top of the plot area and dragging it downwards. Then, she applies formatting to the axes using an Arial 12-point font and to the legend using a Times New Roman 14-point font. To finish off the chart, she adds a WordArt title of "Occupancy Levels" to the top. She then saves and closes the workbook.

4. During last year's Cattle Drive, the Chamber of Commerce conducted a survey to gauge the effectiveness of their advertising efforts. Visitors were asked to fill in a form indicating how they had heard of the event. Wendy has created a chart to summarize the results, but feels that it needs some changes. She opens the EXC5X4 workbook and saves it as "Survey" to her personal storage location.

   Looking over the chart, Wendy sees that the information for Radio advertising is missing. She displays the *Data* worksheet by clicking its sheet tab, adds a new row category for "Radio," and enters a value of 633. Once completed, she switches back to the *Chart* sheet and adds this new data series to the chart. The chart is updated automatically.

   Wendy determines that the chart might be more effective as a three-dimensional bar chart. After converting the chart, Wendy deletes the legend, removes the data labels, and formats the axes to use a larger font. She then selects and increases the size of the chart's plot area. Satisfied with the chart's new appearance, she prints the chart sheet and then saves and closes the workbook. The information package is shaping up nicely! Wendy exits Excel and decides to take the rest of the day off.

Notes

Notes

Notes

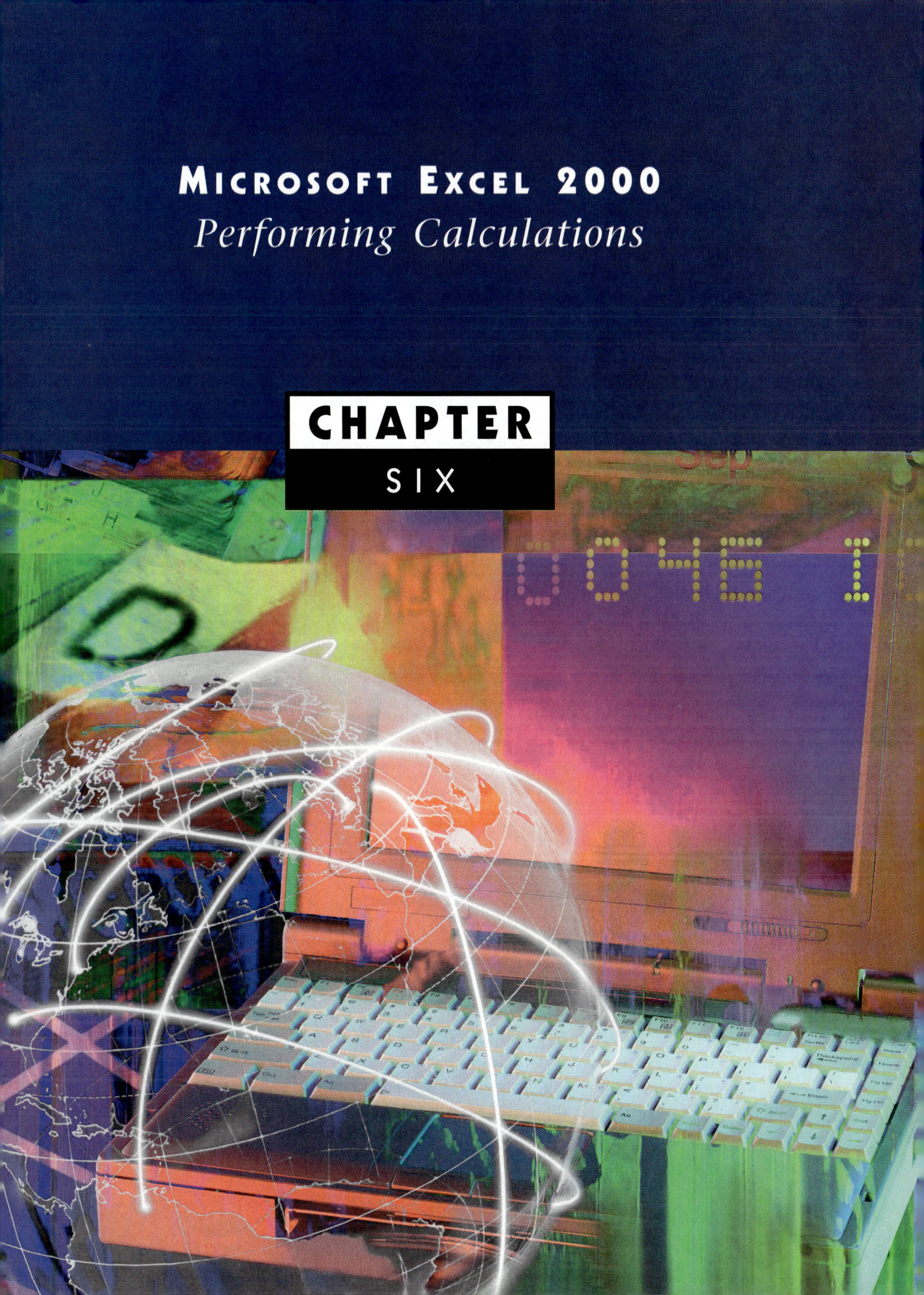

MICROSOFT EXCEL 2000
Performing Calculations
CHAPTER
SIX

Chapter Outline

6.1 Working with Formulas and Functions

6.2 Using Date and Time Functions

6.3 Using Mathematical and Statistical Functions

6.4 Using Text Manipulation Functions

6.5 Using Financial and Logical Functions

6.6 Chapter Review

6.7 Review Questions

6.8 Hands-On Projects

6.9 Case Problems

Learning Objectives

After reading this chapter, you will be able to:

- Construct nested expressions using typing, pointing, the Formula Palette, and the Paste Function dialog box

- Use date and time functions, including DATE, DAY, MONTH, YEAR, WEEKDAY, and TIME

- Use mathematical and statistical functions, including ROUND, RAND, and INT

- Use text functions, including LEN, SEARCH, LEFT, MID, and RIGHT, to extract character strings

- Use text functions, including LOWER, PROPER, and UPPER, to convert the case of an entry

- Use financial functions, including PV, FV, and PMT

- Use the logical IF function to make decisions

Case Study

Synergy Computer Supplies Ltd.

Jackson White graduated with honors from St. John's College in the spring of 1999. It wasn't until last month, however, that he received his first job offer and began working for Synergy Computer Supplies in Baltimore. In the months prior to accepting the position, Jackson studied vigorously to update his skills in Microsoft Excel 2000. Not surprisingly, his dedication and commitment paid off with an offer to become the assistant controller for Synergy.

Synergy's commitment to its customers is what has made the company a smashing success in the past three years. Their growth chart has exceeded even the company founder's expectations. However, the administrative system hasn't kept up with the increased transactions and paper flow in the office. One of Jackson's first duties will be to automate some of the more common procedures being performed by the sales staff. Having just finished an Excel refresher course, Jackson is ready to put the electronic spreadsheet to work for Synergy's staff.

In this chapter, you and Jackson learn how to use a variety of Excel's built-in functions. Specifically, you practice entering date and time values, performing mathematical and statistical calculations, manipulating text labels, analyzing financial transactions, and testing worksheet values using the logical IF function. By the end of this chapter, you will be confident in your ability to construct and enter complex formulas and functions.

6.1 Working with Formulas and Functions

Early on in your discovery of Excel, you learned that entering a formula required typing an equal sign (=) followed by the expression you wanted to evaluate. As you may have already guessed, there is a little more to performing calculations than simply adding and subtracting cell addresses in a worksheet. In this chapter, you practice constructing formulas and implementing Excel's multitude of built-in functions.

A formula is comprised of *operands* and *operators*. An **operand** is a **constant** value (i.e., any number, date, or text entry), a range name, or a cell address that you enter into the formula. An **operator** is the symbol used to determine what calculation to perform on the operand(s). Excel provides four types of calculation operators—arithmetic (which is the focus of this chapter), comparison, text, and reference. When

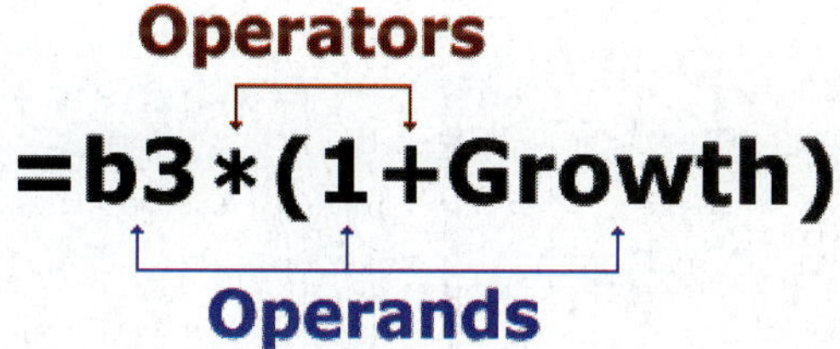

you combine two or more operators in the same expression, Excel performs the calculation according to the operator **order of precedence** shown in Table 6.1. For those instances where an expression contains operators of the same precedence (multiplication and division or addition and subtraction), Excel evaluates the expression from left to right. You can force a portion of an expression to evaluate first, superseding the order of precedence, by placing it within parentheses (as shown above). This process, called *nesting*, is discussed in the first lesson.

Table 6.1

Operators in order
of precedence

Calculated	Symbols	Descriptions
First	%	Percent operator; converts a value to a percentage by dividing it by 100 (e.g., 20% is equal to 0.20)
Second	^	Exponentiation operator; raises the base value to the power specified (e.g., 3^2 is equal to 9 and 4^3 is equal to 64)
Third	* and /	Multiplication and Division operators; performs a calculation using operands on either side of the operator
Fourth	+ and −	Addition and Subtraction operators; performs a calculation using operands on either side of the operator
Fifth	&	Concatenation operator for text; joins two character strings together

The most common methods for entering a formula are *typing* and *pointing*. In typing a formula, the entire expression is typed on the keyboard, including the equal sign, operands, and operators. For entering functions, type the function name and then place its arguments within parentheses. (*Hint:* A useful rule of thumb is to never insert spaces when entering a formula expression.) The pointing method uses both the keyboard and the mouse. After typing the equal sign, the expression is constructed by clicking on the desired cells (operands) and typing the required operators. You can also type a function's name, followed by a left parenthesis, and then use pointing to select the cells or ranges to include as the function's arguments. When finished, remember to place a right closing parenthesis at the end of the function's argument list.

Because entering a function correctly requires that you adhere to its syntax rules, most people prefer to engage the Paste Function dialog box or Formula Palette for assistance. These two tools are especially helpful when you can't remember the name of a particular function or when you need to be reminded of its argument list. Another technique that can help you enter functions is to use range names in place of cell addresses in the argument list. To illustrate, the expression =SUM(Donations) is much easier to read and understand than =SUM(AC12:DC239). In this module, you practice creating, nesting, displaying, and printing formulas and functions.

6.1.1 Nesting Formulas and Functions

FEATURE

Parentheses enable you to control the order by which portions of an expression are evaluated. For example, the formula =4+3*2 is equal to 10, because the order of precedence states that multiplication (3*2) is performed before addition. To force the addition to take place first, insert parentheses into the formula so that it reads =(4+3)*2. The new result is 14. The process of using parentheses to force the order of calculation within an expression is called **nesting.** In addition to affecting the calculation order, parentheses also offer the benefit of making your formula expressions easier to read and understand.

PRACTICE

In addition to nesting calculations, you use Excel's *Range Finder* feature to help identify a formula's operands.

Setup: Ensure that Excel is loaded.

1 Open the data file named EXC611.

2 Save the workbook as "Enderby Wines" to your personal storage location.

3 For review, use the typing method to enter a function in the worksheet:
SELECT: cell B8
TYPE: =sum(b5:b7)
PRESS: ENTER
(*Hint:* Check your results with the screen graphic in Figure 6.1.)

4 Now use the pointing method to enter a formula that references the total payroll value from the "Payroll Costs" table:
SELECT: cell B15
TYPE: =
CLICK: cell I7
PRESS: ENTER
Notice that the expression is built dynamically in Excel's Formula bar as you type and click on cells.

5 To add together the expenses, use the SUM function:
SELECT: cell B17
TYPE: =sum(

6 You may now specify the function's arguments by pointing:
SELECT: cell range from B11 to B16 using the mouse
TYPE:)
PRESS: ENTER

7 To finish the column entries:
SELECT: cell B19
TYPE: =
CLICK: cell B8 (Total Revenue)
TYPE: -
CLICK: cell B17 (Total Expenses)
PRESS: ENTER

8 Nesting allows you to construct more complex expressions. To begin, let's review a cell that contains a nested formula:
SELECT: cell H4
PRESS: F2 EDIT key
Your screen should now appear similar to Figure 6.1. Notice that the formula's worksheet operands are color-coded and that these colors correspond to the cell borders highlighted in the worksheet. This feature of Excel, called **Range Finder,** is especially useful when you need to identify whether a calculation is drawing data from the correct cells. In this formula, an employee's bonus is computed by adding five percent of their salary to one percent of the total revenue for the year.

Figure 6.1

Viewing operands and
operators in a formula
expression

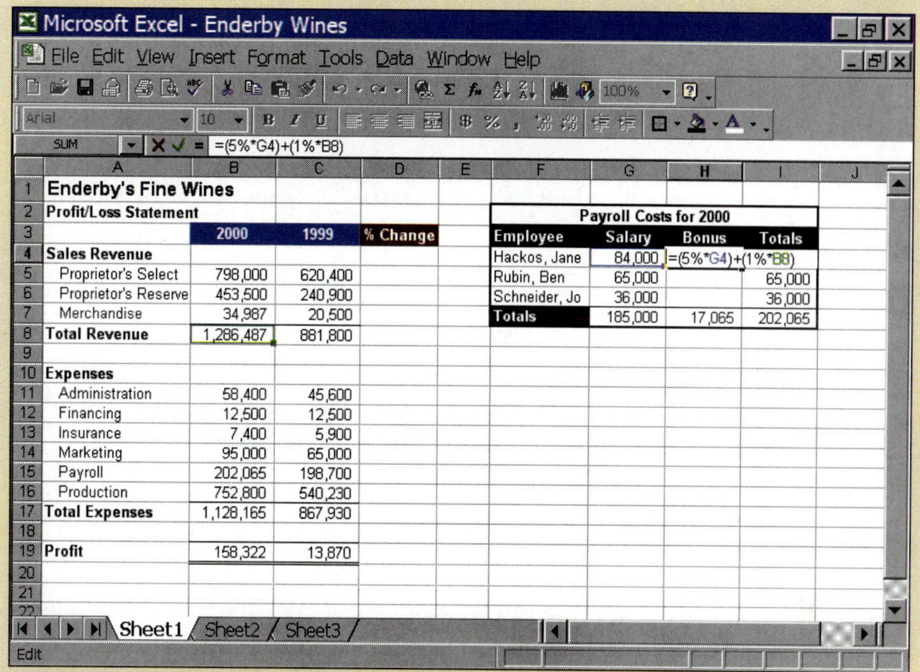

9 Let's enter the bonus calculation as displayed in Figure 6.1 by
typing:
PRESS: ESC to exit the Edit mode for cell H4
SELECT: cell H5
TYPE: =(5%*g5)+(1%*b8)
PRESS: ENTER
Notice that the parentheses group the calculations, making the
formula easier to read.

10 To enter the same formula expression by pointing:
SELECT: cell H6
TYPE: =(5%*
CLICK: cell G6
TYPE:)+(1%*
CLICK: cell B8
TYPE:)
PRESS: ENTER
You may agree that it is easier to type this formula than to keep
reaching for the mouse to click on cells.

 For additional practice in using nesting, calculate the percentage change that occurs between the two years displayed in the income statement.:
SELECT: cell D5
TYPE: =(
PRESS: ← twice to select cell B5
TYPE: -
PRESS: ← once to select cell C5
TYPE:)/
PRESS: ← once to select cell C5
PRESS: ENTER
As demonstrated, it is sometimes easier to point to cells using the keyboard than using the mouse.

 To copy this formula to the remaining cells:
SELECT: cell D5
CLICK: Copy button ([icon]) on the Standard toolbar
SELECT: cell range from D6 to D8
PRESS: CTRL and hold it down
SELECT: cell range from D11 to D17
SELECT: cell D19
Multiple ranges should be highlighted, as shown in Figure 6.2.
(*Hint:* Remember to release the CTRL key before proceeding.)

Figure 6.2

Copying a formula to
several cell ranges

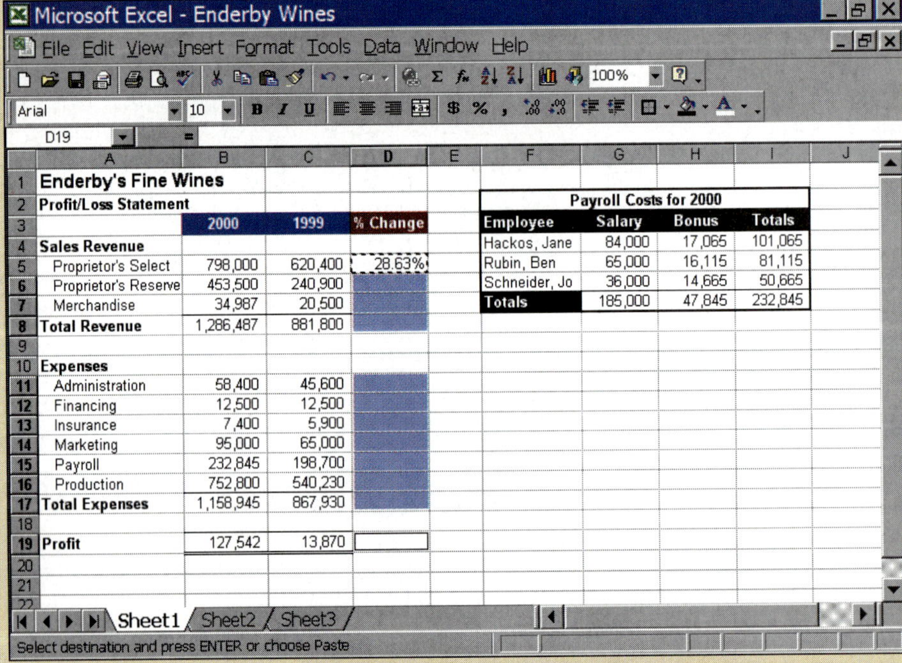

 To complete the copy operation:
CLICK: Paste button ([icon]) on the Standard toolbar

 To remove the highlighting from the worksheet:
PRESS: ESC to remove the dashed marquee
PRESS: CTRL + HOME to move the cell pointer

Save the workbook and keep it open for use in the next lesson.

6.1.2 Displaying and Printing Formulas and Functions

FEATURE

By default, Excel displays only the results of a formula or function in a worksheet cell. But for documentation purposes, you may want to display and print the actual formula expressions. Fortunately, Excel allows you to change the display and print a hard copy of these entries. You can then annotate the printout with handwritten notes and store it away as a paper backup for the original workbook.

METHOD

1. CHOOSE: Tools, Options
2. CLICK: *View* tab
3. SELECT: *Formulas* check box in the *Window options* area
4. CLICK: OK command button
5. CLICK: Print button (🖨) on the Standard toolbar, if desired

PRACTICE

In this lesson, you display formulas in a worksheet and then print the results.

Setup: Ensure that you've completed the previous lesson and that the "Enderby Wines" workbook is displayed.

 To display the Options dialog box (Figure 6.3):
CHOOSE: Tools, Options
CLICK: *View* tab

EXCEL

Figure 6.3

Options dialog box

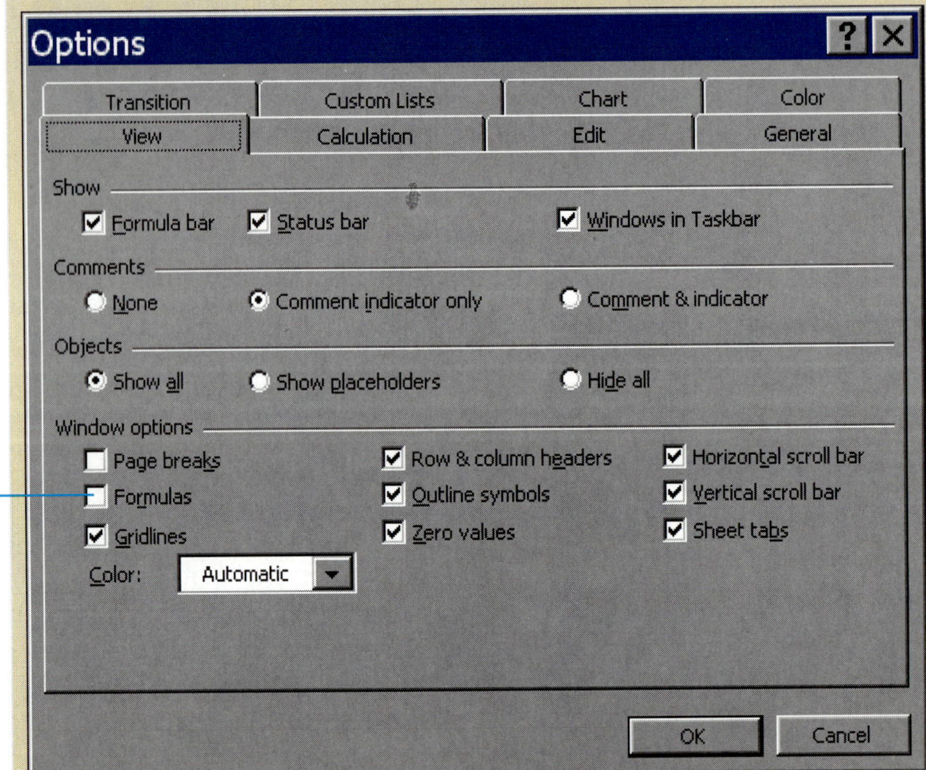

Select this check box to display formulas in your worksheet.

2 To display the formula expressions appearing in cells:
SELECT: *Formulas* check box so that a "✔" appears
CLICK: OK command button
The worksheet should now appear with formulas displayed.

3 With the cell pointer in cell A1, change the width of the first column:
CHOOSE: Format, Column, AutoFit Selection

4 On your own, reduce the widths for columns B, C, and D to eight characters. Then, scroll through the worksheet and review the cell entries.

5 You can customize the worksheet page and then preview how it will appear when printed:
CHOOSE: File, Page Setup
CLICK: *Sheet* tab
SELECT: *Gridlines* check box in the *Print* area
SELECT: *Row and column headings* check box in the *Print* area
CLICK: Print Preview command button
The worksheet appears in the Preview window.

6 Zoom in on the worksheet to view the printed formulas. Your screen should now appear similar to Figure 6.4.

Figure 6.4

Previewing worksheet formulas

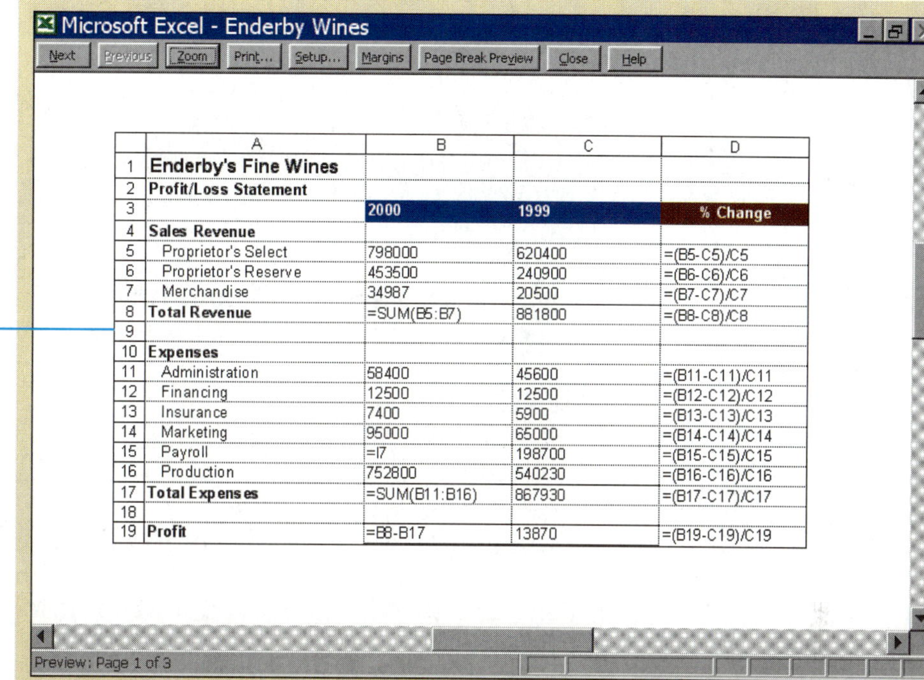

	A	B	C	D
1	**Enderby's Fine Wines**			
2	**Profit/Loss Statement**			
3		2000	1999	% Change
4	**Sales Revenue**			
5	Proprietor's Select	798000	620400	=(B5-C5)/C5
6	Proprietor's Reserve	453500	240900	=(B6-C6)/C6
7	Merchandise	34987	20500	=(B7-C7)/C7
8	**Total Revenue**	=SUM(B5:B7)	881800	=(B8-C8)/C8
9				
10	**Expenses**			
11	Administration	58400	45600	=(B11-C11)/C11
12	Financing	12500	12500	=(B12-C12)/C12
13	Insurance	7400	5900	=(B13-C13)/C13
14	Marketing	95000	65000	=(B14-C14)/C14
15	Payroll	=I7	198700	=(B15-C15)/C15
16	Production	752800	540230	=(B16-C16)/C16
17	**Total Expenses**	=SUM(B11:B16)	867930	=(B17-C17)/C17
18				
19	**Profit**	=B8-B17	13870	=(B19-C19)/C19

Preview: Page 1 of 3

Include the column and row frame areas, along with gridlines, to help you line up information in the worksheet printout.

7 If you have a printer connected to your computer, perform the following instruction. Otherwise, click the Close command button and proceed to the next step:
CLICK: Print command button in the toolbar
CLICK: OK command button

8 To reset the worksheet window:
CHOOSE: Tools, Options
SELECT: *Formulas* check box so that no "✔" appears
CLICK: OK command button

9 Close the workbook without saving the changes.

6.1 Self Check   Provide two reasons for nesting a calculation in a formula expression.

6.2 Using Date and Time Functions

Date and time functions enable you to perform calculations using date and time values and to format, present, and convert results in a variety of ways. In addition to entering a serial date value, you can use the functions in this module to extract the year, month, day, and weekday from a particular date. You also learn to use functions in evaluating date and time expressions.

6.2.1 Entering a Date (DATE)

FEATURE

The DATE function returns a serial date value given three separate arguments for the year, month, and day. Once calculated, you format the result to appear as a date rather than a serial number. The DATE function is especially useful for calculating the difference between two dates and for constructing date values from worksheet entries.

METHOD

=DATE(*year,month,day*)

PRACTICE

You now practice entering the DATE function.

Setup: Ensure that no workbooks appear in the application window.

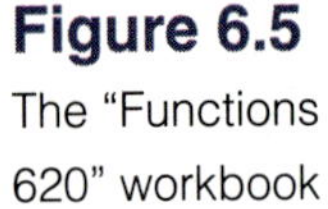 Open the data file named EXC620.

Save the workbook as "Functions 620" to your personal storage location. This workbook (Figure 6.5) provides a summary area for function syntax, sorted alphabetically, followed by an exercise area starting at row 10.

Figure 6.5

The "Functions 620" workbook

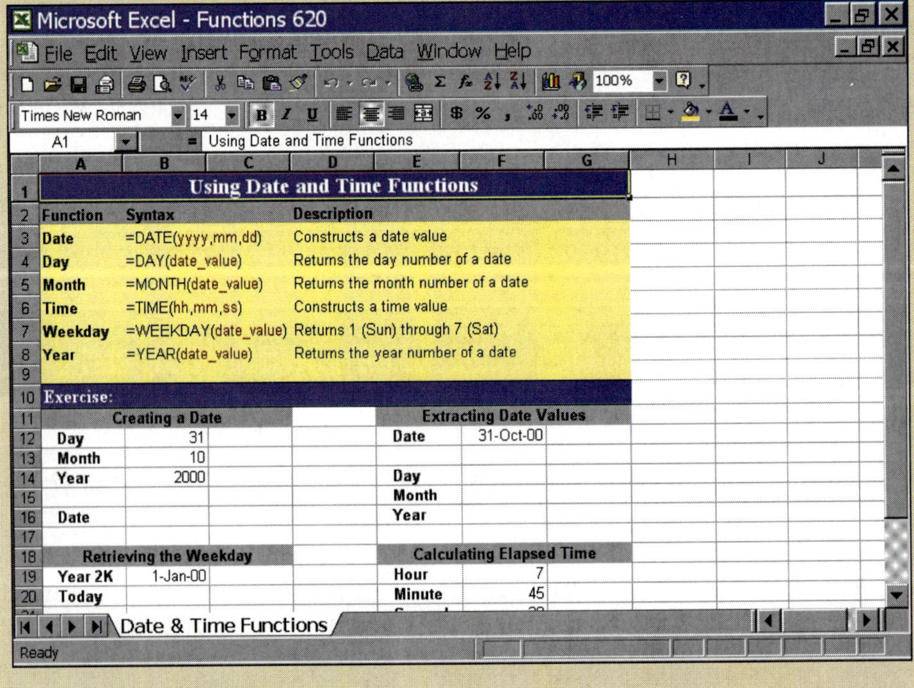

	A	B	C	D	E	F	G
1			**Using Date and Time Functions**				
2	**Function**	**Syntax**		**Description**			
3	Date	=DATE(yyyy,mm,dd)		Constructs a date value			
4	Day	=DAY(date_value)		Returns the day number of a date			
5	Month	=MONTH(date_value)		Returns the month number of a date			
6	Time	=TIME(hh,mm,ss)		Constructs a time value			
7	Weekday	=WEEKDAY(date_value)		Returns 1 (Sun) through 7 (Sat)			
8	Year	=YEAR(date_value)		Returns the year number of a date			
9							
10	**Exercise:**						
11		**Creating a Date**			**Extracting Date Values**		
12	Day	31		Date	31-Oct-00		
13	Month	10					
14	Year	2000		Day			
15				Month			
16	Date			Year			
17							
18		**Retrieving the Weekday**			**Calculating Elapsed Time**		
19	Year 2K	1-Jan-00		Hour	7		
20	Today			Minute	45		

3 After reviewing the function names and descriptions, scroll the window downward so that row 10 appears as the first row at the top of the worksheet.

4 Your objective in this step is to construct a date value from three separate arguments. To begin:
SELECT: cell B16
TYPE: =date(b14,b13,b12)
PRESS: ENTER
Notice that this cell has been formatted to display a date value, 31-Oct-00.

5 To change the date value:
SELECT: cell B13
TYPE: 12
PRESS: ENTER
You now have a dynamic date value that you can adjust by changing its individual arguments.

6 Let's do some date arithmetic. To display the number of days between the date appearing in cell B16 and today, do the following:
SELECT: cell C16
TYPE: =
PRESS: ← once
TYPE: -today()
PRESS: ENTER
Apart from the result being incorrectly formatted as a date, notice that you used a function as an operand in the formula expression.

7 To adjust the cell formatting:
SELECT: C16
CLICK: Comma Style button (,)
The correct answer now appears in cell C16.

8 Save the workbook and keep it open for use in the next lesson.

6.2.2 Extracting Date Values
(DAY, MONTH, and YEAR)

FEATURE
Working backwards from the last lesson, Excel provides three functions that you use to extract the day, month, and year values from
a particular date. These functions are used to display a date's component values separately in a worksheet or to calculate operands
for use in other formulas or functions.

METHOD
=DAY(*date_value*)
=MONTH(*date_value*)
=YEAR(*date_value*)

PRACTICE
You now extract the day, month, and year for a given date value.

Setup: Ensure that the "Functions 620" workbook is displayed.

1 Let's name the source cell to use in the following functions:
SELECT: cell F12
CLICK: in the Name box using the I-beam mouse pointer
TYPE: exDate
PRESS: ENTER

2 To return the day number from the date value:
SELECT: cell F14
TYPE: =day(exDate)
PRESS: ↓

3 To return the month number:
TYPE: =month(exDate)
PRESS: ↓

4 To return the year number:
TYPE: =year(exDate)
PRESS: ENTER

5 Let's change the original exDate value. To insert the current date
using a keyboard shortcut:
SELECT: cell F12
PRESS: CTRL + ;
PRESS: ENTER
Notice that the day, month, and year values are updated as soon
as the new value is entered.

6 Save the workbook and keep it open for use in the next lesson.

6.2.3 Calculating the Day of the Week (WEEKDAY)

FEATURE
The WEEKDAY function calculates the day of the week by returning a number between 1 (Sunday) and 7 (Saturday). For example, the function returns the number 4 if the date argument falls on a Wednesday. Another way of displaying the weekday is to apply the "ddd" or "dddd" custom format option to a standard date value.

METHOD
=WEEKDAY(*date_value*)

PRACTICE
Let's calculate the day of the week for two date values.

Setup: Ensure that the "Functions 620" workbook is displayed.

1 To insert the WEEKDAY function for the date appearing in cell B19:
SELECT: cell C19
CHOOSE: Insert, Function
The Paste Function dialog box appears.

2 To pick the desired function:
SELECT: Date & Time in the *Function category* list box
SELECT: Weekday in the *Function name* list box
CLICK: OK command button
The Formula Palette appears, as shown in Figure 6.6.

Figure 6.6

Entering the
WEEKDAY function

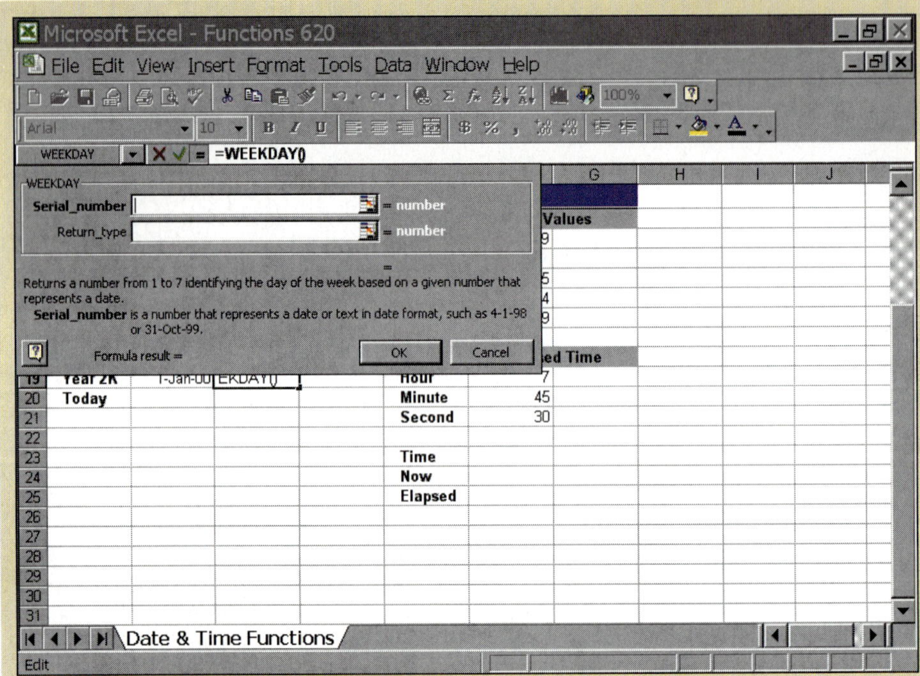

3 In the *Serial_number* text box:
TYPE: b19
Notice that the date's serial value, 36526, appears to the right of
the text box and the result, 7, appears near the bottom of the
Formula Palette.

4 To complete the Formula Palette:
CLICK: OK command button
The answer, 7 (for Saturday), appears in the cell.

5 To demonstrate another method for displaying the weekday, let's
insert the current date:
SELECT: cell B20
PRESS: CTRL + ;
PRESS: ENTER

6 You will now format the cell to display the weekday:
SELECT: cell B20
CHOOSE: Format, Cells
CLICK: *Number* tab
SELECT: Custom in the *Category* list box

7 To create a new custom format:
SELECT: the contents of the *Type* text box using the mouse
PRESS: DELETE to remove the existing entry
TYPE: dddd
CLICK: OK command button
The long name for the current day of the week should appear.
(*Hint:* Use the "ddd" custom format option to display the three-letter abbreviation for the weekday name.)

8 Save the workbook and keep it open for use in the next lesson.

6.2.4 Calculating Elapsed Time (TIME)

FEATURE
Similar to the DATE function, the TIME function returns a time value given three separate arguments for hour, minute, and second. You specify the hour argument using the range 0 to 23, the time argument using 0 to 59, and the second argument using 0 to 59. You can use this function to calculate the elapsed time between two time values.

METHOD
=TIME(*hour,minute,second*)

PRACTICE
In this lesson, you create an expression that calculates the amount of time to elapse between two values.

Setup: Ensure that the "Functions 620" workbook is displayed.

1 To enter the TIME function by typing:
SELECT: cell F23
TYPE: =time(f19,f20,f21)
PRESS: ENTER
The time, 7:45 AM, appears in the formatted cell.

2 You can insert the current time into a cell using a keyboard shortcut:
SELECT: cell F24
PRESS: CTRL + :
PRESS: ENTER

3 To calculate the amount of time that has elapsed between these two time values:
SELECT: cell F25
TYPE: **=f24-f23**
PRESS: ENTER
Notice that the result inherits the source cells' time formatting.

4 To format the cell to display a more appropriate measuring unit:
SELECT: cell F25
CHOOSE: Format, Cells

5 On the *Number* tab of the dialog box:
SELECT: Time in the *Category* list box, if not already selected
SELECT: 37:30:55 in the *Type* list box
CLICK: OK command button
The number of hours, minutes, and seconds to elapse are now displayed. Your worksheet should appear similar, but not identical, to Figure 6.7.

6 Save and then close the workbook.

Figure 6.7

Completing the "Functions 620" worksheet

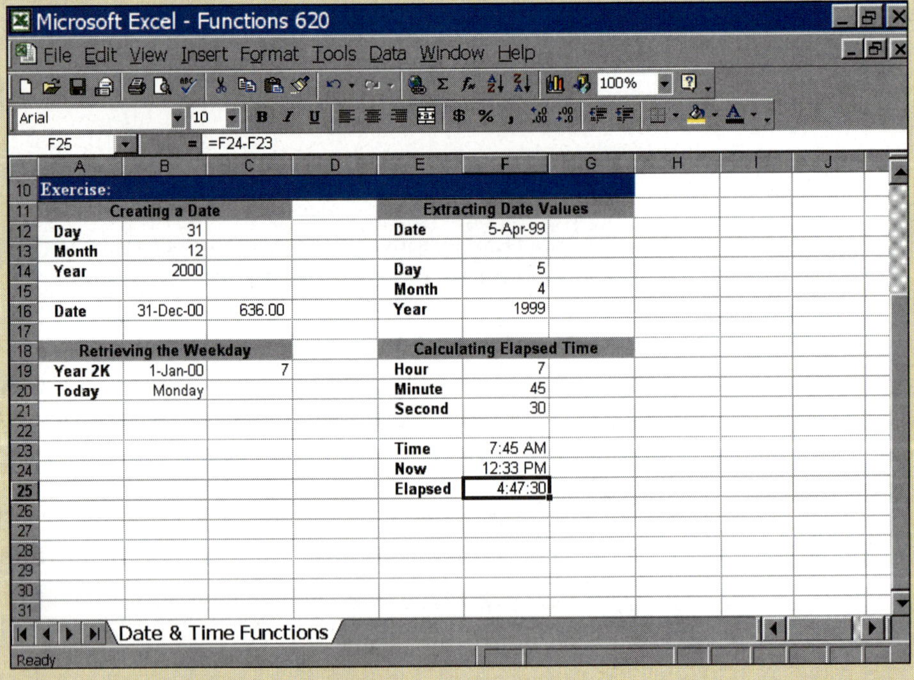

	A	B	C	D	E	F	G
10	Exercise:						
11		Creating a Date				Extracting Date Values	
12	Day	31			Date	5-Apr-99	
13	Month	12					
14	Year	2000			Day	5	
15					Month	4	
16	Date	31-Dec-00	636.00		Year	1999	
17							
18		Retrieving the Weekday				Calculating Elapsed Time	
19	Year 2K	1-Jan-00	7		Hour	7	
20	Today	Monday			Minute	45	
21					Second	30	
22							
23					Time	7:45 AM	
24					Now	12:33 PM	
25					Elapsed	4:47:30	

In Addition	Rather than performing date arithmetic, you can use Excel's
Calculating the Elapsed Number of Days, Months, and Years	DATEDIF(*start_date,end_date,unit*) function to calculate the difference between two dates. You can also choose how the answer is calculated and displayed in terms of the unit value (Years, Months, or Days). There exists no such function for calculating the difference between two times.

6.3 Using Mathematical and Statistical Functions

Excel's mathematical, trigonometric, and statistical functions serve many purposes. Whether you need to calculate the sides of a triangle, generate a list of random numbers, or calculate the standard deviations for an experimental research study, these functions can save you tremendous amounts of time and complexity. Only skimming the surface, you are introduced to the ROUND, RAND, and INT functions in this module. You also use the Paste Special command to convert a formula expression into its resulting value.

6.3.1 Rounding Values (ROUND)

FEATURE

The ROUND function returns the **rounded value** of a cell to the number of digits specified. If the number of digits is greater than 0, the value is rounded to the number of decimal places. If the number of digits is 0, the value is rounded to the nearest integer. If the number of digits is less than 0, the value is rounded to the left of the decimal point.

METHOD

=ROUND(*number,digits*)

PRACTICE

You now practice entering the ROUND function using the Paste Function dialog box.

Setup: Ensure that no workbooks appear in the application window.

1   Open the workbook named EXC630.

2   Save the workbook as "Functions 630" to your personal storage location. This workbook (Figure 6.8) provides a summary area for function syntax, in rows 1 through 6, followed by an exercise area starting at row 7.

Figure 6.8

The "Functions
630" workbook

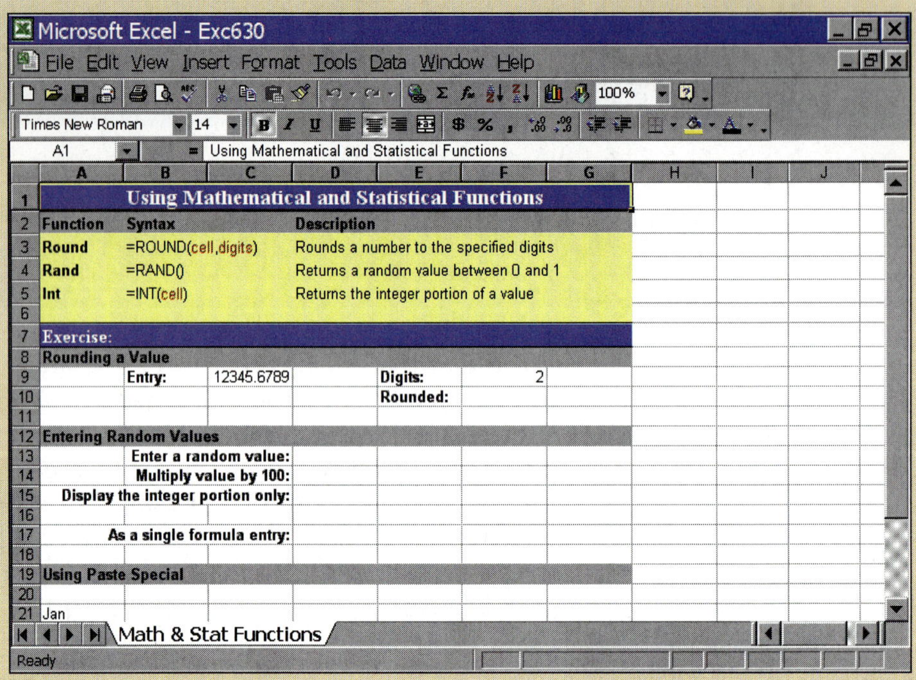

3 Your objective in the next few steps is to round the value
appearing in cell C9 to the number of digits displayed in cell F9.
Let's use the Paste Function dialog box to enter the ROUND
function:
SELECT: cell F10
CLICK: Paste Function button (f_x)

4 In the Paste Function dialog box:
SELECT: Math & Trig in the *Function category* list box
SELECT: ROUND in the *Function name* list box

5 To paste the selected function into the worksheet:
CLICK: OK command button
The Formula Palette appears.

6 In the *Number* text box, select a cell or input a value to round:
CLICK: Collapse Dialog button ([⬚]) in the Formula Palette
CLICK: cell C9
CLICK: Expand Dialog button ([⬚]) near the Formula bar
PRESS: TAB to move to the next text box
Notice that the function being built also appears in the
Formula bar.

7 In the *Num_digits* text box, select a cell or input a value to limit
the number of decimal places displayed:
TYPE: **F9**
The Formula Palette should now appear as shown in Figure 6.9.

Figure 6.9

Entering the ROUND function

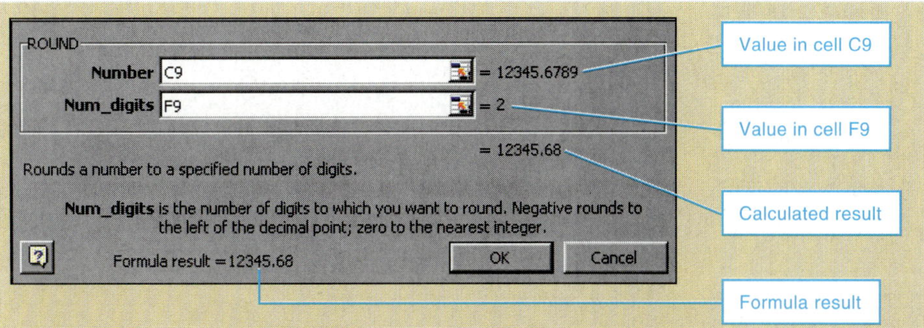

8 To complete the Formula Palette:
CLICK: OK command button
The result, 12345.68, is entered into cell F10.

9 To demonstrate how changing the digits affects the rounded result:
SELECT: cell F9
TYPE: **-2**
PRESS: ENTER
The result in cell F10 is updated to display 12300.

10 Save the workbook and keep it open for use in the next lesson.

6.3.2 Finding Random Values (RAND and INT)

FEATURE

The RAND function is used to calculate a **random number** between 0 and 1. Each time the worksheet is recalculated the RAND function will calculate a new random value. To manually force the worksheet to recalculate, press the F9 CALC key. The INT function returns the **integer value** of a number or cell. You use the INT function to round a number down to the nearest integer.

METHOD
=RAND()
=INT(cell)

PRACTICE

In this lesson, you calculate a random value between 0 and 100 and then return the integer portion of the value.

Setup: Ensure that the "Functions 630" workbook is displayed.

1 To begin, scroll the window downward so that row 7 appears as the first row at the top of the worksheet.

2 The RAND function enables you to generate random data for testing. To enter the function:
SELECT: cell D13
TYPE: `=rand()`
PRESS: ⬇
A value between 0 and 1 should now appear in the cell.

3 To display the random value as a number between 0 and 100:
TYPE: `=`
PRESS: ⬆
TYPE: `*100`
PRESS: ⬇
Notice that Excel updates the random value when you press ⬇.

4 The INT function, unlike ROUND, simply truncates the decimal portion of a value—no rounding takes place. To extract only the integer portion of cell D14, do the following:
TYPE: `=int(`
PRESS: ⬆
TYPE: `)`
PRESS: ENTER
Only the value to the left of the decimal point appears in cell D15.

5 Using a single formula, you can calculate a random value between 0 and 100 that displays to two decimal places only. To illustrate:
SELECT: cell D17
TYPE: `=round(rand()*100,2)`
PRESS: ENTER
A value between 0 and 100 should now appear. Notice that you nest the RAND function as an argument in the ROUND function.

6 To generate new values, do the following:
PRESS: F9 CALC key repeatedly
With each key press, new random values appear in the cells.

7 Save the workbook and keep it open for use in the next lesson.

In Addition
Finding the Absolute Value

The ABS(*value*) function returns the absolute or positive value for a cell, value, or expression. For example, the entry =ABS(-4) returns 4. Most often, you nest another formula or function within the ABS function to force a positive result.

6.3.3   Using Paste Special to Convert Data

FEATURE

After populating cells using the RAND function, you may wish to convert the results into values that no longer change with each recalculation. The Paste Special command enables you to copy a formula to the Clipboard and then paste the result back into the worksheet as a static value. You can also use the Paste Special command to transpose values from a column to row orientation or vice versa.

METHOD

1. SELECT: the desired cell or cell range
2. CLICK: Copy button (⧉)
3. SELECT: the desired target cell
4. CHOOSE: Edit, Paste Special
5. SELECT: *Transpose* check box to change the orientation of data
   SELECT: *Values* option button to convert formulas to values

PRACTICE

In this lesson, you practice transposing values in the worksheet and converting the results of a RAND function to static worksheet values.

Setup: Ensure that the "Functions 630" worksheet is displayed.

1   In the cell range from A21 to A26, the worksheet stores a list of month names. You can use the Paste Special command to transpose this columnar list to display on a single row. Do the following:
SELECT: cell range from A21 to A26

2   To copy the contents of the range to the Clipboard:
CLICK: Copy button (⧉) on the toolbar

3   To transpose the orientation of the selected cell range:
SELECT: cell B20
CHOOSE: Edit, Paste Special
SELECT: *Transpose* check box so that a "✔" appears
The dialog box should now appear similar to Figure 6.10.

Figure 6.10

Using the Paste
Special command

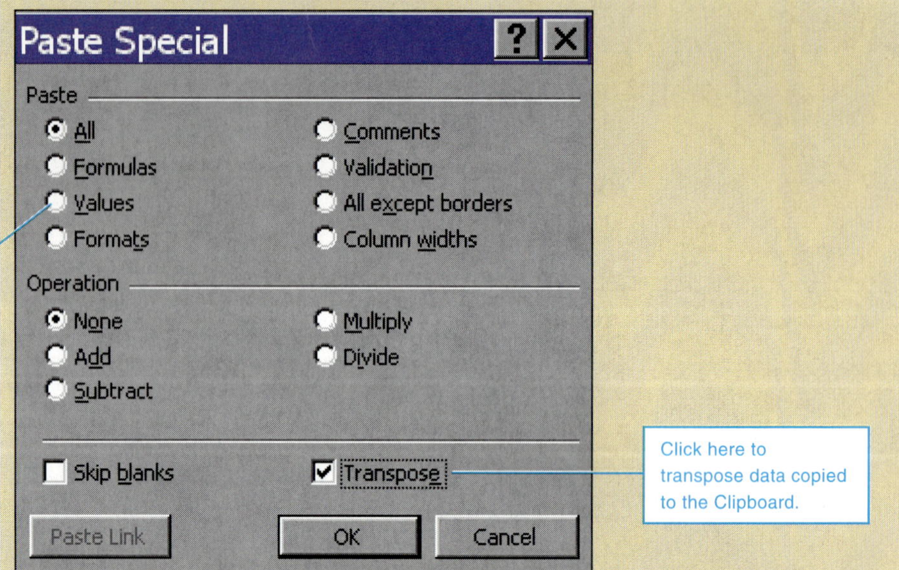

Click here to convert data
copied to the Clipboard to
their static values.

Click here to
transpose data copied
to the Clipboard.

4 To complete the operation:
CLICK: OK command button
PRESS: [ESC] to remove the dashed marquee

5 Let's fill a range with a table of random numbers. In this step,
you learn a shortcut for entering similar entries. Do the following:
SELECT: cell range from B21 to G26
TYPE: `=int(rand()*100)`
Although the entire range is selected, you enter a formula into
the top left-hand cell only.

6 To fill the selected range with the same formula expression:
PRESS: [CTRL] + [ENTER]
Your worksheet should resemble Figure 6.11.

Figure 6.10

Completing multiple entries using CTRL + ENTER

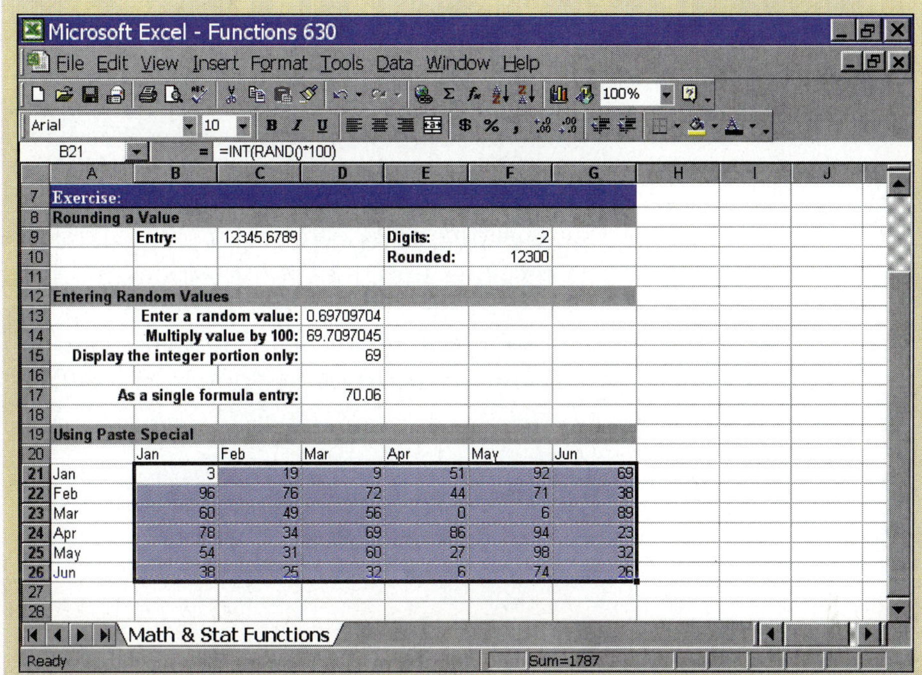

7 With the range still selected and highlighted:
PRESS: F9 CALC key repeatedly
Notice that the values are updated in the table.

8 To convert the selected table of random values to static values:
CLICK: Copy button ()
CHOOSE: Edit, Paste Special
SELECT: *Values* option button in the *Paste* area
CLICK: OK command button
(*Note:* Because the range for copying and pasting is the same, you effectively copy the formulas to the Clipboard and then paste the static values back over top of the same cells.)

9 On your own, press ESC to remove the highlighting and then click on the values in the table. Notice that these cells contain static values, as opposed to the RAND function entered in steps 5 and 6. (*Hint:* Look in the Formula bar to see the contents of the selected cell.)

10 Save and close the workbook.

6.4 Using Text Manipulation Functions

As a competent Excel user, you will most certainly be asked at some point to summarize information that has been entered by less experienced users or has been imported from different applications. Frequently, data from these sources requires "cleaning up" to make it presentable in reports. It is in these circumstances that you will find Excel's text functions to be extremely useful. These functions enables you to compare, convert, format, extract, and combine textual data. In this module, you learn how to manipulate text labels, also called **character strings,** in your worksheet.

6.4.1 Analyzing a String (LEN and SEARCH)

FEATURE

The LEN function returns the number of characters or spaces in a string. For example, the expression LEN("ABC") is equal to 3 and LEN("A B C") is equal to 5. While not used by itself very often, the LEN function helps you in calculating character positions and for extracting text using other functions. The SEARCH function is also used for locating character positions in a string.

METHOD

```
=LEN(text)
=SEARCH(find_text,text,start)
```

PRACTICE

You now practice entering the LEN and SEARCH text functions.

Setup: Ensure that no workbooks appear in the application window.

1   Open the data file named EXC640.

2   Save the workbook as "Functions 640" to your personal storage location. This workbook (Figure 6.12) provides a summary area for function syntax, in rows 1 through 13, followed by an exercise area starting at row 14.

Figure 6.12

The "Functions 640" workbook

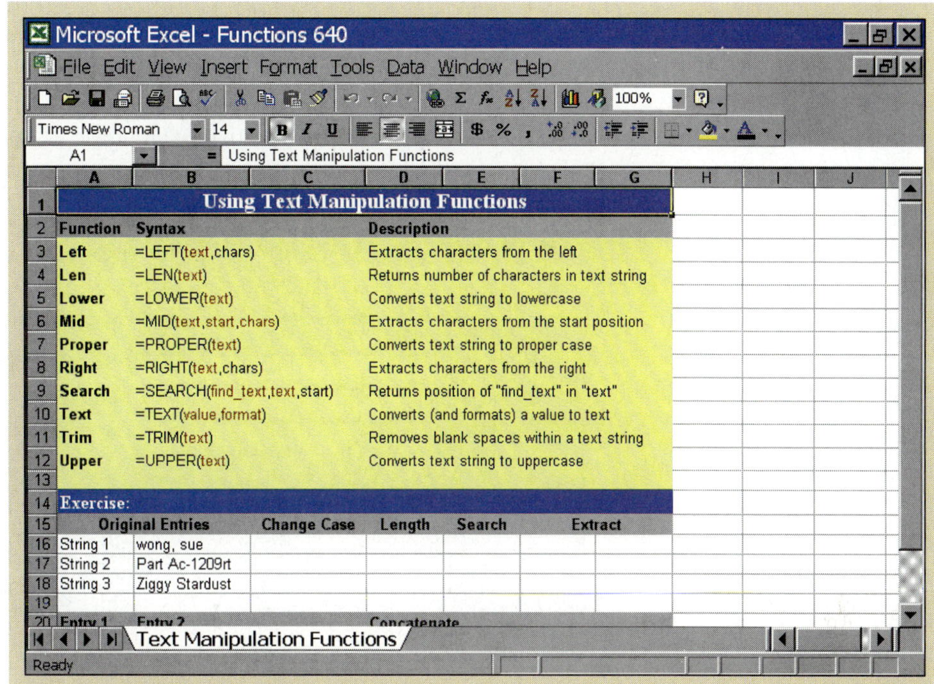

3 After reviewing the function names and descriptions, scroll the window downward so that row 14 appears as the first row at the top of the worksheet.

4 To calculate the length of a text label or string:
SELECT: cell D16
TYPE: =len(b16)
PRESS: ENTER
The result, 9, appears in the cell. Notice that the calculation included the comma and space in addition to the characters stored in cell B16.

5 To copy this formula to the other two rows:
SELECT: cell range from D16 to D18
CHOOSE: Edit, Fill, Down

6 To find the character position of the comma in cell B16:
SELECT: cell E16
TYPE: =search(
CLICK: Edit Formula button (=) in the Formula bar
The Formula Palette appears with the required prompts appearing in boldface lettering.

7 In the *Find_text* text box, enter the text surrounded by quotation marks that you want to search for in the cell:
TYPE: ","
PRESS: TAB

8 In the *Within_text* text box, enter the cell address containing the text label that you want to search:
TYPE: **b16**
The Formula Palette should now appear similar to Figure 6.13. Notice that the result, 5, already appears. In other words, the comma appears at the fifth character position of the contents in cell B16.

Figure 6.13

Entering the SEARCH

function

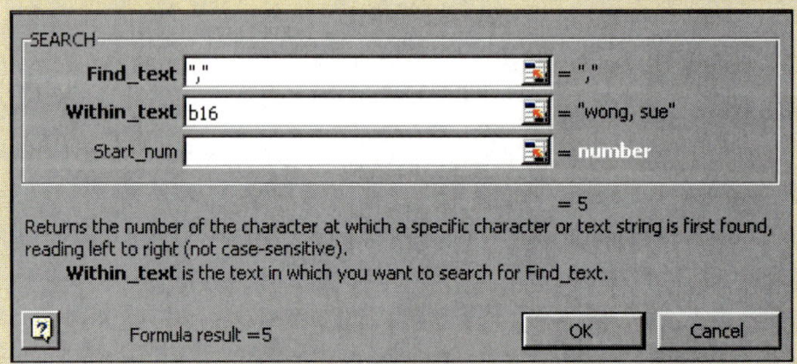

9 To complete the Formula Palette:
CLICK: OK command button

10 To find the character position of an empty space, you enter a space between quotation marks for the *Find_text* argument. In the next two steps, you enter the identical SEARCH function into cells E17 and E18 using the CTRL + ENTER keystroke. Do the following:
SELECT: cell range from E17 to E18
TYPE: **=search(" ",b17)**
Notice that you entered the relative cell address (B17) in order to calculate the search function for the active cell (E17).

11 To complete the operation:
PRESS: CTRL + ENTER

12 Save the workbook and keep it open for use in the next lesson.

6.4.2 Changing the Case (LOWER, PROPER, and UPPER)

FEATURE

Excel provides three functions for changing the case of text labels. The LOWER and UPPER functions return character strings in lowercase and uppercase, respectively. The PROPER function capitalizes the first character in each word of a character string. Once converted to the desired case, you may use the Paste Special command to permanently convert the values to the calculated result.

METHOD

=LOWER(*text*)
=PROPER(*text*)
=UPPER(*text*)

PRACTICE

Using these three functions, you now practice changing the case of text labels in a worksheet.

Setup: Ensure that the "Functions 640" workbook is displayed.

1 To convert the text label in cell B16 to proper case:
SELECT: cell C16
TYPE: =proper(b16)
PRESS: ENTER
The result, "Wong, Sue," appears in cell C16.

2 To convert the text label in cell B17 to uppercase:
SELECT: cell C17
TYPE: =upper(b17)
PRESS: ENTER
The result, "PART AC-1209RT," appears in cell C17. (*Note:* The entry may not fit within the column's display width.)

3 To convert the text label in cell B18 to lowercase:
SELECT: cell C18
TYPE: =lower(b18)
PRESS: ENTER
The result, "ziggy stardust," appears in cell C18.

4 To replace the text labels in column B with the calculated results in column C, do the following:
SELECT: cell range from C16 to C18
CLICK: Copy button (📋)

5 To paste the result of the copied formulas into column B:
SELECT: cell B16
CHOOSE: Edit, Paste Special
SELECT: *Values* option button in the *Paste* area
CLICK: OK command button

6 PRESS: `ESC` to remove the dashed marquee

7 Save the workbook and keep it open for use in the next lesson.

6.4.3 Extracting Characters (LEFT, MID, and RIGHT)

FEATURE

Imagine that you've received a worksheet that needs to be sorted by surname. Unfortunately, all of the data has been entered as "Firstname Lastname." To perform a sort, you must first extract the surname from each cell using a process called **parsing.** Excel provides three functions—LEFT, MID, and RIGHT—for use in parsing or extracting character strings in text labels.

METHOD

=LEFT(*text,characters*)
=MID(*text,start,characters*)
=RIGHT(*text,characters*)

PRACTICE

In addition to applying Excel's LEFT and RIGHT functions for extracting characters, you practice nesting functions in this lesson. Although not demonstrated, the MID function differs in that you provide a starting position for where to begin extracting characters.

Setup: Ensure that the "Functions 640" workbook is displayed.

1 Your first objective is to parse or separate the entry in cell B16 into two cells. To place the person's surname into cell F16:
SELECT: cell F16
TYPE: =left(
CLICK: Edit Formula button (`=`)
The Formula Palette appears for the LEFT function.

2 In the *Text* text box, specify the text that you want to parse:
TYPE: b16
PRESS: `TAB`

3 In the *Num_chars* text box, you enter the number of characters to extract from the first character position. Because you wouldn't know the exact length of each person's first name, you need to nest the SEARCH function within the LEFT function to find the character position of the comma. Do the following:
TYPE: search(",",b16)
Notice that the result, 5, appears to the right of the text box.

4 With the comma appearing at the fifth position, you need to tell the LEFT function to extract one less than this value:
TYPE: -1
The Formula Palette should appear as shown in Figure 6.14.

Figure 6.14

Entering the LEFT function

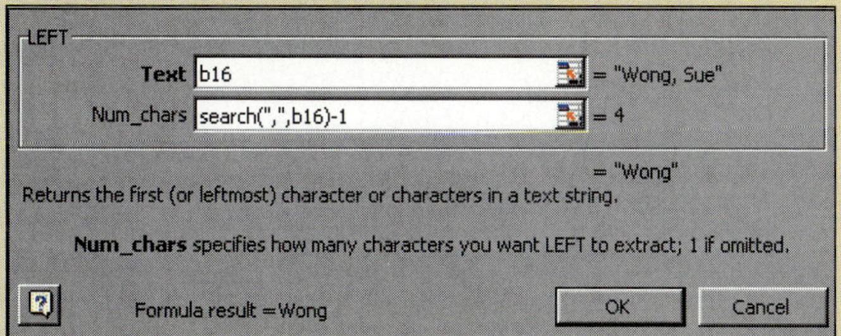

5 To complete the Formula Palette:
CLICK: OK command button

6 To demonstrate the dynamic nature of this function:
SELECT: cell B16
TYPE: Yashin, Steve
PRESS: ENTER
Notice that the function in cell F16 extracts the new last name.

7 To return the first name, you use the RIGHT function and then calculate how many characters to extract from right to left:
SELECT: cell G16
TYPE: =right(
CLICK: Edit Formula button (=)

8 In the *Text* text box:
TYPE: b16
PRESS: TAB

9 In the *Num_chars* text box, you enter the number of characters to extract from the last character position and moving left. To calculate this value, subtract the character position of the space from the length of the string. Do the following:
TYPE: `len(b16)-search(" ",b16)`
CLICK: OK command button
Looking in the Formula bar, notice that there are three functions—RIGHT, LEN, and SEARCH—nested in this one expression!

10 Using the previous steps as your guide, separate the word "Part" from the part number in cell B17 and place the results in cells F17 and G17. Then, parse the name entry in cell B18 so that the first and last names appear separately in cells F18 and G18. Your worksheet should appear similar to Figure 6.15 before proceeding.

Figure 6.15

Parsing text labels

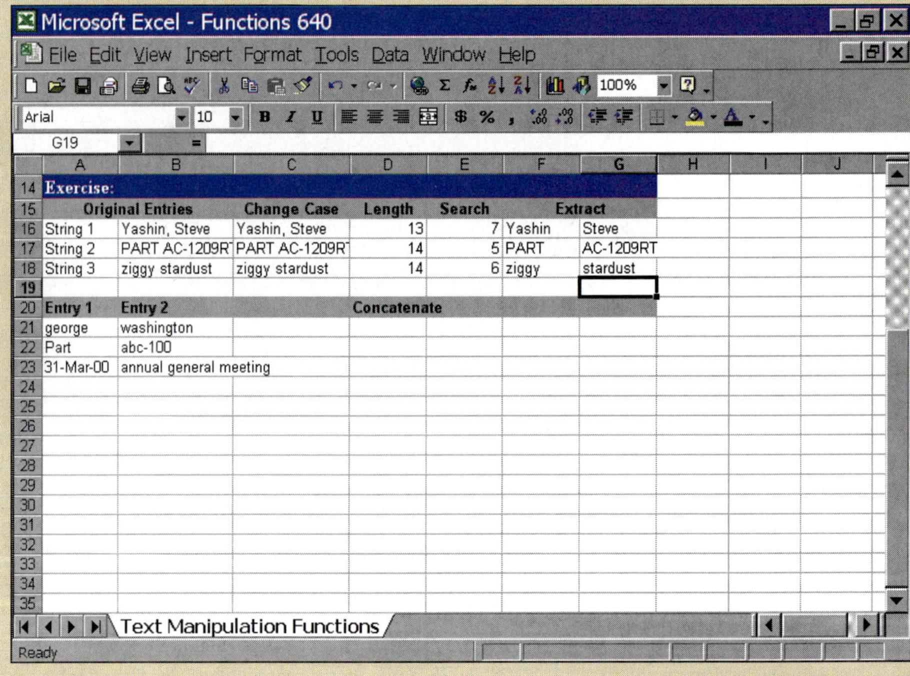

The worksheet shown in Figure 6.15 (Microsoft Excel - Functions 640, sheet "Text Manipulation Functions"):

	A	B	C	D	E	F	G
14	Exercise:						
15		Original Entries	Change Case	Length	Search	Extract	
16	String 1	Yashin, Steve	Yashin, Steve	13	7	Yashin	Steve
17	String 2	PART AC-1209R	PART AC-1209R	14	5	PART	AC-1209RT
18	String 3	ziggy stardust	ziggy stardust	14	6	ziggy	stardust
19							
20	Entry 1	Entry 2		Concatenate			
21	george	washington					
22	Part	abc-100					
23	31-Mar-00	annual general meeting					

 On your own, enter new values into cells B16, B17, and B18 to see the results of your function entries.

 Save the workbook and keep it open for use in the next lesson.

6.4.4 Concatenating Strings (&, TEXT, and TRIM)

FEATURE

In a process opposite to parsing, you can **concatenate** or join two text strings using the ampersand "&" operator or the CONCATE-NATE function. The ampersand is commonly used to join text entries with numeric values in a sentence-like structure. To do so, however, requires that you use the TEXT function to convert the value to a character string. You cannot, in other words, combine a text label with a numeric value directly. The TRIM function is used to remove any trailing blank spaces that may exist at the end of a text label.

METHOD

```
&
=TEXT(value,format)
=TRIM(text)
```

PRACTICE

In this lesson, you join labels and values using the amper-sand and TEXT function.

Setup: Ensure that the "Functions 640" workbook is displayed.

1 Joining two text labels together is an easy task. To do so:
SELECT: cell D21
TYPE: =a21&b21
PRESS: ENTER
Although the two cell entries are combined, notice that there is no space inserted between the first and last names.

2 Let's edit the expression to insert a space:
SELECT: cell D21
PRESS: F2 EDIT key
PRESS: ← three times
The flashing insertion point should be positioned to the immediate right of the ampersand.

3 To add a character space, you must insert another join:
TYPE: " "&
PRESS: ENTER
In the Formula bar, the expression =A21&" "&B21 returns
"george washington" in cell D21.

4 You can also nest functions when joining the cell entries:
SELECT: cell D22
TYPE: =a22&" "&upper(b22)
PRESS: ENTER
Notice that you use the UPPER function to convert the part
number to uppercase before joining it with the contents of cell
A22.

5 In order to join a date value (cell A23) with a text label (cell
B23), use the TEXT function to convert the date to a character
string:
SELECT: D23
TYPE: =proper(b23)&" is on "&text(a23,"mmmm dd,
yyyy")
Notice that the text function uses the same designators for formatting the date value as you would use in creating a custom
number format.

6 To demonstrate the dynamic nature of the last function entry:
SELECT: cell A23
TYPE: 14-Feb-01
PRESS: ENTER
The text string in cell D23 is updated automatically.

7 Save and then close the workbook.

6.4 Self Check   Cell A1 contains a person's area code and phone number in the form
(789)555-1234. What expression would you enter in cell A2 to extract
only the phone number for display?

6.5 Using Financial and Logical Functions

Excel's financial functions enable you to confidently use complex financial formulas in your worksheets. And the best part is that you don't even need to understand the difference between a stock and a bond! Some of the more popular functions are devoted to making investment decisions and working with annuity scenarios. Although it sounds technical, an **annuity** is simply a series of equal cash payments that are made over a given period of time, such as an investment contribution or mortgage payment. In this module, you learn to solve annuity problems using the present value (PV), future value (FV), and loan payment (PMT) functions.

Using Excel's logical and information functions, you can create a worksheet that performs conditional calculations and checks itself for errors. Arguably the most useful of Excel's functions next to AVERAGE and SUM, the IF function lets you test for a condition and then, depending on the result, perform one of two calculations (which may, themselves, contain nested IF functions). While this module does not describe the intricacies of these function categories, the following lessons introduce you to constructing useful and practical expressions.

6.5.1 Calculating Present and Future Values (PV and FV)

FEATURE

The PV function calculates the **present value** of an investment. Restated for the business majors among us, the PV function returns the current value of an annuity given a constant interest rate. The FV function calculates the **future value** of an annuity, such as an IRA or RSP contribution. In other words, the FV function returns the total future value of a series of equal payments made periodically at a constant interest rate.

METHOD

```
=PV(rate,periods,payment)
=FV(rate,periods,payment)
```

PRACTICE

In this lesson, you practice applying the PV and FV functions in realistic scenarios.

Setup: Ensure that no workbooks appear in the application window.

1 Open the data file named EXC650.

2 Save the workbook as "Functions 650" to your personal storage location. This workbook (Figure 6.16) provides a summary area for function syntax, in rows 1 through 7, followed by an exercise area starting at row 8.

Figure 6.16

The "Functions 650" workbook

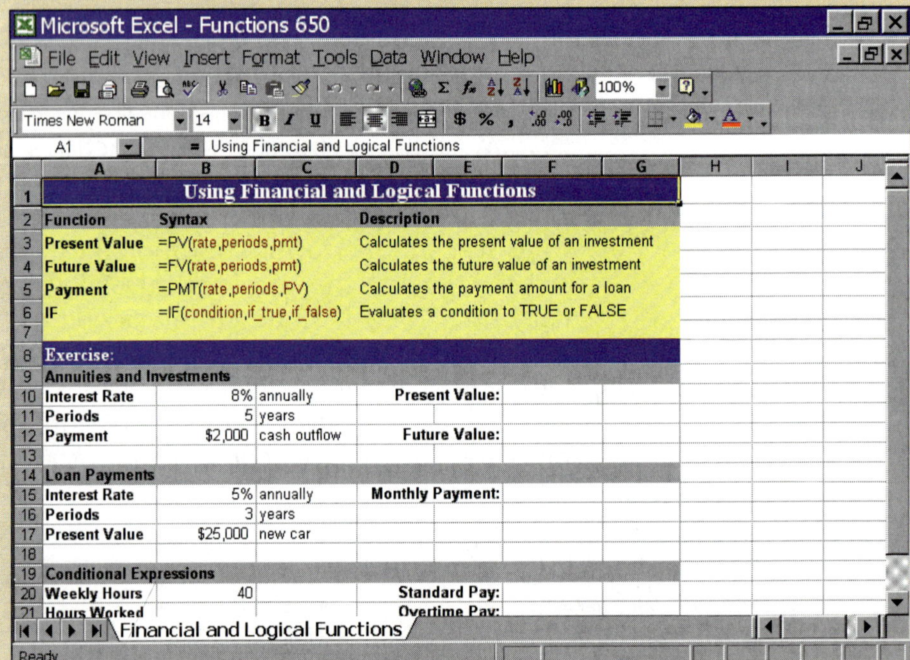

3 Constructing expressions that use several functions or arguments is much easier when you name the required cell ranges:
SELECT: cell B10
CLICK: in the Name box
TYPE: **Rate**
PRESS: ENTER

4 To create named ranges for the next two cells:
SELECT: cell B11
CLICK: in the Name box
TYPE: **Periods**
PRESS: ENTER
SELECT: cell B12
CLICK: in the Name box
TYPE: **Payment**
PRESS: ENTER

5 In this first scenario, an altruistic uncle offers you a choice between receiving $8,500 today or $10,000 in an annuity of $2,000 per year for the next five years. With an interest rate of 8 percent per year, which would be the better offer? To solve this problem, you enter a present value calculation:
SELECT: cell F10
TYPE: **=pv(**
CLICK: Edit Formula button (**=**)

6 In the Formula Palette, you enter the required range names:
TYPE: **Rate** in the *Rate* text box
PRESS: TAB
TYPE: **Periods** in the *Nper* text box
PRESS: TAB
TYPE: **Payment** in the *Pmt* text box
Your screen should now appear similar to Figure 6.17.

Figure 6.17

Entering the PV function

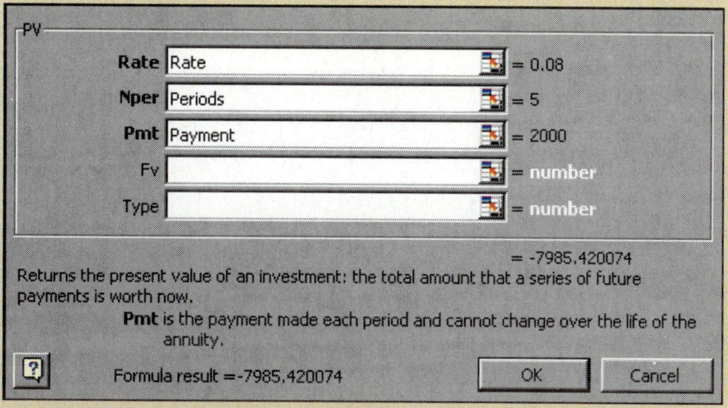

7 To complete the Formula Palette:
CLICK: OK command button
The better offer is receiving $8,500 today, compared to receiving $7,985.42 in today's dollars over the next five years. (*Hint:* With the majority of these calculations, you are concerned with the result's absolute or positive value. Therefore, you can ignore the negative sign or parentheses around the figure.)

 Let's change the scenario slightly. The same uncle offers you a choice between receiving a flat $11,500 five years from now or an annuity of $2,000 per year for the next five years. Which offer is better given an 8 percent interest rate? This problem requires that you enter a future value calculation:
SELECT: cell F12
TYPE: `=fv(Rate,Periods,Payment)`
PRESS: `ENTER`
The better offer is receiving the $2,000 annuity, since its future value is worth $233.20 more than the flat $11,500.

 Save the workbook and keep it open for use in the next lesson.

6.5.2 Calculating Payments (PMT)

FEATURE
The PMT function calculates the payment amount for a loan or mortgage, given a constant interest rate and number of periods. The *rate* argument is the interest rate charged, *periods* is the amortization length, and *pv* is the present value or loan amount. To find the annual payments required for a $100,000 mortgage at 7 percent over 25 years, you enter the function `=PMT(.07,25,100000)`. To calculate the monthly payments, you must divide the annual interest rate by 12 months and multiply the number of periods by 12. Thus, the entry becomes `=PMT(.07/12,25*12,100000)`. You can also determine the total amount of money paid over the term of the loan by multiplying the PMT result by the number of periods used in the calculation.

METHOD
`=PMT(rate,periods,pv)`

PRACTICE
In this lesson, you learn how to calculate a payment for a car loan.

Setup: Ensure that the "Functions 650" workbook is displayed.

1 Your objective in this lesson is to calculate the payment required to purchase a $25,000 car. To begin:
SELECT: cell F15

2 Let's use the Formula Palette to enter the PMT function:
TYPE: =pmt(
CLICK: Edit Formula button (=)

3 In the Formula Palette, specify the required arguments:
TYPE: b15/12 in the *Rate* text box
PRESS: TAB
TYPE: b16*12 in the *Nper* text box
PRESS: TAB
Notice that you divide the annual interest rate by 12 to calculate the monthly rate and multiply the periods (years) by 12.

4 To enter the principal loan amount:
TYPE: b17 in the *Pv* text box
Your screen should now appear as shown in Figure 6.18.

Figure 6.18

Entering the PMT function

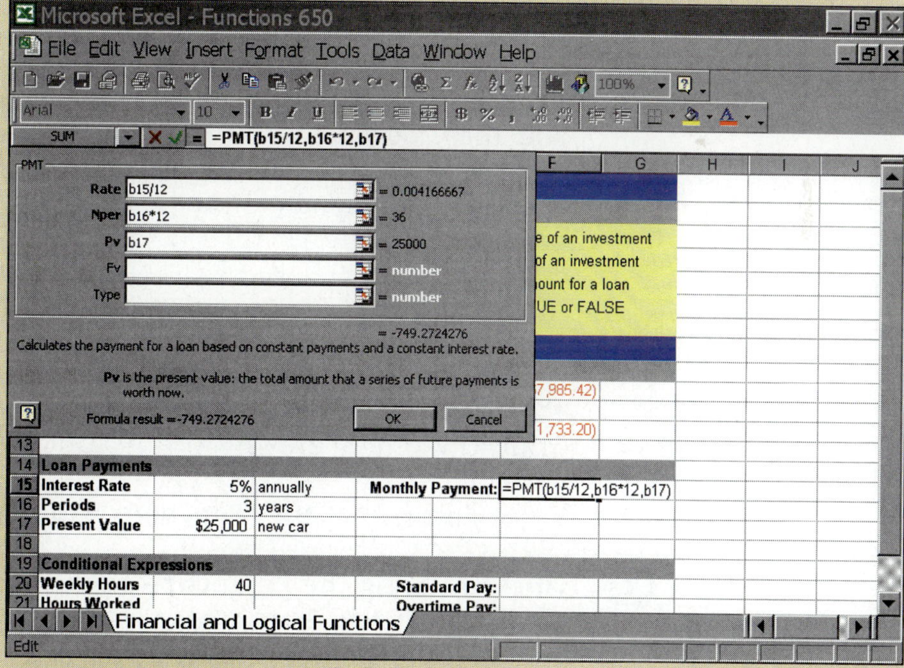

5 To complete the Formula Palette:
CLICK: OK command button
The answer ($749.27) appears in cell F15. The payment appears in parentheses to indicate it is a negative number, since it is a cash outflow from yourself to the bank.

6 On your own, change the values in cells B15, B16, and B17. For example, calculate the monthly payment for a $30,000 car loan given an interest rate of 6 percent.

7 Save the workbook and keep it open for use in the next lesson.

In Addition
Using Other Financial Functions

Excel provides two variations on the PMT function for calculating the principal and interest portions of a PMT result. The PPMT function returns the principal payments and the IPMT function returns the interest payments. There are several other useful functions for evaluating investment decisions, such as NPV for finding the net present value of cash flows and IRR for calculating the internal rate of return. For more information, access the Microsoft Excel Help system.

6.5.3   Making Decisions (IF)

FEATURE
You use the IF function when you need to employ conditional logic in your worksheets. The IF function lets you test for a condition and then, depending on the result, perform one of two calculations. Conditional expressions are entered using the following logical operators: equal (=), not equal (<>), less than (<), less than or equal to (<=), greater than (>), and greater than or equal to (>=).

METHOD
```
=IF(condition,true,false)
```

PRACTICE
You now practice using the IF function.

Setup: Ensure that the "Functions 650" workbook is displayed.

1 After reviewing the IF function's syntax, scroll the window downward so that row 8 appears as the first row at the top of the worksheet.

2 Your objective is to use the IF function to calculate the earnings for a job that pays both standard and overtime wages. To begin, enter an "Hours Worked" number that includes five hours of overtime:
SELECT: cell B21
TYPE: 45
PRESS: ENTER

EXCEL

3 To facilitate entering the IF function, let's name the cell ranges that will be required in calculating the number of hours worked:
SELECT: cell B20
CLICK: in the Name box
TYPE: Weekly
PRESS: ENTER
SELECT: cell B21
CLICK: in the Name box
TYPE: Worked
PRESS: ENTER

4 Now name the cell ranges that supply the pay rates:
SELECT: cell B22
CLICK: in the Name box
TYPE: Standard
PRESS: ENTER
SELECT: cell B23
CLICK: in the Name box
TYPE: Overtime
PRESS: ENTER

5 To enter a calculation that determines the worker's standard pay:
SELECT: cell F20
TYPE: =if(
CLICK: Edit Formula button ([=])

6 In the *Logical_test* text box, enter a condition to test whether there were any overtime hours worked:
TYPE: worked>weekly
PRESS: TAB

7 In the *Value_if_true* text box, specify the calculation to perform if the hours worked exceed the standard weekly hours. In other words, you multiply the number of normal working hours by the standard pay rate:
TYPE: weekly*standard
PRESS: TAB

8 In the *Value_if_false* (no overtime hours) text box, you multiply the actual number of hours worked by the standard pay rate:
TYPE: worked*standard
CLICK: OK command button
The result, 618, is displayed in cell F20.

9 Now calculate the overtime pay. On your own, select cell F21 and then enter the IF function as displayed in Figure 6.19. When finished, click the OK command button to place the function into cell F21.

Figure 6.19

Entering the IF function

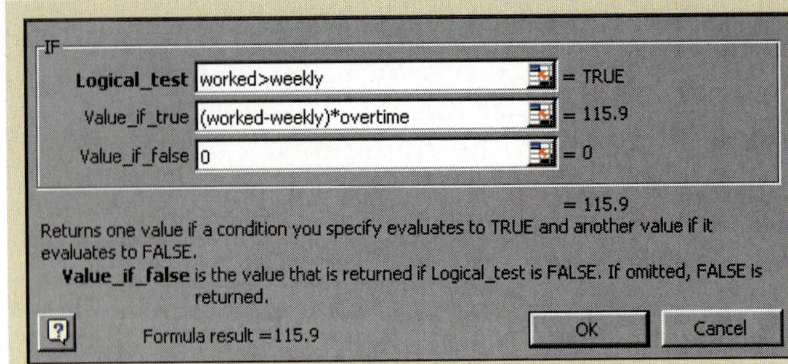

 **10** On your own, adjust the Weekly Hours and the Hours Worked worksheet values to see their effect on the earnings calculation.

11 Save and then close the workbook.

12 Exit Microsoft Excel.

6.5 Self Check   How might you calculate the payment for a mortgage in which the interest rate changed depending on the term chosen?

6.6   Chapter Review

The focus of this chapter centers around creating formulas and using Excel's built-in functions. After a brief description of the operator order of precedence, you learn that nesting portions of a formula expression within parentheses lets you control and force the order of calculation. Also useful in entering functions, you practice nesting date and time functions. There are many date and time functions available. For example, you use date functions to compute a serial date value from data stored in the worksheet and to extract the individual year, month, and day values from a date value. You also use nesting in performing mathematical and statistical calculations. In one lesson, you insert a table of random integer values and then convert the results to static values. Moving from numeric calculations to text manipulation, several functions are introduced for modifying, extracting, and concatenating character strings stored in worksheet cells. You can also use these functions to combine numbers and dates with text labels in the worksheet. From the financial category, you use functions to evaluate investment decisions, solve annuity problems, and calculate loan payments. And, lastly, you use the logical IF function to create conditional expressions and perform calculations based on its results.

6.6.1 Command Summary

Many of the commands and procedures appearing in this chapter are summarized in the following table.

Skill Set	To Perform this Task . . .	Do the Following . . .
Working with Cells	Convert formula results to static values	SELECT: *formula to copy* CLICK: Copy button (image) SELECT: *target location* CHOOSE: Edit, Paste Special SELECT: *Values* option button
	Transpose worksheet values from a column or row orientation	SELECT: *cells to transpose* CLICK: Copy button (image) SELECT: *target location* CHOOSE: Edit, Paste Special SELECT: *Transpose* check box
Working with Formulas and Functions	Display and print formulas in a worksheet	CHOOSE: Tools, Options CLICK: *View* tab SELECT: *Formulas* check box CLICK: OK command button CLICK: Print button (image)

Using Functions	Use date and time functions:
	• Enter a date value
	• Return the day number
	• Return the month number
	• Return the year number
	• Calculate the weekday
	• Enter a time value
		`=DATE(year,month,day)`
		`=DAY(date_value)`
		`=MONTH(date_value)`
		`=YEAR(date_value)`
		`=WEEKDAY(date_value)`
		`=TIME(hour,minute,second)`

	Use mathematical and statistical functions:
	• Round a value to specific digits
	• Return a number between 0 and 1
	• Extract a value's integer portion
	• Extract a value's integer portion
		`=ROUND(number,digits)`
		
		`=RAND()`
		
		`=INT(cell)`
		
		`=INT(cell)`

Continued

Skill Set	To Perform this Task . . .	Do the Following . . .
Using Functions *Continued*	Use text manipulation functions:	
	• Extract text from the left	=LEFT(*text*,*chars*)
	• Return the length of a string	=LEN(*text*)
	• Convert a string to lowercase	=LOWER(*text*)
	• Extract text from the middle	=MID(*text*,*start*,*chars*)
	• Convert a string to proper case	=PROPER(*text*)
	• Extract text from the right	=RIGHT(*text*,*chars*)
	• Return a string's position	=SEARCH(*find*,*text*,*start*)
	• Convert a value to a string	=TEXT(*value*,*format*)
	• Remove trailing spaces in a string	=TRIM(*text*)
	• Convert a string to uppercase	=UPPER(*text*)
	Use financial functions:	
	• Calculate a loan payment	=PMT(*rate*,*periods*,*pv*)
	• Calculate the present value of an annuity	=PV(*rate*,*periods*,*payment*)
	• Calculate the future value of an annuity	=FV(*rate*,*periods*,*payment*)
	Use logical and information functions:	
	• Evaluate a condition to true or false	=IF(*condition*,*true*,*false*)

6.6.2 Key Terms

This section specifies page references for the key terms identified in
this chapter. For a complete list of definitions, refer to the Glossary
provided at the end of this learning guide.

6.7 Review Questions

6.7.1 Short Answer

1. Explain the difference between an *operand* and an *operator*.
2. How do you overrule the operator order of precedence?
3. What two tools help you insert Excel's built-in functions?
4. What is Range Finder and why is it useful?
5. Name one method for documenting the formulas in a worksheet.
6. How do the ROUND and INT functions differ?
7. What does it mean to *transpose* a cell range?
8. Explain the difference between *parsing* and *concatenating*.
9. How might you use the IF function to test more than one condition?
10. List some of the logical operators used to create conditional expressions.

6.7.2 True/False

1. —— Nesting is the process of placing operators between operands.
2. —— The Paste Special command can paste values, formulas, and even transpose the contents of a row or column.
3. —— To display formulas in your worksheet, choose the View, Options command and then select the *Formulas* check box.
4. —— The DATE and TIME functions are similar in that they both accept three arguments.
5. —— The RAND function only works when nested within a ROUND or INT function.
6. —— The PROPER function returns the correct syntax for a function.
7. —— You concatenate text strings together using the ampersand "&."
8. —— The PV and FV functions are used to evaluate annuity problems.
9. —— You must use the Formula Palette to enter the PMT function.
10. —— The IF function is categorized as a "Logical" function.

6.7.3 Multiple Choice

1. The following expression evaluates to 12.
    a. `=3+3*2`
    b. `=(3+3)*2`
    c. `=3+(3*2)`
    d. Both a and b

2. The Excel feature that color-codes an expression's cell references during Edit mode is called:
    a. Range Rover
    b. Cell Finder
    c. Range Finder
    d. Edit Formula

3. Which of the following is not a function in the Date & Time category?
    a. DAYS360
    b. MINUTE
    c. WEEKDAY
    d. WEEKEND

4. The following function displays the number of days remaining until the end of the year:
    a. `=date(year(now(),12,31)-today())`
    b. `=date(year(now(),12,31)-then())`
    c. `=today()-(month(12)+day(31))`
    d. `=date(12,31)-today()`

5. Which is the correct expression for extracting the integer portion of a random number between 0 and 100?
    a. `=INTEGER(RAND*10)`
    b. `=INT(RAND()*100)`
    c. `=RAND(INT()*100)`
    d. `=RAND(ROUND()*100`

6. Which key do you press to recalculate or update a worksheet?
    a. `F2`
    b. `F3`
    c. `F4`
    d. `F9`

7. The following function returns the number 9 in a worksheet cell:
    a. `=extract(",","Tampa Bay, FL")`
    b. `=search(",","Spokane, WA")`
    c. `=len("New York, NY")`
    d. `=search(",","Stockton, CA")`

8. Which of the following best describes the FV function?
   a. Calculates the future value of an annuity.
   b. Evaluates the lump sum payment of a mortgage.
   c. Calculates the discounted present value of an annuity.
   d. Calculates the value of a series of unequal payments.

9. Which of the following is the correct syntax for the IF function?
   a. `=IF(condition,false,true)`
   b. `=IF(condition,true,false)`
   c. `=IF(true,false,condition)`
   d. `=IF(false,true,condition)`

10. Which of the following is not a logical operator?
    a. `>`
    b. `<=`
    c. `=`
    d. `\`

6.8 Hands-On Projects

6.8.1 Grandview College: Gradebook

This exercise practices modifying and enhancing a gradebook worksheet using Excel's built-in functions.

1. Open the data file named EXC681.
2. Save the workbook as "Gradebook" to your personal storage location.
3. Your objective is to create a nested formula that calculates each student's final grade given the weighting factors entered on row 4. To facilitate entering the formula, let's name the required cell ranges:
   SELECT: cell B4
   CLICK: in the Name box
   TYPE: `Quizzes`
   PRESS: ENTER
4. Using the same method, name cell C4 `MidTerm` and cell D4 `Final`. Then, do the following:
   SELECT: cell E6
5. To calculate the weighted course grade for Marjorie Blackwood:
   TYPE: `=(b6*Quizzes)+(c6*MidTerm)+(d6*Final)`
   PRESS: ENTER
   Notice that you placed each weight calculation in parentheses to improve the formula's readability. The result, 62.63, appears.

6. To copy this formula for the remaining students:
   SELECT: cell range from E6 to E17
   CHOOSE: Edit, Fill, Down
7. PRESS: **HOME** to remove the highlighting
   Your worksheet should now appear similar to Figure 6.20.

Figure 6.20

Calculating the final course grades

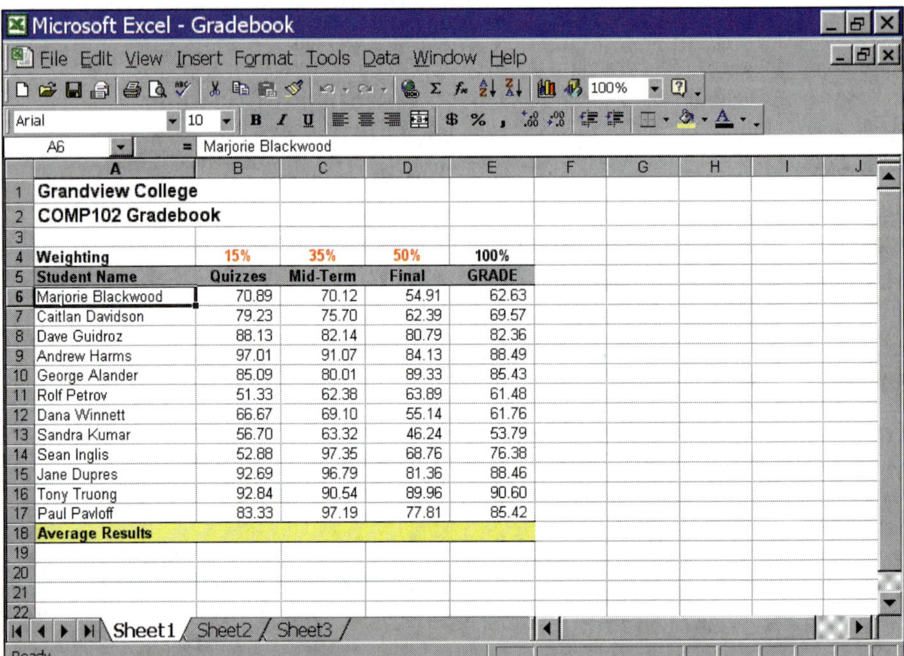

8. To calculate the average results for each course component:
   SELECT: cell range from B18 to E18
   TYPE: `=average(b6:b17)`
   PRESS: **CTRL** + **ENTER**
   The correct function is entered into each cell of the selected range.
9. To display the formulas in the worksheet:
   CHOOSE: Tools, Options
   CLICK: *View* tab
   SELECT: *Formulas* check box
   CLICK: OK command button
10. On your own, review the formulas in the worksheet. Then, save and close the workbook.

6.8.2 Fast Forward Video: Sweepstakes

In this exercise, you create a worksheet that uses Excel's mathematical and statistical functions to generate a value for use in a sweepstakes contest.

1. Open the data file named EXC682.
2. Save the workbook as "Sweepstakes" to your personal storage location.
3. Your first step is to populate the worksheet with a list of 10 random integer values between 0 and 100. To do so:
   SELECT: cell A5
   TYPE: **=int(rand()*100)**
   PRESS: [ENTER]
   A random value appears in the cell.
4. To copy this value down 10 rows in the worksheet:
   SELECT: cell range from A5 to A14
   CHOOSE: Edit, Fill, Down
5. Now let's calculate the average value of this range:
   SELECT: cell D6
   TYPE: **=average(a5:a14)**
   PRESS: [ENTER]
6. Each person who rents a video will have an opportunity to press the [ENTER] CALC key to try to beat the value appearing in cell D5. To demonstrate:
   PRESS: [F9] CALC key repeatedly
   Did you best the value in cell D5?
7. Let's add an IF function that more clearly informs the participant on how they've done:
   SELECT: cell D8
   TYPE: **=if(**
   PRESS: Edit Formula button ([=])
   The Formula Palette appears.
8. In the *Logical_test* text box, you enter the condition to test for. In this case, the winner must achieve an average random value that is greater than the value specified in cell D5. To enter this condition:
   TYPE: **d6>d5**
   PRESS: [TAB]
9. Now enter the text messages to display:
   TYPE: **"Winner!"** in the *Value_if_true* text box
   PRESS: [ENTER]
   TYPE: **"Try Again!"** in the *Value_if_false* text box
   CLICK: OK command button

10. On your own, press the F9 CALC key. How many presses does it usually take to beat the target value? When you are ready to proceed, save and then close the workbook.

6.8.3 Sun Valley Frozen Foods: Payroll Withholdings

Using a retirement plan worksheet for Sun Valley, you now practice entering logical IF functions and calculating future investment values.

1. Open the data file named EXC683.
2. Save the workbook as "Sun Valley Plan" to your personal storage location.
3. For the employee retirement package, Sun Valley has agreed to match each person's annual contribution up to a maximum of 5 percent of their salary. To begin:
   SELECT: cell D5
4. To calculate Sun Valley's contribution to the plan, enter an IF function that determines whether the employee's contribution is greater than 5 percent of their salary. If it is, input the 5 percent contribution limit for Sun Valley. If the contribution isn't greater than 5 percent of their salary, match the employee's contribution.
5. Copy the function that you entered in cell D5 to the remainder of the employee cells in column D.
6. Now let's calculate each employee's retirement nest egg. To begin, enter an annual return rate of 8 percent for the company's investments:
   SELECT: cell B3
   TYPE: **8.00%**
   PRESS: ENTER
7. To make calculating the future values easier, name the required cells. First, name cell B3 **ReturnRate**. Then, name cells E4 **ShortTerm**, F4 **MidTerm**, and G4 **LongTerm**.
8. You use the FV function to determine the investment's growth potential in the timeframe specified in cells E4, F4, and G4. To begin:
   SELECT: cell E5
9. For the total annuity amount, add together the employee and employer contributions. To proceed:
   TYPE: **=fv(**
   CLICK: Edit Formula button (▪)
10. Complete the Formula Palette as follows:

TYPE: **ReturnRate** in the *Rate* text box
PRESS: `TAB`
TYPE: **ShortTerm** in the *Nper* text box
PRESS: `TAB`
TYPE: **-(c5+d5)** in the *Pmt* text box
CLICK: OK command button
Notice that you enter a minus sign before the *Pmt* argument in order to change the final result into a positive. You can also nest the FV function within an ABS function to return its positive value.

11. On your own, enter the FV functions for the MidTerm and LongTerm periods in cells F5 and G5, respectively. Then, copy these three FV functions to the remaining employee rows in the table. Your screen should appear similar to Figure 6.21.

12. Save and then close the workbook.

Figure 6.21

Completing the retirement plan for Sun Valley

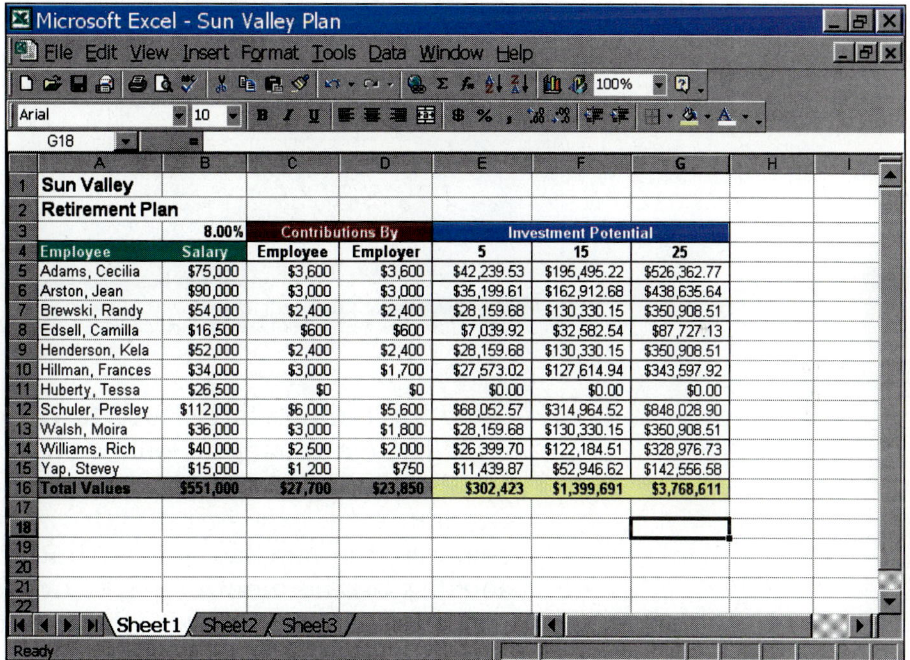

Sun Valley						
Retirement Plan						
	8.00%	Contributions By		Investment Potential		
Employee	Salary	Employee	Employer	5	15	25
Adams, Cecilia	$75,000	$3,600	$3,600	$42,239.53	$195,495.22	$526,362.77
Arston, Jean	$90,000	$3,000	$3,000	$35,199.61	$162,912.68	$438,635.64
Brewski, Randy	$54,000	$2,400	$2,400	$28,159.68	$130,330.15	$350,908.51
Edsell, Camilla	$16,500	$600	$600	$7,039.92	$32,582.54	$87,727.13
Henderson, Kela	$52,000	$2,400	$2,400	$28,159.68	$130,330.15	$350,908.51
Hillman, Frances	$34,000	$3,000	$1,700	$27,573.02	$127,614.94	$343,597.92
Huberty, Tessa	$26,500	$0	$0	$0.00	$0.00	$0.00
Schuler, Presley	$112,000	$6,000	$5,600	$68,052.57	$314,964.52	$848,028.90
Walsh, Moira	$36,000	$3,000	$1,800	$28,159.68	$130,330.15	$350,908.51
Williams, Rich	$40,000	$2,500	$2,000	$26,399.70	$122,184.51	$328,976.73
Yap, Stevey	$15,000	$1,200	$750	$11,439.87	$52,946.62	$142,556.58
Total Values	$551,000	$27,700	$23,850	$302,423	$1,399,691	$3,768,611

6.8.4 Lakeside Realty: Mortgage Table

In this exercise, you practice using Excel's built-in functions in calculating a simple mortgage table.

1. Open the data file named EXC684.
2. Save the workbook as "Mortgage Table" to your personal storage location.
3. Enter a function to display the current date in cell B3. Format the date to display as "dd-mmm-yyyy."

4. In cell B6, enter an IF function using the Formula Palette that calculates the down payment. If the purchase price is greater than $150,000, the down payment required is 10 percent of the purchase price. Otherwise, the down payment is 15 percent of the purchase price.

5. Enter a formula in cell B7 that subtracts the down payment in cell B6 from the purchase price in cell B5. The result is the principal loan amount that you must borrow.

6. In cell B11, enter a PMT function using the Formula Palette that calculates the monthly payment for the principal loan amount, given the periods in cell B10 and the interest rate in cell A11. Because you want to copy this formula, you must make some of the cell references absolute, as shown in Figure 6.22.

Figure 6.22

Completing the PMT function with absolute cell references

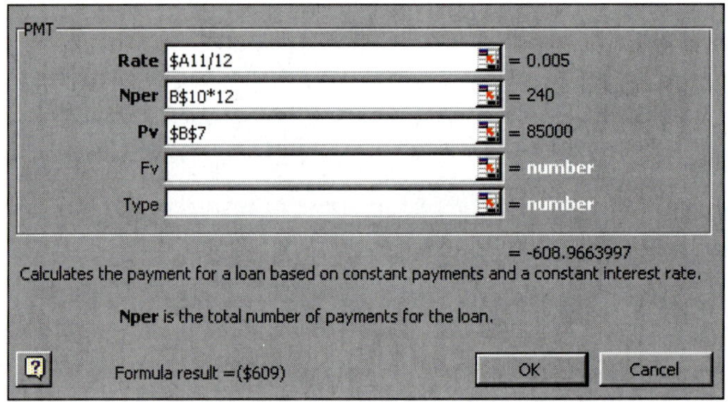

7. Copy the formula in cell B11 to the cell range from B11 to D14. The entire range should now appear filled with payment results.

8. On your own, experiment with various loan scenarios by changing the purchase price. Notice the effect that this variable has on the monthly payment and the required down payment. When you are ready to proceed, change the purchase price to $175,000.

9. Display the formulas in your worksheet. Change the width of columns A and B to 18 characters and the width of columns C and D to 2 characters. Then, send the worksheet to the printer.

10. Save and then close the workbook.

6.8.5 On Your Own: Air Quality Measurements

You will now practice working with named cell ranges and entering built-in functions. To begin, open the EXC685 workbook and then save it as "Air Quality" to your personal storage location.

Using the Name box, review the list of existing named ranges in the worksheet. Experiment with selecting various names to see which cell ranges are referenced. Then, use the Insert, Name, Paste command to create a list of names beginning in cell F1. Adjust the width of columns F and G to view the contents.

Using the range names and appropriate functions, calculate the highest and lowest measurements for each of the three types of air pollution. Then, use the IF function and range names to determine whether a warning needs to be issued for any of the three categories. If the "Highest" value is greater than the "Acceptable" amount, display "YES" in the corresponding "Issue Warning?" cell, otherwise display "NO." (*Hint:* In the IF function, use double quotes around text values that you want to enter into a cell.)

When you are finished, save and then close the "Air Quality" workbook. Then, exit Excel.

6.8.6 On Your Own: Functions-R-Great!

To practice working with date, time, mathematical, statistical, text, financial, and logical functions, open the data file named EXC686 and then save it as "Functions-R-Great" to your personal storage location. This worksheet provides a series of exercises for calculating, parsing, and concatenating data. Work your way down the worksheet until you have completed all ten of the examples. When finished, display the formulas in the worksheet and then modify the page setup options to print using a landscape orientation with gridlines and row and column headings displayed. Lastly, send the worksheet to the printer.

When you are finished, save and then close the "Functions-R-Great" workbook. If you are not proceeding to the case problems, exit Microsoft Excel.

6.9   Case Problems: Synergy Computer Supplies Ltd.

Around the same time that Jackson White accepted the position of assistant controller for Synergy, the company hired several commission salespeople to service their customer base. Having spent a few weeks becoming familiar with the general office procedures and paper flow, Jackson has recommended to his boss that they convert their in-house sales team from a one-write paper-based system to an Excel application. To illustrate his point, he develops a sample workbook and shows how they can create and print invoices. Impressed with the initial attempt, the president has asked him to make some minor modifications and then provide the workbook to two staff members for testing. Jackson is eager to implement his newly learned skills. He is certain that he can make the workbook even faster and easier to use!

In the following case problems, assume the role of Jackson and perform the same steps that he identifies. You may want to re-read the chapter opening before proceeding.

1. Jackson arrives early at the office with his notebook computer in tow. Even before his customary morning coffee, he docks the computer at his workstation, turns on the power, and then launches Microsoft Excel 2000. Unfortunately, Jackson's accounting duties have kept him occupied over the past few days, so he decides to perform a quick review of his sample workbook. He loads the file named EXC690 and then saves it as "Synergy" to his personal storage location.

    Perusing the sample workbook (Figure 6.23), Jackson remembers that he has already entered a fictitious company name and invoice details. However, he hasn't yet entered formulas to calculate the total amounts in column E. To complete the detail area, Jackson selects the cell range from E8 through E11 and then types a formula to multiply the values in the Quantity and Price columns. Instead of pressing (ENTER), he uses the (CTRL) + (ENTER) keystroke to complete the entry for all of the selected cells. In cell E12, Jackson uses the pointing method to enter a SUM function that adds together the results in the Total column. Lastly, he enters the TODAY function in cell B3 and then formats the result to display using the "March 14, 1998" format. Jackson saves the workbook before proceeding.

Figure 6.23

The "Synergy" workbook

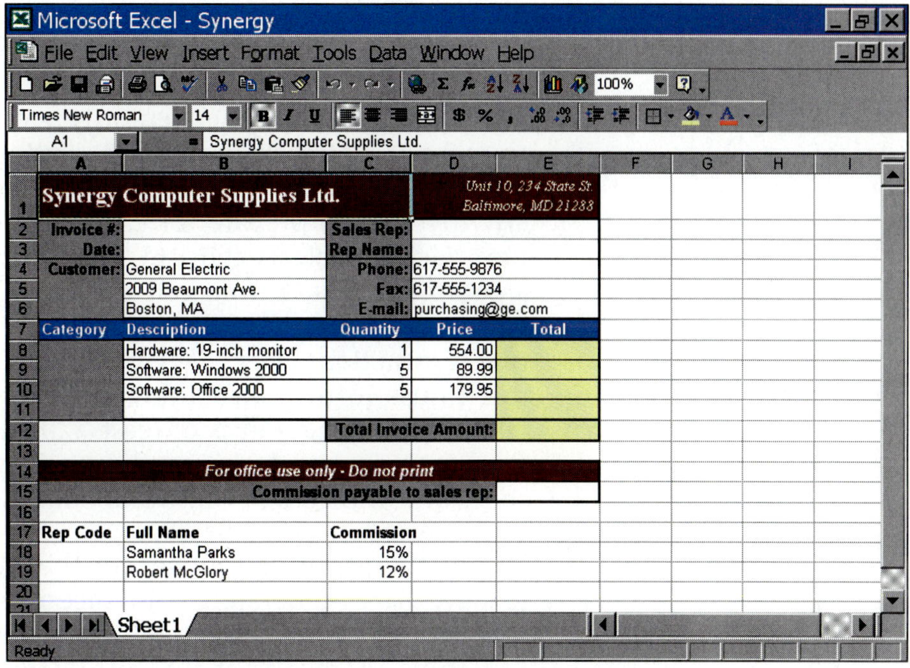

2. Jackson wants to complete the workbook so that two of the sales staff can test it. Before handing it off to them, he ensures that their names appear in cells B18 and B19, next to their commission rates in column C. Although he has only used the LEFT and RIGHT functions in the past, Jackson determines that the MID function can help him create a "Rep Code" automatically for each entry. The function extracts the first three letters of the person's last name and then converts it to display in uppercase letters. For example, Samantha Park's rep code will read "PAR" in cell A18 and Robert McGlory's rep code will read "MCG" in cell A19. Jackson realizes that he needs to nest the MID and SEARCH functions in order to complete this operation. (*Hint:* The MID function is similar in form to the LEFT and RIGHT functions. However, you must locate a starting position for extracting characters.)

    Once finished, Jackson selects cell D2 and enters "PAR" as the Sales Rep in this example. In cell D3, he uses an IF function to see whether the value in cell D2 equals either of the values in cell A18 and A19. If a match is found, Jackson places the appropriate name in cell D3. If no match is found, the text "No rep by that name" is placed into the cell. Jackson saves the workbook before proceeding.

3. According to the sales reps' compensation agreement, they earn a commission on every invoice that they generate. Each sales rep is assigned a commission rate between 10 and 15 percent, depending on his or her seniority with the company. However, to make it worth their while to service the smaller clients, management assures them a minimum commission of $20 on any invoice. To prepare for entering the commission calculation, Jackson selects cell E15. He realizes that he must multiply a commission rate from cell C18 or cell C19 by the total invoice amount shown in cell E12. This calculation requires two IF functions. First, Jackson determines which commission rate to use in the calculation. Second, he ensures that the resulting commission is at least $20. After entering the expression, Jackson checks his work by adjusting values in the worksheet and then saves the workbook.

4. To put the finishing touches on the worksheet, Jackson decides to have Excel generate the invoice number automatically. Each invoice is numbered by combining the current date with the first three characters of the customer's name in uppercase letters. For example, the invoice number in the "Synergy" worksheet should read "yyyymm-CUS-dd." If the date were December 31, 2000, the invoice number would be "200012-GEN-31." With the current date already displayed in cell B3, Jackson proceeds to enter a concatenation formula that combines the date values (using the TEXT function) with the first three characters of the customer's name.

    Pleased with his latest results, Jackson displays the formulas he has entered and then adjusts the column widths in the worksheet. (*Hint:* There are some long formulas in this worksheet!) In preparation for printing, he specifies page setup options to print the worksheet using landscape orientation and with gridlines and row and column headings. After sending the worksheet to the printer, Jackson saves and then closes the workbook. Finally, he exits Excel and calls it a day. And what a day it was!

Notes

Notes

Notes

Notes

MICROSOFT EXCEL 2000
Managing Worksheets and Workbooks
CHAPTER
SEVEN

Chapter Outline

Learning Objectives

After reading this chapter, you will be able to:

- Freeze titles for viewing large worksheets

- Divide the worksheet window into panes

- Outline a worksheet for reporting purposes

- Perform global workbook editing operations

- Navigate, rename, insert, delete, move, and copy worksheets in a workbook

- Consolidate data that is stored in multiple-sheet workbooks and multiple workbook files

Case Study

Home Stretch Hardware

Home Stretch Hardware operates a chain of home-improvement outlets along the east coast. In the last few years, they have opened three new stores and have recently established a central distribution warehouse to reduce inventory holding costs. The lead purchasing agent, Howard Bose, is responsible for monitoring the inventory levels at their distribution warehouse and must provide weekly, monthly, and quarterly summary reports to management. Being relatively experienced in using Excel, Howard has created a large worksheet that contains product, inventory, and supplier information. As well, he has several worksheets that collect and store the data he needs to create summary reports for management.

In this chapter, you and Howard learn several techniques for working more productively in Excel. First, you examine working with large worksheets and learn how to view and outline data. Then, you perform find and replace editing tasks and spell check a worksheet. Finally, you practice manipulating and consolidating information that is stored in various worksheets and workbooks.

7.1 Using Large Worksheets

The workbooks created and used in this learning guide are kept small in order to limit their file sizes and download times from the Internet. Conversely, workbooks used in industry are typically quite expansive, containing multiple worksheets and storing hundreds of rows of data. Furthermore, these worksheets seem to grow larger with each passing year and with each new user. Knowing how to efficiently manage and work with large worksheets directly impacts your productivity.

Some worksheets display row and column titles to serve as a frame of reference for the data contained therein. For example, a worksheet that stores address information might provide column headings labeled surname, address, city, and phone. Unfortunately, as you move the cell pointer around the worksheet, these headings can scroll out of view. Excel provides two solutions that make it easier to use large worksheets. First, you can freeze the titles of a worksheet so that certain columns and rows are always visible. Second, for those worksheets that do not group data neatly under headings, you can divide a worksheet window into two or four independent **panes**. This module shows you how to use these two features to navigate and work within a large worksheet.

You also learn about **outlining** a worksheet in this module. Outlining lets you view your data differently by displaying or hiding worksheet details. For example, a company president might prefer to review the sales results for the organization by region, while the regional managers require a more detailed analysis broken down by salesperson. Using outlines, the worksheets used to generate these reports can be one and the same. Outlining lets you report the same information using different views for different needs. Also in this module, you learn to set print titles and other options for printing large worksheets.

7.1.1 Freezing and Unfreezing Panes

FEATURE

You can freeze specific rows and columns within a worksheet window so that they appear at all times, regardless of where you move the cell pointer. This command is especially useful for those worksheets where the data is arranged in a table layout with row and column headings.

METHOD

1. Position the cell pointer below and to the right of the row(s) and column(s) that you want to freeze.
2. CHOOSE: Window, Freeze Panes to freeze the rows and columns
3. CHOOSE: Window, Unfreeze Panes to unfreeze the panes

PRACTICE

In this lesson, you open an existing worksheet and practice freezing and unfreezing titles.

Setup: Ensure that Excel is loaded.

1 Open the data file named EXC710.

2 Save the workbook as "Indicators" to your personal storage location.

3 SELECT: cell A3

4 To move to the bottom of the worksheet's active area:
PRESS: CTRL + ↓
The cell pointer scoots down to row 64. Notice that the column headings have disappeared from the top of the worksheet window. Do you remember what data is stored in each column? Probably not.

5 Let's return to the top of the worksheet:
PRESS: [CTRL] + [HOME]

6 The column headings for the worksheet are stored in rows 1, 2, and 3. Using panes, Excel enables you to freeze these rows on the screen for display at all times. To illustrate:
SELECT: cell B4
Notice that you selected a cell immediately below the row that you want to freeze (row 3) and to the right of the "Region" column.

7 CHOOSE: Window, Freeze Panes

8 Once again, let's scoot down to the last row in the worksheet:
PRESS: [CTRL] + [↓]
Notice that the column headings do not disappear this time, as shown in Figure 7.1.

Figure 7.1

Freezing titles

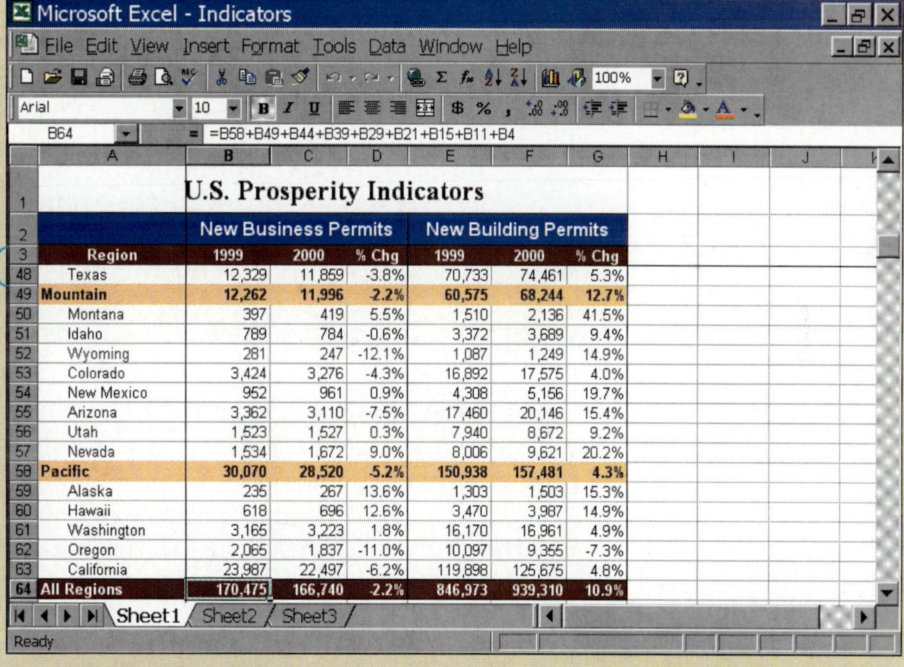

The row numbering skips from 3 to 48

	Region	1999	2000	% Chg	1999	2000	% Chg
48	Texas	12,329	11,859	-3.8%	70,733	74,461	5.3%
49	**Mountain**	**12,262**	**11,996**	**-2.2%**	**60,575**	**68,244**	**12.7%**
50	Montana	397	419	5.5%	1,510	2,136	41.5%
51	Idaho	789	784	-0.6%	3,372	3,689	9.4%
52	Wyoming	281	247	-12.1%	1,087	1,249	14.9%
53	Colorado	3,424	3,276	-4.3%	16,892	17,575	4.0%
54	New Mexico	952	961	0.9%	4,308	5,156	19.7%
55	Arizona	3,362	3,110	-7.5%	17,460	20,146	15.4%
56	Utah	1,523	1,527	0.3%	7,940	8,672	9.2%
57	Nevada	1,534	1,672	9.0%	8,006	9,621	20.2%
58	**Pacific**	**30,070**	**28,520**	**-5.2%**	**150,938**	**157,481**	**4.3%**
59	Alaska	235	267	13.6%	1,303	1,503	15.3%
60	Hawaii	618	696	12.6%	3,470	3,987	14.9%
61	Washington	3,165	3,223	1.8%	16,170	16,961	4.9%
62	Oregon	2,065	1,837	-11.0%	10,097	9,355	-7.3%
63	California	23,987	22,497	-6.2%	119,898	125,675	4.8%
64	**All Regions**	**170,475**	**166,740**	**-2.2%**	**846,973**	**939,310**	**10.9%**

9 PRESS: [→] and hold it down until the columns begin to scroll
You will notice that column A is also frozen into place.

10 PRESS: [CTRL] + [HOME]
Notice that the cell pointer moves to cell B4, instead of cell A1.

 To unfreeze the panes and move the pointer to cell A1:
CHOOSE: Window, Unfreeze Panes
PRESS: CTRL + HOME
The cell pointer now moves freely in the titles area.

 Save the workbook and keep it open for use in the next lesson.

7.1.2 Splitting the Worksheet Window

FEATURE
You can manually split the worksheet's window into two or four
independent panes. To move among the panes, click the mouse
pointer on a cell within the desired pane. This feature makes it easier to view and manage worksheet data that does not fit in a single window.

METHOD
Using the Menu bar:

1. Position the cell pointer below or to the right of the column
    and row where you want the split to occur.
2. CHOOSE: Window, Split to divide the window into panes
3. CHOOSE: Window, Remove Split to remove the panes

Using the mouse:

1. DRAG: the Horizontal split box and the Vertical split box,
    appearing at the end of each scroll bar, to divide the window
    into panes
2. Finalize positioning of the panes by dragging the actual pane
    border that appears inside the worksheet window.
3. Remove a pane by double-clicking its split box.

PRACTICE
You now use two independent window panes to display different
areas in the worksheet.

Setup: Ensure that the "Indicators" workbook is displayed.

1 Let's split the worksheet window into two horizontal panes. Position the mouse pointer over the horizontal split box (above the vertical scroll bar). When positioned correctly, the pointer changes shape.

2 CLICK: left mouse button and hold it down
DRAG: the split box downward to split the window in half

3 Release the mouse button. Notice that you now have two vertical scroll bars for controlling the two panes independently.

4 Clicking a cell that is displayed in a window pane makes that pane active. To move the cell pointer to row 64 in the bottom window pane:
CLICK: on any cell in column A of the lower window pane
PRESS: CTRL + ↓

5 Using the vertical scroll bars, position the contents of the two window panes to appear similar to Figure 7.2. (*Hint:* Before moving the cell pointer within a window pane, click once in the pane to make it active.)

Figure 7.2

Splitting a worksheet window into panes

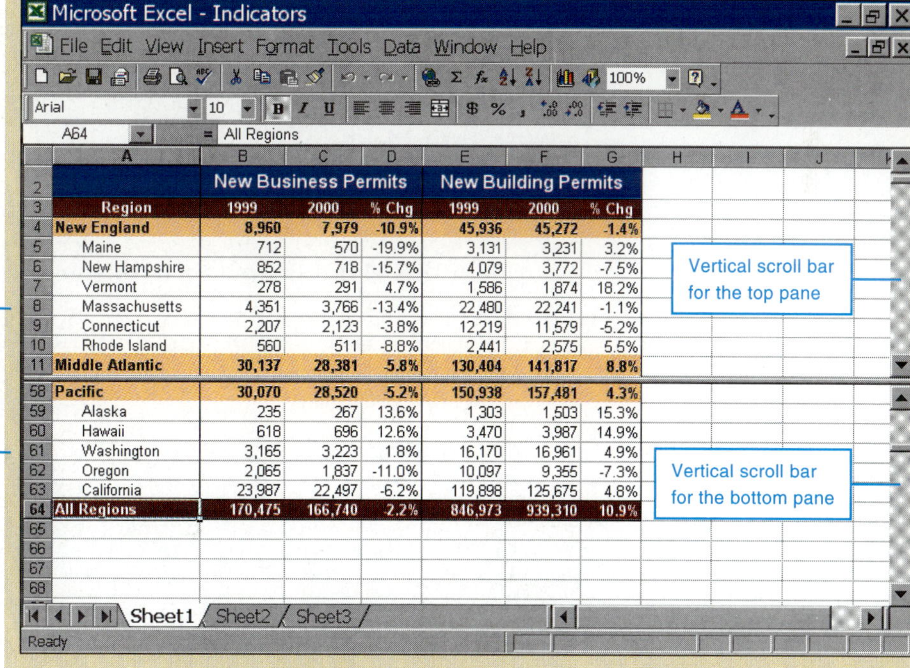

	A	B	C	D	E	F	G	H	I	J
2		New Business Permits			New Building Permits					
3	Region	1999	2000	% Chg	1999	2000	% Chg			
4	New England	8,960	7,979	-10.9%	45,936	45,272	-1.4%			
5	Maine	712	570	-19.9%	3,131	3,231	3.2%			
6	New Hampshire	852	718	-15.7%	4,079	3,772	-7.5%			
7	Vermont	278	291	4.7%	1,586	1,874	18.2%			
8	Massachusetts	4,351	3,766	-13.4%	22,480	22,241	-1.1%			
9	Connecticut	2,207	2,123	-3.8%	12,219	11,579	-5.2%			
10	Rhode Island	560	511	-8.8%	2,441	2,575	5.5%			
11	Middle Atlantic	30,137	28,381	-5.8%	130,404	141,817	8.8%			
58	Pacific	30,070	28,520	-5.2%	150,938	157,481	4.3%			
59	Alaska	235	267	13.6%	1,303	1,503	15.3%			
60	Hawaii	618	696	12.6%	3,470	3,987	14.9%			
61	Washington	3,165	3,223	1.8%	16,170	16,961	4.9%			
62	Oregon	2,065	1,837	-11.0%	10,097	9,355	-7.3%			
63	California	23,987	22,497	-6.2%	119,898	125,675	4.8%			
64	All Regions	170,475	166,740	-2.2%	846,973	939,310	10.9%			
65										
66										
67										
68										

6 Let's enter a new value for Vermont in the top window pane. As you do so, watch the total formula in row 64. Do the following:
SELECT: cell B7
TYPE: **2780**
PRESS: ENTER
The value in cell B64 changes to 172,977. The ability to separate a worksheet into window panes enables you to view the most relevant areas in your worksheet at all times.

7 To quickly remove all panes from the worksheet window:
CHOOSE: Window, Remove Split

8 Save the workbook and keep it open for use in the next lesson.

7.1.3   Outlining a Worksheet

FEATURE
Outlining a worksheet groups related data together and allows you to display or hide the data as a single unit. Excel can automatically outline a worksheet based on the existence of summary formulas, such as the SUM function. When you select a range and issue the Auto Outline command, Excel inserts outline levels at each subtotal formula and for the grand total. Once outlined, you can print a worksheet or plot a chart using only the visible data at a specific level in the outline.

METHOD
1. SELECT: a cell within the worksheet area that you want to outline
2. CHOOSE: Data, Group and Outline, Auto Outline to create an outline
3. CHOOSE: Data, Group and Outline, Clear Outline to remove an outline

PRACTICE
You now practice outlining the contents of an existing worksheet.

Setup: Ensure that the "Indicators" workbook is displayed.

1 To begin, review the contents of this worksheet:
SELECT: cell B4
Looking in the Formula bar, notice that this cell contains a SUM function. In fact, all rows formatted similarly to row 4 provide summary formulas.

2 PRESS: CTRL + ↓

Notice that row 64 contains a formula that adds together all of the subtotal formulas.

3 PRESS: CTRL + HOME

4 Excel uses the existing formulas in a worksheet to determine the best approach for outlining. To begin, you place the cell pointer within the data area that you want to outline and then issue the command:

SELECT: cell A4

CHOOSE: Data, Group and Outline, Auto Outline

Your screen should now appear similar to Figure 7.3. The outlining symbols are described further in Table 7.1.

Figure 7.3

Outlining a worksheet

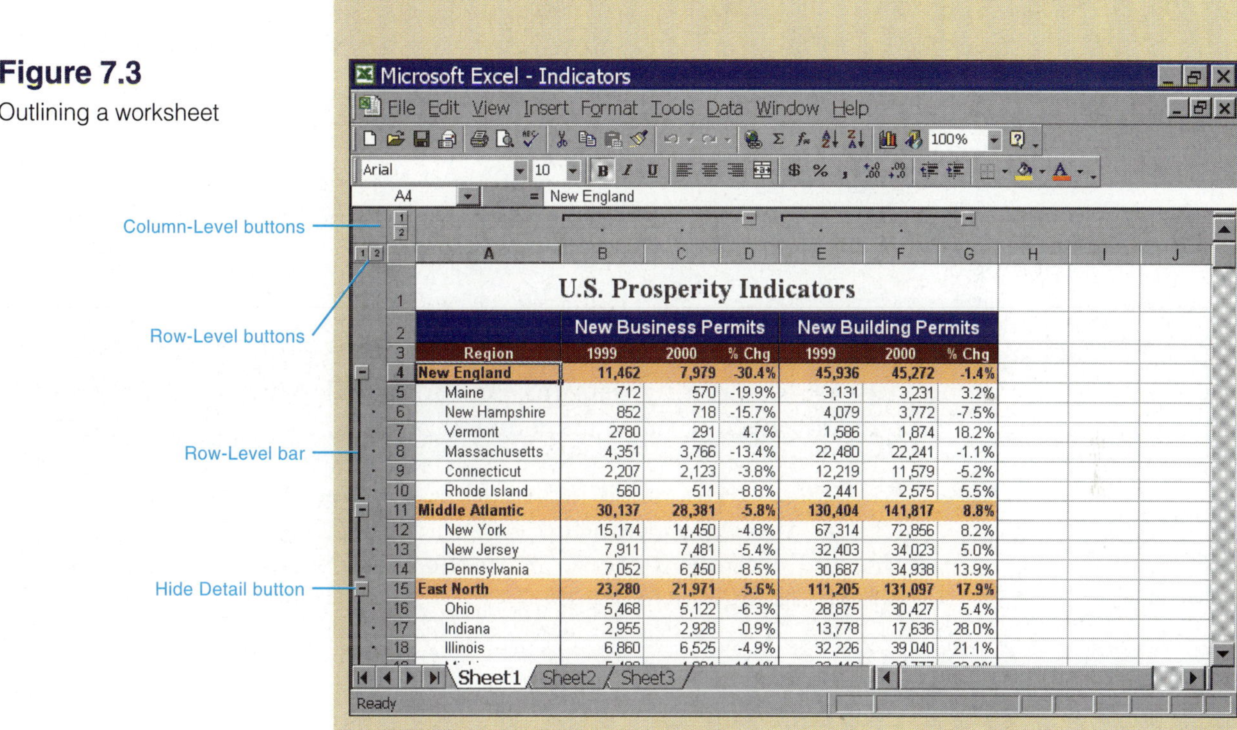

Table 7.1

Outline symbols

Symbol	Description
▣, ▣, ▣, …	Column- and Row-Level buttons let you change the display summary level for the entire worksheet; an outline can have up to eight levels of detail
⊞	Show Detail button lets you expand and display all detail rows and columns for a specific group
⊟	Hide Detail button lets you collapse and hide all detail rows and columns for a specific group
⌐⊟ or ⊟⌐	Row-Level bar shows the detail rows for a specific group; click the bar to hide the detail
─⊟ or ⊟─	Column-Level bar shows the detail columns for a specific group; click the bar to hide the detail

5 To collapse some of the detail in the worksheet:
CLICK: Row-Level 1 button (▣)
All rows containing data for the individual states are hidden; only the Region subtotals remain.

6 To display the detailed information for West North:
CLICK: Show Detail button (⊞) to the left of row 21
Notice that only those states in the West North region are displayed, as shown in Figure 7.4.

Figure 7.4

Collapsing and expanding
an outlined worksheet

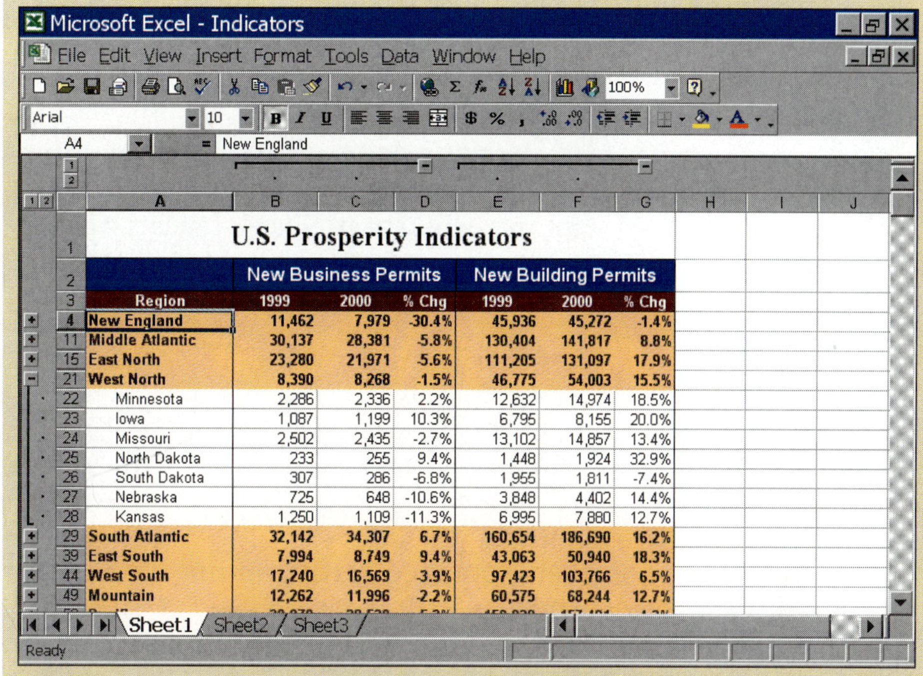

	Region	New Business Permits			New Building Permits		
		1999	2000	% Chg	1999	2000	% Chg
4	New England	11,462	7,979	-30.4%	45,936	45,272	-1.4%
11	Middle Atlantic	30,137	28,381	-5.8%	130,404	141,817	8.8%
15	East North	23,280	21,971	-5.6%	111,205	131,097	17.9%
21	West North	8,390	8,268	-1.5%	46,775	54,003	15.5%
22	Minnesota	2,286	2,336	2.2%	12,632	14,974	18.5%
23	Iowa	1,087	1,199	10.3%	6,795	8,155	20.0%
24	Missouri	2,502	2,435	-2.7%	13,102	14,857	13.4%
25	North Dakota	233	255	9.4%	1,448	1,924	32.9%
26	South Dakota	307	286	-6.8%	1,955	1,811	-7.4%
27	Nebraska	725	648	-10.6%	3,848	4,402	14.4%
28	Kansas	1,250	1,109	-11.3%	6,995	7,880	12.7%
29	South Atlantic	32,142	34,307	6.7%	160,654	186,690	16.2%
39	East South	7,994	8,749	9.4%	43,063	50,940	18.3%
44	West South	17,240	16,569	-3.9%	97,423	103,766	6.5%
49	Mountain	12,262	11,996	-2.2%	60,575	68,244	12.7%

7 To preview how the worksheet will print:
CLICK: Print Preview button ()
Notice that the preview appears identical to the worksheet
display.

8 CLICK: Close command button to return to the worksheet

9 To remove the outline (and all of the associated symbols) from
the worksheet:
CHOOSE: Data, Group and Outline, Clear Outline

10 Save the workbook and keep it open for use in the next lesson.

In Addition

Outlining a Worksheet
Manually

If your worksheet does not contain summary formulas, you need to manually
group the detail sections that you want outlined. Select the desired rows or
columns and then use the Group and Ungroup commands under the Data,
Group and Outline menu option.

7.1.4 Specifying Print Titles and Options

FEATURE

Similar to freezing panes in a worksheet, you can select **print titles** to appear at the top of each printed page. Using data stored in the worksheet, Excel repeats the specified row information whenever a page break is encountered. This feature makes the hard copy printouts for larger worksheets easier to read.

METHOD

1. CHOOSE: File, Page Setup
2. SELECT: *Sheet* tab
3. Specify the desired rows in the *Print titles* area.

PRACTICE

Let's practice setting print titles and printing a large worksheet.

Setup: Ensure that the "Indicators" workbook is displayed.

1 To select the worksheet area to print:
SELECT: cell A4
PRESS: CTRL +*
This keystroke shortcut selects the worksheet's active area.

2 To define the selection as the print area:
CHOOSE: File, Print Area, Set Print Area
(*Note:* Use the Set Print Area command when you need to specify a limited range in the worksheet for printing. In this example, choosing the command was not necessary since you want to print the entire worksheet. However, it is a good habit to set the print area.)

3 To specify a landscape orientation:
CHOOSE: File, Page Setup
SELECT: *Page* tab
SELECT: *Landscape* option button in the *Orientation* area

4 To make the font size appear larger than normal in the printout:
SELECT: 120 in the *% normal size* spin box in the *Scaling* area
CLICK: Print Preview command button
(*Note:* You use Excel's scaling feature to reduce a worksheet's print area to fit on a specified number of pages or to increase a printout's font size for easier reading.)

5 In the bottom left-hand corner of the Preview window, notice that the Status bar reads "Page 1 of 3." (*Note:* Your screen may read "Page 1 of 2" or "Page 1 of 4" for this step, depending on the resolution of your monitor and printer.) To view the next page:
CLICK: Next command button

6 You may have noticed that there are no column headings on page 2 from the title rows in the worksheet. By specifying print titles, you can make your printout more attractive and easier to read. To begin:
CLICK: Close command button
PRESS: CTRL + HOME

7 CHOOSE: File, Page Setup
SELECT: *Sheet* tab

8 In the *Print titles* area of the Page Setup dialog box:
CLICK: Dialog Collapse button (⬚) beside the *Rows to repeat at top* text box
SELECT: cell range from A2 to A3
Notice that only the absolute row numbers "$2:$3" are entered for the range.

9 CLICK: Dialog Expand button (⬚) in the floating range window
Your screen should now appear similar to Figure 7.5.

Figure 7.5

Setting print titles

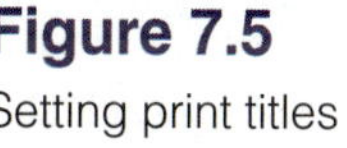

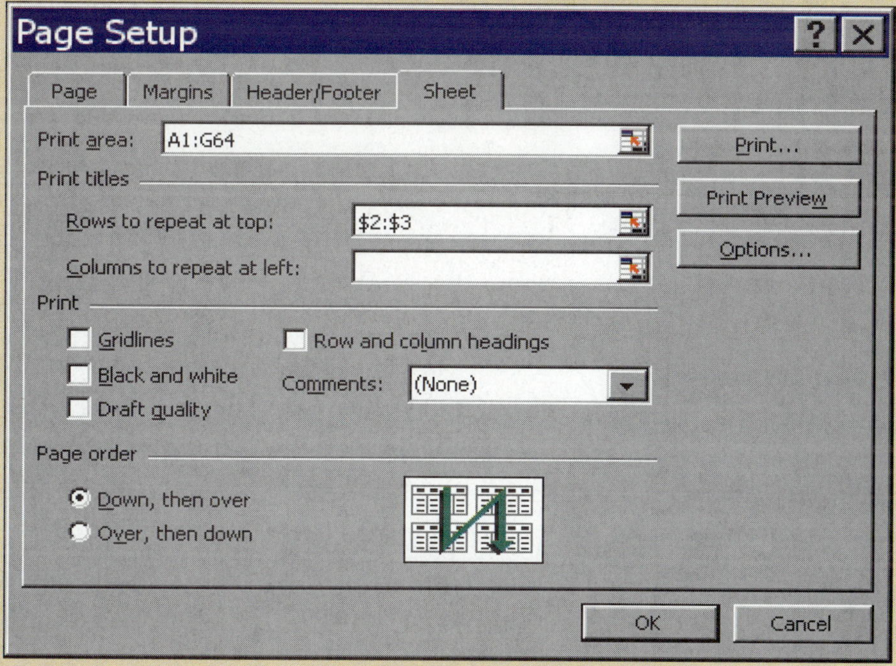

10 To preview your handiwork:
CLICK: Print Preview command button
CLICK: Next command button
Notice that rows 2 and 3 are repeated on the second page.

11 To print the worksheet:
CLICK: Print command button to display the Print dialog box
CLICK: OK command button
(*Note:* If you do not want to print the worksheet, click the Cancel command button in the Print dialog box.)

12 Save the workbook and keep it open for use in the next lesson.

7.1.5 Using the Page Break Preview Mode

FEATURE
After formatting a worksheet and specifying its print options, you can switch display modes to adjust where page breaks occur. In the Page Break Preview mode, you manipulate the location of page breaks by dragging them using the mouse.

METHOD
1. CHOOSE: View, Page Break Preview
2. DRAG: page break lines using the mouse
3. CHOOSE: View, Normal to return to normal viewing

PRACTICE
You now practice adjusting page breaks for the worksheet printout.

Setup: Ensure that the "Indicators" workbook is displayed.

1 To view the worksheet using Page Break Preview mode:
CHOOSE: View, Page Break Preview
(*Note:* If a Welcome to Page Break Preview dialog box appears, click the OK command button to dismiss it.)

2 The right margin and page break borders appear in blue. Position the mouse pointer over the dashed page break line until the pointer changes shape.

3 DRAG: page break line upwards two rows
When you release the mouse, the new page break is set in the window. Figure 7.6 displays one example of a new page break setting.

Figure 7.6

Setting page breaks

"Page 1" watermark helps you line up pages and determine the print order.

Drag the right margin line to set the page border.

Drag the page break line to set the page break.

U.S. Prosperity Indicators						
	New Business Permits			New Building Permits		
Region	1999	2000	% Chg	1999	2000	% Chg
New England	11,462	7,979	###	45,936	45,272	-1.4%
Maine	712	570	-19.9%	3,131	3,231	3.2%
New Hampshire	852	718	-15.7%	4,079	3,772	-7.5%
Vermont	2780	291	4.7%	1,586	1,874	18.2%
Massachusetts	4,351	3,766	-13.4%	22,480	22,241	-1.1%
Connecticut	2,207	2,123	-3.8%	12,219	11,579	-5.2%
Rhode Island	560	511	-8.8%	2,441	2,575	5.5%
Middle Atlantic	30,137	28,381	-5.8%	130,404	#####	8.8%
New York	15,174	14,450	-4.8%	67,314	72,856	8.2%
New Jersey	7,911	7,461	-5.4%	32,403	34,023	5.0%
Pennsylvania	7,052	6,450	-8.5%	30,687	34,938	13.9%
East North	23,280	21,971	-5.6%	111,205	#####	###
Ohio	5,468	5,122	-6.3%	28,875	30,427	5.4%
Indiana	2,955	2,928	-0.9%	13,778	17,636	28.0%
Illinois	6,860	6,525	-4.9%	32,226	39,040	21.1%
Michigan	5,489	4,881	-11.1%	23,416	28,777	22.9%
Wisconsin	2,508	2,515	0.3%	12,910	15,217	17.9%
West North	8,390	8,268	-1.5%	46,775	54,003	###
Minnesota	2,286	2,336	2.2%	12,632	14,974	18.5%
Iowa	1,087	1,199	10.3%	6,795	8,155	20.0%
Missouri	2,502	2,435	-2.7%	13,102	14,857	13.4%
North Dakota	233	255	9.4%	1,448	1,924	32.9%
South Dakota	307	286	-6.8%	1,955	1,811	-7.4%
Nebraska	725	648	-10.6%	3,848	4,402	14.4%
Kansas	1,250	1,109	-11.3%	6,995	7,880	12.7%
South Atlantic	32,142	34,307	6.7%	160,654	#####	###
Maryland	3,310	3,668	10.8%	15,668	18,534	18.3%
Delaware	534	602	12.7%	2,675	2,661	-0.5%
District of Col	595	696	17.0%	2,757	3,457	25.4%
Virginia	3,591	3,779	5.2%	18,557	21,852	17.8%
West Virginia	569	555	-2.5%	2,682	4,239	58.1%
North Carolina	4,007	4,578	14.3%	19,504	25,464	30.6%
South Carolina	1,903	2,014	5.8%	10,175	11,236	10.4%

4 Everything above the page break line appears on the first page and everything below the line appears on the following pages. To preview the worksheet's new settings:
CLICK: Print Preview button ()

5 To return to the normal display:
CLICK: Close command button on the toolbar
CHOOSE: View, Normal

6 Save and then close the workbook.

In Addition
Inserting and Removing a Page Break

To insert a manual page break, position the cell pointer below the row where you wish the page break to occur and then choose the Insert, Page Break command. To remove a manually inserted page break, position the cell pointer in the same location and then issue the Insert, Remove Page Break command.

7.1 Self Check   How would you divide a worksheet window into four panes?

7.2 Manipulating Data in Large Worksheets

When all the data for a worksheet fits on a single screen, the editing tasks are relatively simple. The larger and more complex the worksheet is, the more difficult it is to update. In this module, you learn how to find and replace data in a large worksheet and how to check a worksheet for spelling errors.

7.2.1 Finding and Replacing Data

FEATURE

Excel provides two commands for performing global search and replace operations in a worksheet. The Find and Replace commands enable you to efficiently locate and update the contents of cells. For example, you can easily change the department names in a company directory or increase the prices in a product catalog. If you've ever used word processing software, you're most likely familiar with these two commands already.

METHOD

- CHOOSE: Edit, Find command to locate data in a worksheet
- CHOOSE: Edit, Replace command to replace data in a worksheet

PRACTICE

In this lesson, you practice finding and replacing data in a worksheet.

Setup: Ensure that no workbooks appear in the application window.

1 Open the data file named EXC720.

2 Save the workbook as "Part-Timers" to your personal storage location.

3 The Find command lets you search an entire worksheet for the existence of a few characters, a word, or a phrase. With large worksheets, this command can also be used to move the pointer to a particular cell for editing. To demonstrate:
CHOOSE: Edit, Find
(*Hint:* You can also press CTRL +f to display the Find dialog box.)

4 In the Find dialog box, enter the text you are searching for and then specify where and in what direction to perform the search:
TYPE: **Hunter** in the *Find what* text box
SELECT: By Columns in the *Search* drop-down list box
SELECT: Values in the *Look in* drop-down list box
CLICK: Find Next command button
Your screen should appear similar to Figure 7.7.

Figure 7.7

Find dialog box

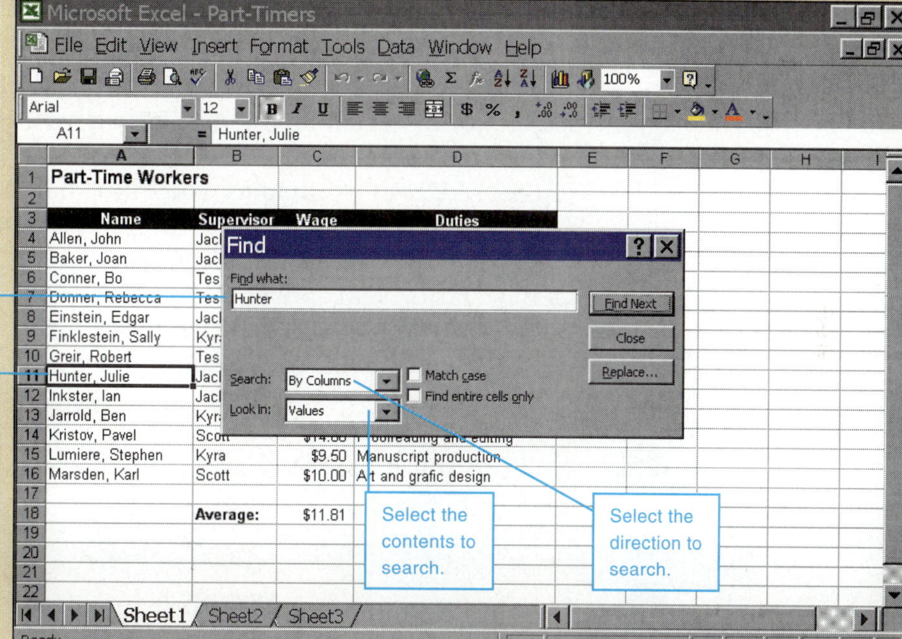

5 If the correct value is found, dismiss the Find dialog box by clicking the Close command button. If you want to continue searching, click the Find Next command button. For this step:
CLICK: Find Next command button
Since the cell pointer does not move, you can safely assume that there are no additional "Hunter" entries in the worksheet.

6 To close the dialog box:
CLICK: Close command button

7 Imagine that one of the supervisors has left the company. You've been asked to replace their name in the worksheet with the name of the newly hired supervisor. To proceed:
SELECT: cell B1
(*Hint:* Although it is not necessary to start at the top of the desired search column, Excel performs searches faster traveling down columns. Given the small size of this workbook, there would be no noticeable speed difference in searching by column or by row.)

8 To replace the name "Jack" with "Andy" in column B:
CHOOSE: Edit, Replace
TYPE: **Jack**
PRESS: TAB
TYPE: **Andy**
Notice that typing replaces the existing selection in the dialog box.

9 You may now proceed by replacing entries one at a time or all at once. For this exercise:
CLICK: Replace All command button
All of the "Jack" entries are replaced by "Andy."

10 Excel can also search for text stored within a cell's formula contents. To demonstrate:
PRESS: CTRL+**f** to display the Find dialog box
TYPE: **C4**
SELECT: Formulas in the *Look in* drop-down list box
CLICK: Find Next command button
The cell pointer stops on the average formula in cell C18. Looking in the Formula bar, notice that one of the arguments is cell "C4."

11 To close the dialog box and return to the top of the worksheet:
CLICK: Close command button
PRESS: CTRL + HOME

12 Save the workbook and keep it open for use in the next lesson.

7.2.2 Spell Checking a Worksheet

FEATURE
The **AutoCorrect** feature can correct hundreds of common typographical and capitalization errors as you type. You will find this feature extremely useful if you habitually misspell particular words. AutoCorrect also helps you enter complex symbols like © and ™ into a cell.

The **Spelling Checker,** a shared utility that appears in all Microsoft Office applications, lets you perform a spelling check on a cell range, a worksheet, or an entire workbook. A spelling check scans cells containing text labels and then displays those words that do not appear in one of its dictionaries. You may then select the proper spelling from a suggested word list or retype the word. If the word is already spelled correctly, you can choose to ignore the word, add the word to a custom dictionary, or insert the word into the AutoCorrect list.

EXCEL

METHOD
- To review the entries available in AutoCorrect:
  CHOOSE: Tools, AutoCorrect
- To perform a spelling check:
  CLICK: Spelling button (▨), or
  CHOOSE: Tools, Spelling

PRACTICE
You now practice using AutoCorrect and spell checking the worksheet.

Setup: Ensure that the "Part-Timers" workbook is displayed.

1 To demonstrate Excel's AutoCorrect feature, let's misspell a word intentionally:
SELECT: cell C1
TYPE: Occassion

2 PRESS: ENTER
Notice that the spelling of the word "occassion" is corrected automatically.

3 To use AutoCorrect to insert special symbols:
SELECT: cell D1
TYPE: (c)
PRESS: Space bar once
AutoCorrect replaces "(c)" with the proper copyright symbol © when you press the Space bar. (*Note:* If you want to keep the "(c)," you can click the Undo button (▨) to reverse the Auto-Correct substitution.)

4 To continue the entry:
TYPE: your name
PRESS: ENTER
(*Note:* Do not take the above instruction literally. Enter your own name and not the text "your name.")

5 To review some of the other entries available in AutoCorrect:
CHOOSE: Tools, AutoCorrect
In the dialog box (Figure 7.8) that appears, there are two columns: *Replace* and *With*. AutoCorrect replaces the entry appearing in the *Replace* column with the entry in the *With* column. You can also use this dialog box to enable and disable several AutoCorrect actions.

Figure 7.8
AutoCorrect dialog box

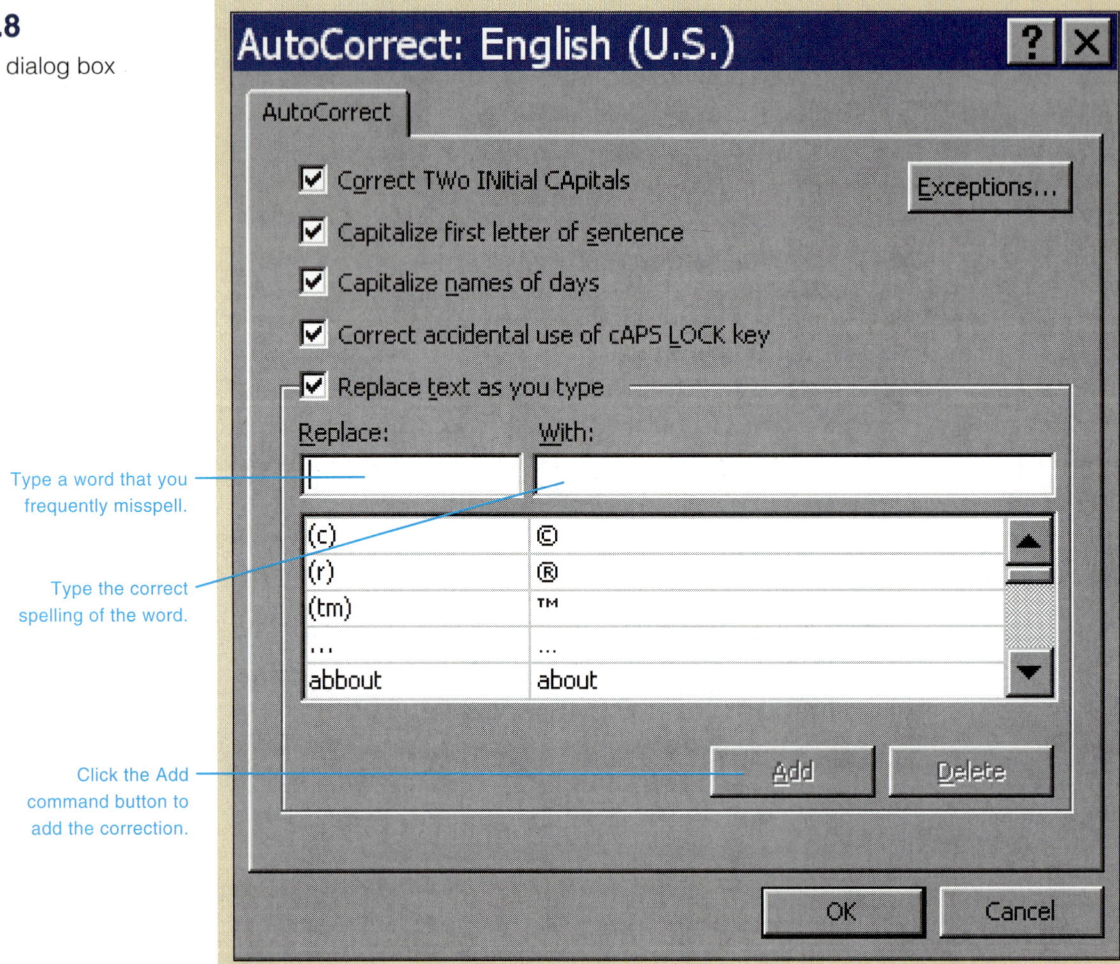

6 To close the AutoCorrect dialog box:
CLICK: OK command button

7 To begin spell checking the entire worksheet:
SELECT: cell A1 to start at the top of the worksheet
CLICK: Spelling button ( )

8 When Excel finds a misspelled word, it displays the dialog box shown in Figure 7.9 and awaits further instructions. To change the word "desin" to the correctly spelled word "design," do the following:
CLICK: Change command button
(*Note:* If this is a word that you frequently misspell, click the AutoCorrect command button to add it to the AutoCorrect list. That way, the next time you misspell the word, Excel corrects your mistake automatically.)

Figure 7.9

Spelling dialog box

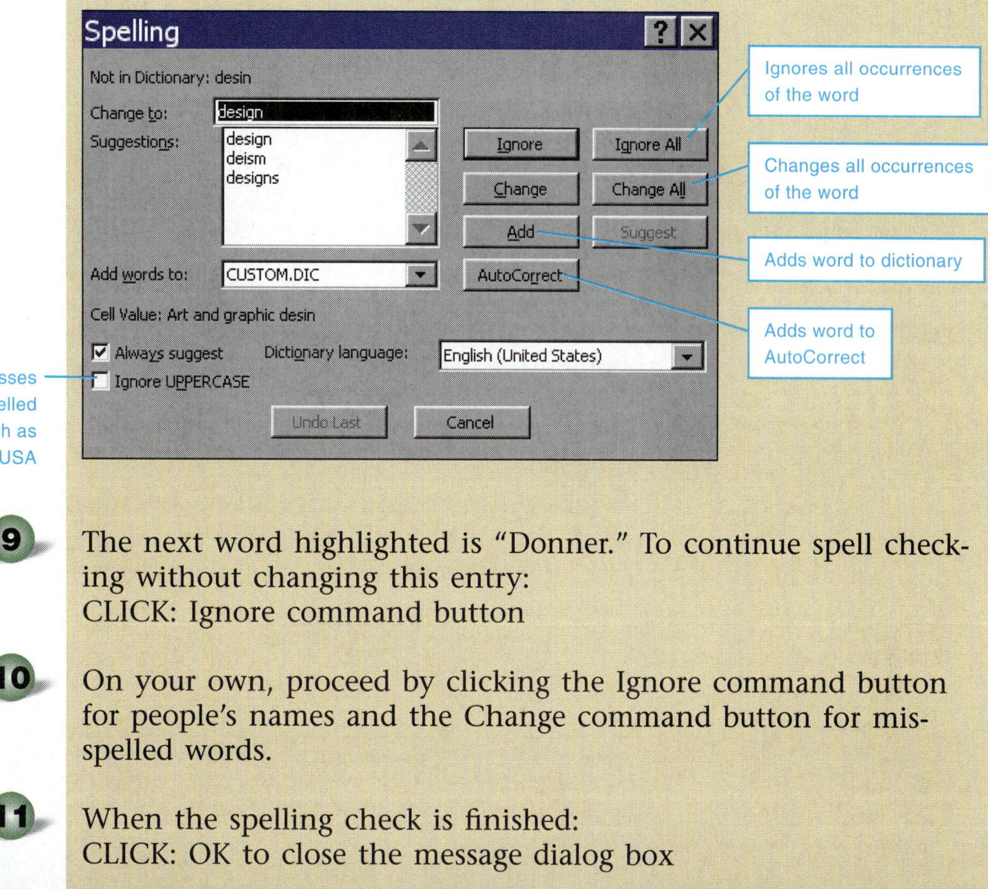

9 The next word highlighted is "Donner." To continue spell checking without changing this entry:
CLICK: Ignore command button

10 On your own, proceed by clicking the Ignore command button for people's names and the Change command button for misspelled words.

11 When the spelling check is finished:
CLICK: OK to close the message dialog box

12 Save and then close the workbook.

7.2 Self Check What characters must you type to have Excel's AutoCorrect feature insert the proper trademark symbol (™)?

7.3 Working with Multiple-Sheet Workbooks

In this module, you learn how to create and navigate a multiple-sheet workbook file. Multiple-sheet workbooks enable you to separate related information onto different pages in a single disk file. For example, a project manager can create a summary report on one worksheet and then place detailed information for each development phase on subsequent worksheets. This three-dimensional (3-D) capability enables you to easily manage and consolidate your information.

7.3.1 Navigating and Renaming Sheets

FEATURE

You access and navigate the sheets in a workbook using tabs that appear at the bottom of the worksheet window. In a new workbook, Excel provides three worksheets named *Sheet1*, *Sheet2*, and *Sheet3*. Besides inserting and deleting sheets, you can rename them to display more descriptive names. When changing the name of a sheet tab, limit your entry to 30 characters, including spaces, and avoid using the asterisk (*), question mark (?), forward slash (/), backslash (\), or colon (:).

METHOD

To move quickly to a particular worksheet, click the desired sheet tab. If the sheet tab is not visible, you may need to scroll the tabs using the tab scroll buttons (shown below). You can also right-click a tab scroll button to display a pop-up menu of the available sheets in the current workbook. To rename a sheet tab, double-click the tab, type a new name, and then press ENTER.

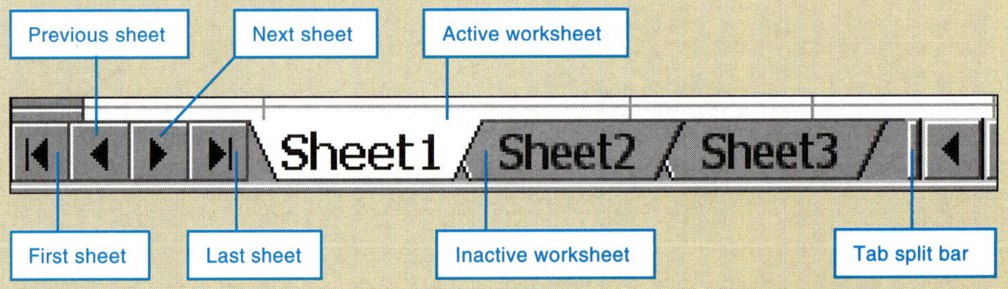

PRACTICE

In this exercise, you practice moving among worksheets and renaming worksheet tabs.

Setup: Ensure that no workbooks are open in the application window.

1   Open the data file named EXC730.

2   Save the workbook as "Tables" to your personal storage location.

3   To familiarize yourself with the workbook's contents:
CLICK: *Sheet2* tab
CLICK: *Sheet3* tab
Notice that the tab for the active worksheet appears with a white background.

4 To navigate among the worksheets:
RIGHT-CLICK: one of the tab scroll buttons
(*Hint:* The tab scroll buttons appear to the left
of the sheet tabs and, when right-clicked, display the pop-up menu shown at the right.)

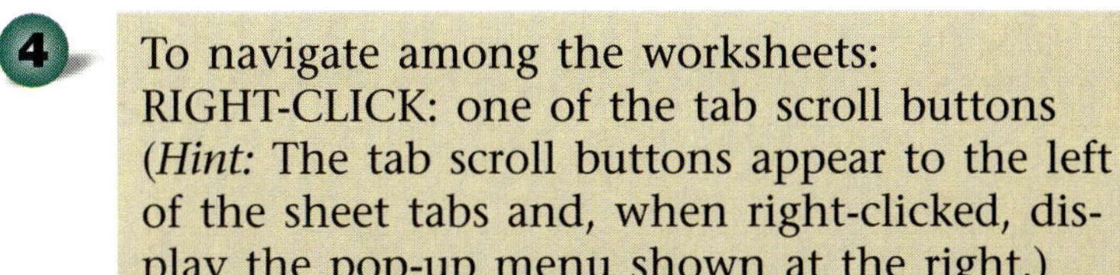

5 To move to the first worksheet:
CHOOSE: Sheet1 in the pop-up menu

6 To rename the Sheet1 worksheet:
DOUBLE-CLICK: *Sheet1* tab
The text within the tab will appear highlighted when selected
properly. (*Hint:* You can also right-click a sheet tab and choose
the Rename command.)

7 TYPE: **Commercial**
PRESS: ENTER

8 To rename the Sheet2 worksheet:
DOUBLE-CLICK: *Sheet2* tab
TYPE: **House**
PRESS: ENTER

9 To rename the Sheet3 worksheet:
DOUBLE-CLICK: *Sheet3* tab
TYPE: **Townhouse**
PRESS: ENTER

10 To move back to the first worksheet:
RIGHT-CLICK: one of the tab scroll
buttons
The pop-up menu now displays more
descriptive names.

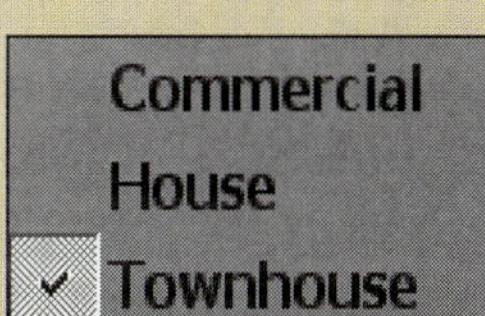

11 CHOOSE: Commercial on the pop-up menu

12 Save the workbook and keep it open for use in the next lesson.

7.3.2 Inserting, Arranging, and Deleting Worksheets

FEATURE

You can insert and delete worksheets and chart sheets inside a workbook file. In addition, you can move, copy, and rearrange the order in which worksheets appear in a workbook. The collection of worksheets and chart sheets in a workbook is known as a *sheet stack*.

METHOD

1. RIGHT-CLICK: a sheet tab
2. CHOOSE: Insert to insert a new worksheet, or
    CHOOSE: Delete to delete the current worksheet, or
    CHOOSE: Move or Copy to move or copy worksheets

PRACTICE

You now practice inserting, copying, moving, and deleting worksheets.

Setup: Ensure that you have completed the previous lesson and that the "Tables" workbook is displayed.

To begin, display the context-sensitive right-click menu for a worksheet tab:
RIGHT-CLICK: *Commercial* tab
Your screen should now appear similar to Figure 7.10.

Figure 7.10

Displaying a sheet tab's right-click menu

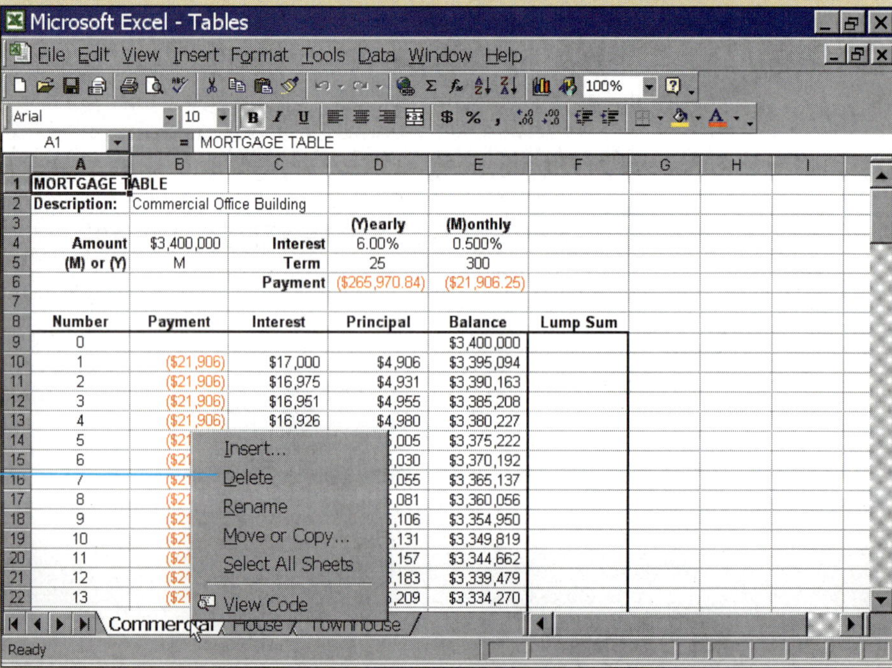

	A	B	C	D	E	F
1	MORTGAGE TABLE					
2	Description:	Commercial Office Building				
3				(Y)early	(M)onthly	
4	Amount	$3,400,000	Interest	6.00%	0.500%	
5	(M) or (Y)	M	Term	25	300	
6			Payment	($265,970.84)	($21,906.25)	
7						
8	Number	Payment	Interest	Principal	Balance	Lump Sum
9	0				$3,400,000	
10	1	($21,906)	$17,000	$4,906	$3,395,094	
11	2	($21,906)	$16,975	$4,931	$3,390,163	
12	3	($21,906)	$16,951	$4,955	$3,385,208	
13	4	($21,906)	$16,926	$4,980	$3,380,227	
14	5	($21		,005	$3,375,222	
15	6	($21		,030	$3,370,192	
16	7	($21		,055	$3,365,137	
17	8	($21		,081	$3,360,056	
18	9	($21		,106	$3,354,950	
19	10	($21		,131	$3,349,819	
20	11	($21		,157	$3,344,662	
21	12	($21		,183	$3,339,479	
22	13	($21		,209	$3,334,270	

Display the right-click menu to manipulate the worksheets and chart sheets in a workbook.

EXCEL

2 To remove the menu from displaying:
PRESS: ESC

3 Before inserting and deleting worksheets, let's practice moving a sheet using the drag and drop method. To begin, ensure that the *Commercial* tab is selected. Then, position the mouse pointer over the *Commercial* tab and do the following:
CLICK: the left mouse button and hold it down
DRAG: *Commercial* tab to the right until the downward pointing triangle appears to the right of the *Townhouse* tab, at the end of the sheet stack

4 Release the mouse button when positioned correctly to complete the move operation.

5 On your own, move the *House* tab in between the *Townhouse* and *Commercial* tabs. The *House* tab will appear active when dropped.

6 To create a duplicate of an existing worksheet:
RIGHT-CLICK: *House* tab
CHOOSE: Move or Copy

7 The current workbook's filename already appears in the *To book* drop-down list. To complete the copy operation:
SELECT: (move to end) in the *Before sheet* list box
SELECT: *Create a copy* check box
CLICK: OK command button
A new sheet tab appears named *House (2)*. You will remove this duplicate worksheet in the next few steps.

8 A workbook's sheet tabs share the window with the horizontal scroll bar. You can adjust how much room is devoted to each by dragging the tab split bar that is sandwiched between the two. On your own, practice dragging and releasing the tab split bar. (*Hint:* Refer to the graphic in Lesson 7.3.1.) After reducing the space available to the sheet tabs, click the tab scroll buttons to navigate back and forth.

9 SELECT: *House (2)* tab

10 To delete this worksheet:
RIGHT-CLICK: *House (2)* tab
CHOOSE: Delete
CLICK: OK command button
The worksheet is removed from the workbook.

 To insert a worksheet:
RIGHT-CLICK: *Commercial* tab
CHOOSE: Insert
The Insert dialog box appears as shown in Figure 7.11.

Figure 7.11

Insert dialog box: *General* tab

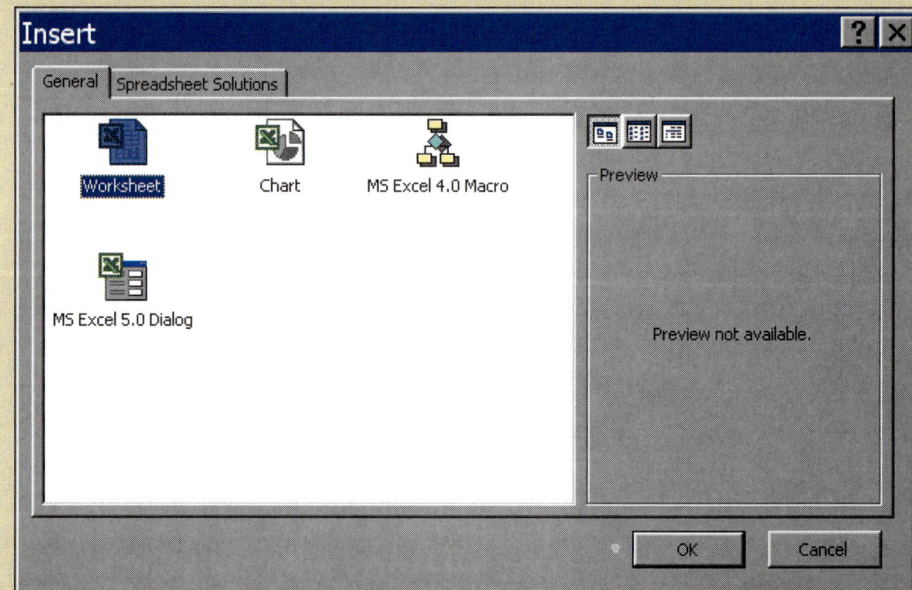

 On the *General* tab:
SELECT: Worksheet icon
CLICK: OK command button
A blank worksheet, named *Sheet1*, appears to the left of the *Commercial* tab. (*Note:* New sheets are numbered incrementally. Therefore, the worksheet tabs will be named *Sheet2*, *Sheet3*, and so on.)

 DRAG: *Sheet1* tab to the left of the *Townhouse* tab

 Let's rename this tab for use as a summary worksheet:
DOUBLE-CLICK: *Sheet1* tab
TYPE: Summary
PRESS: ENTER

 DRAG: tab split bar to the right until all sheet tabs are visible

 Save the workbook and keep it open for use in the next lesson.

7.3.3 Creating Hyperlinks in a Worksheet

FEATURE

The Web might not be so famous if it were not for hyperlinks. They provide an easy way to "drill-down" through layers of information to find what you are looking for. With a single mouse click on a hyperlink, you can go from viewing a company's annual report to viewing its performance ratios, charts and graphs, or competitor's results. (And with another mouse click, you may even display a list of the company's majority shareholders along with links to their Web sites.)

With Excel 2000, you can connect a worksheet to other Excel workbooks, to other Office documents, or to data stored on the Internet. Your connections can be simple—linking together the worksheets in a single workbook or complex—linking a worksheet to a database stored on your company's intranet. When you click a hyperlink that appears on a worksheet, two different scenarios can result. If the hyperlink contains an URL address for your intranet or an Internet Web site, your Web browser software is launched and automatically attempts to establish a connection. On the other hand, if the hyperlink contains a reference to another workbook or Office document, the document is retrieved and displayed in its source application.

METHOD

1. SELECT: a cell for which you want to insert a hyperlink
2. CLICK: Insert Hyperlink button (⬛), or
   CHOOSE: Insert, Hyperlink
3. TYPE: *desired prompt* in the *Text to display* text box
4. SELECT: an option in the *Link to* area
5. Specify the connection parameters for the hyperlink.

PRACTICE

Let's create a simple table of contents for navigating the workbook using hyperlinks.

Setup: Ensure that you have completed the previous lessons and that the "Tables" workbook is displayed.

1   On your own, enter the information displayed in Figure 7.12 on the *Summary* worksheet. Ensure that the text labels appear in cells B3, B4, and B5.

Figure 7.12

Creating a table of contents

	A	B	C	D
1	**Workbook Table of Contents**			
2				
3	**1**	Townhouse Mortgage Table		
4	**2**	House Mortgage Table		
5	**3**	Commercial Mortgage Table		
6				

2 SELECT: cell B3
This cell contains the text "Townhouse Mortgage Table."

3 To create a hyperlink using the contents of this cell:
CLICK: Insert Hyperlink button ( )

4 In the *Link to* area of the Insert Hyperlink dialog box:
CLICK: Place in This Document button
The dialog box should now appear as shown in Figure 7.13.

Figure 7.13

Insert Hyperlink dialog
box: *Place in This
Document* button

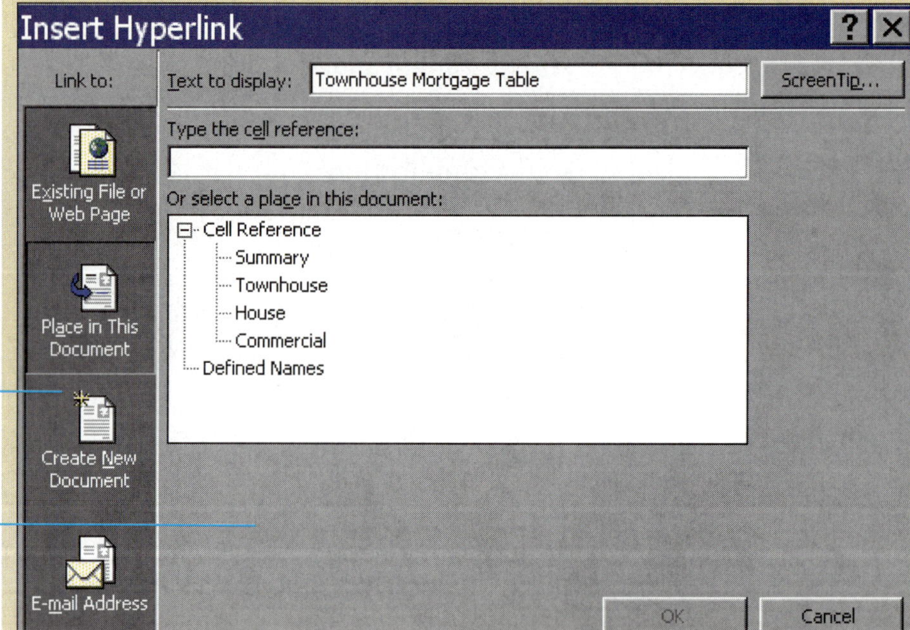

Click the type of link that you want to create.

The information displayed changes depending on the type of link selected.

5 To establish a hyperlink to the *Townhouse* tab:
SELECT: Townhouse in the tree-style list box
Notice that cell A1 is entered as the target cell reference automatically.

6 To complete the operation:
CLICK: OK command button
You will notice that the cell entry appears blue and with an underline. This is the common formatting style for displaying and using hyperlinks in Web browser software.

7 To move to the *Townhouse* tab using the hyperlink, position the mouse pointer over cell B3. Notice that the pointer changes shape to a hand. To initiate the hyperlink:
CLICK: cell B3

8 CLICK: *Summary* tab to return to the table of contents worksheet
Notice that the cell entry now appears purple to show that the link has been selected.

9 On your own, create hyperlinks in cells B4 and B5 for the other two worksheets. Make sure that you test the hyperlinks before proceeding.

10 Save the workbook and keep it open for use in the next lesson.

7.3.4　Grouping Worksheets for Formatting

FEATURE

You can group worksheets together to assist in creating and formatting identical worksheets. When you select more than one sheet tab, **Group mode** is automatically turned on and all the commands that you issue affect all of the selected worksheets. For example, Group mode allows you to change a column's width in one worksheet and have that same modification made to all sheets in the workbook file.

METHOD

- To activate Group mode, select multiple worksheets by clicking their tabs while holding down the CTRL key. (*Hint:* To select multiple contiguous sheets, hold down the SHIFT key.)
- To turn Group mode off, right-click on any selected tab and then choose the Ungroup Sheets command from the shortcut menu.

PRACTICE

In this exercise, you practice selecting multiple worksheets and then formatting them as a group.

Setup: Ensure that you have completed the previous lesson and that the "Tables" workbook is displayed.

1 In reviewing the three primary worksheets, you may have noticed that they are identical in layout and appearance. By using the same worksheet structure, you can easily format and enhance all of the worksheets as a single unit or group. To illustrate:
CLICK: *Townhouse* tab to make it active

2 To make this worksheet easier to use for novices, you will highlight the cells in which users are allowed to enter and change data. Rather than formatting each sheet separately, let's group them together:
PRESS: CTRL and hold it down
CLICK: *House* tab
CLICK: *Commercial* tab
(*Note:* Remember to release the CTRL key.) All three sheet tabs appear active with a white background. Also, the Title bar displays the word "[Group]" beside the workbook's filename.

3 With all three tabs selected (and active), most commands that you perform in the displayed worksheet will now be applied to the entire group of worksheets. Do the following:
SELECT: cell range from B4 to B5
PRESS: CTRL and hold it down
SELECT: cell range from D4 to D5
(*Note:* Remember to release the CTRL key.)

4 To change the background cell color for the selected cells:
CLICK: down arrow attached to the Fill Color button (⬛▾)
CLICK: a pale yellow color
SELECT: cell B4
Your screen should now appear similar to Figure 7.14. Notice the three active tabs that are selected and grouped for formatting.

Figure 7.14

Formatting worksheets
as a group

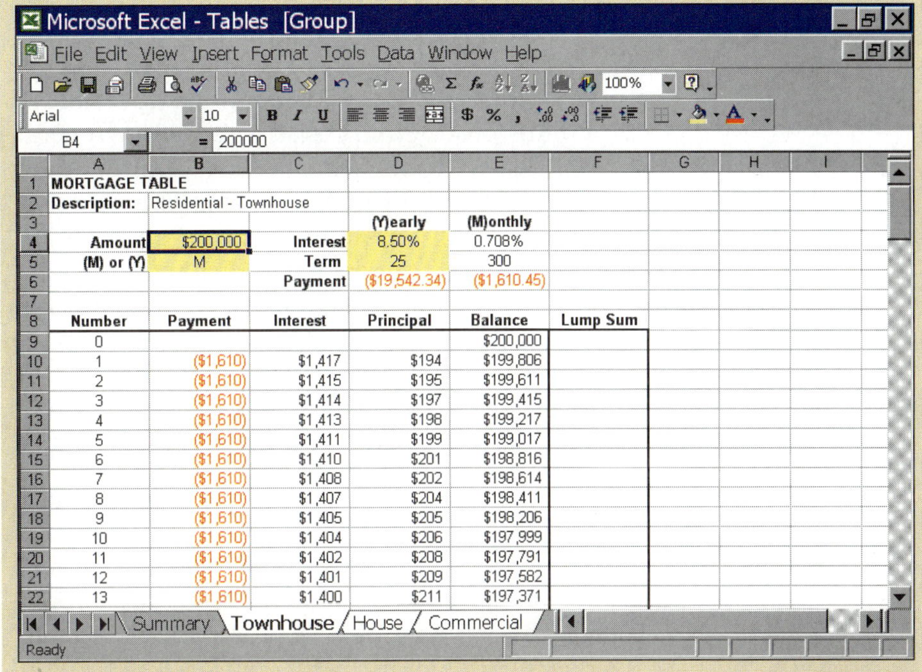

5. Let's ungroup the worksheets.
RIGHT-CLICK: *Townhouse* tab
CHOOSE: Ungroup Sheets

6. To review your handiwork:
CLICK: *House* tab
CLICK: *Commercial* tab
Notice that the background fill color has been applied to the grouped worksheets and that cell B4 is the active cell in all of them.

7. Save and then close the workbook.

In Addition	As you would in formatting multiple worksheets, you can select a group of worksheets and then click the Print button () or choose the File, Print command. Only the worksheets that are part of the selected group are printed.
Printing Multiple Worksheets	

7.3 Self Check   How would you rename a chart sheet and then move it to the end of a sheet stack in a workbook?

7.4 Consolidating Your Data

Whether you need to combine revenues from several regions or calculate productivity statistics across several departments, Excel's consolidation tools allow you to better manage, organize, and present your information. Excel enables you to **consolidate** or merge data stored in different worksheets and workbooks. There are two methods for consolidating worksheet data. First, you can enter formulas and functions that reference cells from other worksheets. Second, you can use Excel's Data, Consolidate command. In this module, you learn how to consolidate data stored in a multiple-sheet workbook and in multiple workbook files.

7.4.1 Consolidating a Multiple-Sheet Workbook

FEATURE

For smaller applications, you can combine or summarize data that is stored across multiple worksheets in a workbook. Dividing data among worksheets enables you to group and manage data logically and then merge data for performing summary calculations and creating reports.

METHOD

1. Select the cell where you want the result to appear.
2. CHOOSE: Data, Consolidate
3. Specify the cell ranges that you want to consolidate.

PRACTICE

You now consolidate data in a multiple-sheet workbook using formulas and the Data, Consolidate command.

Setup: Ensure that no workbooks are open in the application window.

1 Open the data file named EXC741.

2 Save the workbook as "Sauderson" to your personal storage location.

3 Review the four worksheets that are stored in this workbook: Summary, Shift1, Shift2, and Shift3.

4 To begin, you will create a simple addition formula to consolidate the data stored on the three subsidiary worksheets. Do the following:
SELECT: cell B4 on the *Summary* tab
This is the cell where you want the consolidation result to appear.

5 To build the formula expression:
TYPE: =
CLICK: *Shift1* tab
CLICK: cell B4
Notice that =**Shift1!B4** appears in the Formula bar. The exclamation point separates the sheet name from the cell address.

6 To continue:
TYPE: +
CLICK: *Shift2* tab
CLICK: cell B4
TYPE: +
CLICK: *Shift3* tab
CLICK: cell B4
The Formula bar now reads
=**Shift1!B4+Shift2!B4+Shift3!B4**.

7 To enter the formula into the cell:
PRESS: `ENTER`
The result, 75, appears in cell B4 on the *Summary* tab. (*Hint:* You can copy this formula to the remaining cells to complete the worksheet.)

8 Another method for creating a consolidation formula is to use the SUM function. This function works well when the structural layout of subsidiary worksheets is identical. Do the following:
SELECT: cell B5 on the *Summary* tab
TYPE: =**sum(**
CLICK: *Shift1* tab
CLICK: cell B5
The Formula bar now reads =**sum(Shift1!B5**.

9 To continue:
PRESS: `SHIFT` and hold it down
CLICK: *Shift3* tab
TYPE: **)**
The Formula bar now reads =**sum('Shift1:Shift3'!B5)**.
Notice that the formula references a three-dimensional range.

10 To enter the formula into the cell:
PRESS: `ENTER`
The result, 30, appears in cell B5 on the *Summary* tab.

11 Lastly, you may find using the Consolidate command easier than the previous methods. Do the following:
SELECT: cell range from B4 to H7
CHOOSE: Data, Consolidate
Your screen should now appear similar to Figure 7.15.

Figure 7.15

Consolidate dialog box

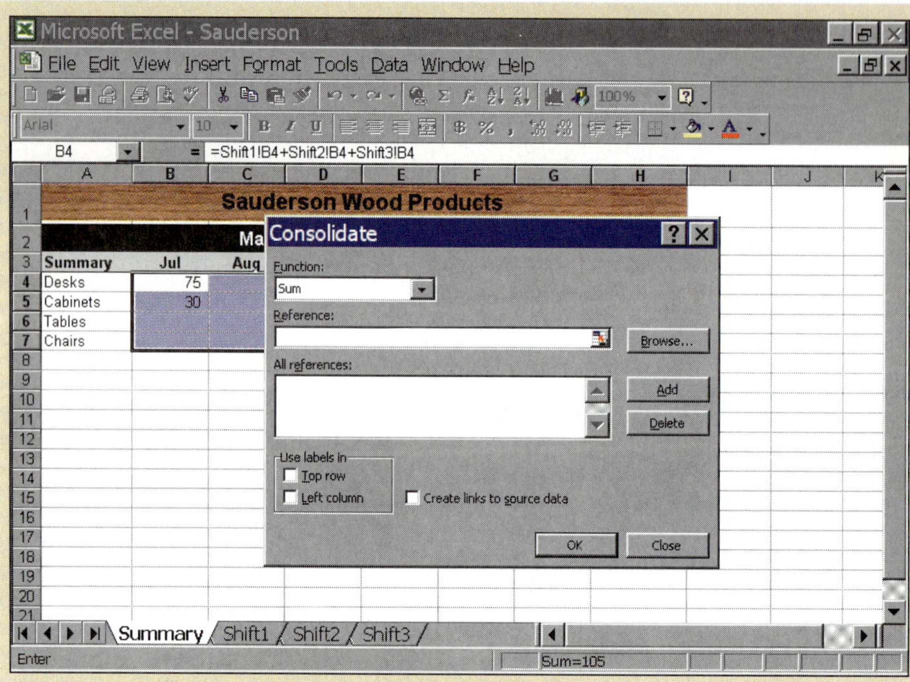

12 In the *Function* drop-down list box:
SELECT: Sum, if it is not already selected
(*Hint:* You can also select from a number of alternative functions
for summarizing data stored in subsidiary worksheets.)

13 In the *Reference* text box, enter the data range for the first shift:
CLICK: Dialog Collapse button (⬚)
CLICK: *Shift1* tab
SELECT: cell range from B4 to H7
CLICK: Dialog Expand button (⬚)
CLICK: Add command button
The cell range selected is added to the *All references* list box.

14 Enter the data range for the second shift:
CLICK: Dialog Collapse button (⬚)
CLICK: *Shift2* tab
Notice that the proper range is already highlighted.

15 To continue:
CLICK: Dialog Expand button (⬚)
CLICK: Add command button

16 Enter the data range for the third shift:
CLICK: Dialog Collapse button (⬚)
CLICK: *Shift3* tab
CLICK: Dialog Expand button (⬚)
CLICK: Add command button
The dialog box should now appear similar to Figure 7.16.

Figure 7.16

Consolidating data from
multiple worksheets

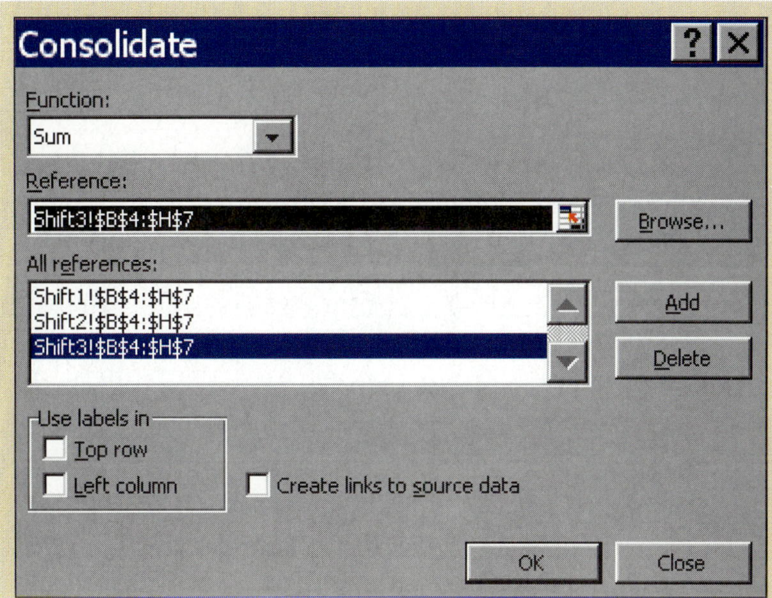

17 To complete the dialog box:
CLICK: OK command button
The *Summary* tab is displayed with the result of the consolidation.

18 On your own, select a few cells in the data area of the *Summary* tab. Except for the entries in cells B4 and B5, notice that the cells contain static values. In order to keep the summary sheet updated, you would need to perform the Consolidate command each time a value changes on a subsidiary worksheet. The entries in cells B4 and B5, on the other hand, contain formulas that will automatically reflect changes in these cells. (*Note:* There is an option in the Consolidate dialog box that allows you to establish formula links to the source data.)

19 On your own, change some of the values on the subsidiary worksheets and then do the following:
SELECT: *Summary* tab
SELECT: cell range from B4 to H7
CHOOSE: Data, Consolidate
Notice that the past references already appear in the dialog box.

20 To update the Summary worksheet:
CLICK: OK command button
The results are now updated in the summary sheet.

21 Save and then close the workbook.

7.4.2 Consolidating Multiple Workbooks

FEATURE

You can link and consolidate separate workbook files into a summary workbook. Linking workbooks has two major advantages over using one large multiple-sheet workbook. First, the subsidiary workbooks are smaller in size and, therefore, easier to maintain and manage on a daily basis. Second, the subsidiary workbooks are not restricted to the same computer or network as the summary workbook. For example, each department may control its own workbook and then submit a file once a month for consolidation, perhaps on a diskette or via the Internet.

METHOD

1.   Open the summary and subsidiary workbooks.
2.   Organize the workbook windows within the application window.
3.   Enter a formula in the summary workbook that references cells in the subsidiary workbooks or choose the Data, Consolidate command.

PRACTICE

You now combine and summarize data that is stored in two individual workbooks.

Setup: Ensure that no workbooks are open in the application window.

1

Let's begin by opening and then saving the workbooks that will be used in this lesson. Do the following:

- Open the file named EXC742a and save it as "Group1" to your personal storage location.
- Open the file named EXC742b and save it as "Group2" to your personal storage location.
- Open the file named EXC742c and save it as "Groups" to your personal storage location.

2 To view all of the worksheets in the document area:
CHOOSE: Window, Arrange
The dialog box shown at the right appears.

3 In the Arrange Windows dialog box:
SELECT: *Tiled* option button
CLICK: OK command button
Your screen should now appear similar to Figure 7.17.

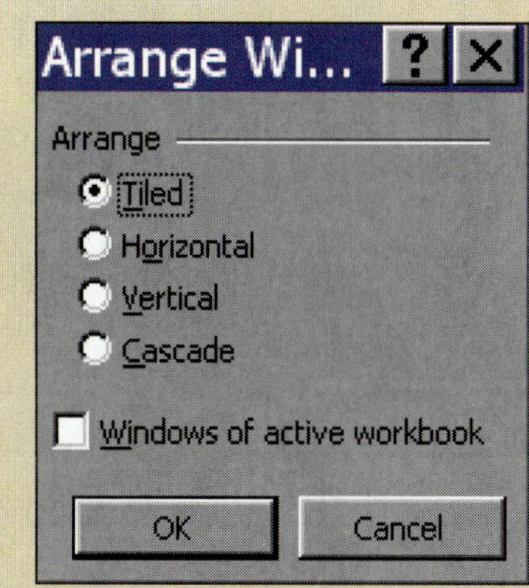

Figure 7.17
Arranging workbook windows

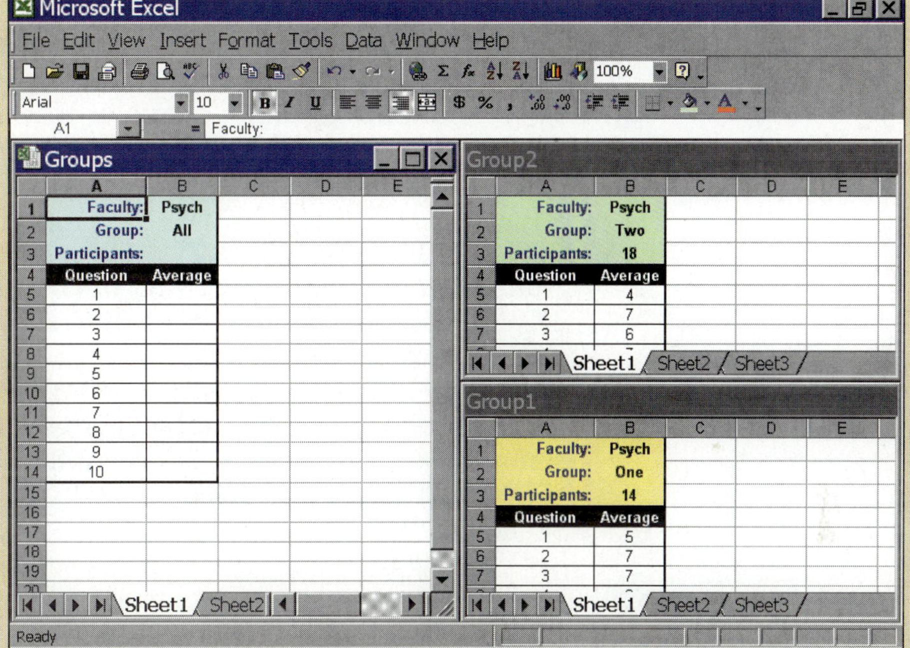

4 To move among the open workbooks, you position the mouse pointer on a visible part of the desired window and click once. You can also choose the workbook's name from the Window menu option. On your own, practice clicking on each window's Title bar to make it active. Notice that the window's scroll bars also appear. When you are ready to proceed, make the Groups workbook active.

5 You will now enter a formula that adds together values from the Group1 and Group2 workbooks and then displays the result in cell B3. Do the following:
SELECT: cell B3 in the Groups workbook

6 To enter the formula expression:
TYPE: =
CLICK: the Title bar for the Group1 workbook
CLICK: cell B3 in the Group1 workbook
The Formula bar now reads =[Group1.xls]Sheet1!$B$3.
Notice that the workbook's filename is enclosed in square brackets and that the sheet name is separated from the absolute cell address using an exclamation point.

7 To continue:
TYPE: +
CLICK: the Title bar for the Group2 workbook
CLICK: cell B3 in the Group2 workbook
PRESS: ENTER
The result, 32, is displayed in cell B3 of the Groups workbook.

8 To illustrate the dynamic nature of the link:
SELECT: Group1 workbook
SELECT: cell B3
TYPE: 24
PRESS: ENTER
Notice that the result in cell B3 of Groups has been updated to 42 automatically. (*Hint:* For this interactive linking to occur, all of the workbooks should be open.)

9 Let's consolidate the two subsidiary workbook's data into the summary area for Groups. Do the following:
SELECT: Groups workbook
SELECT: cell range from B5 to B14

10 To calculate the average results for data stored in the two workbooks:
CHOOSE: Data, Consolidate
SELECT: Average in the *Function* drop-down list box

11 In the *Reference* text box, enter the data range for Group1:
CLICK: Dialog Collapse button (▣)
SELECT: Group1 workbook
SELECT: cell range from B5 to B14
CLICK: Dialog Expand button (▣)
CLICK: Add command button
The workbook's location, filename, sheet name, and cell range are added to the *All references* list box.

12 To enter the data range for Group2:
CLICK: Dialog Collapse button ()
SELECT: Group2 workbook
SELECT: cell range from B5 to B14
CLICK: Dialog Expand button ( )
CLICK: Add command button
The Consolidate dialog box should now appear similar to Figure 7.18.

Figure 7.18

Consolidating data from multiple workbooks

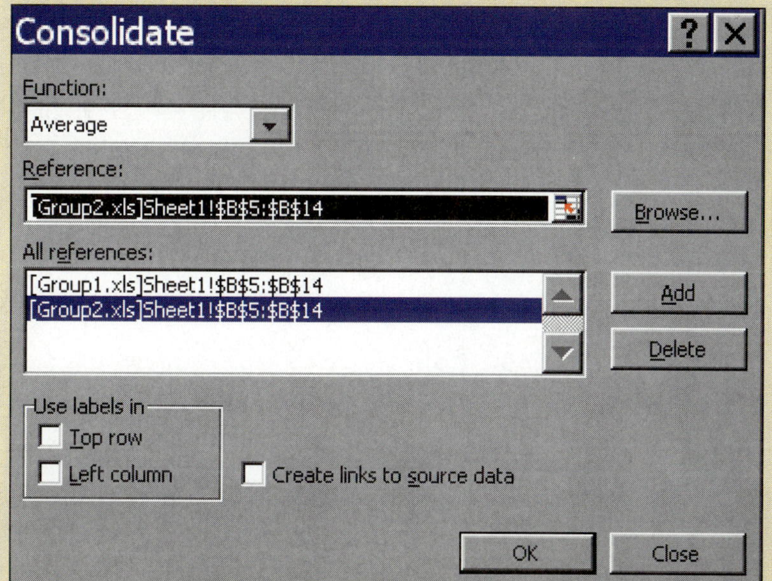

13 To ensure that the Groups workbook is updated to reflect changes made in its subsidiary workbooks:
SELECT: *Create links to source data* check box

14 To proceed with the consolidation:
CLICK: OK command button

15 You may have noticed that Excel automatically generates an outline for the Groups workbook. On your own, click on the Row-Level 2 (2) button to view more detail and then review the contents of the cells. When you are ready to proceed, collapse the detail by clicking on the Row-Level 1 (1) button.

16 To close and save all of the workbooks at the same time:
PRESS: SHIFT and hold it down
CHOOSE: File, Close All
(*Hint:* The Close All command only appears when the SHIFT key is depressed.)

17 Release the [SHIFT] key. Then, do the following:
CLICK: Yes to All command button
All three of the open workbooks are saved and then closed.

In Addition Sending a Workbook via E-mail	Without leaving Excel, you can send a worksheet to another user for consolidation using electronic mail (e-mail). This feature assumes that you communicate with other users via a modem, network, or Internet connection. Once configured, you simply click the E-mail button () on the Standard toolbar or choose the File, Send To, Mail Recipient command. Rather than embedding the worksheet inside the mail message, you can send the worksheet as an attachment to a standard mail message.

7.4.3   Asking the Office Assistant for Help

FEATURE
The Office Assistant is your personal and customizable computer guru. When you need to perform a task that you're unsure of, call up the Assistant and then type your question into the balloon area. When you click the Search button, the Office Assistant analyzes your request and provides a suggested list of helpful topics. Furthermore, the Assistant watches your keystrokes and mouse clicks to ensure that you are using the software productively and efficiently.

METHOD
To display the Office Assistant:

- CLICK: Office Assistant button (▣), or
- CHOOSE: Help, Show Office Assistant

To hide the Office Assistant:

1. RIGHT-CLICK: *the Assistant character*
2. CHOOSE: Hide from the pop-up menu

PRACTICE
You now practice using the Office Assistant.

Setup: Ensure that no workbooks are open in the application window.

1 To display a new workbook:
CLICK: New button (□)

2 If the worksheet window does not appear maximized:
DOUBLE-CLICK: its Title bar

3 Let's ask the Office Assistant how to link workbooks:
CLICK: Office Assistant button (②)
An Assistant character appears on the screen.

4 Using the mouse (and referring to Figure 7.19):
DRAG: the Assistant character to the middle of the worksheet window
(*Note:* Clicking on the Office Assistant with the left mouse button will toggle the balloon's display on an off. For this exercise, ensure that the balloon is displayed.)

Figure 7.19

Displaying and moving
the Office Assistant

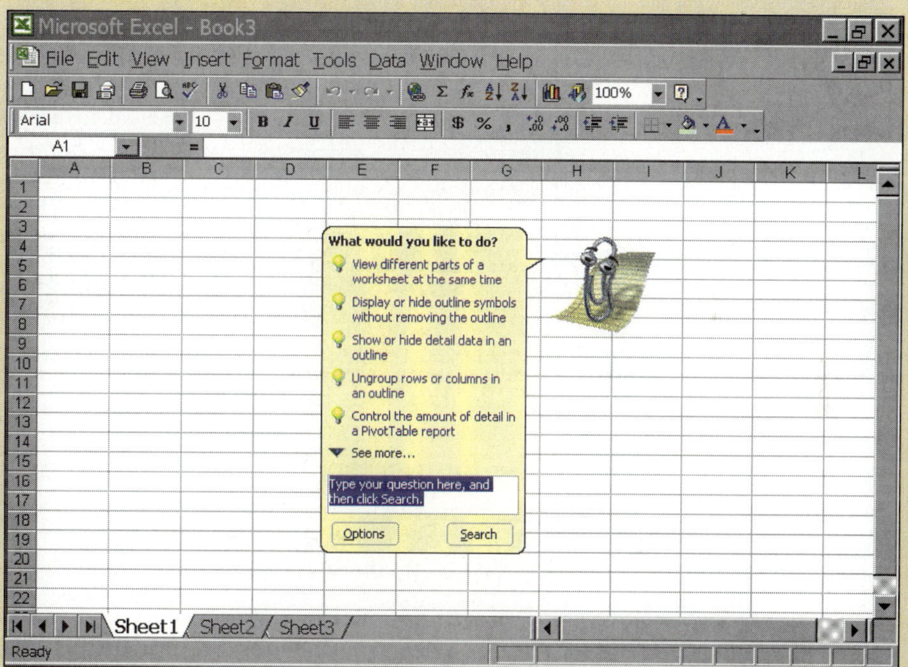

5 To ask the desired question:
TYPE: **How do I link workbooks?**
CLICK: Search button

6 The Assistant provides several potential topics that you can use to clarify your request. To do so:
CLICK: *About using formulas to calculate values on other worksheets and workbooks* option

7 After a few moments, the Help system is launched and the desired topic is displayed (Figure 7.20). To remove the Assistant character from the screen:
RIGHT-CLICK: the Assistant character
CHOOSE: Hide

Figure 7.20

Displaying the Help system

Click this icon to display the Help contents frame.

Click this icon to print the displayed Help topic.

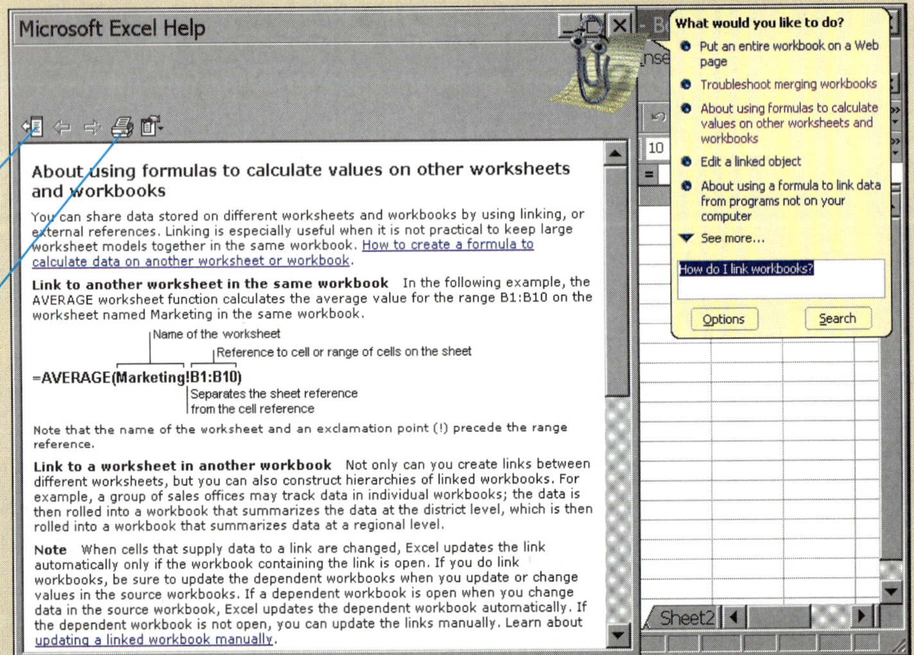

8 To close the Help system window:
CLICK: its Close button (☒)

9 Close the workbook without saving the changes.

10 Exit Microsoft Excel.

7.4 Self Check   Name two advantages for separating your work into multiple workbooks.

7.5 Chapter Review

You have covered some sophisticated, yet practical, features of Excel in this guide. This chapter introduced you to some additional commands and features that can help increase your productivity in building and using worksheets and workbooks. You learned how to freeze titles on the screen, open windows to view different parts of a worksheet, outline your data for display and reporting, create multiple-sheet workbooks, and consolidate data from various sources. All of these features assist you in performing and managing your work more efficiently.

7.5.1 Command Summary

Many of the commands and procedures appearing in this chapter are summarized in the following table.

Skill Set	To Perform this Task . . .	Do the Following . . .
Working with Worksheets and Workbooks	Freeze and unfreeze rows and columns as panes on the screen	CHOOSE: Window, Freeze Panes CHOOSE: Window, Unfreeze Panes
	Split the worksheet window into panes and then remove the split	CHOOSE: Window, Split CHOOSE: Window, Remove Split
	Rename a worksheet or chart sheet	DOUBLE-CLICK: its sheet tab TYPE: *new name*
	Insert a worksheet or chart sheet	RIGHT-CLICK: a sheet tab CHOOSE: Insert
	Delete a worksheet or chart sheet	RIGHT-CLICK: its sheet tab CHOOSE: Delete
	Group worksheets together	SELECT: the first sheet tab PRESS: CTRL and hold it down CLICK: additional tabs for inclusion
	Consolidate data that is stored in a multiple-sheet workbook or in multiple workbooks	CHOOSE: Data, Consolidate

Continued

Skill Set	To Perform this Task . . .	Do the Following . . .
Working with Worksheets and Workbooks *Continued*	Arrange worksheet windows in the Excel application window	CHOOSE: Window, Arrange
	Spell check a worksheet	CLICK: Spelling button ( ), or CHOOSE: Tools, Spelling
	View the AutoCorrect entries	CHOOSE: Tools, AutoCorrect
Working with Cells	Find data in a worksheet	CHOOSE: Edit, Find
	Replace data in a worksheet	CHOOSE: Edit, Replace
	Define a hyperlink in a cell	SELECT: the desired cell CLICK: Insert Hyperlink button ( )
Displaying and Formatting Data	Apply and remove outlining in a worksheet	CHOOSE: Data, Group and Outline, Auto Outline CHOOSE: Data, Group and Outline, Clear Outline
Page Setup and Printing	Change the page orientation and scaling	CHOOSE: File, Page Setup SELECT: *Page* tab
	Specify print titles from the worksheet for printing	CHOOSE: File, Page Setup SELECT: *Sheet* tab
	Insert a page break	CHOOSE: Insert, Page Break
	Remove a page break	CHOOSE: Insert, Remove Page Break
	View and set page breaks using Page Break Preview mode	CHOOSE: View, Page Break Preview DRAG: the desired page break lines
	Return from Page Break Preview mode to normal viewing	CHOOSE: View, Normal

Continued

Skill Set	To Perform this Task . . .	Do the Following . . .
Working with Files	Save and close multiple open workbook files	PRESS: SHIFT and hold it down CHOOSE: File, Close All
	Ask the Office Assistant for help	CLICK: Office Assistant button (), or CHOOSE: Help, Show Office Assistant
	Hide the Office Assistant character	RIGHT-CLICK: the character CHOOSE: Hide
	Send a workbook via e-mail	CLICK: Send Email button (), or CHOOSE: File, Send To, Mail Recipient

7.5.2 Key Terms

This section specifies page references for the key terms identified in this chapter. For a complete list of definitions, refer to the Glossary provided at the end of this learning guide.

AutoCorrect, *p. 340*

consolidate, *p. 354*

Group mode, *p. 351*

outlining, *p. 326*

panes, *p. 325*

print titles, *p. 334*

Spelling Checker, *p. 340*

7.6 Review Questions

7.6.1 Short Answer

1. What is the main difference between freezing titles on a worksheet and dividing a window into panes?
2. How does outlining help you in working with large worksheets?
3. How do you replace all occurrences of one value in a worksheet with another value?
4. What is the purpose of the AutoCorrect feature?
5. How do you change the name of a sheet tab?

6. How do you move a tab in a workbook's sheet stack?
7. Name two ways you might use hyperlinks in a worksheet.
8. In a consolidation formula, what symbol(s) separates a worksheet's name from the cell address? A workbook's name from the sheet tab?
9. What are four options for arranging open workbooks in Excel's application window?
10. When using the Data, Consolidate command, what must you do to ensure that the summary results are updated dynamically?

7.6.2   True/False

1. —— To unfreeze the horizontal and vertical worksheet panes, choose the Window, Undo command.
2. —— You can divide a worksheet window into two, three, or four panes.
3. —— Excel can outline a worksheet automatically based on the existence of summary formulas, such as the SUM function.
4. —— To specify print titles in a worksheet, you enter a row range, such as **$1:$4**, into the appropriate text box.
5. —— You can manipulate page breaks using the mouse when viewing the worksheet in Page Break Preview mode.
6. —— To rename a sheet tab in a workbook, hold down the CTRL key while clicking once on the sheet tab.
7. —— Chart sheets must appear to the right of worksheets in a workbook's sheet stack.
8. —— The currently displayed or active worksheet's tab appears white.
9. —— If you create a hyperlink that contains an URL address, Excel launches your Web browser software to display the link.
10. —— Using the Data, Consolidate command, you can summarize data by summing or averaging the contents of various cell references.

7.6.3   Multiple Choice

1. To freeze the titles appearing in rows 1 through 3 and columns A and B in a worksheet, you must first place the cell pointer in this cell prior to choosing the Freeze Panes command.
   a. B3
   b. B4
   c. C3
   d. C4

2. To split a worksheet window using the mouse:
    a.   DRAG: horizontal or vertical scroll bars
    b.   DRAG: horizontal or vertical split boxes
    c.   DRAG: tab scroll buttons
    d.   DRAG: tab split bar

3. Which of the following will display all of the detail rows in a worksheet that is outlined to three levels?
    a.   CLICK: Level 1 button (1)
    b.   CLICK: Level 3 button (3)
    c.   CHOOSE: Data, Group and Outline, Outline All
    d.   CHOOSE: Data, Group and Outline, Expand All

4. To insert a manual page break in a worksheet, position the cell pointer and then:
    a.   CHOOSE: Insert, Page Break
    b.   CHOOSE: Edit, Insert Page Break
    c.   CHOOSE: View, Insert Page Break
    d.   PRESS: CTRL + ENTER

5. Which of the following is *not* a legitimate combination of options for finding data in a worksheet?
    a.   Search by Columns and Look in Values
    b.   Search by Rows and Look in Formulas
    c.   Search by Columns and Look in Objects
    d.   All of the above are legitimate options.

6. By default, a new workbook in Excel contains how many worksheets?
    a.   1
    b.   2
    c.   3
    d.   16

7. Which of the following is *not* a legitimate option for establishing a hyperlink?
    a.   Place in This Document
    b.   Existing File or Web Page
    c.   E-mail Address
    d.   All of the above are legitimate options.

8. Which of the following modes lets you apply formatting commands to more than one worksheet in a multiple-sheet workbook?
    a.   Edit mode
    b.   Format mode
    c.   Group mode
    d.   Multiple mode

9. To help move about the worksheets in a workbook, you right-click this set of buttons to display a menu of the sheet names.
   a. tab scroll buttons
   b. split box buttons
   c. split bar buttons
   d. toolbar buttons

10. Which of the following is *not* a function that is available in the Consolidate dialog box?
    a. Average
    b. Count
    c. Pmt
    d. Sum

7.7 Hands-On Projects

7.7.1 Grandview College: Student List

In this exercise, you practice navigating a large worksheet, freezing panes, and finding and replacing data.

1. Open the data file named EXC771.

2. Save the workbook as "Student List" to your personal storage location.

3. First, let's look over the worksheet in order to become familiar with its contents. Do the following:
   PRESS: CTRL + ↓ to move to the last row in the list
   PRESS: CTRL + → to move to the last column in the last row

4. PRESS: CTRL + HOME to move back to cell A1

5. To adjust the view magnification:
   PRESS: CTRL + SHIFT + →
   CLICK: down arrow attached to the Zoom button (100% ▾)
   CLICK: Selection
   You should now see columns A through H on the screen.

6. To reinstate the view magnification:
   CLICK: CTRL + HOME
   CLICK: down arrow attached to the Zoom button (100% ▾)
   CLICK: 100%

7. To ensure that the column headings and student surnames are always displayed, let's freeze the appropriate rows and columns:
SELECT: cell C2
CHOOSE: Window, Freeze Panes

8. You can now scroll to any portion of the worksheet without the row and column titles disappearing. To illustrate:
PRESS: **CTRL** + ➡ to move to the last column in the current row
PRESS: **CTRL** + ⬇ to move to the last row in the list
Notice that row 1 and columns A and B are always visible.

9. To remove the window panes (frozen titles):
CHOOSE: Window, Unfreeze Panes
PRESS: **CTRL** + **HOME**

10. To find a student's information:
PRESS: **CTRL** + **f**
TYPE: **Getz**
CLICK: Find Next command button
The cell pointer moves directly to row 17.

11. To close the Find dialog box:
CLICK: Close command button

12. You've just been notified that one of the Department names in column F is going to change. To update the list:
SELECT: cell F1
CHOOSE: Edit, Replace

13. In the Replace dialog box that appears:
TYPE: **Business Admin** in the *Find what* text box
PRESS: **TAB**
TYPE: **Commerce** in the *Replace with* text box
SELECT: By Columns in the *Search* drop-down list box
CLICK: Replace All command button
All the changes are made to the matching worksheet cells.

14. Save and then close the workbook.

7.7.2 Fast Forward Video: Rental Summary

You now practice working with a multiple-sheet workbook. In addition to renaming and moving the sheet tabs, you format the worksheets using Group mode.

1. Open the data file named EXC772.
2. Save the workbook as "Video Outlets" to your personal storage location.
3. On your own, click on the three sheet tabs to familiarize yourself with the contents of the workbook. You will notice that the worksheets are identical in format and style.
4. To begin, let's give the sheet tabs more meaningful names:
    DOUBLE-CLICK: *Sheet1* tab
    TYPE: **Downtown**
    PRESS: ENTER
5. To rename the Sheet2 worksheet:
    DOUBLE-CLICK: *Sheet2* tab
    TYPE: **Coldstream**
    PRESS: ENTER
6. To rename the Sheet3 worksheet:
    DOUBLE-CLICK: *Sheet3* tab
    TYPE: **Westside**
    PRESS: ENTER
7. Let's now arrange the tabs so that they appear in alphabetical order. First, select the *Coldstream* tab to make it active:
    CLICK: *Coldstream* tab
8. Then, position the mouse pointer over the *Coldstream* tab and do the following:
    CLICK: the left mouse button and hold it down
    DRAG: *Coldstream* tab to the left until the downward pointing triangle appears to the left of the *Downtown* tab, at the beginning of the sheet stack
9. After releasing the mouse button, the sheet tabs are arranged into their new order. You will now use Group Mode to apply formatting to all of the worksheets. Do the following:
    PRESS: CTRL and hold it down
    CLICK: *Downtown* tab
    CLICK: *Westside* tab
    All three sheet tabs should appear selected with the word "[Group]" displaying in the Title bar. You can now release the CTRL key.
10. To format the cells containing totals:
    SELECT: cell range from D4 to D10
    PRESS: CTRL and hold it down
    SELECT: cell range from B10 to C10
    Make sure that you release the CTRL key.

11. To apply boldface and a text color to the selected cells:
    CLICK: Bold button (**B**) twice
    SELECT: a blue color from the Font Color button (A⋅)
    SELECT: cell A2 to remove the highlighting
12. Let's ungroup the worksheets.
    RIGHT-CLICK: *Coldstream* tab
    CHOOSE: Ungroup Sheets
13. To review the worksheets:
    CLICK: *Downtown* tab
    CLICK: *Westside* tab
    Notice that the cell formatting has been applied to the
    grouped worksheets and that cell A2 is the active cell in
    all of them.
14. Save and then close the "Video Outlets" workbook.

7.7.3 Sun Valley Frozen Foods: Inventory Averages

In this exercise, you practice combining and summarizing data that
is stored in two individual workbooks.

1. Make sure there are no workbooks open in the application
   window. Then, do the following:
   - Open the data file named EXC773a and save it as
     "SVFF Q1" to your personal storage location.
   - Open the data file named EXC773b and save it as
     "SVFF Q2" to your personal storage location.
   - Open the data file named EXC773c and save it as
     "SVFF Avg" to your personal storage location.
2. To arrange all of the workbooks in the document area:
   CHOOSE: Window, Arrange.
   SELECT: *Tiled* option button
   CLICK: OK command button
   Your screen should now appear similar to Figure 7.21.

Figure 7.21

Arranging open
workbook windows

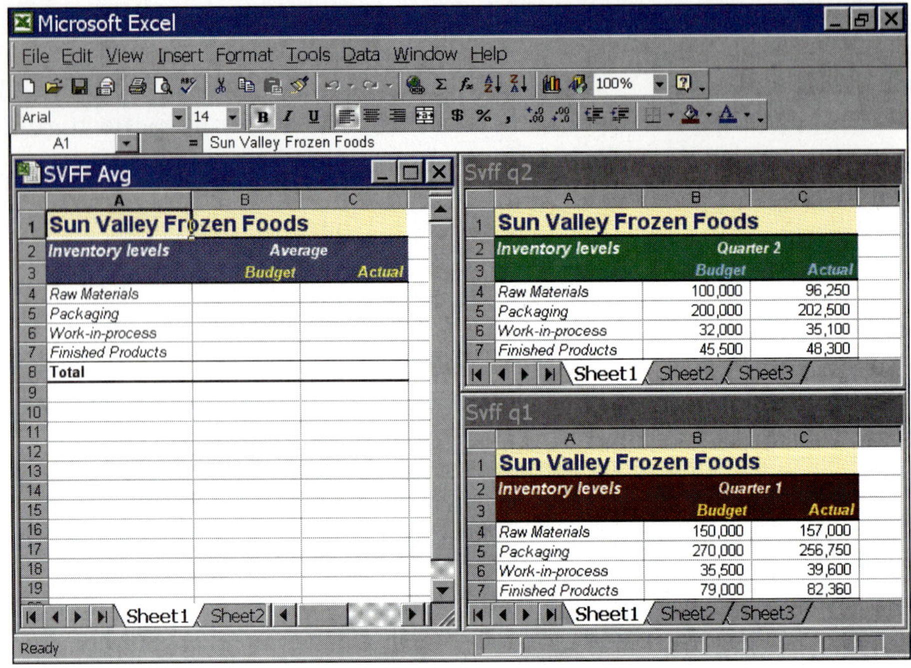

3. To calculate the average of the quarterly workbooks, do the
   following:
   SELECT: cell range from B4 to C8 in the "SVFF Avg" workbook
4. Let's use Excel's Consolidate command:
   CHOOSE: Data, Consolidate
   SELECT: Average in the *Function* drop-down list box
5. In the *Reference* text box, enter the data range for SVFF Q1:
   CLICK: Dialog Collapse button (⊞)
   CLICK: Title bar of the "SVFF Q1" workbook
   SELECT: cell range from B4 to C8
   CLICK: Dialog Expand button (⊞)
   CLICK: Add command button
   The reference should appear similar to the following:
   `'[SVFF Q1.xls]Sheet1'!$B$4:$C$8`. The single quotes are
   required since there is a space in the filename.
6. On your own, add the same cell range for the "SVFF Q2"
   workbook to the *All references* list box.
7. To ensure that the "SVFF Avg" workbook is updated to reflect
   changes made in the two subsidiary workbooks:
   SELECT: *Create links to source data* check box
   CLICK: OK command button
   The calculated average values should now appear in the "SVFF
   Avg" workbook.
8. To maximize the "SVFF Avg" workbook and display some
   details:
   DOUBLE-CLICK: its Title bar
   CLICK: Row-Level 2 (☐) button

9. Return to viewing the summary information only.

10. To save and close all workbooks:
PRESS: (SHIFT) and hold it down
CHOOSE: File, Close All
CLICK: Yes command button when prompted

7.7.4 Lakeside Realty: Project Management

This exercise lets you practice consolidating separate subsidiary workbook files into a summary workbook. Your objective is to consolidate the subcontractor data for two development projects.

1. Make sure there are no workbooks open in the application window. Then, do the following:
    - Open the data file named EXC774a and save it as "Project1" to your personal storage location.
    - Open the data file named EXC774b and save it as "Project2" to your personal storage location.
    - Open the data file named EXC774c and save it as "ProjSumm" to your personal storage location.
2. Enter your name in cell E2 of the ProjSumm workbook.
3. To arrange the windows:
CHOOSE: Window, Arrange.
SELECT: *Tiled* option button
CLICK: OK command button
4. SELECT: cell B7 in the ProjSumm workbook
5. Enter a consolidation formula that adds together the values stored in cell B7 of the Project1 and Project2 workbooks.
6. Modify the formula expression in cell B7 to contain relative cell addresses rather than absolute cell addresses. (*Hint:* Remove the "$" symbols from the formula in cell B7 of the ProjSumm workbook.)
7. Copy the formula in cell B7 to the cell range from B7 to M16 in the ProjSumm workbook. Then, press (ESC) to remove the dashed marquee.
8. To freeze the window panes:
PRESS: (CTRL) + (HOME)
SELECT: cell B7
CHOOSE: Window, Freeze Panes
9. To move the cell pointer to the Year-to-Date column:
PRESS: (CTRL) + (→)
Your screen should now appear similar to Figure 7.22.
10. Save and close all of the workbooks using the Close All command.

Figure 7.22

Completing the
ProjSumm workbook

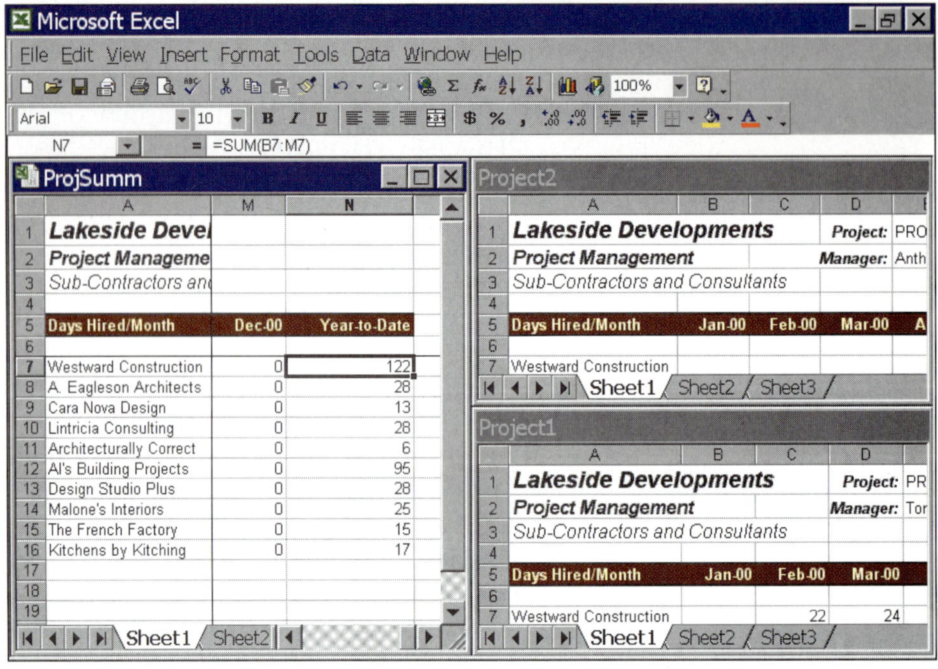

7.7.5 On Your Own: Consolidated Income Statement

This exercise lets you practice working with a multiple-sheet workbook. To begin, open the data file named EXC775. Then, save the workbook as "Division Income" to your personal storage location. After reviewing the worksheets in the workbook, rename the sheet tabs to display the division name appearing in cell A1 of each worksheet. Now, change the order of the worksheets to appear as: *Seaboard, Southern,* and *Central.*

Create a copy of the *Seaboard* worksheet and position it as the first sheet in the workbook. Change the text in cell A1 of the new sheet to "Summary" and rename the sheet tab to display the same name. Using Group Mode, change the font in cell A1 of all the worksheets to Times New Roman. When you are finished, ungroup the sheets.

Replace the Revenue and Expense figures in the *Summary* worksheet with formulas that will consolidate the information from the three Division worksheets. When you are finished, save and then close the "Division Income" workbook.

7.7.6   On Your Own: A New Multiple-Sheet Workbook

The objective of this exercise is to create a new multiple-sheet workbook from scratch. The workbook should contain the following sheets: *Music, Movies,* and *Books.* For the Music worksheet, enter a title in row 1 and column headings in row 3 for Title, Artist, Year, Producer, Label, and Rating. For the Movies worksheet, enter a title and column headings for Title, Actors, Year, Director, Producer, and Rating. For the Books worksheet, enter a title and column headings for Title, Author, Year, ISBN, Publisher, and Rating. Format all of the worksheets using Group mode, and then add some sample information to the worksheets. Include data for the Rating column using a scale from 1 to 5, with 1 being poor and 5 being excellent.

Insert a new worksheet at the front of the sheet stack called *Contents.* Place three hyperlinks on this worksheet that navigate to the sheet tabs in the workbook when clicked. Beside each hyperlink, enter a formula that calculates and displays the average rating value for that particular worksheet. Then, enter a summary formula beneath the hyperlink area that averages these three rating subtotal values. When you are finished, save the workbook as "My Ratings" and then close the workbook. If you are not proceeding to the case problems, exit Microsoft Excel.

7.8   Case Problems: Home Stretch Hardware

Home Stretch Hardware has recently established a distribution warehouse to service their chain of retail outlets. Howard Bose, a purchasing agent working out of the warehouse, monitors and tracks the overall inventory levels. In addition to his regular duties, Howard must prepare and submit management reports to the executive committee of Home Stretch Hardware. Fortunately, Howard has already developed worksheets containing the requisite information, but he now needs to use some of Excel's productivity features to manage and summarize the data.

In the following case problems, assume the role of Howard and perform the same steps that he identifies. You may want to re-read the chapter opening before proceeding.

1. At 3 P.M. today, Howard must meet with a sales representative from EJ Morris, one of Home Stretch's suppliers. To prepare for the meeting, he decides to review the EJ Morris product line in a worksheet that he has developed. He opens the EXC781 data file and then saves it as "EJ Morris" to his personal storage location. He immediately notices that the worksheet has not been updated for some time. Acme Distribution, one of Home Stretch's old suppliers, is still listed on the worksheet. Howard corrects this mistake by updating all occurrences of "Acme Distribution" with their new supplier "ACE Supplies." Next, he modifies the display so that the column headings and the SKU column are always visible when scrolling. At this point, he moves the cell pointer to the bottom right-hand corner of the list using the CTRL + ↓ and CTRL + → keystrokes. The worksheet appears similar to Figure 7.23. Howard keeps the worksheet open for use in his next task.

Figure 7.23

Updating and displaying a large worksheet

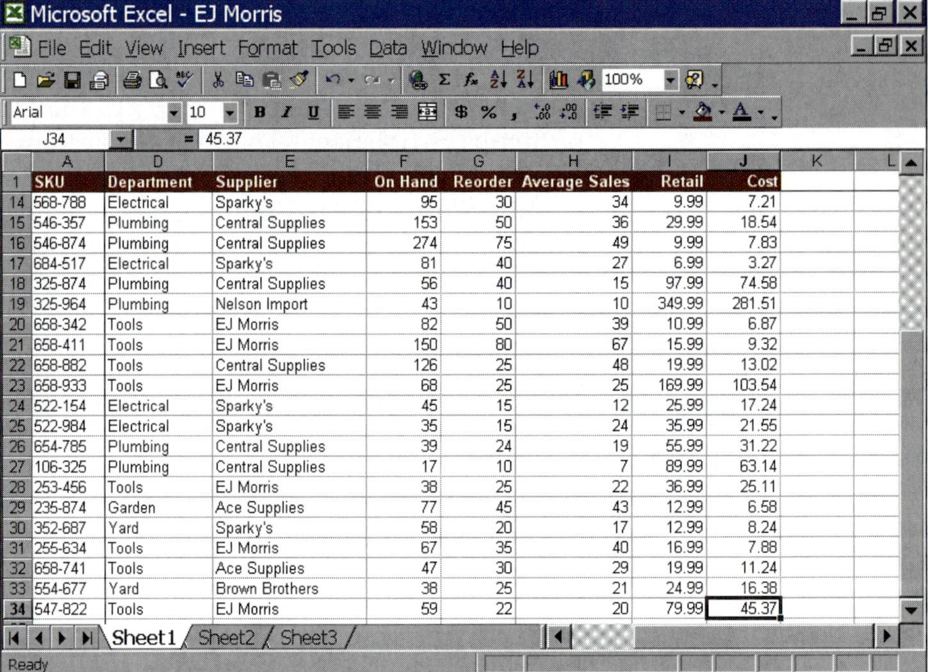

	SKU	Department	Supplier	On Hand	Reorder	Average Sales	Retail	Cost
14	568-788	Electrical	Sparky's	95	30	34	9.99	7.21
15	546-357	Plumbing	Central Supplies	153	50	36	29.99	18.54
16	546-874	Plumbing	Central Supplies	274	75	49	9.99	7.83
17	684-517	Electrical	Sparky's	81	40	27	6.99	3.27
18	325-874	Plumbing	Central Supplies	56	40	15	97.99	74.58
19	325-964	Plumbing	Nelson Import	43	10	10	349.99	281.51
20	658-342	Tools	EJ Morris	82	50	39	10.99	6.87
21	658-411	Tools	EJ Morris	150	80	67	15.99	9.32
22	658-882	Tools	Central Supplies	126	25	48	19.99	13.02
23	658-933	Tools	EJ Morris	68	25	25	169.99	103.54
24	522-154	Electrical	Sparky's	45	15	12	25.99	17.24
25	522-984	Electrical	Sparky's	35	15	24	35.99	21.55
26	654-785	Plumbing	Central Supplies	39	24	19	55.99	31.22
27	106-325	Plumbing	Central Supplies	17	10	7	89.99	63.14
28	253-456	Tools	EJ Morris	38	25	22	36.99	25.11
29	235-874	Garden	Ace Supplies	77	45	43	12.99	6.58
30	352-687	Yard	Sparky's	58	20	17	12.99	8.24
31	255-634	Tools	EJ Morris	67	35	40	16.99	7.88
32	658-741	Tools	Ace Supplies	47	30	29	19.99	11.24
33	554-677	Yard	Brown Brothers	38	25	21	24.99	16.38
34	547-822	Tools	EJ Morris	59	22	20	79.99	45.37

2. Because the conference room does not have a computer, Howard must print the worksheet to take into the meeting. First, he unfreezes the panes and moves the cell pointer to cell A1. Using the Page Setup dialog box, Howard ensures that the first row in the worksheet will appear on each page of the printout. He then changes the printout to a landscape orientation and scales the size of the print upwards to 140 percent of normal. Lastly, Howard previews the worksheet printout. Satisfied that the hard copy will serve him well in the meeting, Howard prints the worksheet. He then saves and closes the workbook.

3. A senior vice president has asked Howard to prepare a report that summarizes inventory levels by department for the years 1999 and 2000. Furthermore, she wants to see the details for only the Garden and Yard departments. Howard realizes he can use Excel's outlining feature on an existing worksheet to produce the report.

Howard opens the data file called EXC783 and then saves it as "Stretch Summary" to his personal storage location. After moving the cell pointer into the table area, he chooses the Auto Outline command to create an outline based on the formulas appearing in the worksheet. Next, he collapses the outline so that the product details are hidden for all departments but "Garden" and "Yard." The worksheet appears similar to Figure 7.24.

Figure 7.24

Collapsing and
displaying an outline

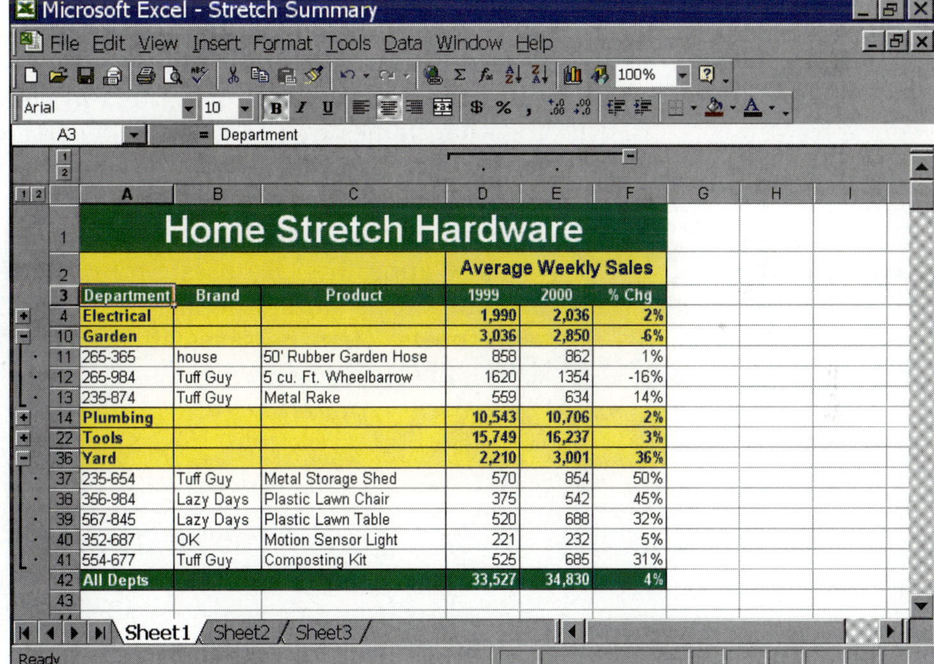

	Department	Brand	Product	1999	2000	% Chg
					Average Weekly Sales	
3	Department	Brand	Product	1999	2000	% Chg
4	Electrical			1,990	2,036	2%
10	Garden			3,036	2,850	-6%
11	265-365	house	50' Rubber Garden Hose	858	862	1%
12	265-984	Tuff Guy	5 cu. Ft. Wheelbarrow	1620	1354	-16%
13	235-874	Tuff Guy	Metal Rake	559	634	14%
14	Plumbing			10,543	10,706	2%
22	Tools			15,749	16,237	3%
36	Yard			2,210	3,001	36%
37	235-654	Tuff Guy	Metal Storage Shed	570	854	50%
38	356-984	Lazy Days	Plastic Lawn Chair	375	542	45%
39	567-845	Lazy Days	Plastic Lawn Table	520	688	32%
40	352-687	OK	Motion Sensor Light	221	232	5%
41	554-677	Tuff Guy	Composting Kit	525	685	31%
42	All Depts			33,527	34,830	4%

Satisfied that the worksheet displays the summarized information requested by the senior vice president, Howard prints a copy of the worksheet. As a last step, he saves and then closes the workbook.

4. Since Howard did such a nice job with the previous summary report, the executive committee has asked him to produce a weekly summary of inventory transactions for the three non-seasonal departments. To begin, Howard locates a workbook containing the requisite information. He opens the data file named EXC784 and then saves it as "Weekly Summary" to his personal storage location. In reviewing the workbook, Howard notices that each department appears on its own worksheet.

   To make the workbook easier to use, Howard renames the sheet tabs to display the department names. In order to create a summary worksheet, he places a copy of the *Electrical* worksheet at the beginning of the sheet stack. He then renames the worksheet "Summary" and modifies its title in cell A1. Lastly, he creates hyperlinks in cells A10, A11, and A12 to the other tabs in the sheet stack.

   After testing the hyperlinks, Howard decides against using the Consolidate command in favor of entering a simple SUM function. The formula that he enters in cell B3, for example, sums together values from the three departmental worksheets. After entering the formula, Howard uses the Edit, Fill, Down command to extend the calculation to cells B4 through B7. Finally, Howard decides that he needs to make the worksheets more visually appealing. He uses Group mode to apply formatting to all four sheets simultaneously. Once finished, he ungroups the worksheets. Then he saves and closes the workbook. Lastly, he exits Microsoft Excel.

Notes

Notes

Notes

Notes

Answers to Self Check Questions

1.1 Self Check How do you turn the adaptive menus feature on or off? Choose the Tools, Customize command and then ensure that no "✔" appears in the *Menus show recently used commands first* check box.

1.2 Self Check Explain why a phone number is not considered a numeric value in an Excel worksheet. Although it contains numbers, a phone number is never used to perform mathematical calculations.

1.3 Self Check Why is worksheet editing such a valuable skill? Most worksheets in use today are revisions and updates of older worksheets. As a novice user, you often spend more time updating existing worksheets than constructing new ones.

1.4 Self Check In the Open and Save As dialog boxes, how do the List and Details views differ? What two other views are accessible from the Views button? The List view uses a multicolumn format. The Details view displays one file per row. Furthermore, the Details view displays other information, including the file size, type, and modification date. The two other views are Properties and Preview.

2.1 Self Check Which of the "Auto" features enables you to sum a range of values and display the result in the Status bar? AutoCalculate

2.2 Self Check Which method would you use to copy several nonadjacent worksheet values for placement into a single column? The Office Clipboard would provide the fastest method. After displaying the Clipboard toolbar, you would clear the Clipboard and collect up to 12 items in the desired sequence. Then, you would move to the target range and paste these items into a single column.

2.3 Self Check Why must you be careful when deleting rows or columns? Because if you delete the entire row or column, you may inadvertently delete data that exists further down a column or further across a row. Ensure that a row or column is indeed empty before deleting it.

3.1 Self Check What is the basic difference between using the Underline button (U) and the Borders button (▦)? When you apply an underline to a cell, only the words in the cell appear underlined. When you apply a border underline to a cell, the entire cell is underlined. Also, borders may be applied to each side of a cell, such as top, bottom, left, and right.

3.2 Self Check   How might you ensure formatting consistency among related worksheets and workbooks? Use the same predefined AutoFormat style to format data in all of the worksheets.

3.3 Self Check   How does the Print Preview display mode differ from the Web Page Preview display mode? Print Preview appears in the Excel application window and displays the workbook as it will appear when printed. Web Page Preview uses the computer's default Web browser to display an HTML rendering of the current worksheet.

3.4 Self Check   How would you create a custom footer that displayed your name against the left page border and your company's name against the right page border? In the Page Setup dialog box, you would click the Custom Footer command button on the *Header/Footer* tab. Then, you would enter your name into the left text box and your company's name into the right text box of the Footer dialog box.

4.1 Self Check   Why is "AD1999" an unacceptable name for a cell range? You cannot name a cell range using an actual cell reference on the worksheet.

4.2 Self Check   When might you use the Formula Palette or Paste Function dialog box to enter a function into the worksheet? If you need help entering the arguments in the correct order or if you cannot remember a function's name or proper syntax, you can use these tools to refresh your memory or to assist you in completing the task.

4.3 Self Check   What must you do when selecting the print range for a worksheet that contains an embedded chart? Because charts do not appear in cells on a worksheet, you must ensure to select the print range to include these graphic objects. For example, select the cells that appear underneath the embedded chart that you want to print.

5.1 Self Check   What are the two ways that you can indent a cell entry? You indent a cell's contents using the *Alignment* tab of the Format Cells dialog box. You can also click the Increase Indent (▣) and Decrease Indent (▣) buttons on the toolbar.

5.2 Self Check   How would you change the default font for an entire workbook to be 12-point, Times New Roman? You can modify the Normal style for the workbook using the Format, Style command. Click the Modify command button in the Style dialog box and then make the required changes in the Format Cells dialog box. After you return to the worksheet, all cells based on the Normal style will appear formatted with the new font.

5.3 Self Check How would you place a "STOP" sign on a worksheet using the techniques described in this module? Click the AutoShapes button on the Drawing toolbar and then select an Octagon shape from the Basic Shapes menu. After placing the object onto the draw layer, apply a red fill color. Then, add and center the text "STOP" inside the object and format the word to appear white and boldface.

5.4 Self Check What are the three media types that you can insert into a worksheet using the Microsoft Clip Gallery dialog box? The three media types, as witnessed by the tabs in the dialog box, are *Pictures*, *Sounds*, and *Motion Clips*.

5.5 Self Check What must you remember when selecting nonadjacent ranges in preparation for the Chart Wizard or to add to a chart's plot area? You must ensure that the ranges are the same shape and size.

5.6 Self Check What might you do differently in formatting a chart for printing as opposed to formatting a chart for displaying online? When formatting a chart for printing, you must concern yourself with the quality of output capable at the printer. Therefore, you may use patterns and shading levels instead of colors. For online or computer-based presentations, the use of colors in charts works well to differentiate the various elements.

6.1 Self Check Provide two reasons for nesting a calculation in a formula expression.
1. To force the calculation to perform before another calculation, as dictated by the operator order of precedence.
2. To make a formula expression easier to read and understand.

6.2 Self Check Name two methods for calculating and displaying the day of the week (e.g., Wednesday).
1. Use the WEEKDAY function and then translate the return value (1 to 7) to the appropriate weekday value.
2. Use the Format command to apply a custom number format using either the "ddd" or "dddd" option.

6.3 Self Check What are the results of the functions INT(4.55) and ROUND(4.55,0)?
- INT(4.55) returns the number 4
- ROUND(4.55,0) returns the number 5

6.4 Self Check Cell A1 contains a person's area code and phone number in the form (789)555-1234. What expression would you enter in cell A2 to extract only the phone number for display? Here is one formula expression that solves the stated problem: =RIGHT(A1,LEN(A1)-SEARCH(")",A1))

6.5 Self Check How might you calculate the payment for a mortgage in which the interest rate changed depending on the term chosen? You would use a nested IF function to calculate the *Rate* argument in the PMT function.

7.1 Self Check How would you divide a worksheet window into four panes? You can drag both the horizontal and vertical split boxes to create panes. Once you have finished specifying horizontal panes for example, you can then divide the worksheet window into vertical panes. You can also use the Window, Split command.

7.2 Self Check What characters must you type to have Excel's AutoCorrect feature insert the proper trademark symbol (™)? You type (tm) and then press the Space bar.

7.3 Self Check How would you rename a chart sheet and then move it to the end of a sheet stack in a workbook? You rename and move a chart sheet just as you would a worksheet. In other words, double-click the chart sheet's tab and type a new name. Press **ENTER** to accept the entry. Then, drag the sheet tab to the far right in the sheet stack.

7.4 Self Check Name two advantages for separating your work into multiple workbooks. First, the workbooks are typically smaller than a single multiple-sheet workbook. Second, the workbooks are not limited to being stored on the same computer or network.

Glossary

absolute cell address Cell reference in a worksheet that does not adjust when copied to other cells. You make a cell address absolute by placing dollar signs ($) before the column letter and row number, such as $C$4.

adaptive menus The dynamic menu bars and toolbars that are personalized to the way you work. Microsoft Office 2000 watches the tasks that you perform in an application and then displays only those commands and buttons that you use most often.

annuity A series of equal cash payments made over a given period of time.

application window In Windows, each running application program appears in its own application window. These windows may be sized and moved anywhere on the Windows desktop.

arguments The parameters used in entering a function according to its *syntax*. Arguments may include text, numbers, formulas, functions, and cell references.

AutoCalculate In Excel, a software feature that sums the selected range of cells and displays the result in the Status bar.

AutoComplete In Excel, a software feature that assists you in entering data into a worksheet by filling in letters from existing entries in the column as you type.

AutoCorrect In Excel, a software feature that corrects common typing and spelling mistakes automatically as you type. It also enables you to enter complex symbols quickly and easily.

AutoFill In Excel, a software feature that enables you to copy and extend a formula or data series automatically in a worksheet.

AutoFit In Excel, a software feature that calculates the optimal row height or column width based on existing data in the worksheet.

AutoFormat A software feature that applies professionally designed formatting styles to your documents.

AutoShapes Ready-made graphic objects that you can add to your worksheet using the Drawing toolbar and then format and customize to suit your needs.

AutoSum A software feature that automatically inserts a formula for adding values from a surrounding row or column of cells.

bar chart   A chart that compares one data element to another data element using horizontal bars. Similar to a *column chart.*

cell   The intersection of a column and a row.

cell address   The location of a cell on a worksheet given by the intersection of a column and a row. Columns are labeled using letters. Rows are numbered. A cell address combines the column letter with the row number (for example, B9 or DF134).

cell alignment   The positioning of data entered into a worksheet cell in relation to the cell borders.

cell layer   The layer for worksheet cells; this layer holds data, calculated expressions, formatting attributes, and other information.

cell pointer   The cursor on a worksheet that points to a cell. The cell pointer is moved using the arrow keys or the mouse.

cell range   One or more cells in a worksheet that together form a rectangle.

character strings   Any combination of letters, symbols, and numerals that is not a numerical or date value.

chart sheet   A sheet tab or page within a workbook file that is used to create, modify, and display a chart graphic.

Chart Wizard   A linear step progression of dialog boxes that leads you through creating a chart in Excel.

Clip Gallery   A shared application in Microsoft Office that lets you manage clip art images, pictures, sounds, animation, and video clips and insert them into a worksheet's draw layer.

column chart   A chart that compares one data element with another data element and can show variations over a period of time.

concatenate   In Excel, joining together characters from separate cells or strings using the ampersand "&" operator to form a single cell entry; combining characters to form a string.

consolidate   The process of combining smaller worksheet files into a single summary worksheet, making it easier to manage large amounts of data.

constant   Any number, date, or text value that is entered directly into a cell, as an operand in a formula, or as an argument in a function. An unchanging value that the user cannot adjust or modify. Opposite of a *variable.*

custom format   A combination of formatting codes that when placed in a particular sequence enhance the display of numeric and date values. You construct and store custom formats on the *Number* tab of the Format Cells dialog box.

document window   In Excel, each open *workbook* appears in its own document window. These windows may be sized and moved anywhere within the application window.

drag and drop   A software feature that allows you to copy and move information by dragging information from one location to another using the mouse.

draw layer   The invisible surface that exists above the *cell layer* and holds inserted or embedded graphic objects and charts.

embedded chart   A chart that is placed on the draw layer of a worksheet.

fill handle   The small black square that is located in the bottom right-hand corner of a cell or cell range. You use the fill handle to create a series or to copy cell information.

font(s)   All the characters of one size in a particular *typeface*; includes numbers, punctuation marks, and uppercase and lowercase letters.

footer(s)   Descriptive information (such as page number and date) that appears at the bottom of each page of a document.

Format Painter   A software feature that enables you to copy only the formatting attributes and styles from one location to another.

formula   A mathematical expression that typically defines the relationships among various cells in a worksheet or table.

Formula Palette   The dialog box, appearing beneath the Formula bar, that provides assistance for entering a function's *arguments* using the correct syntax.

functions   Built-in shortcuts that can be used in formulas to perform calculations.

future value   The value in future dollars of a series of equal cash payments.

graphic file   A computer graphic, created by an artist or scanned from an existing picture, that you can insert into your worksheets.

gridlines   The lines on a worksheet that assist the user in lining up the cell pointer with a particular column letter or row number.

Group mode   In Excel, a special mode for working with multiple-sheet workbooks; enables you to perform commands on a single sheet and have those commands reflected in all other sheets in the file.

header(s) Descriptive information (such as page number and data) that appears at the top of each page of a document.

HTML An acronym for Hypertext Markup Language, which is the standardized markup language used in creating documents for display on the World Wide Web.

hyperlinks In terms of Internet technologies, a text string or graphics that when clicked take you to another location, either within the same document or to a separate document stored on your computer, an intranet resource, or onto the Internet.

in-cell editing In Excel, the feature that enables you to revise text labels, numbers, dates, and other entries directly within a cell. To activate in-cell editing, you double-click a cell.

integer value The value of a number to the left of the decimal point. For example, the integer of 123.987 is 123.

Internet A worldwide network of computer networks that are interconnected by standard telephone lines, fiber optics, and satellites.

intranet A private local or wide area network that uses Internet protocols and technologies to share information within an institution or corporation.

Legend A key for deciphering the data series appearing in the plot area of a chart.

line chart A chart that plots trends or shows changes over a period of time.

macro virus A malicious program that attaches itself to a document or template and performs instructions that may damage files on your computer.

margins Space between the edge of the paper and the top, bottom, left, and right edges of the printed document.

Microsoft Map A shared application in Microsoft Office that enables you to create and plot an embedded map from geographic data stored in a worksheet.

mixed cell address Cell reference in a worksheet that includes both *relative* and *absolute cell references*. For example, the address C$4 provides a "relative" column letter and an "absolute" row number.

Name box The text box appearing at the left-hand side of the Formula bar that displays the current cell address and that enables you to navigate quickly to any cell location in the worksheet.

natural language formula In Excel, a type of *formula* that allows you to use the column and row labels within a worksheet in building a mathematical expression.

Office Clipboard   A program, in Microsoft Office 2000, that allows you to copy and move information within or among Office 2000 applications. Unlike the Windows Clipboard, the Office Clipboard can store up to 12 items and then paste them all at once.

operand   In Excel, a constant value, range name, or cell address that you use in building formula expressions.

operator   In Excel, a symbol used to determine what calculations to perform on operands. Excel provides four types of operators—arithmetic, comparison or logical, text, and reference.

order of precedence   The sequential order in which formula expressions are evaluated is determined by the use of parentheses and the operator *order of precedence*.

outlining   In Excel, the process of grouping data together on a worksheet in order to hide (collapse) or display (expand) detailed information.

panes   When a worksheet window has been divided into separate areas using the Window, Freeze Panes command or the Window, Split command, these areas are called *window panes* or *panes*. A worksheet can have a maximum of four panes at any one time.

parsing   In Excel, dividing a single cell entry or text string across multiple cells; extracting a character or characters from a string. To parse data in Excel, you use functions from the Text category.

pie chart   A chart that shows the proportions of individual components compared to the whole.

Places bar   The strip of icon buttons appearing in the Open and Save As dialog boxes that allow you to display the most common areas for retrieving and storing files using a single mouse click.

plot area   The area for plotting values in a chart. The plot area contains the axes and data series.

present value   The value in present-day dollars of a series of equal cash payments made sometime in the future.

print titles   Row and column data that is stored in a worksheet and used to display repeating header information across page breaks for printed output.

random number   In Excel, a value between 0 and 1 that results by chance, but with equal probability of any other value between 0 and 1.

Range Finder   An Excel feature that color-codes the operands and arguments (cell ranges) used in a formula or function for easy reference.

range name   A name that is given to a range of cells in the worksheet. This name can then be used in formulas and functions to refer to the cell range.

Redo command   A command that makes it possible to reverse the effects of an Undo command.

relative cell address   Default cell reference in a worksheet that automatically adjusts when copied to other cells.

rounded value   The value of a number rounded to a specific number of decimal places. For example, the number 2.378 rounded to a single decimal returns the number 2.4.

scanner   A hardware device that converts an existing paper-based image, such as a photograph or drawing, into a computer image that is stored digitally on the disk.

scatter plot chart   A chart that shows how one or more data elements relate to another data element. Also called *XY charts*.

series   A sequence of numbers or dates that follows a mathematical or date pattern.

sizing handles   The white boxes that appear around an object that is selected on the *draw layer*. You use the sizing handles to increase or decrease the size of an object.

Spelling Checker   A shared proofing tool in Microsoft Office 2000 that you use to check your workbooks for typing errors and spelling mistakes.

style   A set of formatting specifications that are named and stored with the workbook in which they were created.

syntax   The rules, structure, and order of *arguments* used in entering a formula or function.

template   A workbook or document that has been saved to a special file and location so that it may be used again and again as a model for creating new documents.

typeface(s)   The shape and appearance of characters. There are two categories of typefaces: serif and sans serif. Serif type (for example, Times Roman) is more decorative and, some say, easier to read than sans serif type (for example, Arial).

Undo command   A command that makes it possible to reverse up to the last 16 commands or actions performed.

variable   A temporary value or storage location in memory for data that can be adjusted and modified.

Windows Clipboard   A program, in Windows, that allows you to copy and move information within an application or among applications. The Windows Clipboard temporarily stores the information in memory before you paste the data in a new location.

wizard   A program or process whereby a series of dialog boxes lead you step-by-step through performing a procedure.

WordArt   A shared application in Microsoft Office that lets you manipulate and apply special effects to text and then insert the text into a worksheet.

workbook   The disk file that contains the *worksheets* and *chart sheets* that you create in Excel.

worksheet   A sheet tab or page within a workbook file that is used to create, modify, and display a worksheet grid of columns and rows.

World Wide Web   A visual interface to the Internet based on *hyperlinks*. Using Web browser software, you click on hyperlinks to navigate resources on the Internet.

X-axis   The horizontal or category axis that shows the categories for which the chart is making comparisons.

XY charts   Charts that show how one or more data elements relate to another data element. Also called *scatter plot diagrams*.

Y-axis   The vertical or value axis in a two-dimensional chart that shows the value or measurement unit for making comparisons among the various categories.

Appendix: Microsoft Windows Quick Reference

Using the Mouse and Keyboard

Microsoft Windows provides a graphical environment for working in your application, such as Microsoft Word, Excel, Access, or Power-Point. As you work with Windows applications, you will find that there are often three different ways to perform the same command. The most common methods for performing commands include:

- Menu — Choose a command from the Menu bar or from a right-click menu.
- Mouse — Position the mouse pointer over a toolbar button and then click once.
- Keyboard — Press a keyboard shortcut (usually [CTRL] + *letter*).

Although you may use a Windows application with only a keyboard, much of a program's basic design relies on using a mouse. Regardless of whether your mouse has two or three buttons, you will use the left or primary mouse button for selecting screen objects and menu commands and the right or secondary mouse button for displaying right-click menus.

The most common mouse actions include:

- Point — Slide the mouse on your desk to position the tip of the mouse pointer over the desired object on the screen.
- Click — Press down and release the left mouse button quickly. Clicking is used to select a screen object, activate a toolbar command, and choose menu commands.
- Right-Click — Press down and release the right mouse button. Right-clicking the mouse pointer on a screen object displays a context-sensitive menu.
- Double-Click — Press down and release the mouse button twice in rapid succession. Double-clicking is used to select screen objects or to activate an embedded object for editing.
- Drag — Press down and hold the mouse button as you move the mouse pointer across the screen. When the mouse pointer reaches the desired location, release the mouse button. Dragging is used to select a group of screen objects and to copy or move data.

You may notice that the mouse pointer changes shape as you move it over different parts of the screen. Each mouse pointer shape has its own purpose and may provide you with important information. There are four primary mouse shapes that appear in Windows applications:

arrow	Used to choose menu commands and click toolbars buttons.
hourglass	Informs you that the application is occupied and requests that you wait.
I-beam	Used to set the position of the insertion point and to modify and edit text.
hand	Used to select hyperlinks in the Windows-based Help systems, in Microsoft Office documents, and on the Web.

Aside from being the primary input device for entering information, the keyboard offers shortcut methods for performing some common commands and procedures.

Starting Windows

Because Windows is an operating system, it is loaded into the computer's memory when you first turn on the computer. To start Windows, you must do the following:

1. Turn on the power switches to the computer and monitor. After a few seconds, the Windows desktop will appear. (*Note*: If you are attached to a network, a dialog box may appear asking you to enter your User name and Password. Enter this information now or ask your instructor for further instructions.)
2. A Welcome dialog box may appear providing information about the operating system's major features. If the Welcome dialog box appears on your screen:
   CLICK: Close button (☒) in the top right-hand corner of the Welcome window
3. If additional windows appear open on your desktop:
   CLICK: Close button (☒) in the top right-hand corner of each window

EXCEL

Parts of a Dialog Box

A dialog box is a common mechanism in Windows applications for collecting information before processing a command. In a dialog box, you indicate the options you want to use and then click the OK button when you're finished. Dialog boxes are also used to display messages or to ask for the confirmation of commands. The following shows an example of the Print dialog box, which is similar across Windows applications.

Print dialog box

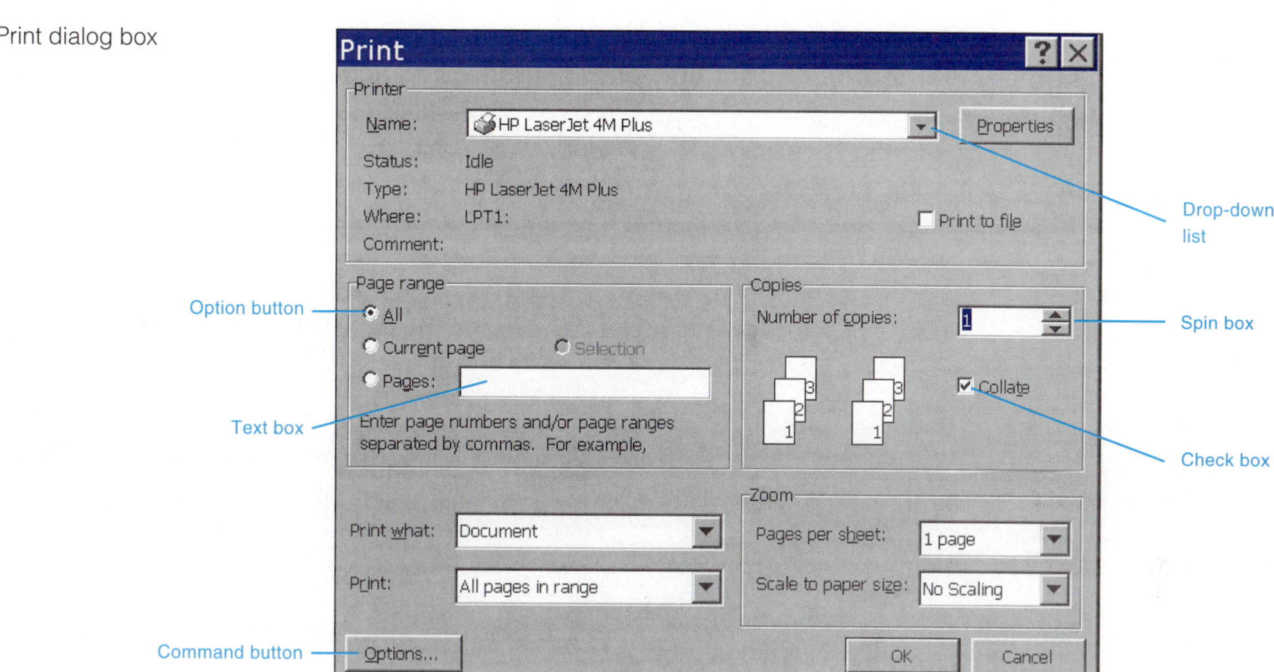

A dialog box uses several types of controls or components for collecting information. We describe the most common components in the following table.

Dialog box components

Name	Example	Action
Check box	Always Never	Click an option to turn it on or off. The option is turned on when an "✔" appears in the box.
Command button	OK Cancel	Click a command button to execute an action. Click OK to accept your selections or click Cancel to exit the dialog box.

Name	Example	Action
Drop-Down list box		Make a choice from the list that appears when you click the down arrow next to the box; only the selected choice is visible.
List box		Make a choice from the scrollable list; several choices, if not all, are always visible.
Option button		Select an option from a group of related options.
Slide box		Drag the slider bar to make a selection, like using a radio's volume control.
Spin box		Click the up and down arrows to the right of the box until the number you want appears.
Tab		Click a named tab at the top of the window to access other pages of options in the dialog box.
Text box		Click inside the text box and then type the desired information.

Most dialog boxes provide a question mark icon ([?]) near the right side of the Title bar. If you have a question about an item in the dialog box, click the question mark and then click the item to display a pop-up help window. To remove the help window, click on it once.

Getting Help

Windows applications, such as Microsoft Office 2000 applications, provide a comprehensive library of online documentation. This section describes these help features and how to find more detailed information.

Obtaining Context-Sensitive Help

In Windows applications, you can often retrieve context-sensitive help for menu options, toolbar buttons, and dialog box items. *Context-sensitive help* refers to a program's ability to present helpful information reflecting your current position in the program. The help information is presented concisely in a small pop-up window that you can remove with the click of the mouse. This type of help lets you access information quickly and then continue working without interruption. The following table describes some methods for accessing context-sensitive help while working in Windows applications.

Displaying context-sensitive help information

To display...	Do this...
A description of a dialog box item	Click the question mark button ([?]) in a dialog box's Title bar and then click an item in the dialog box. Alternatively, you can often right-click a dialog box item and then choose the What's This? command from the shortcut menu.
A description of a menu command	Choose the Help, What's This? command from the menu and then choose a command using the question mark mouse pointer. Rather than executing the command, a helpful description of the command appears in a pop-up window.
A description of a toolbar button	Point to a toolbar button to display a pop-up label called a ToolTip.

Getting Help in Office 2000

Getting Help from the Office Assistant

In Office 2000 applications, the Office Assistant is your personal computer guru and is available by default when your application is first installed. When you need to perform a task that you're unsure of, simply click the Assistant character and then type a phrase such as "How do I obtain help" in the Assistant balloon. The Assistant analyzes your request and provides a resource list of suggested topics, as shown to the right. Simply click a topic to obtain additional information.

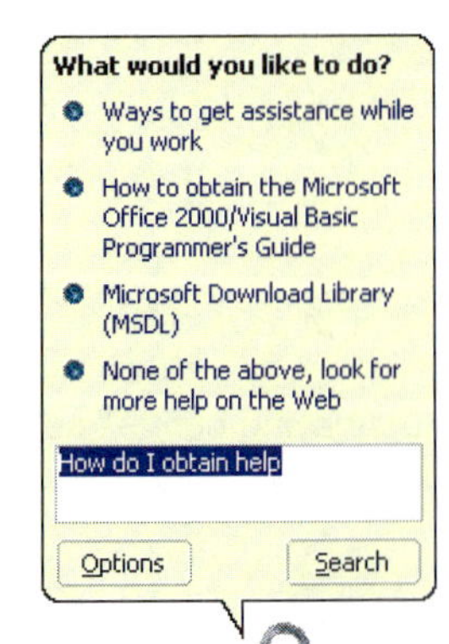

The Assistant also watches your keystrokes and mouse clicks as you work and offers suggestions and shortcuts to make you more productive and efficient. If you find the Office Assistant to be distracting, you can turn it off by choosing "Hide the Office Assistant" from the Help menu. To redisplay it, simply choose "Microsoft *Application* Help" or "Show the Office Assistant" from the Help menu.

Getting Help from the Help Window

You may prefer to obtain a complete topical listing of your application's help system. To do this, you must first disable the Office Assistant by clicking the Options button in the Assistant balloon, clearing the *Use the Office Assistant* check box, and then pressing (ENTER). Once the Office Assistant is disabled, simply choose "Microsoft *Application* Help" from the Help menu to display the Help window. If the *Contents*, *Answer Wizard*, and *Index* tabs don't appear, click Show (⬅) in the window's toolbar.

The Help window, shown below, provides three different tools, each on its own tab, to help you find the information you need quickly and easily. You can read the Help information you find onscreen or print it out for later reference by clicking the Print button (🖨) in the window's toolbar. To close the Help window, click its Close button (✖).

Example Help window

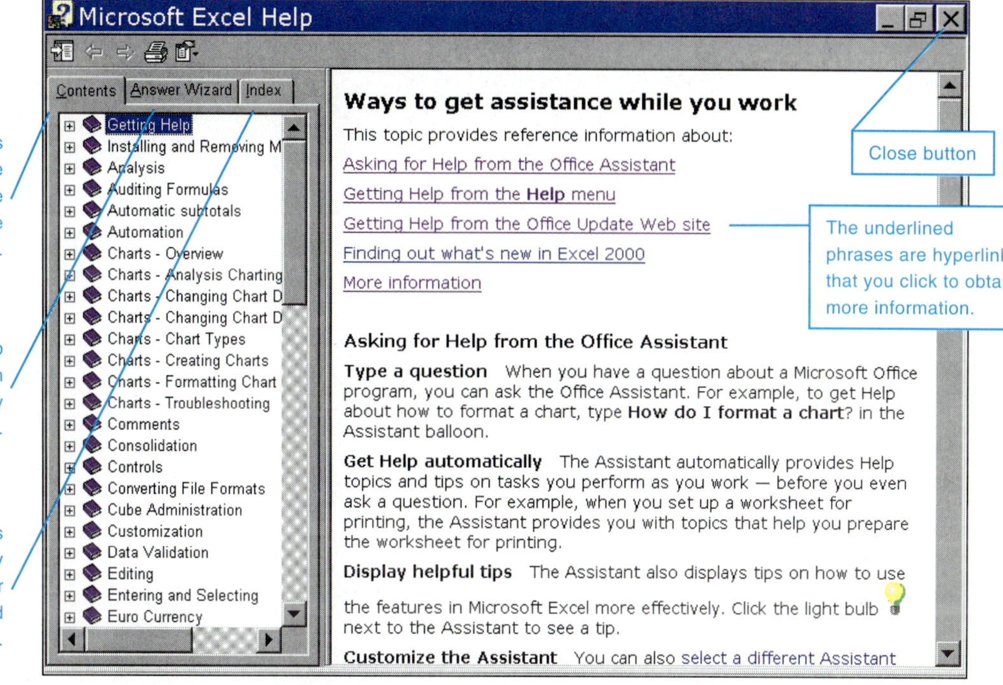

The *Contents* tab is currently selected. Use this tab to display the Table of Contents for the entire Help system.

The *Answer Wizard* tab enables you to obtain help information by typing in questions.

The *Index* tab enables you to display topics by selecting keywords or typing in words and phrases.

Close button

The underlined phrases are hyperlinks that you click to obtain more information.

Getting Help from the Office Update Web Site

Microsoft's Office Update Web site provides additional technical support and product enhancements. You can access this site from any Office application by choosing "Office on the Web" from the Help menu.

EXCEL

Index